THE RISE AND FALL OF BUSINESS FIRMS

At the intersection between statistical physics and rigorous econometric analysis, this powerful new framework sheds light on how innovation and competition shape the growth and decline of companies and industries.

Analyzing various sources of data including a unique micro-level database which collects historical data on the sales of approximately 5,000 firms and 130,000 products in 21 countries, the authors introduce and test a model of innovation and proportional growth, which relies on minimal assumptions and accounts for the empirically observed regularities. Through a combination of extensive stochastic simulations and statistical tests, the authors investigate to which extent their simple assumptions are falsified by empirically observable facts.

Physicists looking for application of their mathematical and modeling skills to relevant economic problems as well as economists interested in the explorative analysis of extensive data sets and in a physics-oriented way of thinking will find this book a key reference.

S. V. BULDYREV is Professor of Physics at Yeshiva University. His research interests span theoretical and computational statistical physics and its applications to various complex systems, physical chemistry, material science, and biological physics.

F. PAMMOLLI is Professor of Economics and Management at Polytechnic University of Milan. He served as the Founding Rector of the IMT School for Advanced Studies and is currently a member of the Investment Committee of the European Fund for Strategic Investments at the European Investment Bank in Luxembourg. His research interests span the analysis of a variety of complex industrial and technological systems, with particular reference to pharmaceuticals and the life sciences.

M. RICCABONI is Professor of Economics and Director of the PhD Track in Economics, Networks, and Business Analytics at the IMT School for Advanced Studies Lucca. His current research focuses on industrial organization, network analysis, and the economics of innovation, with particular reference to the life sciences.

H. E. STANLEY is William Fairfield Warren Distinguished Professor and Director of the Center for Polymer Studies at Boston University. He is one of the founding fathers of econophysics, a pioneer of interdisciplinary science, and has made seminal contributions to the field of statistical physics. He is a member of the US National Academy of Sciences and a recipient of numerous awards throughout his career.

"This is a superb and fascinating book. The distribution of firms' growth rates exhibits a large number of regularities, including some that are very hard to explain. The authors are pioneers in that enterprise, combining empirical and theoretical work. This team of economists and physicists provides a model for a future way to do economics."

Xavier Gabaix,
Pershing Square Professor of Economics and Finance, Harvard University

"*The Rise and Fall of Business Firms* offers a lucid reconstruction and extension of the exciting developments that fundamentally reshaped our understanding of how firms grow and evolve, brought to you by the scientists responsible for the key discoveries. A must for anyone interested in the deep laws that govern economic processes."

Albert-László Barabási,
Robert Gray Dodge Professor of Network Science at Northeastern University

"There is a long tradition of physicists being interested in and contributing to economics. That tradition continues here in *The Rise and Fall of Business Firms.* The book is based on generalized proportional growth models for the dynamics and stochastics of the growth and decline of business firms. For further studies, the book points out where more detailed specific inter-related complexities (such as among products, markets, and technologies) can be incorporated. The theoretical analysis paired with empirical data provides valuable insight for firms to understand their past trajectory and future choices."

Michael F. Schlesinger,
Office of Naval Research

THE RISE AND FALL OF BUSINESS FIRMS

A Stochastic Framework on Innovation, Creative Destruction, and Growth

S. V. BULDYREV
Yeshiva University

F. PAMMOLLI
Polytechnic University of Milan

M. RICCABONI
IMT Institute for Advanced Studies Lucca

H. E. STANLEY
Boston University

CAMBRIDGE
UNIVERSITY PRESS

CAMBRIDGE
UNIVERSITY PRESS

University Printing House, Cambridge CB2 8BS, United Kingdom

One Liberty Plaza, 20th Floor, New York, NY 10006, USA

477 Williamstown Road, Port Melbourne, VIC 3207, Australia

314–321, 3rd Floor, Plot 3, Splendor Forum, Jasola District Centre, New Delhi – 110025, India

79 Anson Road, #06–04/06, Singapore 079906

Cambridge University Press is part of the University of Cambridge.

It furthers the University's mission by disseminating knowledge in the pursuit of education, learning, and research at the highest international levels of excellence.

www.cambridge.org
Information on this title: www.cambridge.org/9781107175488
DOI: 10.1017/9781316798539

First published 2020

Printed in the United Kingdom by TJ International Ltd, Padstow Cornwall

A catalogue record for this publication is available from the British Library.

ISBN 978-1-107-17548-8 Hardback

To our families

If the very same regularity appears among diverse phenomena having no obvious common mechanism, then chance operating through the laws of probability becomes a plausible candidate for explaining that regularity.

Ijiri and Simon (1977, p. 3)

At the core of the discussion is a concern as to how we can distinguish between apparent regularities that just happen to crop up in same single data set from those regularities whose happening reflects some underlying law.

Sutton (2000, pp. 16–17)

Less is more.

Ludwig Mies Van der Rohe

Contents

Preface

It all began in Lausanne, when John Sutton invited us for a session on the growth of firms at the European Conference of the Econometric Society. That meeting was the beginning of a deep friendship and intense collaboration. At that time, John Sutton's work on innovation, firm growth, and industry structure, together with that of Herbert A. Simon, the founding father of the stochastic tradition in the analysis of the growth of business firms, was already a fundamental source of inspiration.

For more than 15 years, the four of us traveled between Boston, Lucca, and Milan, combining hard work with vibrant discussions on the most disparate themes. Gene's enthusiasm and generosity have sustained us to "get the work done," to overcome every difficulty, and to focus our gaze on "The Book," as if gazing on a polar star. We remember our ideas drafted on the blackboards at the Center of Polymer Studies at Boston University, the long conversations and collaborations with Kazuko Yamasaki, Kaushik Matia, Dongfeng Fu, Linda Ponta, and with the great students and scholars that animated Gene's Laboratory. These are all memories of our Φιλία, to look back on with a smile and a content heart. Soon, Sergey fell in love with the ancient town of Lucca, where he spent many months working on the book, secluded in the ancient monasteries of San Francesco and San Micheletto, and whose walls he encircled by jogging, thinking, and discussing with Fabio on the puzzles of preferential growth.

Sole and Stefano deserve a special mention for their hospitality at Il Mecenate, first under The Fig Tree in Gattaiola and then in Piazza San Francesco, where heated discussions took place.

Gene and Sergey want to thank their colleague and coauthor Michael A. Salinger without whose guidance it would have been impossible for them to enter the field of economics. Gene and Sergey are also grateful to Shlomo Havlin, their most frequent coauthor, whose interest in applying concepts of statistical physics to complex systems has stimulated their research for four decades. Last, but not least, we are in debt to those who participated in the creation of the new field of Econophysics in the late 1990s: Luis A. Nunes Amaral, Rosario N. Mantegna, Heiko Leschhorn, Philipp Maass, and especially Gene's son, Michael Stanley, who was a high school student at the time, and whose fascination with Zipf's law ignited the interest of his father.

Over the years, we have had the privilege to learn from exceptional colleagues who have influenced us with their writings, comments, caveats, critiques, and suggestions. We would like to mention here Xavier Gabaix, Didier Sornette, Laszlo Barabasi, and Angelo Maria Petroni.

Several colleagues have contributed to our research in the field, while others have read and commented on the content of this book. Special mention goes to Nicola Nottoli, who has designed the cover of our first PNAS article and has inspired us in the selection of the cover for the book, as well as to Gianni de Fabritiis, Jakub Growiec, Alex Petersen, Orion Penner, Greg Morrison, Armando Rungi, Marco Bee, Stefano Schiavo, and, for the most recent comments, Andrea Flori, Alessandro Spelta, Salvatore di Novo, and Stefano Martinazzi. We would also like to thank Mark Buchanan, Giorgio Gnecco, Simone Scotti, Andrea Vindigni, Stefano Gattei, Aymeric Stamm, and Daniele Regoli for their critical reading and valuable comments to earlier versions of the manuscript.

Andrea Morescalchi and Valentina Tortolini are our young, distinguished, coauthors of Chapter 4. Valentina has followed the entire preparation of the manuscript, always combining research endurance with admirable patience.

The Merck Foundation supported, with a multiyear unrestricted grant, Fabio's and Gene's research on innovation and industrial dynamics in pharmaceuticals. We say a big thank you to Lou Galambos, Jeff Sturchio, Brian Healy, Goffredo Freddi, Zoe Bell, and Leslie Hardy. A special thought goes to William Looney for his friendship and wisdom. Sarah Morrison, Wessen Maruwge, and Marina Eskin made an excellent contribution to the editing of the manuscript.

The data that we have had access to thanks to IMS International (now IQVIA) have been a key enabling condition for our research on the nuts and bolts of firm growth.

The research presented in this book was also funded by the National Science Foundation, the Italian Ministry of Education, University and Research (Crisis Lab Project), and the CERM Foundation.

This book is dedicated to our families.

1

Introduction

This book aims at characterizing some fundamental features of processes of Schumpeterian innovation and "creative destruction" (Schumpeter 1934) driven by firms through the development of new ideas and the launch of new products (see Nelson 1959; Ziman 1977; Freeman 1982; Winter 1984; Dosi 1988; David 1992; Aghion and Howitt 1992; Aghion and Durlauf 1998; Mokyr 2005).

Firms are the key actors of our representation of the relationship between innovation, growth, and instability.

In particular, we found inspiration from a provocative thought experiment by Herbert Simon:

> Suppose that [...] a mythical visitor from Mars [...] approaches the Earth from space, equipped with a telescope that reveals social structures. The firms reveal themselves, say, as solid green areas with faint interior contours marking out divisions and departments. Market transactions show as red lines connecting firms, forming a network in the spaces between them. [...] A message sent back home, describing the scene, would speak of *large green areas interconnected by red lines*. It would not likely speak of *a network of red lines connecting green spots*.
>
> *(Simon 1991, page 30)*

Despite the indisputable dominant role of firms in modern economies, and notwithstanding a few notable exceptions, the mainstream economic thought still considers firms as green peas (see Penrose 1959; Teece 1982; Teece et al. 1994). To fill this research gap, we point our telescope right at the core of the large green areas and their interior contours, and we focus on how small and large multiproduct firms shape the evolution of industry structure and contribute to economic growth.

The top 10 largest employers in the United States account for more than 5% of the total employment in the private sector, and the top 20 US companies combined have more employees than all job losses caused by the Great Recession at its peak in 2009. Furthermore, firm-level events of growth and decline related to the top 100 U.S. firms explain about one-third of aggregate fluctuations in output growth (Gabaix 2009), while industry-specific events account for at least half of macroeconomic volatility (Atalay 2017).

Firm turnover and innovation shape economic dynamics at higher levels of aggregation, and the growth and decline of business firms associated with technological innovations, market selection, and demand evolution affect real business cycles and economic growth (see Fu et al. 2005; Gabaix and Ibragimov 2011; Acemoglu et al. 2012; Carvalho and Gabaix 2013; Acemoglu and Cao 2015).

A crucial aspect of real-world firms vividly painted by Simon is that they are not elementary units of analysis, but they have "interior contours marking out divisions" (Simon 1991). Firms producing and selling multiple products across markets and countries dominate the global economy. Although the majority of firms produce a single product, multiproduct firms represent more than 90% of the total output in the United States (Bernard et al. 2010). Walmart, the largest company in the world with 2.3 million employees, sells more than 4.2 million products in 11.7 thousand retail units. Amazon, the second largest company in the world in terms of workforce, sells around 356 million products all around the world.

Data availability at the micro level of individual products and narrowly defined markets make it now possible to investigate the nuts and bolts of firm size dynamics, measuring the relative contribution of relevant elements, such as product adding, growing, declining, dropping, and switching.

Against this background, we present here a set of facts and a theoretical framework on the growth and decline of business firms.

We build on our own work in the field from the past two decades (Stanley et al. 1996; Amaral et al. 1998; Lee et al. 1998; Bottazzi et al. 2001; De Fabritiis et al. 2003; Fu et al. 2005; Buldyrev et al. 2007; Riccaboni et al. 2008; Growiec et al. 2008, 2018) and on a research tradition that dates back to Robert Gibrat to introduce a parsimonious theoretical framework, which, we believe, accounts for a vast set of observed empirical regularities and their interplay (Gibrat 1931; Ijiri and Simon 1977; Sutton 1997, 2007).

Specific features of our approach have been outlined in earlier publications (see, for exemple, Fu et al. 2005; Growiec et al. 2018). However, this book represents an original contribution in that, together with significant revisions and extensions of our previous work on the subject, it provides a comprehensive view of our framework for the analysis of the growth and decline of business firms.

We consider both the scale and scope of firms (Chandler 1990). Firms grow by increasing the size and scope of their activities. One mechanism of growth, which has been largely investigated in the literature, concerns expansion and productivity gains of already existing activities, while a second fundamental driver is associated with entry of new firms as well as with innovation and diversification by established firms across new products and markets (see Carsten and Neary 2010; Arkolakis and Muendler 2012; Autor et al. 2017).

In our journey, we combine analytical techniques that are well established in statistical physics and in economics.

On the one hand, we present firms as systems composed of units and products, and we are interested in establishing which relationships display scaling phenomena (Stanley 1971; Montroll 1987; Kadanoff 1991; Mantegna and Stanley 1995; West 2017) across multiple levels of aggregations of the economic system (i.e., products, firms, industries, and national economies). The identification of consistent patterns, statistical regularities, and scaling laws, i.e., common properties of a set of plots of one quantity against another one across data sets, time frequencies, and time periods, has sustained our process of theory formation by providing discipline on the shape of invariant measures and on their interplay (see Brock 1999).

On the other hand, we aim at estimating some key conditional densities/predictive distributions that are significantly influenced by relevant explanatory mechanisms so that they can discriminate across otherwise equally plausible data generating processes (Barro 1991, 1996; Brock and Durlauf 1999; Durlauf and Quah 1999).

Overall, this book aims at providing a unifying interpretative framework for a set of otherwise disconnected empirical facts and regularities, which hold across empirical domains and timeframes, irrespective of differing features (Schmalensee and Willing 1989; Sutton 1997; Caves 1998; Klepper and Thompson 2006; Sutton 2007). In particular, while focusing on the key role of firms in shaping innovation, we also account for a list of relevant and related "stylized facts" (analogously to Klette and Kortum 2004) that have been observed in a number of quite diverse settings:

(I) *Size distributions of firms are highly skewed in their upper tails.* An extensive literature has investigated the properties of size distributions of varying skewness (Schmalensee and Willing 1989; De Wit 2005; Rossi-Hansberg and Wright 2007*a*). While exact shapes of size distributions are still debated (De Fabritiis et al. 2003; Luttmer 2010; Bottazzi et al. 2011), the Pareto and the lognormal distributions are retained as benchmarks. In some cases, following Gibrat's Law, the size distribution of firms has been found to be approximately lognormal for a broad range of data (Gibrat 1931; Sutton 1997). Alternatively, following Pareto, other scholars have shown that in a double logarithmic scale, empirical size distributions are well approximated by a straight line in the upper tail (Simon and Bonini 1958; Ijiri and Simon 1977). Other studies have found that the size distribution of firms is a power law distribution with a specific exponent, so that the number of firms with a size greater than a given value S is inversely proportional to S

(the so-called Zipf's Law, see Steindl 1987; Gabaix 1999; Axtell 2001; Solomon and Richmond 2001; Saichev et al. 2009; Johansen and Sornette 2010; Luttmer 2011, 2012; Carvalho and Grassi 2015).

(II) *Small, young firms have a lower probability to capture economic opportunities and, as a consequence, to grow and survive; but those small firms that do survive tend to grow faster than large firms.* Among larger firms, growth rates tend to be unrelated to past growth or to firm size (Mansfield 1962; Jovanovic 1982; Evans 1987b; Hall 1987; Dunne et al. 1989; Perline et al. 2006; Rossi-Hansberg and Wright 2007*b*; Luttmer 2011), while growth rates for the small surviving firms decrease with size.

(III) *The distribution of firms' growth rates is not Gaussian, but "tent-shaped."* While, for many decades, the literature on the growth of firms has focused on the relation between size and the corresponding expected growth rate, a scaling law was recently observed, which reveals rare events involving extremely large positive and negative shocks, uncovering a double-exponential distribution close to the origin, with power law tails (Stanley et al. 1996; Bottazzi et al. 2001; Fu et al. 2005; Perline et al. 2006; Buldyrev et al. 2007; Bottazzi et al. 2011; Growiec et al. 2018). In particular, Fu and colleagues (Fu et al. 2005) have shown that once the tent-shaped distribution emerges at the product and firm level, it becomes a stable feature of processes of growth at higher levels of aggregation within the economy up to the level of a country's gross domestic product (GDP) (Lee et al. 1998; Fu et al. 2005).

(IV) *Conditioning on firm size, the volatility of growth rates exhibits a decreasing pattern* (see also the seminal papers by Hymer and Pashigian 1962; Mansfield 1962; Evans 1987b; Stanley et al. 1996; Bottazzi et al. 2001; Sutton 2002; Riccaboni et al. 2008; Bottazzi et al. 2011; Koren and Tenreyro 2013). In recent years, it has been found that the standard deviation of firms' growth rates decays with firm size as a power law, with a power of approximately $-0.15/-0.25$. In other words, large firms have a lower volatility of growth but they seem to be more unstable than the central limit theorem would predict. The negative size-variance relationship has been observed at different aggregation levels up to the GDP level (Lee et al. 1998; Fu et al. 2005; Castaldi and Dosi 2009; Koren and Tenreyro 2007, 2013). This fact, together with the heavy tail size distribution of firms, is the basis of the "granularity hypothesis" put forward by several researchers (Gabaix 2009; Gabaix and Ibragimov 2011; Carvalho and Gabaix 2013), according to which the individual shocks experienced by large firms can propagate aggregating into large GDP shocks (see Aoki and Hawkins 2010; Barro and Jin 2011; Aoki and Yoshikawa 2012; Solomon and Golo 2014; Carvalho and Grassi 2015) and contribute to the evolution of economic cycles.

Obviously, departures from these stylized facts will be found in the literature (Perline et al. 2006). Nevertheless, the fact that these empirical patterns hold for multiple and diverse data sets, contexts, time frames, and levels of aggregation suggests that context-specific modelling is of little help and that some primitive and general mechanisms should be investigated instead (Ijiri and Simon 1964, 1977; Sutton 1997).

In particular, we propose that any candidate model of firm growth should be tested simultaneously along all of the dimensions I–IV. Any coherent interpretative framework on the size and growth of business firms should match at least this minimum set of robust empirical facts since they characterize relevant restrictions on the space of plausible interpretative hypotheses. In fact, as stated by Brock, scaling and universality characterize "unconditional objects" (Brock 1999). The robustness of stable laws becomes then an issue, since a very large class of stochastic processes can lead to the same steady state distribution. By simultaneously considering multiple facts and their relations, we reduce the set of plausible generative processes. We then evaluate the accuracy of our conclusions through a considerable amount of statistical tests and simulations on the interplay between different predictions in order to account for as many consistent patterns as possible.

In the literature, the choice of the regularities to be matched by theoretical models has been rather partial, while facts have been somehow vaguely defined, e.g., "the size distribution of firms is highly skewed" or "the variance of growth rates is higher for smaller firms" (see Klette and Kortum 2004, p. 989). When authors have aimed at endogenizing economic forces behind firm dynamics in a general equilibrium setting, they have focused on specific predictions, along with a subset of the relevant dimensions (see Lentz and Mortensen 2008; Akcigit and Kerro 2010).

The framework that we introduce here is statistical in nature (Ijiri and Simon 1977; Slanina 2014). We do not explicitly model firms as entities obeying a maximizing behavior (Lucas 1978; Jovanovic 1982; Ericson and Pakes 1995; Luttmer 2007; Rossi-Hansberg and Wright 2007*b*; Luttmer 2011, 2012; Carvalho and Grassi 2015). Instead, we derive some coherent predictions on facts and relations from a core of "robust and primitive" features of the stochastic environment in which firms operate (Sutton 2007).

In particular, we aim to unravel some fundamental features of processes of index innovation, competition, and growth by means of assumptions that are both parsimonious and plausible. To generate falsifiable hypotheses, we begin by introducing the simplest possible model, which represents the growth and decline of business firms in relation to innovation "capture and loss" of elementary business opportunities. The neoclassical tradition within the stochastic framework focuses on equilibrium properties and on steady-state distributions (see, e.g.,

Jovanovic 1982; Klette and Kortum 2004; Koren and Tenreyro 2013). Our work is complementary to this tradition, since our objective is to study the properties of a growing economy in which the number of firms and products increases in time.

In our approach, time plays a key role as in any evolutionary process and, as a consequence, a steady state is present only as a limiting case.

Following John Sutton (2007), we assume that strategic interaction, product interdependence, and market forces are at work at the local level of specific markets, while firms diversify their activity across multiple lines of business and products. Each individual business opportunity is like an "island," large enough to fit just a single firm.

We come to a simplified representation of innovation and competition as the process through which firms conquer and lose "green islands" of variable sizes. A rule of proportional growth is then applied to both the number of units/products taken by each firm and to the size of each business unit, measured by its sales performance.

To summarize, we rely on two key first-approximation assumptions based on the seminal ideas presented by Ijiri and Simon, and by Gibrat (Gibrat 1931; Ijiri and Simon 1964, 1977):

(A) *Innovation: entry and exit (Simon's model).* The number of units (product lines) in a firm grows in proportion to the number of already exisisting units, while there is a positive probability that a new unit is captured by an entrant firm;

(B) *Proportional growth of existing units (Gibrat's model).* Each unit of a firm fluctuates in size at a proportional rate, which is independent of its size, while it operates in a given, independent market.

As we will show in Chapter 3, Simon's and Gibrat's models, taken separately, cannot account for the stylized facts I–IV listed earlier.

The combination of the two models in a single generalized proportional growth (GPG) framework is the key idea of this book (see also Growiec et al. 2018).

We introduce the smallest possible number of parameters, which play a straightforward role and allow direct checks of model consistency across various domains, featuring different regimes of innovation and growth.[1] Then, through a process of successive approximations, we derive relevant sub cases. Although GPG is a minimalist benchmark, it has a rich parametric space. Simon's model relies on three essential parameters: the rate of entry of new units, λ, which is a proxy of

[1] For a complementary approach, see Nelson and Winter (2002) on evolutionary theorizing in economics change, and Malerba et al. (2018) on the role of rich, history-friendly models in accounting for the evolution of industries. In addition, Robert Axtell (1999; Axtell and Guerrero 2019) relies upon agent-based approaches to account for the evolution of industry structure.

the arrival of innovation; the rate of exit of existing units, μ, which provides a simplified representation of the other side of "creative destruction" and the rate of entry of new firms, ν, which maps new small companies pursuing innovative ideas. The Gibrat side of the GPG framework, in turn, has three essential parameters: the mean growth rate of individual units, m_η; the dispersion of unit growth rate, V_η; and the dispersion of unit sizes, V_ξ, which in the simplest benchmark case have a lognormal distribution as a result of Gibrat's multiplicative growth process. The mean size of units, m_ξ, which in the benchmark model is the same for all units, is not an essential parameter as it can be regarded as a unit size.

We explore the impact of each parameter of GPG on the stylized facts I–IV presented earlier, and investigate the case of multiple levels of aggregation, i.e., when firm divisions are made up by multiple products sold in independent submarkets, or when firms aggregate to contribute to industrial sectors and national economies.

The framework and the evidence presented in this book show how the growth of complex economic organizations can be accounted for by a primitive representation of the arrival of new products and the underlying competitive environment in which they grow, shrink, and die.

In our mapping between models and data, we rely on different techniques, including simulations, econometric analysis, and data visualitazion (Tukey 1977).

The book is organized as follows. In Chapter 2, we present the key motivating evidence for the four stylized facts I–IV that have been discussed earlier. In Chapter 3, we develop our framework and derive its predictions. Statistical tests to compare predictions with empirical data are discussed in Chapter 4, where we rely on multiple data sources. In particular, we focus on PHID (PHarmaceutical Industry Database), a unique dataset which covers about one million products and thousands of firms in the pharmaceutical industry worldwide (for detailed investigations on the evolution of the pharmaceutical industry, see Orsenigo 1989; Gambardella 1995; Pammolli 1996; Sutton 1998; Matraves 1999; Henderson et al. 1999; Mc Kelvey et al. 2004).

PHID has allowed us to study how the size and growth of each individual firm is influenced by the rate of arrival, number, size, and growth of its products. Even though similar data are now available for different industries (see Argente et al. 2018), the pharmaceutical industry is an ideal setting to test a model on size and growth of firms. In particular, as it has been shown by Sutton (1998, chapter 8), the long-term evolution of the pharmaceutical industry has been constantly shaped by innovation, while the industry consists of a large number of products and therapeutic classes, which identify almost independent submarkets (Sutton 2007).

In Chapter 5, we complement the analysis of Chapter 4 and test the empirical accuracy and plausibility of our assumptions, as well as the sensitivity and robustness of our predictions. We focus on some unrealistic components of our framework and outline the corresponding violations of the benchmark, which is obviously an approximation that does not aim to reproduce the entire fine structure of the observed phenomena. Our analysis in Chapter 5 shows the key function of the benchmark to sustain a strategy of successive approximations. In fact, we have designed our framework starting from the simplest possible assumptions, followed by building upon its simplicity, parsimony, generality, and falsifiability (Popper 1961; Simon 1968) to encompass additional mechanisms that can lead to finer approximations, auxiliary hypotheses, and more accurate representations within specific domains.

2

Empirical Regularities

In this chapter, we present some descriptive statistics on the size and growth of business firms, which refer to facts I–IV presented in the Introduction and constitute the elementary evidence underlying our further investigations.

2.1 Background

In 1931, the French engineer Robert Gibrat proposed a simple stochastic framework to account for the empirically observed firm size distributions (Gibrat 1931; Sutton 1997; De Wit 2005; Coad 2009).

Gibrat made the following assumptions: (i) the number of firms is fixed; (ii) each firm faces the same growth rate distribution, i.e., the growth rate R of a company is independent of its size and of other firm characteristics (*law of proportionate effect*, LPE); (iii) the growth rates of a company are uncorrelated over time; and (iv) growth rates of different firms are independent of each other.

Following Stanley et al. (1996), Gibrat's idea can be expressed by a simple stochastic process:

$$S_{t+\Delta t} = S_t \eta_{t+\Delta t}, \tag{2.1}$$

in which S_t and $S_{t+\Delta t}$ are firm sizes at times t and $(t + \Delta t)$, respectively, and $\eta_{t+\Delta t}$ is an uncorrelated positive random number. Moreover, $\eta_{t+\Delta t}$ satisfy the hypothesis of the central limit theorem (CLT), namely, η_t is independent in t and we assume that $\log \eta$ has finite mean and variance. Hence, $\log S_t$ follows a random walk, and for sufficiently large time intervals $u \gg \Delta t$, the growth rates:

$$R_u \equiv \frac{S_{t+u}}{S_t} \tag{2.2}$$

follow a lognormal distribution. If companies are assumed to be born approximately at the same time (t_0) and to have approximately the same initial size (S_0)

(i.e., companies are differentiated only by the random sequence η), then the distribution of company sizes is also lognormal. In fact, by taking the logarithm of Equation (2.1), one can express the distribution of $\log S_t$ as the convolution of $(t - t_0)/\Delta t$ distributions of $\log \eta$.

Gibrat's Law of proportionate effect has reached widespread popularity for two main reasons.[1] First, the stochastic properties of LPE have been shown to be broadly consistent with the dynamic patterns of firm growth and decline, which have been observed in many countries and industrial sectors over time. Second, Gibrat's Law postulates one simple and plausible process that generates a skewed size distribution with a bulk of small- and medium-sized firms and few larger ones, which is approximately consistent with the observed size distribution of firms (Kalecki 1945; Steindl 1965; Prais 1976; Stanley et al. 1995; Hart and Oulton 1996). The lognormal distribution of firm sizes is not a steady-state solution, because its parameters go toward infinity as time goes to infinity (Sutton 1997; Sornette and Cont 1997). For this reason, Kalecki examined a modified process in which the expected rates of growth increase slightly less than proportionally, leading to a steady-state lognormal distribution with a constant variance (Kalecki 1945). This approach is justified by the presence of constraints to firm growth (such as finite assets, limited resources, or bounded market sizes) that prevent firms from growing indefinitely. More recently, this argument has been used to justify the tendency of firms to evolve toward an "optimal" firm size (*mean reversion effect*, Rossi-Hansberg and Wright 2007*b*). Alternatively, frictions can prevent firms from becoming too small, i.e., a lower bound for sizes enforced by a reflecting barrier might exist. In this case, the corresponding stochastic process, known as the Kesten process (Kesten 1973; Sornette and Cont 1997), generates a power law distribution of firms (Axtell et al. 2008; Gabaix 2009) or business unit sizes (Takayasu et al. 2014).

In sum, a Gibrat's growth process with frictions that prevent firms from becoming too large, à la Kalecki, generates a stable lognormal distribution, whereas adding to Gibrat's Law a barrier to prevent firms from becoming too small, à la Kesten, generates a stable power law distribution.

Over the years, the benchmark of Gibrat's Law has sustained an extensive set of empirical studies, aiming to scrutinize the empirical validity of its assumptions and predictions. These studies have contributed to unravel a series of departures. First, some of the main assumptions of Gibrat's Law are violated in most empirical settings: (a) the number of firms varies over time due to entry, exit, mergers, acquisitions, and spin-offs; (b) firms have idiosyncratic features, such as the quality

1 Similar processes have been popularized in general science under different names such as *preferential attachment*, *the rich get richer*, or *the Matthew effect*.

of management, competences, and resources, which motivate some stability of differential performances; (c) firms interact strategically with each other when they compete and they are connected in production, financial, and strategic collaboration networks.

After more than 50 years of research, there is now considerable empirical evidence that challenges the assumptions and predictions of Gibrat's Law. Gibrat's Law assumes the absence of any relation between the expected percentage growth rates and firm size as well as between the variance of percentage growth rates and size. However, the growth rate has been found to be dependent on size. First, firm survival increases either with firm size, holding firm age constant, or with age, holding size constant (Dunne et al. 1989; Evans 1987a; Hall 1987; Sutton 2007). Second, the variance of firm growth declines with firm size, holding firm age constant (Hymer and Pashigian 1962; Mansfield 1962; Dunne et al. 1989; Stanley et al. 1996; Bottazzi et al. 2001; Sutton 2002; Riccaboni et al. 2008), and declines with firm age, holding firm size constant (Dunne et al. 1989).

The negative relationship between the volatility of growth rate and size (see Section 2.2) can be accounted for by the fact that large and established firms are likely to be more diversified. Singh and Whittington have stated that the decline of the standard deviation of growth with size is not as rapid as it would be if the firms consisted of independently operating divisions (Hymer and Pashigian 1962; Singh and Whittington 1975). The latter would imply that standard deviation decays as $\sigma(r) \sim S^{-1/2}$. Such a departure might have been seen as coherent with the common-sense view that the performance of different parts of a firm are related to each other, as stated by Mansfield:

> The growth rate of a large firm can be viewed as the mean of the growth rates of its smaller "components" (e.g., plants). Note that, if the growth rates of the components (plants or other) were independent, the standard deviation would be inversely proportional to the square root of a firm's size. But, since they tend to be located in the same region and have other similarities in common, one would expect the growth rates of such components to be positively correlated. Thus, the standard deviation would not be expected to decrease as rapidly with increases in size as the square-root formula suggests.
>
> *(Mansfield 1962, p. 1034)*

The tradition of considering a firm as a portfolio of internal units dates back to the mid-1950s and has recently been revitalized by the view of firms as aggregations of products sold in different submarkets (see, for instance, Sutton's *island model* (Sutton 1998) and the *quality ladder* model by Klette and Kortum (2004) which focuses on the fundamental role of innovation in the evolution of industry structure).

Results from studies on the relationship between firm size and growth rate are not fully conclusive. For example, the mean growth rate of a firm has been found to slightly increase with size, if firm assets are considered (Singh and Whittington 1975). However, other authors have shown that when the number of employees is used to measure the size of a company, the mean growth rate declines slightly with firm size (Evans 1987a; Hall 1987). Dunne and colleagues have insisted on the effect of firm failure rate and diversification on the relation between size and mean growth rate. They have concluded that the mean growth rate is negatively correlated with size for single-unit firms, while it increases modestly with size in case of multi-unit firms because their lower failure rates overshadow the reduction in the growth of nonfailing firms (Dunne et al. 1989).

Gibrat's Law also implies that the growth rates of a firm are uncorrelated over time. Although this implication is testable, the empirical results in the literature are not conclusive. Sing and Whittington observed positive first-order correlations in the one-year growth rates of a company (persistence of growth) (Singh and Whittington 1975), whereas Hall did not find any correlation (Hall 1987). The possibility of negative correlations (regression toward the mean) has also been suggested by others scholars (see Leonard 1986; Friedman 1992). For an empirical investigation of different patterns of autocorrelation of firm growth rates, see Bottazzi et al. (2001), who were inspired also by the work of Quah (1996).

Overall, if the Gibrat's Law has been rejected in its general formulation, it still holds as a long-run regularity for large and mature firms (Lotti et al. 2009).

Against this background generated by Gibrat, we now briefly summarize the main known empirical facts about the size and growth of firms.

2.2 Size Distributions

In order to investigate the distribution of company sizes we first need to define and measure firm size. If all companies produce the same product (e.g., steel), we can use a physical output to measure firm size (e.g., tons). When firms produce different goods for which no common physical output measure is available, one solution is to use the dollar value of output, i.e., a firm's total sales. Alternatively, one can measure the value of input factors (labor, capital, raw materials, etc.). Though we might expect systematic differences between alternative measures, we focus on a set of empirical regularities that are similar across different measures.

Our first set of data is taken from the Compustat files for all publicly traded firms in the United States from 1950 to 2010 (values adjusted to 1950 US $). The Compustat data cover approximately one half of total employment in the manufacturing sector in the United States, although they cover less than 1 percent of all firms and cannot be used to estimate the shape of the entire size distribution (Axtell 2001).

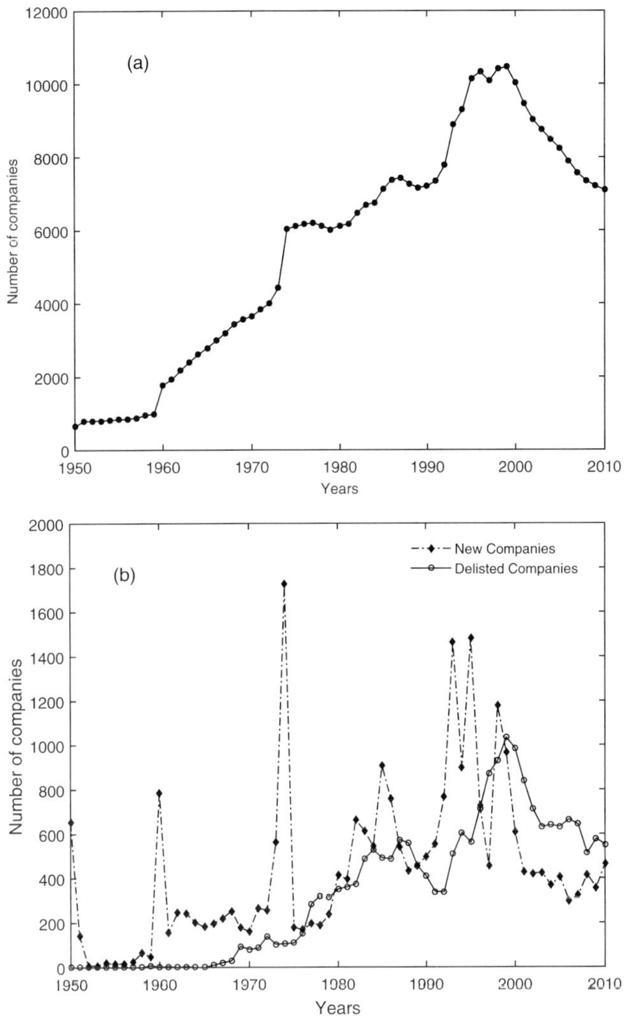

Figure 2.1 Number of publicly traded manufacturing companies (a) and numbers of companies entering and exiting the market (b) in the United States from 1950 to 2010. Data source: Compustat

Figure 2.1 shows the total number of firms in the Compustat database for different years. We also plot the number of both *new* and "dying" companies (i.e., companies that leave the database because of a merger, a change of name, or a bankruptcy). Clearly, the population of firms undergoes market turnover proxied by flows of firm entry and exit. In particular, a significant market "shakeout" (Klepper 1996) happened at the turn of the millennium when the number of firms first grew to a peak and later fell to a lower level.

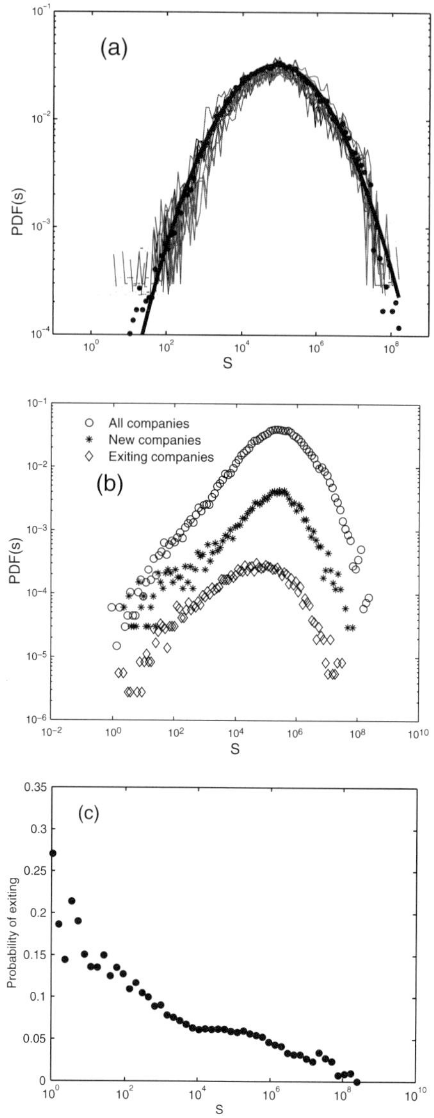

Figure 2.2 (a) Probability density of the logarithm of the sales for publicly-traded manufacturing companies (with standard industrial classification index of 2000–3999) in the United States, every four years from 1950 to 2010. From 1950, sales are deflated by the Gross National Product (GNP) price deflator. Solid circles show the average over the 60 years, while the black line represents the lognormal fitting. (b) Normalized probability density of the logarithm of sales for all of the manufacturing companies, for the companies entering the market, and for the companies exiting the market averaged over the time period from 1950 to 2010. The PDFS for entering and exiting companies are shifted down by factors of 1/10 and 1/100, respectively. (c) Plot of the fraction of exiting companies by size. We define this probability as the yearly ratio of exiting companies of a given size over the total number of companies of that size. Panels (a), (b), and (c) are inspired by panels (a) and (b) in figure 2 in Amaral et al. (1997) taking a longer observation period. Data source: Compustat

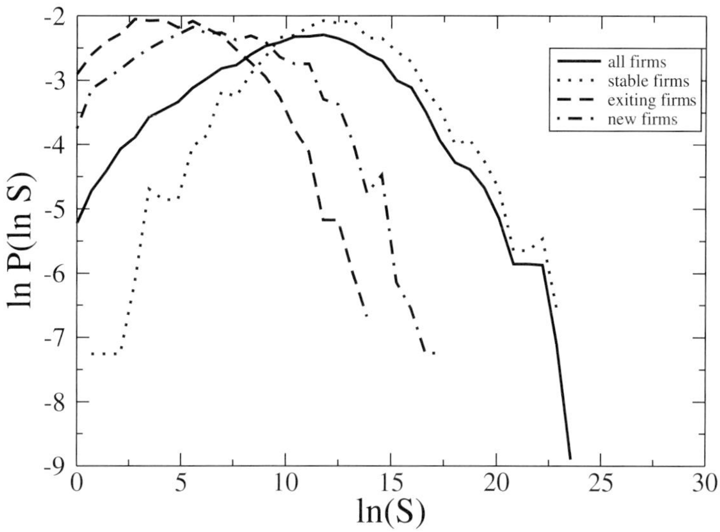

Figure 2.3 The distribution of firm sizes in the pharmaceutical industry. The size distribution of *all firms* includes all pharmaceutical firms that were active in the years 1994–2003. *Stable firms* are long-lived firms which have been active for at least 10 years. The distribution of *stable firms* approaches a lognormal shape (a parabola in double-log scale). *New firms* are new-born companies in their first year. The size distribution of new firms is shifted to the left with smaller mean and variance and larger skewness as compared to long-lived firms. Finally, *exiting firms* are companies in the year preceding their exit. Just before their exit, companies are considerably smaller than long-lived firms. Data Source: PHID

Figure 2.2a shows the distribution of firm sizes for every four years from 1950 to 2010.

At first inspection, the size distribution seems to be stable over the 60 years of observation despite an increase in market turnover. Namely, we cannot detect significant changes in the mean, variance, and tails of the distributions over the observation period. This stability is surprising, since there is no theoretical reason to expect that the size distribution of firms would remain stable. In fact, the economy was growing and the composition of output was changing, driven by technological progress and social-economic transformations. A remarkable feature of most industries and markets is that at any given moment, the bulk of firms is concentrated at smaller sizes, but there are also a number of larger firms, leading to a skewed or heavy-tailed size distribution. The stability of heavy-tailed size distributions is important. In fact, as already noticed, Equation (2.1) implies that the size distribution of companies should become broader with a linearly increasing variance over time. Therefore, we must conclude that other factors have important roles, such as, for instance, firm entry and exit, or frictions that prevent firms from becoming too large or too small.

At closer inspection, we can detect another departure from Gibrat's Law, that is, the firm size distribution is not lognormal. As shown in Figure 2.2a, the body of the distribution can be approximated by a lognormal, but the tails seem to follow a different behavior. Again, this fact could be a consequence of the selection bias associated with the Compustat data, which collects information on publicly traded companies (Hall 1987; Axtell 2001).

Here, moving toward deeper inspections of individual industries, we refer to the Pharmaceutical Industry Database (PHID). In Figure 2.3 we show the size distribution for all pharmaceutical companies worldwide. After a first visual inspection, the size distribution seems approximatively lognormal for long-lived companies.

Gibrat did not take into account the appearance of new firms. Figure 2.2b shows that the size distribution of new publicly traded firms is similar to the distribution of existing firms. However, Compustat covers only newly traded companies (Hall 1987). When we look at the entire size distribution of firms, as in the case of the pharmaceutical industry (Figure 2.3), new entities tend to be smaller than existing companies.

In addition, Figure 2.2c shows that the probability that a company leaves the market depends negatively on its size.

2.3 The Distribution of Growth Rates

Since the Gibrat's benchmark implies a multiplicative process for the growth of companies, it is natural to study the logarithm of sales:

$$s_t \equiv \ln S_t \tag{2.3}$$

and the corresponding growth rate:

$$r \equiv \ln R = \ln \frac{S_{t+1}}{S_t}, \tag{2.4}$$

which corresponds to Equation (2.2), where r indicates the one-year growth rate of firms between year t and $t+1$.

Since the 1960s, the empirical literature has been piling up sound evidence on the dependency of firm growth rates on size and age of firms, conditional on firm survival. In recent years, the growing availability of detailed micro-level data about the evolution of the size of all firms in specific countries and industries has provided valuable insight into the empirics of firms' growth. For example, we now know that, among surviving firms, the mean and variance of growth rates decrease with increasing size and age, also after controlling for other factors that influence firm survival and performance (Klepper and Thompson 2006; Sutton 2007). Figure 2.4 shows the relationship between firm size (S) and growth rate (r) for

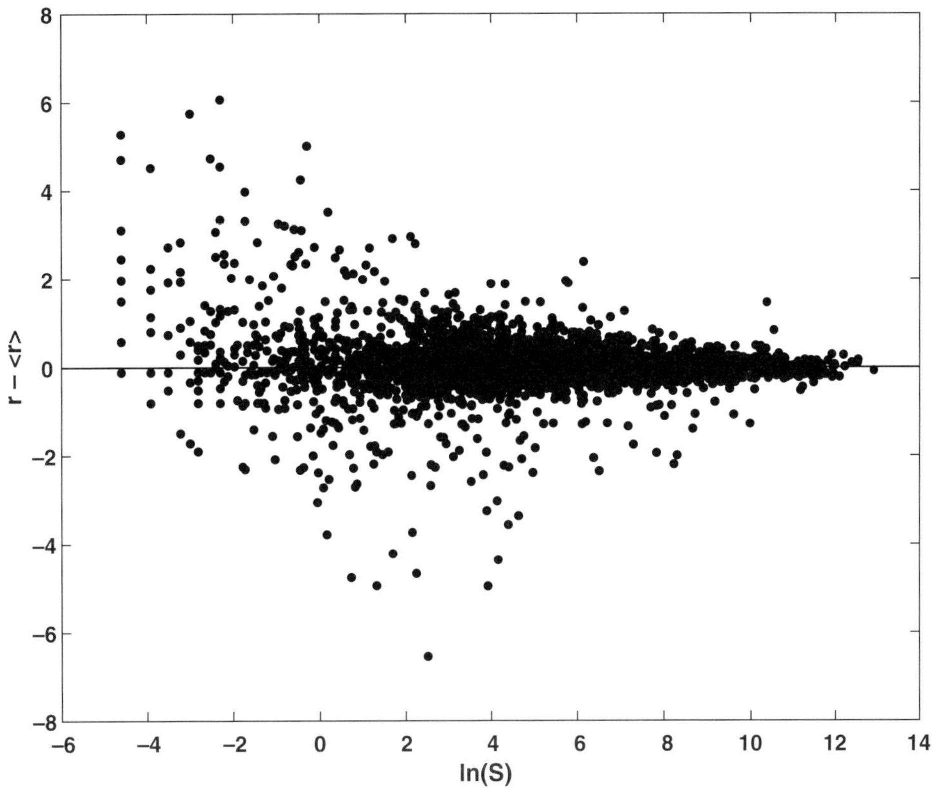

Figure 2.4 The figure shows the yearly firm growth rate minus the average firm growth rate (about 0.11) ($r - \langle r \rangle$) versus log-size ($\ln(S)$), for manufacturing firms in the United States during the years 2009–2010; USD, thousands. Data source: Compustat

manufacturing firms in the United States (Hall 1987). According to Gibrat's Law, firm growth rates should be evenly distributed above and below the horizontal axes with the same width along all sizes, which is clearly not the case here. First, Figure 2.4 suggests that the variance of growth rates depends on firm size (heteroskedasticity). More precisely, the variance of growth rates declines with size. Second, we notice a prevalence of positive growth for small firms, which vanishes for medium and large firms, suggesting that the average growth rate could correlate negatively with firm size. Should small firms be more likely to exit when they experience negative growth shocks, this would explain the prevalence of positive growth rates for small firms in Figure 2.4. This issue, known as "sample censoring", combined with the observed heteroskedasticity, has been a major focus of empirical research since the 1980s, with the goal of understanding whether the departures from Gibrat's Law depend on any of these effects.

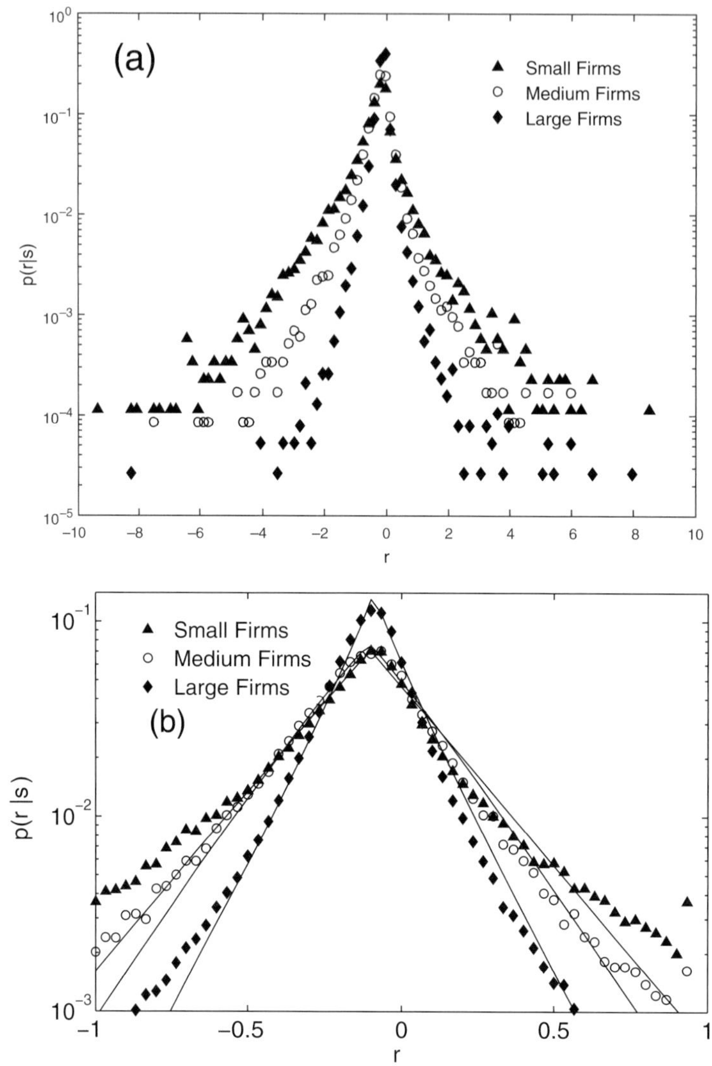

Figure 2.5 (a) Probability density $p(r|s)$ of the growth rate $r \equiv \ln(S_{t+1}/S_t)$ for all publicly traded manufacturing firms in the United States present in the Compustat with Standard Industrial Classification index of 2000–3999. The distribution shows all annual growth rates observed during the 60-year period between the years 1950 and 2010. Data for three different groups of firms are shown: small, medium, and large firms. (b) Same as in (a), but with a magnified scale near the peak. The solid lines are Laplace fits to the empirical data close to the peak. Visual inspection shows that the tails are somewhat "fatter" than what is predicted by Equation (2.5). Data source: Compustat

Another prediction of Gibrat's Law is that the logarithmic growth rate of firms (r) is normally distributed. Stanley and colleagues brought to the attention of the scientific community the fact that the logarithmic growth rate distribution is not

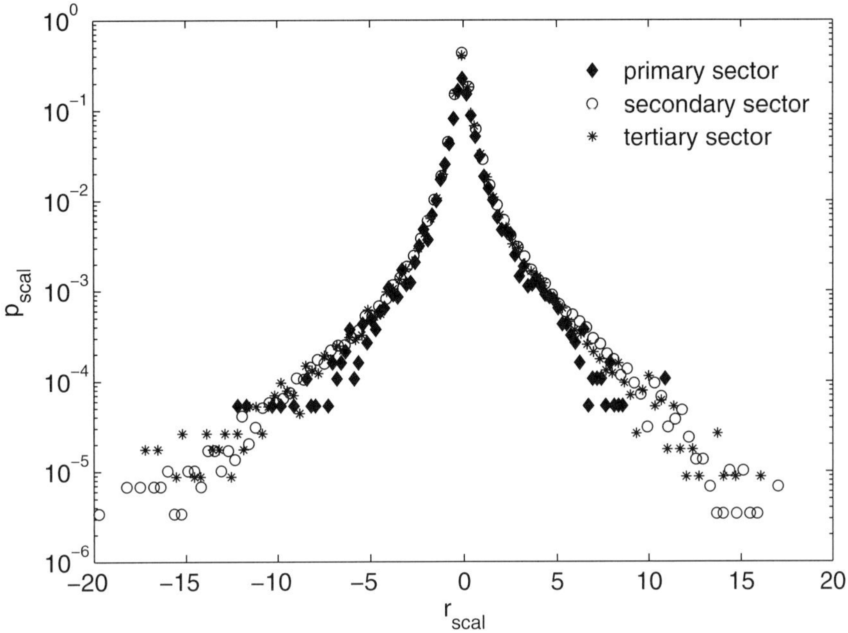

Figure 2.6 Probability density function of scaled growth rate by industrial sectors. The scaled growth rate is calculated as $r_{\text{scal}} = [r - \bar{r}]/\sigma(r)$. Data source: Compustat

Gaussian but displays a "tent-shaped" distribution (Stanley et al. 1996). Figure 2.5 shows the distribution $p(r|s)$ of the growth rates of the Compustat list of firms from 1950 to 2010 for small, medium-sized, and large firms. In this case, the definition of firm size is based on the number of employees: a small firm has less than 100 employees, a medium-sized firm has between 100 and 500 employees, and a large firm has more than 500 employees. Note that all distributions in Figure 2.5 are far from being Gaussian. The distributions of logarithmic growth rates have both a sharper peak around the mean and heavier tails than a normal distribution. Therefore, extreme (positive and negative) events of growth are much more likely to occur than predicted by Gibrat's Law, especially for small firms. In a single word, the growth distribution is leptokurtic, i.e., it has excess positive kurtosis as compared to the normal distribution. In particular, a Laplace distribution, which is widely used to fit financial data (Kotz et al. 2001), provides a good first approximation (Stanley et al. 1996)[2]:

$$p(r|s) = \frac{1}{\sqrt{2}\sigma(s)} \exp\left(-\frac{\sqrt{2}\,|r - \bar{r}(s)|}{\sigma(s)}\right). \tag{2.5}$$

[2] For the description of the Laplace distribution, see also Appendix E.

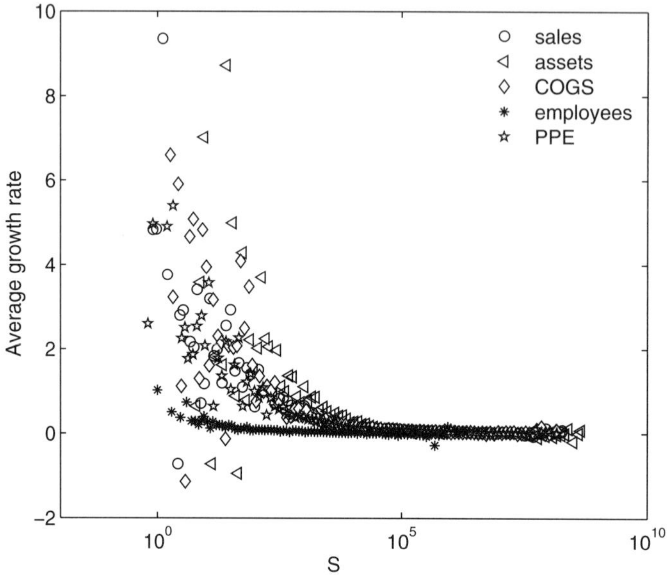

Figure 2.7 Average growth rate over a 60-year period $\bar{r}$, for different measures of firm size: sales, assets, cost of goods sold (COGS), employees, plant property, and equipment (PPE) against firm size. The figure is inspired by figure 3 in Amaral et al. (1997). Data source: Compustat

The straight lines shown in Figure 2.5 are calculated from the average growth rate $\bar{r}(s)$ and the standard deviation $\sigma(s)$ is obtained as in Amaral et al. (1997).

The tails in Figure 2.5 seem to be fatter than predicted by Equation (2.5). This deviation is the opposite of what one would find in the case of a Gaussian distribution.

Thus, the body of the distribution for companies of different sizes can be described by a Laplace distribution, but the growth rate distribution for small companies shows fatter tails.

For a first assessment of the robustness of these results, we classify firms according to their main sector of activity: agriculture, manufacturing, and services. It is visually apparent in Figure 2.6 that the same behavior holds for different sectors of the economy.

Mean Growth Rate

Figure 2.7 displays the average growth rate, $\bar{r}$, as a function of initial size, s, over several years. Despite the level of noise, the data highlight a negative dependency of the mean growth rate on firm size.

The figure also suggests that the results do not change when we consider alternative measures of firm size.

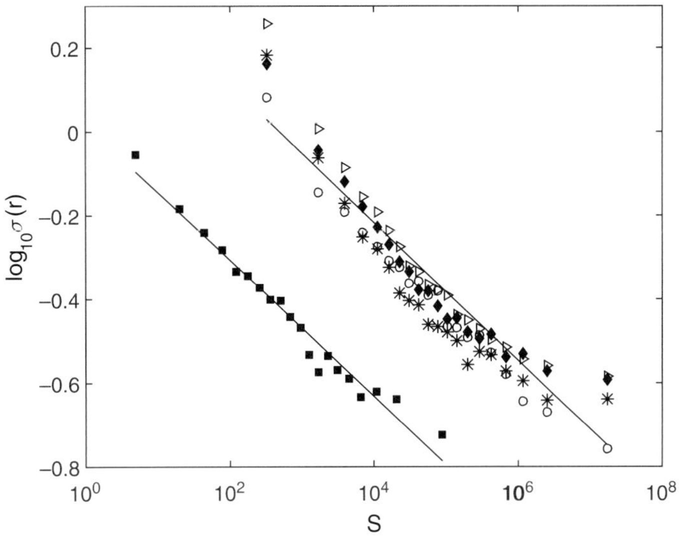

Figure 2.8 Standard deviation of the annual growth rates for different definitions of firm size as a function of firm initial size. Least squares power law fits were made for all quantities leading to the estimates of β: 0.18 ± 0.06 for "assets," 0.17 ± 0.07 for "sales," 0.17 ± 0.03 for "number of employees," 0.16 ± 0.06 for "cost of goods sold," and 0.17 ± 0.03 for "plant, property and, equipment". The straight lines are guides for the eye and have a slope of 0.17. The figure is inspired by figure 4 in Amaral et al. (1997). Data source: Compustat

The data analyzed here are obtained from the Compustat database of all US publicly traded industrial firms. One may argue that the negative dependence of the average growth rate on size is due to the selection bias of the Compustat database for small fast growing firms, e.g., successful startups. Indeed, Bottazzi et al. (2011) did not find a significant dependence of the average growth rate on size for all French firms. On the other hand, data on all pharmaceutical firms (PHID) confirm strong negative dependence of the average growth rate on size for small firms (see Figures 4.13 and 5.16b). Perline and coauthors (2006) are in agreement with this finding for small US firms from US Census data. As we will see in Chapter 3, the existence of this negative relationship crucially depends on the intensity of innovation, and it holds only if small firms producing one product or consisting of one business unit have a high probability to launch a new product or to open a new unit.

Standard Deviation of Growth Rates

The relationship between the standard deviation of growth, $\sigma(r)$, and firm size, S ("size-variance relationship") has been found to be approximated by the scaling law (Stanley et al. 1996; Bottazzi et al. 2001; Sutton 2002; Riccaboni et al. 2008):

$$\sigma(r) \sim S^{-\beta}, \tag{2.6}$$

which in log–log scale implies a linear dependence with slope β:

$$\ln(\sigma(r)) \sim -\beta s, \tag{2.7}$$

where, for sales, $\beta = 0.17 \pm 0.07$ (see Figure 2.8). Figure 2.8 displays $\sigma(r)$ *versus* S, and we can see that Equation (2.6) is indeed not falsified by the data.[3]

The relationship between $\sigma(r)$ and s seems to hold across different measures of s: (i) assets; (ii) cost of goods sold (COGS); (iii) property, plant, and equipment (PPE); and (iv) number of employees, as in Amaral et al. (1997). Figure 2.8 shows the standard deviation of these different measures of firm size. Considering, for instance, the number of employees, we see that the data on the number of employees are linear across roughly five orders of magnitude from firms with less than 10 employees to firms with almost 10^5 employees. The slope $\beta = 0.16 \pm 0.06$ is similar, within the error bars, to that for sales.

In this chapter, we have presented some known broad empirical facts on the size and growth of business firms, which seem to hold across different data sets and empirical domains.

In the next chapter we introduce a simple probabilistic framework as a plausible benchmark to account for the observed empirical regularities.

[3] Perline et al. (2006) analyze data from the Census Bureau Statistics of US Businesses, and find that the volatility increases with the numbers of employees. As we will see in Chapter 3, our framework accounts for this result in a certain region of its parameter space.

3

Innovation and the Growth of Business Firms

A Stochastic Framework

3.1 Introduction

In this chapter, we present a generalized proportional growth (GPG) model of innovation and growth, which we have been partially outlined also in previous works (Fu et al. 2005; Growiec et al. 2018). We keep the model as parsimonious as possible, and we assume that all its variables are independent and uncorrelated. Then, we derive its predictions to investigate which of the stylized facts (I–IV) defined in Chapter 1 are falsified in each particular domain of the parametric space. The basic idea of the model is that the firm is not an "indivisible atom" of the economic system but consist of a number of units, each pursuing a separate business opportunity.

We refer to the notion of business units, which we interpret as *independent submarkets*, followinging John Sutton's hypothesis according to which submarkets are composed of product sets, each of which satisfies different needs and requires distinct Research and Development (R&D) efforts and technical expertise (Sutton 1998). Firms thus diversify their activities across submarkets.

In a nutshell, we assume that innovating firms capture new business opportunities (products) in proportion to the number of their existing business units. Some business opportunities are captured by new start-up firms. The sizes of products grow and shrink in time following innovation, demand fluctuations, and competition. Our goal here is to model this process of innovation and growth with the minimal set of assumptions and parameters.

The chapter is structured as follows: Section 3.2 describes the key assumptions of our theoretical framework. Sections 3.3–3.7 present the key consequences of our assumptions under different regimes of innovation and growth. In Sections 3.3–3.7, we refer the interested reader to the appendices, where detailed analytical derivations, when possible, or computer simulations, are presented. Section 3.8 summarizes the results.

3.2 Assumptions

In this section, we present the key assumptions of GPG. We introduce two main assumptions:

A The number of units in a firm grows in proportion to the number of existing units (proportional growth in the number of elementary units);
B The size of each unit grows in proportion to its size, independently of other units (proportional growth in size).

While Assumption (A) was first applied to firm growth by Simon (see Simon 1955), Assumption (B) is known as Gibrat's Law. Assumption (A) can be detailed as follows (see also Fu et al. 2005):

(1) At time t, the industry is populated by $N(t)$ firms. Each firm i consists of $K_i(t)$ units, while $N_K(t)$ indicates the number of firms with exactly K units. By definition,

$$N(t) = \sum_{K=0}^{\infty} N_K(t). \tag{3.1}$$

The sum in Equation (3.1) starts from zero in order to take into account the firms that went out of business by closing all their units. The total number of units in the industry, $n(t)$, is

$$n(t) = \sum_{K=0}^{\infty} K N_K(t) \equiv \langle K(t) \rangle N(t), \tag{3.2}$$

where $\langle K(t) \rangle$ is the average number of units per firm. According to our assumption, at time $t = 0$ there are $N_K(0)$ firms consisting of K units. We denote the initial number of firms and units as $N(0)$ and $n(0) \equiv n_0$, respectively. Accordingly, we introduce

$$\langle K \rangle = n_0/N(0) = \langle K(0) \rangle, \tag{3.3}$$

which indicates the initial average number of units per firm at time $t = 0$. We define the initial firm size distribution, measured in terms of the number of units, as $P_K^o = N_K(0)/N(0)$, where P_K^o is the probability for a randomly selected firm from a population of firms at $t = 0$ to have exactly K units. Our main goal is to find

$$P_K(t) = N_K(t)/N(t), \tag{3.4}$$

the probability for a randomly selected firm to have exactly k units at any $t > 0$.

(2) At each infinitesimally small time interval Δt, each existing unit can create, with probability $\lambda \Delta t$, a new unit, which is placed in the same firm as the existing unit. Here, λ is the birth rate of new units. It follows that the average number of units added during Δt is $\Delta_\lambda n = \lambda n(t)\Delta t$ and these newly created units belong to firm i with probability p_i, proportional to the number of units, $K_i(t)$, in firm i: $p_i = K_i(t)/n(t)$.
(3) At each infinitesimally small time interval Δt, an existing unit is deleted, with probability $\mu \Delta t$. Here, μ is the death rate of existing units. It follows that the average number of units deleted during Δt is $\Delta_\mu n = \mu n(t)\Delta t$ and these units are deleted from firm i with probability p_i, proportional to the number of units, $K_i(t)$, in firm i: $p_i = K_i(t)/n(t)$.
(4) At each infinitesimally small time interval Δt, each existing unit can create a new *firm* with probability $\nu' \Delta t$. Here, ν' is the birth rate of new firms. As a consequence, the average number of firms created during Δt is $\Delta_\nu N = \nu' n(t)\Delta t$. We assume that the probability of a new firm to have exactly k units is P'_K.[1] Thus, for each time interval, the average number of units added due to the entry of new firms is $\Delta_\nu n = \nu n(t)\Delta t$, where

$$\nu \equiv \nu' \sum_K P'_K K = \nu' \langle K \rangle' \tag{3.5}$$

and $\langle K \rangle'$ is the average number of units in new firms.

A similar model was formulated by Klette and Kortum (see Klette and Kortum 2004), who derived the size distribution of firms in the case of zero net growth $\psi = \lambda - \mu + \nu = 0$. Interestingly, these four assumptions bring to mind a model of asexual reproduction of colonies of primitive organisms, with birth rate $\lambda + \nu$ and death rate μ, in which a newborn organism can form a separate colony with probability $\nu/(\nu + \lambda)$. Analogous models were popular in theoretical ecology in the mid twentieth century (Darwin 1953).[2] One of these models was treated anaytically by a British mathematician, D. G. Kendall (1948). A significant difference is that in the Kendall model no new colonies (interpreted as species) are created ($\nu = 0$).

One can alternatively think that units are firm divisions. In this case, each division can split, during a unit time interval, to form a new division with probability $\lambda + \nu$, and the new division can then split into a new firm with probability $\nu/(\lambda + \nu)$ (see also Amaral et al. 1998). A similar model of firm growth with positive λ, μ, and ν has been presented in (Luttmer 2011), where firm units are interpreted as

[1] It is natural to assume that the startups begin with only one product, but for the sake of generality, we include a probability that a new firm may begin with more than one product quantified by P'_K.
[2] For an extensive reference to ecological models in the analysis of processes of economic growth, see (Ricolfi 2014).

"blueprints," and the total growth rate of the economy ψ is related to the growth of consumption.

Proportional growth with no entry of new firms ($\nu = 0$) is well known in general probability theory, where firms would be represented as urns and units as balls, and in physics, where urns are quantum states and balls are quantum particles (Feller 1968; Ijiri and Simon 1975). The Bose–Einstein process, in which bosons (indistinguishable quantum particles with integer spin) are added one by one to a system with N possible quantum states, is of particular interest. For distinguishable and noninteracting classical particles obeying Maxwell–Boltzmann statistics, the probability to find a state with exactly K particles is given by a binomial distribution that, in the limit of infinitely large number of particles and states, $n \to \infty$ and $N \to \infty$, converges to the Poisson distribution $P_K = \langle K \rangle^K \exp(-\langle K \rangle)/K!$, where $\langle K \rangle$ is the average number of particles per state $\langle K \rangle = n/N$. This result is what one would normally expect when $n = \langle K \rangle N$ balls are placed at random in N urns. Surprisingly, for the case of bosons, the result is the geometric distribution: $P_K = \langle K \rangle^K/(\langle K \rangle + 1)^{K+1}$. Interestingly, Kendall showed that a geometric distribution arises if the probability for a ball to be placed in an urn with K particles is proportional to K. This process is also known as Polya's urn scheme (Feller 1968; Garibaldi and Scalas 2010). Thus, somehow, this means that bosons attract each other in the absence of any classical interaction. This attraction (the so-called exchange force) has a pure quantum nature coming from the symmetry of the boson wave-function with respect to permutation of particles, which are indistinguishable (Griffiths 2005). Accordingly, throughout this chapter we refer to the proportional growth with $\nu = 0$ as a Bose–Einstein process.

All equations in this chapter describe the behavior of the mathematical expectations of certain quantities obtained by averaging over the ensemble of all realizations. The behavior of each realization can deviate significantly from the behavior of the ensemble average. In fact, the analytical solution to the problem of finding the probability distribution $P_k(t) = N_k(t)/N(t)$ of number of units in a firm at time t given Assumptions (1)–(4) is based on treating discrete variables, such as, for example, the total number of units in the system $n(t)$, as continuous variables, which are the mathematical expectations of actual discrete random variables (see Cox and Hinkley 1979). This approach is rigorous only in the limit of infinite number of firms and units. Its results differ from the results obtained for a finite system in the same way as the Poisson distribution differs from the binomial distribution in the problem of random assignment of n balls to N urns. When the number of urns and balls in the system goes to infinity, keeping the average number of balls per urn finite, the binomial distribution converges to the Poisson distribution (Feller 1968). By using continuous variables we obtain the Poisson distribution directly from the differential equations relating the time derivatives of the continuous variables.

Since convergences of the distributions describing a finite system to their limits in the infinite system may vary in speed, we always verify our analytical results by computer simulations of a finite system.

We now borrow notions from the elementary theory of linear differential equations to derive the time evolution of two key characteristics of an industry, i.e., the number of units $n(t)$ and the number of firms $N(t)$. By summing up positive contributions to the growth of number of units $\lambda n(t)\Delta t$ and $\nu n(t)\Delta t$ defined in Assumptions (2) and (4), and the negative contribution $-\mu n(t)\Delta t$ from Assumption (3), we find the net increase in the number of units $\Delta n(t)$ during the time interval Δt:

$$\Delta n(t) = (\nu + \lambda - \mu)n(t)\Delta t, \tag{3.6}$$

which, in the limit of $\Delta t \to 0$, is equivalent to a linear differential equation:

$$\frac{dn}{dt} = (\nu + \lambda - \mu)n(t). \tag{3.7}$$

Consequently, by solving this equation with the initial condition $n(0) = n_0$, we predict an exponential growth[3] of the system (industry, economy) in time:

$$n(t) = n_0 e^{(\nu+\lambda-\mu)t}. \tag{3.8}$$

On the other hand, the number of firms $N(t)$, according to Assumption (4), obeys a differential equation:

$$\frac{dN}{dt} = \nu' n(t), \tag{3.9}$$

where $n(t)$ is already determined by Equation (3.8). By substituting $n(t)$ into Equation (3.9), integrating and applying the initial condition $N(0)$, we obtain:

$$N(t) = \frac{\nu'}{\nu + \lambda - \mu}(n(t) - n_0) + N(0). \tag{3.10}$$

As a consequence, if the net growth rate $\psi = \nu + \lambda - \mu > 0$ is positive, the system will grow exponentially. If $\psi < 0$, the system will shrink exponentially and eventually, when $n(t)$ becomes of the order of unity, (3.8) and (3.10) will not approximate the behavior of a finite system. However, the model will give reliable predictions also for $\psi < 0$ so long as the number of units, $n(t)$, is sufficiently large.

These derivations are made under the assumption that parameters λ, μ, and ν are constants. In reality, these parameters fluctuate over time due to external factors, for example, fluctuations of demand or economic cycles. A good approximation is

[3] Note that the rates λ, μ, and ν for real systems are small, corresponding to a few percentage points per year. Therefore, Equation (3.8) can be well approximated by a linear function for realistic observation periods.

provided by replacing the instantaneous values of $\lambda(t)$, $\mu(t)$, and $\nu(t)$ with the time averages of these quantities, e.g. $\lambda = \int_0^t \lambda(\tau)d\tau/t$. In any real economic system, however, the instantaneous values of these parameters are not known. We measure the average values of the parameters counting the number of units and firms added and deleted from the industry in a certain observation period of time, for example, one year (see Chapter 5 for a practical example). Thus, it is desirable to express growth in terms of the total number of units $n(t)$, the number of units added to the existing firms $n_\lambda(t)$, the number of units added together with the new firms $n_\nu(t)$, and the number of units deleted from the system $n_\mu(t)$. It is clear that

$$n(t) = n_\lambda(t) - n_\mu(t) + n_\nu(t) + n_0 \tag{3.11}$$

no matter how these parameters depend on time. For constant λ, μ, and ν, we have:

$$n_\lambda(t) = \lambda(n(t) - n_0)/(\nu + \lambda - \mu), \tag{3.12}$$

$$n_\mu(t) = \mu(n(t) - n_0)/(\nu + \lambda - \mu), \tag{3.13}$$

$$n_\nu(t) = \nu(n(t) - n_0)/(\nu + \lambda - \mu), \tag{3.14}$$

We introduce the death–birth ratio[4] as

$$\alpha(t) \equiv \frac{n_\mu(t)}{n_\lambda(t)}. \tag{3.15}$$

For constant values of λ and μ, $\alpha = \mu/\lambda$. Another important parameter is the overall growth factor,

$$F(t) \equiv n(t)/n_0. \tag{3.16}$$

We can make a variable substitution and use F instead of t. We show in Appendix 7.1 (Chapter 7) that all quantities of interest can be expressed in terms of F, α, and the firm-unit birth ratio

$$b(t) \equiv \frac{n_\nu(t)}{n_\lambda(t) - n_\mu(t)}. \tag{3.17}$$

For constant ν, λ, and μ, $b = \nu/(\lambda - \mu)$. To analyze the case $\nu > 0$, it is convenient to introduce also a modified growth factor

$$R \equiv F^{1/(b+1)}. \tag{3.18}$$

Note that for $\nu = 0$, $R = F$. In the remaining parts of the book, we use R rather than F to describe the growth rate. For constant values of λ, μ, and ν, $R = \exp[(\lambda - \mu)t]$. Thus, all of the results of the model can be approximated in terms of $n_\lambda(t)$, $n_\mu(t)$,

[4] As shown in Appendix 7.1 (see Chapter 7), the solution to the problem with $\nu > 0$ is based on the solution to the problem for $\nu = 0$, (Kendall 1948), for which α is an intrinsic parameter. The solution for $\nu > 0$, given by Equation (7.58), uses α independently of ν.

and $n_\nu(t)$, avoiding the instantaneous parameters $\lambda(t)$, $\mu(t)$, and $\nu(t)$. In particular, we will show that if the ratios of $n_\lambda(t)$, $n_\mu(t)$, and $n_\nu(t)$ are constant:

$$\frac{n_\lambda(t)}{\lambda} = \frac{n_\mu(t)}{\mu} = \frac{n_\nu(t)}{\nu} = f(t), \tag{3.19}$$

where $f(t)$ is a positive differentiable function and P'_k is independent of time, then this approximation becomes exact. Indeed, by combining Equations (3.11) and (3.19), we obtain

$$n - n_0 = \psi f, \tag{3.20}$$

where $\psi = \lambda - \mu + \nu$ (as before), and

$$\frac{dn_\lambda}{df} = \lambda, \tag{3.21}$$

$$\frac{dn_\mu}{df} = \mu, \tag{3.22}$$

$$\frac{dn_\nu}{df} = \nu, \tag{3.23}$$

$$\frac{dn}{df} = \psi. \tag{3.24}$$

Note that $f = (F - 1)n_0/\psi$. By introducing a new variable τ such that $f = n_0[\exp(\psi\tau) - 1]/\psi$, we obtain $df = n_0 \exp(\psi\tau)d\tau = (\psi f + n_0)d\tau = nd\tau$ and hence

$$\frac{dn}{d\tau} = \psi n, \tag{3.25}$$

$$\frac{dn_\lambda}{d\tau} = \lambda n, \tag{3.26}$$

$$\frac{dn_\mu}{d\tau} = \mu n, \tag{3.27}$$

$$\frac{dn_\nu}{d\tau} = \nu n, \tag{3.28}$$

which is equivalent to the original Equation (3.7) and Assumptions (2–4) for a renormalized time $\tau = \ln F/\psi$ and constant ν, μ, and λ.

In a nutshell, Assumptions (1–4) should be interpreted as follows. On the one hand, existing firms play an important role in the introduction and the exploitation of new business opportunities (see also Sutton 1997; Klette and Kortum 2004).[5]

[5] Sutton generalizes Simon's original model by considering the case in which the probability that a currently active firm will respond to an opportunity is nondecreasing with firm size (Sutton 1997).

On the other hand, a positive rate of entry ($\nu > 0$) implies that a given positive fraction of new business opportunities is introduced by new firms that enter the market.

We do not explicitly model firm disappearance here. In our model, firm exit occurs when a firm loses all of its units due to the process described in Assumption (3). Although such firms, due to proportional growth rules, will never grow again, for mathematical convenience we do not delete them, but denote them by the term $N_0(t)$. The disappearance of large firms due to merger or bankruptcy is not explicitly included in our model. However, it can be implicitly taken into account if we assume that ν' is the *net* entry rate (entry minus exit), which, in a growing economy, is positive in the long run.

The second set of Assumptions (B) regarding the proportional growth of unit sizes includes (see also Fu et al. 2005; Riccaboni et al. 2008):

(5) At time t, supposed discrete, each firm i is made up of $K_i(t)$ units of size $\xi_j(t)$, $j = 1, 2, \ldots K_i(t)$, where $\xi_j(t) > 0$ are identically distributed variables extracted from the distribution P_ξ. Accordingly, the size of a firm i is denoted by $S_i(t) \equiv \sum_{j=1}^{K_i(t)} \xi_j(t)$. We assume that $\xi_j(t)$ are independent from each other and from any other variable characterizing firm i, such as the number of products $K_i(t)$ or its age. We also assume that $\mathrm{E}[\ln \xi_j(t)] \equiv m_\xi$ and $\mathrm{Var}[\ln \xi_j(t)] = \mathrm{E}[(\ln \xi_j(t))^2] - m_\xi^2 \equiv V_\xi$ are finite. Here and below, $\mathrm{E}[x]$ and $\mathrm{Var}[x]$ are the mathematical expectation and the variance of a random variable x, respectively.

(6) For each time interval Δt, the size of each unit j is decreased or increased by a random factor $\eta_j(t) > 0$, such that

$$\xi_j(t + \Delta t) = \xi_j(t)\, \eta_j(t + \Delta t). \tag{3.29}$$

We assume that $\eta_j(t)$, the growth factor of unit j, is a random variable taken from a given probability distribution P_η. We assume that $\mathrm{E}[\ln \eta_j(t)] \equiv m_\eta$, while $\mathrm{Var}[\ln \eta_j(t)] \equiv V_\eta$. We also assume that $\eta_j(t)$ for different times t and different j are independent from each other and that η_j are independent from ξ_j, K_i, and from all other random variables that characterize the firm i.

(7) The size of each new unit arriving at time t is drawn randomly from the distribution of unit sizes P_ξ (cf. Assumption(5)).

An intuitive representation of the structure of our framework is presented in Figure 3.1.

Based on Assumptions (5–7), we conclude the following: first, the sizes of elementary units fluctuate independently of each other, as if each unit occupies a separate market niche. Second, any shift in the demand curve affects all units *proportionately*, while their growth rate variance is not size-dependent. Third,

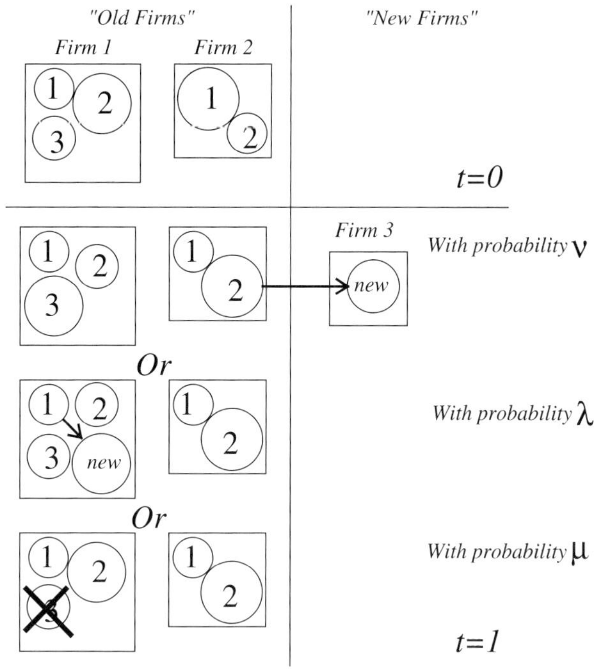

Figure 3.1 A schematic representation of the model of proportional growth. At time $t = 0$, there are $N(0) = 2$ firms (□) and $n(0) = 5$ units (◯) (Assumption 1). The area of each circle is proportional to the size ξ of the unit, and the size of each firm is the sum of the areas of its constituent units (see Assumption 5). At the following time step, $t = 1$, a new unit is created or deleted. With probability ν, each existing unit can create a new unit, which is assigned to a new firm, firm 3 in this example, (Assumption 4). The size of the new unit is taken from the distribution of the existing units (Assumption 7). With probability λ, each existing unit can create a new unit which is assigned to the same existing firm. (Assumption 2). In this example, because the numbers of existing units in firms 1 and 2 are 3 and 2, respectively, given the new unit is created, it will be assigned to firm 1 with probability 3/5 or to firm 2 with probability 2/5. Each unit can be deleted with probability μ. Given that one unit is deleted, it will be deleted from firm i with a probability proportional to its number of units $K_i(t)$. Finally, at each time step, each circle k grows or shrinks by a random factor η_k (Assumption 6). The figure is reproduced from figure 1 in Fu et al. (2005).

elementary units cannot be moved from one firm to another. Finally, any increase in the size of the existing units is unaffected by the arrival of a new unit. In other words, the average size and number of units within a firm are assumed to be independent from each other.

The economic rationale behind this set of assumptions has been outlined in the work of Growiec et al. (2018). First, in a growing economy, the average *net* growth rate of elementary unit sales is positive ($E[\eta] > 1$). This assumption does not preclude processes of creative destruction, obsolescence effects, or the existence of product life cycles. Second, the assumption that new units are, on average, comparable in size to already existing units captures the disembodied component of technical change: if the overall rate of technical progress is positive, as it is when $E[\eta] > 1$, then it is natural to expect that not only existing units but also new units benefit from it. Otherwise, new units would become increasingly smaller compared with the established ones, and the average age of units would determine firm size, an assumption which is at odds with the evidence. The combination of Assumptions (4) and (7) suggests the new firms consisting of one new unit sometimes can be very large, because P_ξ can be very broad. This assumption (unrealistic from the first glance) is supported by empirical studies (Hellerstein and Koren 2019).

A Critique of Our Model

The simplicity of our framework implies a cost in terms of adherence to reality.

First, we rule out the possibility of competition within independent submarkets. Firm and product turnover is modeled through entry and exit, while market share turnover induced by competitive dynamics within submarkets, is not treated explicitly.

Second, our framework does not provide a theory of selection, i.e., it does not feature any mechanism that predicts the discontinuation of the least successful products, or predicts which producers, due to a single or a few unsuccessful products, are forced to exit (Amaral et al. 1998; Luttmer 2012).

Third, the model does not explicitly represent the life cycle of products (Bottazzi et al. 2001; Argente et al. 2018). The sizes of elementary units are allowed to vary according to a multiplicative process, irrespective of the age of the unit. The initial period of fast growth of a newly created unit and the fast decay of an old unit prior to its exit could be easily represented by a single act of creation and deletion, respectively.

Fourth, since unit sizes change according to Gibrat process (Assumptions 5 and 6), the variance of unit size distribution tends to grow indefinitely over time. On the other hand, according to Assumption (7), the sizes of new units are taken from a distribution that coincides with the distribution of all units, new and old. This apparent contradiction can be resolved if we consider that all units have finite lifetimes, and the distribution of their sizes does not have time to fully evolve. In GPG, the average lifetime of a unit is the inverse rate of destruction $1/\mu$, introduced in Assumption 3. Thus $\mu > 0$ is an important stabilizing factor without which the set of Assumptions (5–7) would be self-contradicting. In principle, Assumptions (7) and (5) can be replaced by one assumption, namely that the distribution of sizes of new units is given, while the distribution of all units can be computed based on μ

from Assumption (3) and $P_\eta(\eta)$ from Assumption (6). However, this simplification would increase the complexity of the model beyond analytical tractability, without any reasonable gain in understanding processes leading to the size distribution of units. Accordingly, one should regard the set of Assumptions (5–7) as an instantaneous snapshot with a minimal set of parameters.

Fifth, Assumption (6) implies that our model ignores autocorrelations and cross-correlations in the evolution of unit sizes. Including autocorrelation is not an easy task and generally the solution cannot be presented in closed form (Brockwell and Davis 2009) except in the easier cases of autoregressive models. Autoregressive (AR) and moving average (MA) models, with their combinations, ARMA and ARIMA, define a large framework to include serial correlations in GPG and provide a theoretical setting to include non-Markovian effects such as delay dependency (see for instance, Douc et al. (2014)). Cross-correlations among growth rates of units can be introduced, for example, in the hierarchical model developed by Stanley et al. (1996) and Buldyrev et al. (1997); Chapter 7, Appendix 7.4).

Sixth, GPG depends on three frequencies of innovation (λ) closure (μ) of business units and creation of new firms (ν). All these parameters are assumed to have constant ratios or, as we will see in Section 5.1, they weakly depend on time. A natural extension would be to replace the deterministic dependency by a stochastic one, including one or more stochastic factors accounting for the variation of these frequencies in time. The mathematical framework to deal with this issue is the Cox process or self-exciting point processes (Lando 1998). In his seminal paper, Hawkes introduces and studies self-exciting point processes, whose conditional intensity function depends on the previous times of the process itself (Hawkes 1971; see also Lewis and Shedler 1979, Bremaud 1981, and Ogata and Vere-Jones 1984). Including Hawkes processes into GPG opens an interesting research field, to model clustering effects in innovation dynamics.

Seventh, GPG uses a continuous Poisson process to model the addition and deletion of units, while using a discrete multiplicative process to model the Gibrat process of changing unit sizes. It would be natural to study these two processes on equal footing, formulating the Gibrat process as a continuous geometric Brownian motion (Cox and Miller 1968; Luttmer 2012) and, thus, reformulate GPG in a fully continuous framework.

Notwithstanding these limitations, we believe that the simplicity of our framework provides a relevant benchmark for further anaytical developments.

Outline of the Predictions of GPG

In the next sections, we derive the predictions of the model with respect to stylized facts I–IV, outlined in Chapter 1:

(I) The size distribution of firms $P(S)$;
(II) The size–mean growth rate relationship, characterized by the shape of the conditional average growth rate $E(r|S)$ presented as a function of firm size, S;
(III) The distribution of firm logarithmic growth rates $P_r(r)$,[6] where

$$r_i \equiv \ln\left(\frac{S_i(t+\Delta t)}{S_i(t)}\right); \tag{3.30}$$

(IV) The size-variance relationship, characterized by the shape of the conditional standard deviation of the growth rate $\sigma(r|S)$ presented as a function of firm size, S, and whether this relationship can be approximated as a power law $\sigma(r|S) \sim S^{-\beta}$.

In our analysis, we refer to the logarithmic definition of growth rates, since its distribution $P_r(r)$ has a symmetric shape spanning from $-\infty$ to ∞. However, we also study the nonlogarithmic growth rate,

$$r'_i \equiv \frac{S_i(t+\Delta t)}{S_i(t)} - 1, \tag{3.31}$$

which simplifies the study of $E(r'|S)$ and $\sigma(r'|S)$, since $E(r')$ is independent of firm size for some of the cases of the model listed below (see Table 3.1).[7] Moreover, for these specific cases, the variance of non-logarithmic growth rate $\mathrm{Var}(r'|S)$ can be related to the Herfindahl concentration index (H-index), which for a firm composed of K units is defined as:

$$H = \frac{\sum_j^K \xi_j^2}{\left(\sum_j^K \xi_j\right)^2}. \tag{3.32}$$

The inverse H-index is a good measure of the number of "important" units, which provide a significant contribution to firm size

$$K_e = 1/H. \tag{3.33}$$

When all units are equal, $\xi_j = \xi > 0$ and $K_e = K$. When the sizes of all units except one are equal to zero, $K_e = 1$. In the context of our analysis, $K_e = 1/H$ indicates the effective number of units.

We first list all subclasses of the model, each of which implies a qualitatively different mode of behavior, and then study them sequentially. These subclasses and their properties are summarized in detail in Section 3.8 and listed in Table 3.1.

[6] The distribution of the growth rates depends on the observation period Δt. As we see in Chapter 2, according to Gibrat's hypothesis, this distribution converges to a Gaussian distribution for large Δt.
[7] When the firm exits $S(t+1) = 0$ and, in this case, $r' = -1$, taking into account the exiting firms. This correction is called Mansfield correction (see Mansfield 1962).

Table 3.1 *The summary of the main analytical and numerical results of the GPG framework. The cases denoted by A1–C3 correspond to the most important cases illustrated by the figures. GPG* is a variant of GPG in which the changes in the number of units in a firm, during an observation period* Δt*, are neglected when growth rates are computed. The case of stable economy is treated in (Klette and Kortum 2004) who investigate zero net growth* $\psi = \lambda + \nu - \mu = 0$*. In the cases (B1), (C1), and (D) marked by* $**$*, the exponent* β*, describing the size-growth rate variance relationship* $\sigma_r \sim S^{-\beta}$*, weakly depends on S but in a large range of S can be approximated by Equation (3.116), which, for empirically reasonable width of unit-size distribution,* V_ξ *takes values in between* 0.1 *and* 0.3.

Case	Key assumptions	$P(K)$	Size distribution
Pure Gibrat (A0)	$\nu = 0,\ \lambda = 0,\ \mu = 0,\ V_\eta > 0$	One-point	Lognormal
Bose-Einstein (A1)	$\nu = 0,\ \lambda > \mu \geq 0, V_\eta = 0,\ V_\xi = 0,$	Exponential or Γ	Exponential or Γ
Simon, $t = \infty$ (A2)	$\nu > 0,\ \lambda > \mu \geq 0,\ V_\eta = 0,\ V_\xi = 0$	Power Law	Power law
Simon $t < \infty$ (A2t)	$\nu > 0,\ \lambda > \mu \geq 0,\ V_\eta = 0,\ V_\xi = 0$	Power Law with exp. cutoff	Power law with exp. cutoff
Stable economy (A3)	$\nu > 0,\ \psi = 0,\ V_\eta = 0,\ V_\xi = 0$	Logarithmic with exp. cutoff	Logarithmic with exp. cutoff
GPG, no firm entry (C1)	$\nu = 0,\ \lambda > \mu \geq 0,\ V_\eta > 0,\ V_\xi > 0$	Exponential or Γ	Skewed lognormal
GPG, firm entry (C2)	$\nu > 0,\ \lambda > \mu \geq 0,\ V_\eta > 0,\ V_\xi > 0$	Power Law with exp. cutoff	Lognormal with Power law tail
GPG, stable (C3)	$\nu > 0,\ \psi = 0,\ V_\eta > 0,\ V_\xi > 0$	Logarithmic with exp. cutoff	Skewed lognormal
GPG, two level (D)	$\nu > 0,\ \lambda > \mu \geq 0,\ V_\eta > 0,\ V_\xi > 0$	Power law tail	Lognormal with Power law tail

Case	Key assumptions	Growth distr.	Size-mean growth	Size-variance
Pure Gibrat (A0)	$\nu = 0,\ \lambda = 0,\ \mu = 0,\ V_\eta > 0$	Lognormal	Flat	Flat
Bose-Einstein (A1)	$\nu = 0,\ \lambda > \mu \geq 0, V_\eta = 0,\ V_\xi = 0,\ t = \infty$	tent-shape $\sim r^{-3}$	Flat	$\beta = 1/2$
Simon, $t = \infty$ (A2)	$\nu > 0,\ \lambda > \mu \geq 0,\ V_\eta = 0,\ V_\xi = 0$	Atoms	Flat	$\beta = 1/2$
Simon $t < \infty$ (A2t)	$\nu > 0,\ \lambda > \mu \geq 0,\ V_\eta = 0,\ V_\xi = 0$	Atoms	Flat	$\beta = 1/2$
Stable economy (A3)	$\nu > 0,\ \psi = 0,\ V_\eta = 0,\ V_\xi = 0$	Dome-shaped	Flat	$\beta = 1/2$
GPG*, no firm entry (B1)	$\lambda \to 0,\ \mu \to 0,\ \nu = 0,\ V_\eta > 0,\ V_\xi > 0$	Tent-shaped $\sim r^{-3}$	Flat	$0 < \beta < 1/2$**
GPG*, firm entry (B2)	$\lambda \to 0,\ \mu \to 0\ \nu > 0,\ V_\eta > 0,\ V_\xi > 0$	Lognormal	Flat	Nonmonotonic
GPG*, stable (B3)	$\lambda \to 0, \mu \to 0,\ \nu > 0,\ \psi = 0,\ V_\eta > 0,\ V_\xi > 0$	Dome-shaped $\sim r^{-1}$	Flat	Nonmonotonic
GPG no firm entry (C1)	$\nu = 0\ \lambda > \mu \geq 0,\ V_\eta > 0,\ V_\xi > 0$	Tent-shaped $\sim r^{-3}$	Decreasing	$0 < \beta < 1/2$**
GPG, firm entry (C2)	$\nu > 0,\ \lambda > \mu \geq 0,\ V_\eta > 0,\ V_\xi > 0$	Lognormal with tails	Decreasing	Nonmonotonic
GPG, stable (C3)	$\nu > 0,\ \psi = 0,\ V_\eta > 0,\ V_\xi > 0$	Dome-shaped with tails	Decreasing	Nonmonotonic
GPG, two level (D)	$\nu > 0,\ \lambda > \mu \geq 0,\ V_\eta > 0,\ V_\xi > 0$	Tent-shaped $\sim r^{-3}$	Decreasing	$0 < \beta < 1/2$**

The subclasses are denoted by a letter-digit combination, which will be used as a reference throughout this chapter:

(A0) *Gibrat process*: Firm size grows proportionally, while $\lambda = \mu = \nu = 0$.

(A1) *Bose–Einstein process*: Firms are made up by elementary units of equal size, which do not grow with time. ($V_\xi = V_\eta = m_\eta = 0$). The number of units can change ($\lambda > 0$, $\mu > 0$), but no new firms are created ($\nu = 0$).

(A2) *Simon process*: Firms are made up of elementary units of equal size, which do not grow with time ($V_\xi = V_\eta = m_\eta = 0$). The number of units can change ($\lambda > 0$, $\mu > 0$) and new firms enter the market with some probability $\nu > 0$. A variant of this case is (A3), which represents a stable economy $\lambda + \nu - \mu = 0$.

(C1) *Gibrat–Bose–Einstein process*: The distribution of the unit sizes is produced by Gibrat's Law of proportional growth ($V_\xi > 0$, $V_\eta > 0$, $m_\eta \neq 0$). The number of units in the firm can also change ($\lambda > 0$, $\mu > 0$, but $\nu = 0$).

(C2) *Gibrat–Simon process with entry*: The distribution of the unit sizes is produced by Gibrat's Law of proportional growth ($V_\xi > 0$, $V_\eta > 0$, $m_\eta \neq 0$). The number of units in the firm can also change ($\lambda > 0$, $\mu > 0$) and the new firms can be created $\nu > 0$. Again, here we can consider a special case (C3) of stable economy: $\lambda + \nu - \mu = 0$.

(D) *Gibrat–Bose–Einstein–Simon process with two levels of aggregation and entry*: This is the most advanced model, which assumes that firms and their units follow the Simon process, but each unit of a firm consists of a large number of elementary units, which follow the Bose–Einstein and the Gibrat process.

In addition to the cases (C1), (C2), and (C3), we introduce their simplified versions (B1), (B2), and (B3) when we study growth rates. In (B1), (B2), and (B3), when we compute growth rates, we neglect contributions due to changes in the number of units in the firm, i.e., when during an observation period Δt, $\lambda \Delta t \ll V_\eta$, and $\mu \Delta t \ll V_\eta$. As we will show in Chapter 7, Appendix 7.2 for these cases, $\text{Var}(r') = \text{Var}(\eta) H$.

For each case, we assess whether the Stylized Facts (I)–(IV) presented in Chapter 1 are well captured by the corresponding subclass of the model.

3.3 Gibrat

Case (A0) $\lambda = \mu = \nu = 0$ *but* $V_\eta > 0$, $V_\xi > 0$, $m_\eta \neq 0$

According to Gibrat's Law, the expected value of the growth rate of a business firm is proportional to its current size. Gibrat's Law assumes that: (i) the growth rate R of a company is independent of its size; (ii) the successive growth rates of a company are uncorrelated in time; and (iii) companies do not interact with each other.

The corresponding stochastic process is given by

$$S_{t+\Delta t} = S_t \eta_{t+\Delta t}, \tag{3.34}$$

where $S_{t+\Delta t}$ and S_t are the size of the company at time $(t + \Delta t)$ and t, respectively, and $\eta_{t+\Delta t} > 0$ is a random number with some narrow distribution centered around unity, uncorrelated for different time intervals. Hence, $\log S_t$ follows a simple random walk and, for sufficiently large time intervals $u \gg \Delta t$, the growth rates

$$R_u \equiv \frac{S_{t+u}}{S_t}, \tag{3.35}$$

are lognormally distributed.

Indeed,

$$S_{t+u} = \eta_{t+\Delta t} \cdot \eta_{t+2\Delta_t} \cdot \ldots \cdot \eta_{t+M\Delta t} \cdot S_t = R_u S_t, \tag{3.36}$$

where $M = u/\Delta t \gg 1$. Taking the logarithm of both sides of Equation (3.36) and denoting $s_i = \ln S_{t+i\Delta t}$, $r_i = \ln \eta_{t+i\Delta}$, and $r_u = \ln R_u$, we obtain

$$s_M = s_0 + r_1 + r_2 + r_3 + \ldots r_M \tag{3.37}$$

and

$$r_u = r_1 + r_2 + r_3 + \ldots r_M, \tag{3.38}$$

where r_i can be seen as steps of a random walk. If we let $\mathrm{E}(r_i) = m_\eta$ and $\mathrm{Var}(r_i) = V_\eta$, and assume η_t as independent, then, according to the central limit theorem, the distribution of the sum of M independent random variables r_i converges as $M \to \infty$ to the normal distribution with mean $M m_\eta$ and variance $M V_\eta$, which is described by a probability density function (hereinafter PDF) with a familiar bell-shaped curve:

$$P(r_u) = \frac{1}{\sqrt{2\pi M V_\eta}} \mathrm{e}^{-\frac{(r_u - M m_\eta)^2}{2 M V_\eta}}. \tag{3.39}$$

Note that the convergence occurs for any distribution of η_t if the variance of its logarithm, V_η, is finite. Thus, R_u follows a lognormal distribution,

$$P(R_u) = \frac{1}{R_u \sqrt{2\pi M V_\eta}} \mathrm{e}^{-\frac{(\ln R_u - M m_\eta)^2}{2 M V_\eta}}, \tag{3.40}$$

which behaves as an approximate power law $1/R_u$ in the broad range of R near the maximum of the Gaussian distribution, $\exp(M m_\eta)$ (Montroll and Shlesinger 1982). Note that the convergence of $P(R_u)$ occurs only near the maximum $R_u = M m_\eta$.

The tails deviate significantly from lognormal for any M. Due to this deviation the mean and variance of R_u are not given by the formulas for the exact lognormal distribution

$$\mathrm{E}(R_u) = [\mathrm{E}(\eta)]^M \neq \exp[M(m_\eta + V_\eta/2)], \tag{3.41}$$

$$\mathrm{Var}(R_u) = [\mathrm{E}(\eta^2)]^M - [\mathrm{E}(\eta)]^{2M} \neq \exp[2M(m_\eta + V_\eta)] - \exp[2M(m_\eta + V_\eta/2)], \tag{3.42}$$

unless the distribution of η is already lognormal. In fact, the moment generating function of the lognormal distribution does not exist and, therefore, the lognormal distribution is not uniquely determined by its moments (Heyde 1963).

If we assume that all firms are born at approximately the same time and have approximately the same initial size S_0, then the distribution of their sizes at time t is approximately lognormal:

$$P(S) = \frac{1}{S\sqrt{2\pi V_\eta t/\Delta t}} e^{-\frac{(\ln(S/S_0) - m_\eta t/\Delta t)^2}{2V_\eta t/\Delta t}}. \tag{3.43}$$

In the case of a pure Gibrat growth process, firms are indivisible into units ($\lambda = \mu = \nu = 0$ and $K_i = 1$). Hence, each firm consists of exactly one unit, which follows Gibrat's Law. Thus, the logarithmic sales of each firm fluctuate idiosyncratically over time with a positive variance ($V_\eta > 0$).

When there are no new business opportunities, the size distribution of firms coincides with the size distribution of units: $P(S) = P(\xi_i)$. The logarithmic growth rate distribution for one time step Δt is the same as the distribution of $\ln \eta_i$, while for longer observation periods it converges to the Gaussian distribution (3.39).

The size–mean growth rate and the size-variance relationships found in this case provide an important benchmark for further comparisons: irrespective of firm size, the mean of the logarithmic growth rate is constant at $\mathrm{E}(r|S) = \mathrm{E}(r) = m_\eta$, while its variance is constant at $\sigma^2(r|S) = \sigma^2(r) = V_\eta$. Thus, the parameter β in the relationship of the form $\sigma(r|S) \propto S^{-\beta}$ is zero. For the majority of the economic databases studied, $\beta > 0$. Hence, the pure Gibrat process cannot correctly explain the size-variance relationship.

As stated earlier, an application of the central limit theorem to the logarithm of growth rates η_t yields a prediction of the firm size distribution approaching the lognormal in the limit of $t \to \infty$, regardless of the actual distribution of the growth rates $\ln \eta_i$. The problem with this prediction is that, over time, the variance of the firm size distribution increases in proportion to time. As already shown by Fu and colleagues (Fu et al. 2005) and anticipating the results presented in Chapter 4, this prediction is not supported by data. Moreover, size distributions of firms significantly deviate from the lognormal distribution. As we have observed in

Chapter 2, a more striking departure from Gibrat's predictions is the distribution of firm growth rates, which is not lognormal but has a marked tent shape. Thus, most probably, the approximately lognormal size distribution of firms is not a result of a Gibrat process, but rather a consequence of different subsectors with different typical firm sizes, as outlined by Amaral et al. (1998). When the size of a firm is determined by the product of many independent factors, an approximately lognormal distribution may arise not because of a temporal random multiplicative process, but instead, because of a multiplication of these factors in the spirit of the central limit theorem (Montroll and Shlesinger 1982). This hypothesis is supported if the sizes of newly created units follow a broad distribution, which can be approximated by the lognormal law (see Chapter 4). Note also that almost any broad distribution (for example, an exponential distribution with a slow decay), when presented in logarithmic terms, shows a maximum near which the logarithm of the PDF can be approximated by a parabola, and hence, the distribution itself can be (mistakenly) approximated by a lognormal distribution.

In a nutshell, we can conclude that a pure Gibrat process in which the firms consist of a single unit while $\lambda = \mu = \nu = 0$, is unrealistic.

3.4 Bose–Einstein

Case (A1) $\lambda > 0,\ \mu \geq 0,$ *but* $\nu = V_\eta = V_\xi = m_\eta = 0$

In this section, we derive the predictions of our framework when new business opportunities are captured by existing firms ($\nu = 0,\ \lambda > 0,\ \mu \geq 0$) while all units have the same size, which do not change in time: ($m_\eta = V_\eta = V_\xi = 0$). This is the urn scheme with a fixed number of urns when the probability of adding a ball to an urn is proportional to the number of balls it contains (proportional growth, Kendall 1948; Ijiri and Simon 1977; De Vany and Walls 1996; Fu et al. 2005; Bottazzi and Secchi 2006; Yamasaki et al. 2006). This scheme is also known as Polya's urn scheme or the Bose–Einstein process (Feller 1968)), since quantum particles with integer spin, bosons, when added to a system with a fixed number of quantum states (represented by urns) occupy the urns as if they follow the proportional growth rule.

If, initially, all firms consist of exactly one unit ($N(0) = n_0$), then, for large t, many firms will lose all their units and become inactive, while the conditional distribution of the number of units, K, in active firms converges (as shown in Appendix 7.1 of Chapter 7) to a geometric distribution (Kendall, 1948; Fu et al., 2005; Yamasaki et al., 2006),

$$P_K = \frac{1}{\kappa(t) - 1}\left(1 - \frac{1}{\kappa(t)}\right)^K, \tag{3.44}$$

where

$$\kappa(t) \equiv \frac{n_\lambda(t) + n_0}{n_0} = \frac{R - \alpha}{1 - \alpha}. \tag{3.45}$$

Note that $n_\lambda(t)$ is the total number of new units that enter the economy in the time interval $(0,\ t]$. Thus, parameter $(\kappa - 1) = n_\lambda(t)/n_0 = (R - 1)/(1 - \alpha)$ provides an indication of the amount of innovation. Interestingly, when all firms initially consist of one unit, $\kappa(t)$ is equal to the average number of units in the active firms.

According to Equation (3.15), a number of units $n_\mu(t) = (\mu/\lambda)n_\lambda(t)$ are lost during the same period of time, determining the number of active firms, $N_a(t)$, surviving in the economy at time t as shown in Equation (7.30)

$$N_a(t) = n_0 \frac{n(t)}{n(t) + n_\mu(t)} \to n_0 \frac{\lambda - \mu}{\lambda} = n_0(1 - \alpha) \quad \text{for} \quad t \to \infty. \tag{3.46}$$

To summarize, we see an interesting division of the roles of destruction and innovation: the death–birth ratio, $\alpha = n_\mu(t)/n_\nu(t)$, determines the fraction of active and inactive firms, while the innovation factor, $\kappa - 1 = n_\lambda(t)/n_0$ determines the conditional distribution of number of units in active firms. When n_0 is sufficiently large, Equation (3.44) is valid also if $\mu > \lambda$. However, in this case, the number of active firms shrinks to zero when $t \to \infty$ and the results of the model lose their physical meaning. The exact derivation of these facts is provided in Chapter 7, Appendix 7.1.

The continuous limit approximation of $\kappa \to \infty$ in Equation (3.44) is given by the exponential distribution

$$P_K = \frac{\mathrm{e}^{-K/\kappa}}{\kappa}. \tag{3.47}$$

If we assume that at time t all units are approximately of the same size ($V_\xi = V_\eta = 0,\ m_\eta > 0$), then the PDF of firm size S is also exponential

$$P(S) = \frac{\mathrm{e}^{-S/\langle S\rangle}}{\langle S\rangle}, \tag{3.48}$$

where $\langle S\rangle = \kappa\langle\xi\rangle$ is the average firm size. Note that the average size of an active firm is exponentially growing with time together with the economy and, hence, the system is never at equilibrium, even when the number of active firms is stable.

So far, we assumed that, initially, each firm has one unit. In Chapter 7, Appendix 7.1, we derive the corresponding solution for any initial distribution. If the initial distribution P_K is geometric, it remains geometric for the entire evolution of the process. For other types of initial distributions, the convergence to a geometric distribution does not occur. To investigate the shape of the distribution for $t \to \infty$, we introduce a continuous variable $x = K/\kappa(t)$. If M is the number of units in the largest firm at $t = 0$, then, as we will see in Equation (7.41), the probability density $P(x)$ can be expressed as a finite linear combination of gamma distributions (see Growiec et al. 2018):

$$P(x) = \sum_{r=1}^{M} e^{-x} \frac{x^{r-1}}{(r-1)!} (1-\alpha)^{r-1} C_r, \tag{3.49}$$

where $C_r > 0$ are constants. When the death–birth ratio approaches unity, ($\alpha = \mu/\lambda \to 1$), $P(x)$ converges to an exponential distribution. Intuitively, this result reflects a high business unit turnover, in which, with time, the original P_K is wiped out and the geometric distribution is restored. The distribution P_k for the case when all of the firms initially consist of either one unit or three units is presented in Figure 3.2, which shows an excellent agreement between theory and simulations.

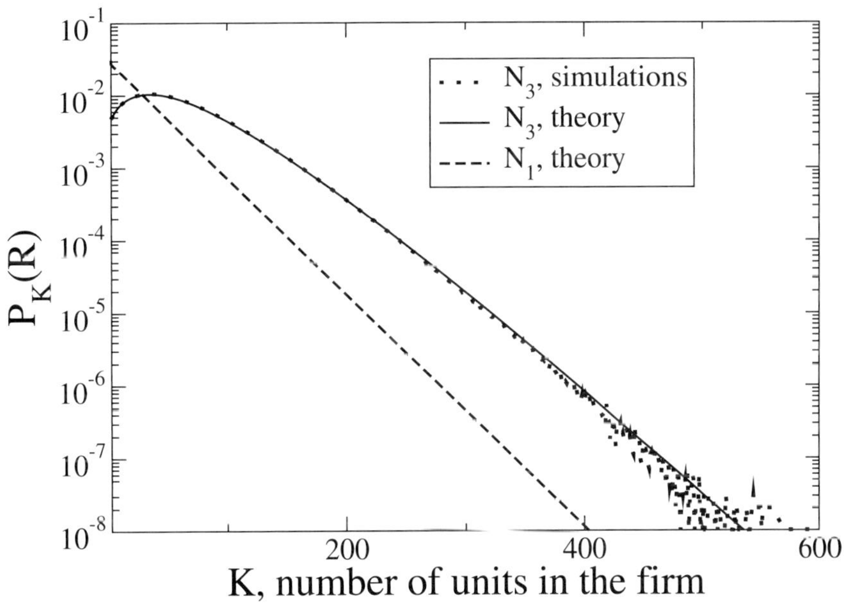

Figure 3.2 The distribution $P_k(R)$ when $\nu = 0$ (no new firm entry), $\alpha = 0.25$, $R = n(t)/n_0 = 21$ for the case when initially all firms have exactly three units: $N = N_3 = 100$, $n_0 = 300$, and for the case when initially all firms have one unit: $N = N_1 = 100$, $n_0 = 100$. For the case $N = N_3$, exponential decay with a slope $\ln(1 - 1/\kappa(t)) = \ln[(R-1)/(R-\alpha)] = -0.037$, is preceded by a power law increase, while for the case $N = N_1$ we see a pure geometric distribution characterized by the same slope. The simulations are averaged over 10^6 realizations of the stochastic process.

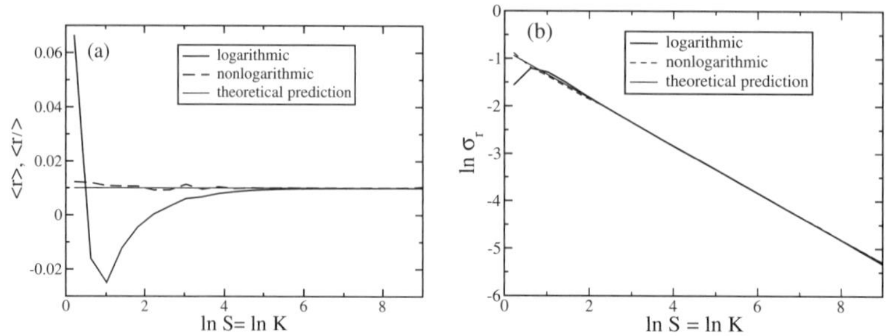

Figure 3.3 (a) The dependence of the average growth rate on firm size for the pure Bose–Einstein process with $\lambda = 0.1$, $\mu = 0.09$, $\Delta t = 1$ for logarithmic and nonlogarithmic growth rates. The logarithmic growth rate is nonconstant due to the nonlinear behavior of the logarithm, but the limiting values for logarithmic and nonlogarithmic growth rates converge for large S to a theoretical prediction $(\lambda - \mu)\Delta t$. (b) The size-variance relationship for the pure Bose–Einstein process with $\lambda = 0.1$, $\mu = 0.09$, $\Delta t = 1$ for logarithmic and nonlogarithmic definitions of the growth rates. Both definitions are well approximated by $\sigma_r = \sqrt{(\lambda + \mu)/S}$, which gives $\beta = 1/2$.

Having derived the size distribution of firms for the Bose–Einstein process, we now discuss the properties of the growth rate distribution. Even when $V_\eta = m_\eta = V_\xi = m_\xi = 0$, the Bose–Einstein process generates a non-trivial behavior for the growth rate distribution. During Δt, the average growth rate for large firms ($S \to \infty$) converges to $m_r = \ln[n(t + \Delta t)/n(t)]$ due to proportional growth. When Δt is small, then approximating $m_r = \ln[n(t + \Delta t)/n(t)] \approx [n(t + \Delta t) - n(t)]/n(t) \approx \Delta t(dn/dt)/n(t)$ and using Equation (7.47) we obtain for $\nu = 0$

$$m_r \approx (\lambda - \mu)\Delta t, \tag{3.50}$$

Simulation results confirm this equation as shown in Figure 3.3(a). Note that the logarithmic definition of the growth rate produces a spurious negative bump for small values of K, which is generated by the nonlinear behavior of $\ln(x)$, which decreases when $x < 1$ much faster than when it increases for $x > 1$. Consequently, the nonlogarithmic average growth rate provides a better characterization of the size–mean growth rate relationship.

Equations (7.72)–(7.73) will show that, for $K \to \infty$, the distribution $P_r(r|K)$ of firms' growth rates converges to a Gaussian distribution:

$$P_r(r|K) = \frac{\sqrt{K}}{\sqrt{2\pi V_r}} \exp\left(-\frac{(r - m_r)^2 K}{2V_r}\right) \tag{3.51}$$

with mean m_r and variance V_r/K, where

$$V_r = \left[1 - \frac{n(t)}{n(t + \Delta t)}\right] \frac{\lambda + \mu}{\lambda - \mu}. \tag{3.52}$$

By approximating $n(t + \Delta t)$ for small Δt and using Equation (3.7), we obtain $V_r \approx (\lambda + \mu)\Delta t$ [Figure 3.3(b)]. Accordingly, $\sigma(r|K) = \sqrt{V_r}/K^{-1/2}$ and, thus, the size-variance relationship is governed by the exponent $\beta = 1/2$. Once we know $P_r(r|K)$ and the distribution of the number of units P_K given by Equation (3.44), we can find the PDF of growth rates of the entire set of firms:

$$P_r(r) \equiv \sum_{K=1}^{\infty} P_K P_r(r|K). \tag{3.53}$$

For the exponential or geometric P_K, the PDF can be approximated for sufficiently small $|r - m_r|\kappa(t)$ by

$$P_r(r) = \frac{\sqrt{\kappa(t)}}{2\sqrt{2V_r}}\left(1 + \frac{\kappa(t)}{2V_r}(r - m_r)^2\right)^{-\frac{3}{2}}, \tag{3.54}$$

which can be obtained by replacing summation by integration in Equation (3.53). Details of this procedure are discussed in Section 3.6. Note that approximation given by Equation (3.54) implies power law tails $P(r) \sim r^{-3}$ and, thus, does not have a finite variance. The exact distribution, which is based on summation, has a more complex form and cannot be expressed in elementary functions. However, the approximation of Equation (3.54) is valid for $|r - m_r| < \sqrt{V_r}$. For large $|r - m_r|$, the distribution $P_r(r)$ can be approximated by a Gaussian distributionwith variance V_r. The derivation of these results is presented in Chapter 7, Appendix 7.2. Figure 3.4 compares the simulation results with the prediction of Equation (3.54) for small $\lambda\Delta t$ and $\mu\Delta t$. In this scale, there is no visible difference between approximation (3.54) and the expression based on the exact summation.

The smooth growth rate distribution shown in Figure 3.4 is valid only for sufficiently large $\kappa(t)$, for which the contribution of small firms consisting of a few units is negligible. Otherwise, growth rates of firms with a small number of elementary units, corresponding to the logarithms of the rational numbers $\ln(1/2), \ln(2/3), \ldots,$ $\ln(2), \ln(3/2)$, etc., will stand out, generating a discontinuous histogram with spikes corresponding to the point masses of the PDF visible at the outskirts of Figure 3.4. These spikes are not due to the insufficient number of realizations which often make the tail of the histogram irregular. On the contrary, they become even more pronounced for a larger number of realizations. A similar phenomenon produces a non-monotonic behavior of the nonlogarithmic growth rates in Figure 3.3(a) for small values of $S = K$. For example, for small λ and μ, the average growth rate of a firm consisting of one unit will be $\langle r \rangle = \lambda \ln(2)$, while for a firm consisting of two units will be $\langle r \rangle = -2\mu \ln(2) + 2\lambda \ln(3/2)$.

In summary, the pure Bose–Einstein process gives origin to an exponential distribution of firm sizes, has no dependence of average growth rate on size and has

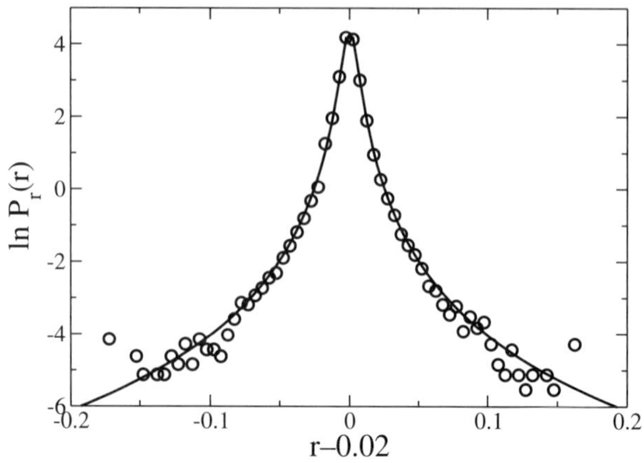

Figure 3.4 The growth rate distribution for $\kappa = 10^4$, $\mu = 0.08$, $\lambda = 0.1$ and $\Delta t = 1$ given by Equation (3.54) and results of computer simulations with 10^5 realizations of the Bose–Einstein process.

a power law size-variance relationship with $\beta = 1/2$. None of these predictions is supported by known empirical evidences for industrial firms. As a step forward from the Gibrat process, the Bose–Einstein process reproduces the tent-shape distribution of the growth rates (see Figure 3.4).

A Multiplicative Shock Model

A combination of the Bose–Einstein process and the Gibrat process was suggested by Bottazzi and Secchi (2006). The model aims to provide an explanation of the tent-shape distribution of firms' growth rates. Unfortunately, the model does not have a clear empirical justification and generates erroneous predictions on size distribution, size-variance relationship and dependence of the growth rates on firm size. The model postulates that the system consists of N firms, each of which participates in a Gibrat process, as described in Equations (3.37) and (3.38), where $r_1, r_2, \ldots$ are called shocks. It is assumed that in any time interval Δt exactly N shocks are introduced into the system, but these shocks are distributed to different firms with different probabilities. Thus the number of shocks $M_i(u)$, absorbed by firm i at time u is different for different firms. The total number of shocks introduced into the system in time u is $M_{total}(u) = \sum_{i=1}^{N} M_i(u)$ grows linearly with u: $M_{total}(u) = Nu/\Delta t$. In principle, the assumption that in any time interval Δt exactly N shocks are introduced into the system is unnecessary. One can always use M_{total} instead of time, and introduce artificial system time $u = \Delta t M_{total}/N$. It is assumed that $M_{total}(u)$ shocks are distributed among the N firms according to the Bose–Einstein process, so that at time $u = 0$ each firm has exactly one initial shock $M_i(0) = 1$, while the new shocks are assigned to each firm in proportion to the existing number of shocks $M_i(u)$. This assumption is unrealistic because preferential growth is not related to the current firm size $S_i(u)$ but happens in a sort of artificial "volatility space," where volatility of a firm is defined as the number of shocks absorbed by the firm until time u. Those already volatile firms that manage to absorb more shocks than the others become even more volatile. Since shocks can be either positive or negative, volatility is not directly related to firm size. This assumption leads to the geometric distribution of M_i, which for $\kappa = M_{total}(u)/N = u/\Delta t \to \infty$ converges to the exponential distribution of Equation (3.47). It is then straightforward to prove that the sum of M_i independent random variables r_k with finite mean m_η and variance V_η converges for $\kappa \to \infty$ to a Laplace distribution (see Kotz et al. 2001):

$$P(r_u) = \frac{1}{\sqrt{2}\sigma_r} \exp\left(\frac{-\sqrt{2}|r_u - \kappa m_\eta|}{\sigma_r}\right), \tag{3.55}$$

where $\sigma_r = 2\sqrt{\kappa V_\eta} = 2\sqrt{V_\eta u/\Delta t}$ is the standard deviation of the growth rate. Note that this distribution retains its tent-shape form for any u, but it grows wider with time in proportion to $\sqrt{u}$. While the model successfully reproduces stylized fact III defined in Chapter 1, namely the tent-shape distribution of the growth rates, its predictions are falsified by stylized facts I, II, and IV. Indeed, assuming that initially all firms have approximately the same size S_0, the distribution of the logarithm of the size should coincide with the distribution of r_u for $u = t$ and, thus, for any time t it will exibit a tent-shape distribution with mean $\ln S_0 + m_\eta t/\Delta t$ and variance $2\sqrt{V_\eta t/\Delta t}$. However, as shown by empirical evidences presented in Chapter 2, the shape of the double logarithmic plots of the empirical distributions of firm sizes do not resemble a tent, but rather a parabola (See e.g., Figure 2.2, violation of stylized Fact I) and does not spread with time as predicted by the model.

Due to the nature of the multiplicative process described in Equation (3.37), the growth rate of the firms in the model is totally independent of the initial firm size $S_i(0)$. Hence, the exponent of the size variance relationship $\beta = 0$ and the average growth rate is independent of firm size (violation of stylized Fact II observed in the majority of databases).

If we observe the system at time $t > 0$, assuming that at time $t = 0$ all the firms were equal in size and evolve with positive average logarithmic growth rate $m_\eta > 0$, the average size of a firm with many shocks is larger than the average size of a firm with a few shocks. Thus, the average growth rate of large firms will be larger than the corresponding value for small firms, because, according to the proportional growth rule, the large firms will encounter more shocks in the future than small firms. Indeed, the average size of a firm which by time t has experienced M shocks, is given by $\langle \ln S \rangle_M = \ln S_0 + M m_\eta$. In the following time interval u, this firm will receive on average Mu/t shocks and its average logarithmic growth rate will be $r_u = Mm_\eta u/t = (\langle \ln S \rangle_M - \ln S_0)u/t$. Accordingly, the average logarithmic growth rate will grow logarithmically with firm size, which is unrealistic (violation of stylized Fact II).

Recently, a stochastic evolutionary model which reproduces the tent-shape distribution of the firm growth rates has been developed (Dosi et al. 2016). This model is based on a geometric Brownian motion in the productivity space. Positive shocks in productivity accumulate to produce a fat-tail growth rate distribution due to "learning," which is based on past performance. Productivity is then related to the change in the size of the market share of the firm via an elasticity relationship. The authors verify the robustness of their results in a multidimensional parametric space. The model reproduces stylized Facts I, III, and IV. Whether it can reproduce stylized Fact II remains to be seen. Also, if learning creates long range temporal autocorrelations in the growth of firms, these correlations can be compared with the empirically observed ones; for example, see Bottazzi et al (2001).

3.5 Simon

Case (A2) $\lambda > 0,\ \mu \geq 0,\ \nu > 0,$ *but* $V_\xi = V_\eta = m_\eta = 0$*)*

The firm growth model developed by Herbert A. Simon and coauthors (Ijiri and Simon 1977) builds on Yule (1925) and allows for the net entry of new firms ($\nu > 0$), as well as for a positive net entry of business opportunities $\lambda - \mu > 0$. The model assumes that there is no Gibrat process that can change the sizes of units: $V_\xi = V_\eta = m_\eta = 0$. When the system is given an infinite time for evolution ($t \to \infty$), the distribution of the number of units per firm converges asymptotically, for large K, to the distribution with a power law (Pareto) tail:

$$P_K = \frac{1}{K^{2+b}}[C + o(1)], \tag{3.56}$$

where

$$b = \frac{\nu}{\lambda - \mu}, \tag{3.57}$$

while $C > 0$ is a constant and $o(1) \to 0$, as $K \to \infty$ (Ijiri and Simon 1975; Fu et al. 2005; Yamasaki et al. 2006; Luttmer 2011).

Since there is no randomness at the unit level, the size distribution $P(S)$ is the same as P_K. For asymptotically large S, its PDF is given by

$$P(S) = \frac{1}{S^{2+b}}[C + o(1)], \tag{3.58}$$

i.e., it follows an approximate power law with an exponent $\tau = 2 + b$. In contrast with the exponential distribution predicted by the Bose–Einstein process, it does not have a scale $\kappa(t)$ that grows with time and, thus, it is called a scale-free distribution in physics. It is not the classical Pareto distribution described in Equation (6.128), which is exactly a power law for $S \geq S_0$ and zero for $S < S_0$. In statistical literature S_0 is called scale, while in physics literature it is called lower cutoff. In terms of a Pareto distribution, the exponent $\gamma = \tau - 1$ is called shape.

Pareto-like distributions are very abundant in biological and social sciences. Many different models lead to Pareto-like distributions among which are a scaling amplification model (Montroll and Shlesinger 1982; Montroll 1987), a hierarchical model (Buldyrev et al. 2003), a random multiplicative process with repelling boundary (Dokholyan et al. 1997; Sornette and Conty 1997), and a mixture of random multiplicative process with exponentially distributed evolution times (Reed 2001; Reed and Hughes 2002; Luttmer 2012). Simon process provides yet another explanation. All these models predict arbitrary values of exponent τ, which depends on the parameters of the models. The advantage of the Simon process is that it naturally predicts $\tau \approx 2$, which is equivalent to the well-known Zipf's Law (Zipf 1949). Indeed, when the firm-unit birth ratio b, remaining positive, approaches zero from above ($b \to 0_+$), Equation (3.56) simplifies to $P_K \sim 1/K^2$.

Zipf's law describes the size distributions of many ecological and socio-economic systems (West 2017), such as the size of bird colonies, the wealth of the world's richest individuals, the distribution of city populations, and even the word frequencies in a text written in any language (Simon 1955). Indeed, many complex systems of interest to physicists, biologists, and economists share two basic features in their growth dynamics (Zipf 1949; Gabaix 1999; Barabasi and Albert 1999; Solomon and Richmond 2001; Buldyrev et al. 2003; Caldarelli 2007; Malevergne et al. 2009; Saichev et al. 2009): (i) they are not in a steady state but are growing; and (ii) their elementary units are born and agglomerate to form classes, which grow in size according to a rule of proportional growth. These two common features of complex systems are captured by the Simon model. Thus, it is not surprising that this model is successful in providing a general and parsimonious description, which encompasses all these heterogeneous phenomena. As it was already pointed out by (Yamasaki et al. 2006), in biological systems, units can be bacteria and classes can be bacterial colonies. In economic systems, units can be products and classes can be firms. In social systems, units can be human beings and classes can be cities. In the theory of complex networks, which describes systems ranging from interacting proteins in the cell to the network of Internet providers, the class is a node and its units are the endpoints of the edges connecting it to its neighbors in the network.

The probability distribution function $P(S)$ of the class size S of the systems mentioned above has been shown to follow a universal scale-free behavior $P(S) \sim S^{-\tau}$ with $\tau \approx 2$ (Zipf 1949; Barabasi and Albert 1999; Gabaix 1999; Solomon and Richmond 2001; Buldyrev et al. 2003; Malevergne et al. 2009; Saichev et al. 2009). Other possible values of τ are discussed and reported elsewhere (Newman 2005). In particular, in the Barabasi–Albert preferential attachment model (Barabasi and Albert 1999) of the Internet, preferential attachment growth, $\tau = 3$, which follows from Equation (3.57) because, in their model, it is assumed that at any time step a new node is created simultaneously with the edge that connects it to an existing node selected according to the preferential attachment rule. In the terminology of the Simon growth process, a new node is a new class with one unit, which corresponds to the endpoint of the new edge; hence, $\nu = \nu' = 1$. However, the other end of this edge is counted as a unit of a class representing the existing node to which this new edge is connected; hence $\lambda = 1$. Since no edges are removed, $\mu = 0$. Thus, $b = \nu/\lambda = 1$ and $\tau = 2 + b = 3$. In this process, adding new units to the existing classes and creating new classes are not independent. However, as we will see in Chapter 7, Appendix 7.1, the derivation of Equation (3.56) does not require independence of these two processes.

At the time when Zipf was developing his pioneering work, available socio-economic data usually consisted of a few hundred classes, and they did not allow the construction of a PDF of a size distribution. On the other hand, the complementary cumulative distribution function (CCDF),

$$\mathcal{P}(S) = \int_S^\infty P(s)ds, \tag{3.59}$$

can be approximated with higher accuracy as a monotonic decreasing step function with each step of size $1/N$, corresponding to an existing class of size S. Thus, $N\mathcal{P}(S) = \mathcal{R}(S)$ is the rank of a class in the list of classes sorted in descending order of their sizes. Zipf plotted the size of the class versus its rank $S(\mathcal{R})$ on log–log paper and, for many different systems obtained straight lines with slope $-\zeta \approx -1$, corresponding to power law dependence $S \sim \mathcal{R}^{-\zeta}$, which is equivalent to $\mathcal{P} = S^{-1/\zeta}$. Accordingly, the PDF, which is the derivative of the CCDF with a minus sign, is given by $P(S) \sim S^{-1-1/\zeta} \approx S^{-2}$.

Here, following Yamasaki et al. (2006), we present a simplified derivation of $\tau \approx 2$ based on the Simon model in the limit of small b. At any time t_0, the number of units in existing firms is $n(t_0)$. Suppose that a new class, consisting of one unit, is born at time t_0. According to the proportional growth rule, if we assume that b is small and neglect the effect of the influx of new classes on $n(t)$, at any future moment of time $t > t_0$, then the ratio of the average number of units, $\kappa(t, t_0)$, in a class born at t_0 to the total number of units, $n(t)$, will always remain equal to $1/n(t_0)$, as it has been at the moment of its birth. Thus, $\kappa(t, t_0) = n(t)/n(t_0)$

and, therefore, classes born at times $t > t_0$ tend to have a smaller average size $S \sim \kappa(t, t_0)$ than older classes. If classes are sorted according to their size, then the rank $\mathcal{R}(S)$ of a class born at time t_0 is approximately equal to the number of classes $N(t_0)$ existing at time t_0. In its turn, $N(t_0)$ is proportional to $n(t_0)$ because the new classes are born with a constant probability specified by ν, λ, and μ. Hence, $\mathcal{R} \sim n(t_0)$. Thus, at time t, the size $S(\mathcal{R})$ of a class with the rank $\mathcal{R}$ is $S(\mathcal{R}) \sim \kappa(t, t_0) = n(t)/n(t_0) \sim n(t)/\mathcal{R}$. Since the factor $n(t)$ is the same for all classes that exist at time t, $S(t) \sim \mathcal{R}^{-1}$, coherently with the standard formulation of Zipf's Law (Zipf 1949), according to which the size of a class is inversely proportional to its rank. If we take into account the influx of new classes, then $\kappa(t, t_0)/n(t) < 1/n(t_0)$. Using elementary calculus (Chapter 7, Appendix 7.1), we can show that $S(\mathcal{R}) \sim \mathcal{R}^{-1-b}$, which includes $S \sim \mathcal{R}^{-1}$ as a limiting case for $b \to 0$. Hence, $P(S) \sim S^{-2-b}$.

A Simon Process with Finite Evolution Time

We now relax the assumption $t \to \infty$. We will refer to this subcase as (A2t) in the summary table (Table 3.1). If we stop the process at a finite time to account for real-world behavior, we observe nontrivial truncation effects. We first notice that the power law distribution of P_K can only form if the time period is infinite. If the time horizon is finite, the process is truncated at an approximately exponential cutoff point (Fu et al., 2005).

For most of the systems discussed earlier, P_K has an exponential cutoff for large K, i.e., it changes its behavior from a power law decay to an exponential decay. This phenomenon is often assumed to be a finite size effect of the specific databases. Several models (Champernowne 1953; Ijiri and Simon 1977; Gabaix 1999; Reed 2001; Buldyrev et al. 2003) explain $\tau \approx 2$, but not the exponential cutoff of P_K. Moreover, an appropriate model should predict the transition from the Pareto distribution $P_K \sim K^{-\tau}$ for $\nu > 0$ to the exponential one $P_K \sim \exp(-K/\kappa)$ for $\nu = 0$.

In fact, as it was shown first by Yamasaki et al. (2006), the exponential cutoff of the power law can be the effect of the finite time interval considered for the evolution of the system. The functional form of P_K is determined by different variants of the model, changing from a pure exponential to a pure power law (with $\tau \approx 2$), via a power law with an exponential cutoff.

By using generating functions, we analytically find P_K in the Simon model for all of its parameters: λ, μ, ν, P_K^o, and P'_K (Chapter 7, Appendix 7.1). Our derivation is based on the fact that the distribution $P'_K(t, t_0)$ of the number of units in the classes created at time t_0 follows the Bose–Einstein process. The only difference is being that these classes acquire only a fraction of the new units, which is, proportional to the number of units in these classes at their birth. Thus, $P'_K(t, t_0)$ converges to a geometric distribution, characterized by an average number of units $\kappa(t, t_0)$. The total distribution of units in all classes can be obtained by summing up all $P'_K(t, t_0)$,

$$P_K(t) = P_K^o(t)\frac{N(0)}{N(t)} + \frac{1}{N(t)}\int_0^t dN(t_0)P_K'(t,t_0), \tag{3.60}$$

where $P_K^o(t)$ is the distribution of units in the old classes existing at $t = 0$, and the integral yields the distribution $P_K'(t)$ in all new classes created later. Integration in Equation (3.60) converts the geometric distribution into a power law with an exponential cutoff (Appendix 7.2). By introducing a modified growth factor of the economy,

$$R(t) = \left(\frac{n(t)}{n_0}\right)^{1/(1+b)} = e^{t(\lambda-\mu)}, \tag{3.61}$$

we can show (Appendix 7.1) that the distribution of the number of units in the old classes, present at $t = 0$, decays exponentially for large K,

$$P_K^o(t) \sim \exp[-(1-\alpha)K/R(t)]. \tag{3.62}$$

The distribution of units in the new classes undergoes a crossover from a power law distribution of Equation (3.56) for $K \ll R$ to an exponential one for $K \gg R$

$$P_K'(t) \sim \exp[-(1-\alpha)K/R(t)]/K, \tag{3.63}$$

which, due to the extra factor $1/K$, decays faster than the distribution of the old classes.

When $t \to \infty$ and $R \to \infty$, the distribution of the number of units acquires a pure power law tail. When units are not removed ($\mu = 0$) and when each new class has only one unit, $P_K'(t)$ becomes a beta-distribution,

$$P_K(\infty) = (1+b)B(b+2,K) = \frac{(b+1)(K-1)!}{(b+2)(b+3)\cdots(b+1+K)}. \tag{3.64}$$

This result was first obtained by Simon for the distribution of words in a text (Simon 1955). It is also known as Yule's distribution (Garibaldi and Scalas 2010).

As mentioned earlier, in the absence of the Gibrat process, all units are of equal size, $\langle\xi\rangle$, and thus, when $S = K\langle\xi\rangle$, the $P(S)$ distribution is proportional to P_K. To compute $P(S)$, we simply rescale P_K given in Equation (3.56). We conclude that the firm size distribution $P(S)$ is a Pareto-like distribution with an exponential cutoff, which gradually shifts to larger and larger sizes as $t \to \infty$. This is one of the most important predictions of our benchmark, which is observed in the majority of the so-called scale-free distributions. In fact, the scale, R, is hidden in the exponential cut-off.

A Stable Economy

An interesting limiting case is the case (A3) of a stable economy, which is realized when $\lambda - \mu < 0$, but $\psi = \nu + \lambda - \mu = 0$ (Klette and Kortum 2004). The condition of Klette and Kortum, $\lambda < \mu$ is a special case of the Simon model. Empirical observations show that this restriction is not necessarily true (see Chapter 5). Here, old firms shrink on average, but, due to the influx of new innovative firms capturing new business opportunities, the total number of active firms and business opportunities stays constant. The growth factor of the economy $R(t) = \exp(-\nu t)$ decreases with time and equal to $R(t) = \exp(-n_\nu(t)/n_0)$ if expressed in terms of the number of units introduced due to the entry of new firms $n_\nu(t)$. In this case, as $t \to \infty$, the number of active firms converges to

$$N_a = N(0) \ln \left[\frac{\alpha}{\alpha - 1} \right] (\alpha - 1), \tag{3.65}$$

and the distribution of units in the active firms becomes inversely proportional to $K\alpha^K$. Note that the death–birth ratio $\alpha > 1$. In the simple case, when all new firms have initially one unit, the distribution of the number of units converges for $t \to \infty$ to the logarithmic distribution

$$P_K = \frac{1}{K\alpha^K \ln[\alpha/(\alpha - 1)]}, \tag{3.66}$$

which for $\alpha \to 1$ becomes inversely proportional to K for a wide range of values of K. These results were obtained by (Kendall 1948) for a slightly different model

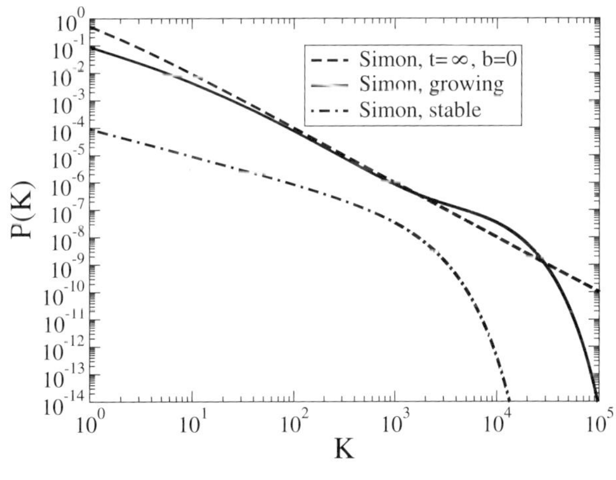

Figure 3.5 The distribution of the number of units P(K) for the preferential attachment model with new firm entries $\nu > 0$, $\lambda > 0$: Classical Simon–Zipf case (A2) given by Equation (3.64) for $t \to \infty$, $b \to 0$, $\alpha = 0$ (dashed line); Growing Simon case (A2t): $\alpha = 0.9$, $b = 0.1$, $n(t)/n_0 = 1101$ (bold line); Stable Simon case (A3): $\alpha = 1.001$, $b = -1$, $n_\nu(t)/n_0 = 10$ (dashed-dotted line). In all cases, the system initially consists of $N(0) = 100$ firms with 1 unit each. The new firms always consist of 1 unit.

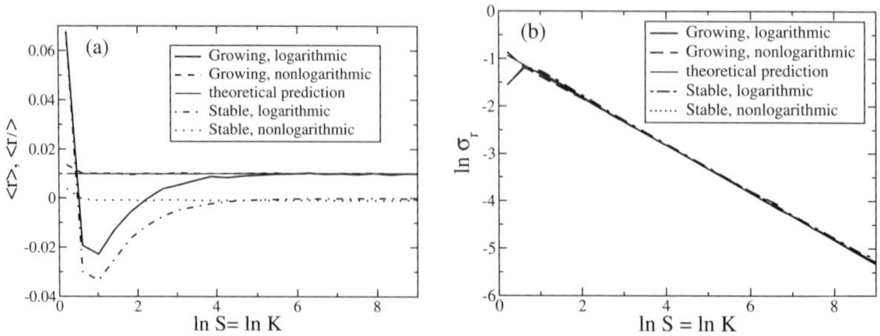

Figure 3.6 (a) The dependence of the average growth rate on firm size for the pure Simon process with the same set of parameters as in Figure 3.5 and for the case of a stable economy with $\lambda = 0.1$ and $\mu = 0.1001$, for logarithmic and nonlogarithmic growth rates. The logarithmic growth rate is nonconstant due to the nonlinear behavior of the logarithm, but the limiting values for logarithmic and nonlogarithmic growth rates converge for large S to the theoretical prediction $(\lambda - \mu)\Delta t$. (b) The size-variance relationship for the Simon process with the same set of parameters for logarithmic and non-logarithmic definitions of the growth rates. Both definitions are very well approximated by $\sigma_r = \sqrt{(\lambda + \mu)/S}$, which gives $\beta = 1/2$.

and are rederived in the context of our model in Appendix 7.1. Typical examples of P_K, produced by the Simon growth process, are presented in Figure 3.5.

Growth Rates in the Simon Model

As for the size-mean growth and size-variance relationships, the Simon model for large S closely follows the Bose–Einstein model with no firm entry (Figure 3.6). The distribution of the number of units in the firm is a power law $P_K \sim K^{-2-b}$, which rapidly increases for $K \to 0$ (much faster than the exponential distribution). Therefore, P_K is dominated by newly created firms consisting of a few units. Accordingly, adding or subtracting units from these firms changes their size by factors $2, 3/2, 4/3, 1, 3/4, 2/3, 1/2, \ldots$. These discrete values dominate the behavior of the distribution of the growth rates (Figure 3.7). Of course, this phenomenon exists only when all units have the same size. If the distribution of new units is broad enough, the growth rate distribution becomes continuous with flat tails and a big spike in the center. That is to say, distribution the does not reproduce the empirically observed tent-shaped distribution for the growth of business firms. In particular, the $1/r^3$ behavior of the tails created in the case of the Bose–Einstein process (due to the flat distribution of the number of units for small $K/\kappa \to 0$) is lost. For a stable Simon process, the P_K distribution for small K increases as K^{-1}, which is slower than for the Simon process in a growing economy, for which $P_K \sim K^{-2+b}$. Thus, for a stable Simon process, we observe a small build-up of the tent-shape for small values of r.

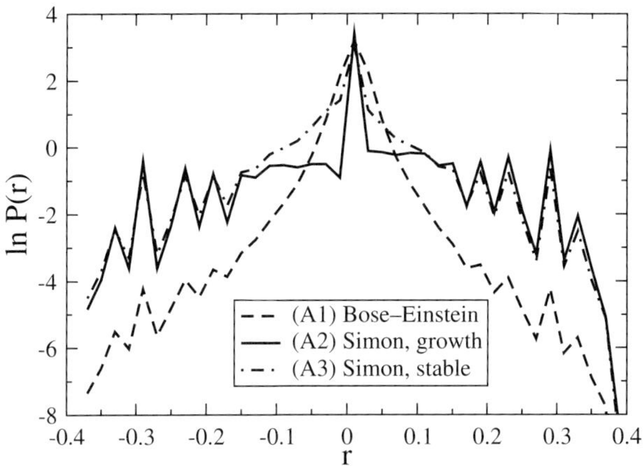

Figure 3.7 The distribution of the firm growth rates for the growing and stable Simon cases with the same set of parameters as in Figure 3.5, in comparison with the Bose–Einstein process. The irregularities of the distribution present in all three cases, especially pronounced for growing and stable Simon cases, are not due to small number of realizations but are the consequences of adding units to, or subtracting units from, the small firms consisting of a few units. The resulting growth rate distribution consists of discrete values corresponding to $\ln 1/2$, $\ln 2/3$, $\ln 2/1$, $\ln 3/2$, ... etc.

In conclusion, the Simon growth process generates the Pareto size distribution observed in many complex systems, while it fails to reproduce empirical findings on growth rates. An interesting agent based model was developed by (Axtell 1999), who models firms as growing and shrinking of aggregates of individuals, who max imize their utility functions by switching from one firm to another. Although some of its assumptions seem unrealistic, the model reproduces the four stylized facts we have presented in Chapter 1. The relation between this model, whose complex dynamics leads to proportional growth, and GPG, deserves further investigation

3.6 Generalized Proportional Growth (GPG)

Cases (B, C) $\lambda > \mu \geq 0,\ \nu = 0,\ V_\xi > 0,\ V_\eta > 0,\ m_\eta \neq 0$

Size Distribution, Stylized Fact I

In the previous Sections, we have studied separately the Gibrat proportional growth mechanism on unit sizes and the Simon growth mechanism on the number of units in a firm. We now combine the two processes and assume that firms consist of many business units, which are not equal in size, and their sizes can change according to Gibrat's Law of proportional growth. The Gibrat model predicts that sizes of units ξ and their growth rates η obey the lognormal distributions:

$$P_\xi(\xi) = \frac{1}{\xi\sqrt{2\pi V_\xi}} \mathrm{e}^{-\frac{(\ln \xi - m_\xi)^2}{2V_\xi}}, \tag{3.67}$$

and

$$P_\eta(\eta) = \frac{1}{\eta\sqrt{2\pi V_\eta}} \mathrm{e}^{-\frac{(\ln \eta - m_\eta)^2}{2V_\eta}}, \tag{3.68}$$

where $V_\xi > 0$ and $V_\eta > 0$.

According to Assumption (5), the size of a firm consisting of K units is the sum of the sizes ξ_j of its units, which are independent random variables drawn from the same distribution, $P_\xi(\xi)$, for all firms independent of K. Thus, in general, for a given distribution of unit sizes $P_\xi(\xi)$, and a given distribution of number of units P_K in the firm, the distribution of firm sizes is given by

$$P(S) = \sum_{K=1}^{\infty} P_K P(S|K), \tag{3.69}$$

where P_K is the distribution of the number of units in each firm determined by the Bose–Einstein process or the Simon processes, and

$$P(S|K) = P_\xi^{(K)}(S) \tag{3.70}$$

is the distribution of the sum of K independent random variables ξ_j, which is equal to the convolution $P_\xi^{(K)}(S)$ of K probability density functions P_ξ. Unfortunately, convolution of lognormal distributions cannot be expressed in elementary functions. For a large logarithmic variance V_ξ, the standard deviation of the lognormal distribution is much larger than the mean μ_ξ,

$$\sigma_\xi = \mu_\xi \sqrt{\exp(V_\xi) - 1}, \tag{3.71}$$

where

$$\mu_\xi = \exp(m_\xi + V_\xi/2). \tag{3.72}$$

When the mean of the sum of K lognormal distributions, $\mu_\xi K$, is much larger than the standard deviation of that sum, $\sigma_\xi\sqrt{K}$, we see a convergence of the sum to a Gaussian distribution (Figure 3.8). This convergence happens when $\sqrt{K} > \sqrt{\exp(V_\xi) - 1}$, which for large V_ξ is equivalent to $K > \exp(V_\xi)$. In the empirically observed databases, $V_\xi \approx 5$. Hence, the convergence only occurs in firms when $K \gg 100$. When $K \ll 100$, the distribution $P(S|K)$ resembles the original lognormal distribution (Figure 3.8).

When there is no entry of new firms, $\nu = 0$, P_K is a geometric distribution with $\langle K \rangle = \kappa$ (Section 3.4). When $\kappa \gg \exp(V_\xi)$, the resulting distribution $P(S)$ in Equation (3.69) will resemble P_K, i.e., the exponential distribution. In contrast,

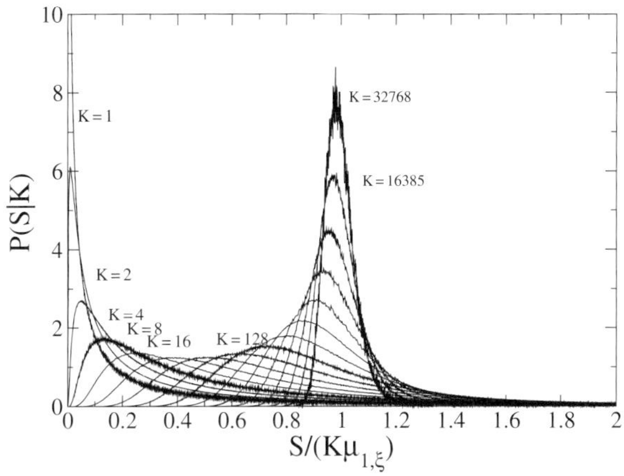

Figure 3.8 The convergence of the sum of $K = 2^n$ lognormal random variables with variance $V_\xi = 5$ (normalized by its mathematical expectation, $K\mu_{\xi},$) to a Gaussian distribution. One can see that for small K, the peak of the distribution is achieved at small S and the width of the peak is narrow. In fact, the distribution is not concentrated because its right tail decreases very slowly. As K increases, the peak shifts to the right and broadens. However, the right tail vanishes and the distribution starts to resemble a Gaussian distribution. When $K > \exp(V_\xi) = 148$, the peak starts to become narrower again and the distribution starts to concentrate near $K\mu_\xi$.

in the presence of entry of new firms, $\nu > 0$, P_K is a power law given by Equation (3.56). Here, $\langle K \rangle = 1/b$ is independent of system size because the distribution is dominated by new firms with a small number of units. Even in the limit $b \to 0$ when the first moment of the power law distribution $1/K^2$ diverges, the actual distribution always has an exponential cutoff R given by Equation (3.61). Thus, $\langle K \rangle \sim \ln R = (\lambda - \mu)t$ grows linearly with time and, hence, it remains small. Therefore, in the case of entry of new firms, the distribution of firm sizes does not converge to a power law if V_ξ is large, because the fraction of large firms in the power law distribution is very small, causing the Pareto tail of P_K to sink below the broad distribution of companies with a small number of units. However, for small V_ξ, we observe the emergence of a Pareto tail in the size distribution. Figure 3.9 illustrates these heuristic arguments through simulations.

Figure 3.10 shows typical examples of size distributions for different P_K: exponential distribution (the Bose–Einstein process), Pareto distribution (the Simon model in a growing economy), and logarithmic distribution (the Simon model in a stable economy). We can see that the $P_S(S)$ in the case of the Simon growth model resembles the empirical distributions presented in Chapter 2 (compare, in particular, Figure 2.2 with Figure 3.10).

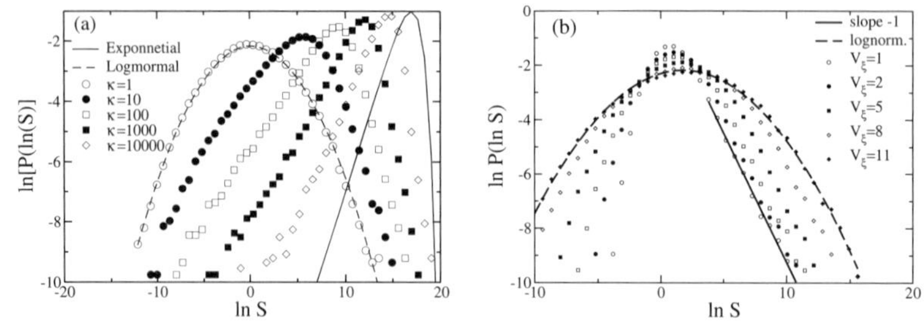

Figure 3.9 Firm size distribution for (a) the Bose–Einstein–Gibrat model with no entries $\nu = 0$, case (C1); and (b) the Simon–Gibrat model with entries $\nu > 0$, $b = 0.001$ case (C2). (a) As the scale of the exponential distribution κ increases, the distribution changes from the lognormal distribution with $V_\xi = 5$ and $m_\xi = 0$ to an exponential distribution, which in a double logarithmic scale has a functional form $y = x - \ln\kappa - \exp(x - \ln\kappa)$, characterized by a straight line with slope 1 for small x and an exponential cut-off for large scales. (b) As the logarithmic variance of the unit size distribution V_ξ decreases, the firm size distribution changes from the lognormal distribution to a distribution with a right power law tail S^{-2-b}, which is characterized by a straight line $y = (-1 - b)x$ in the double logarithmic plot. Here, we use b = 0.001, hence, the slope is very close to -1.

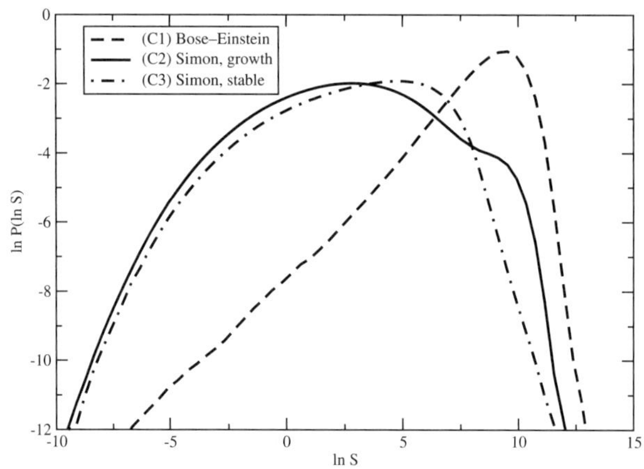

Figure 3.10 The distribution of the logarithm of firm sizes for the three cases of P_K: the Bose–Einstein process (C1), (P_K is geometrical as in Figure 3.9 with $\kappa = 1000$, the Simon growth process (C2), (P_K as in Figure 3.5, case A2t) and the Simon stable process (C3), (P_K as in Figure 3.5, case A3). $V_\xi = 5$, a value that has been found in several empirical databases.

Concentration and Inequality

One implication of our study of size distributions is related to the possibility to analyze the effect of innovation on concentration and inequality. Inequality can be measured by the Gini index (Gini 1936) defined as

$$G = \frac{\sum_{K=1,L=1}^{\infty} P_K P_L |K - L|}{2\sum_{K=1}^{\infty} K P_K} \tag{3.73}$$

for a discrete random variable K or as

$$G = \frac{\int_0^{\infty}\int_0^{\infty} P(x)P(y)|x - y|dxdy}{2\int_{x=0}^{\infty} xP(x)dx} \tag{3.74}$$

for a continuous random variable x. For Gibrat's model, in which the distribution of unit sizes converges to a lognormal distribution

$$P(\xi) = \frac{1}{\xi\sqrt{2\pi V_\xi}} \exp\left[-\frac{(\ln\xi - m_\xi)^2}{2V_\xi}\right], \tag{3.75}$$

where the logarithmic variance V_ξ grows linearly with time, the Gini index is equal to $\mathrm{erf}(\sqrt{V_\xi}/2)$,[8] and thus quickly approaches its highest possible value of 1, indicating concentration in a very few largest units. However, since for $\mu > 0$, the average lifetime of units is fixed, in GPG, the Gini index of units is also fixed.

For the Bose–Einstein process case, $(\nu = 0, V_\xi = 0)$, when there is no innovation and no inequality in terms of unit sizes, the size distribution in terms of number of units is geometric (Equation 3.44) and, thus, the Gini index increases with time: $G = (1 - 1/\kappa)/(2 - 1\kappa)$. If $\nu > 0$, the size distribution converges to a steady state distribution with a Pareto tail, characterized with a power law decay $P_K \sim K^{-2-b}$. For the pure Pareto distribution with no exponential cutoff, $G = 1/(1 + 2b)$. In reality, since Simon's model never produces the pure Pareto distribution, for each value of b, G increases from $1/2$ for $R = 1$ to a greater value $G(b, \infty)$ for $R \to \infty$, such that $1 > G(b, \infty) > 1/(1 + 2b)$. For large b, the convergence is very fast, but $G(b, \infty)$ is close to $1/2$, while for small b, the convergence is very slow, but $G(b, \infty)$ is close to 1 (Figure 3.11(a)). For $b \to 0$ and $R \to \infty$, the inequality grows to its highest level and the Gini coefficient $G \to 1$. We denote the Gini coefficient for the Simon model $G(\lambda, \mu, \nu, R)$.

In GPG, with $V_\xi > 0$, Case (C2), the Gini coefficient, due to the combined effect of P_K and V_ξ stays almost constant, while $G(\lambda, \mu, \nu, R) > \mathrm{erf}(\sqrt{V_\xi}/2)$ (Figure 3.11(b)). As V_ξ grows, $\mathrm{erf}(\sqrt{V_\xi}/2)$ becomes larger than $G(\lambda, \mu, \nu, R)$ and the Gini coefficient starts to increase, but $G(\lambda, \mu, \nu, R, V_\xi)$ and converges to 1 for $V_\xi \to \infty$, but slower than $\mathrm{erf}(\sqrt{V_\xi}/2)$. Usually, a good convergence can be found for $V_\xi \geq 25$. For realistic value of V_ξ, i.e, $5 < V_\xi < 10$, we can see a strong competition between the two effects. In summary, in the absence of innovation and given the broad distribution of unit sizes, industrial concentration is dominated by inequality among unit sizes. In this setting, Schumpeterian creative destruction

[8] $\mathrm{erf}(x)$ is the error function (Greene 2012).

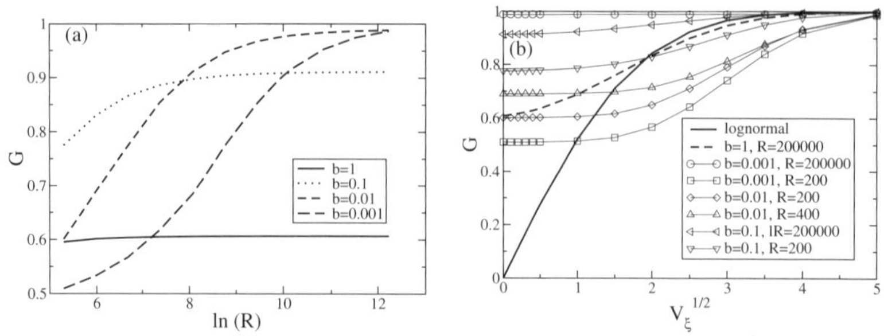

Figure 3.11 (a) Dependence of the Gini index on R for the Simon model, case (A2t), with different values of b. (b) Dependence of the Gini index on V_ξ for the GPG model with different values of b and R.

captured by parameter μ prevents V_ξ from growing indefinetly. Some further analysis of the determinants of concentration and inequality will be discussed in Chapter 5.

Dependence of the Growth Rate Distribution on Firm Size

We now analyze stylized Facts II, III, and IV. When Gibrat's growth of unit size is combined with the proportional growth of the number of units, it is relatively straightforward to find the distribution of the firm growth rates $P_r(r|K)$, which is the conditional distribution of growth rates of firms with a given number of units, K, determined by the distributions $P_\xi(\xi)$ and $P_\eta(\eta)$. It is simple to find both the mean $m_r(K) \equiv \langle r(K) \rangle$ and the variance $\sigma_r^2(K)$ of this distribution as a function of K.

The resulting distribution of the growth rates of all firms is given by

$$P_r(r) \equiv \sum_{K=1}^{\infty} P_K P_r(r|K), \tag{3.76}$$

where P_K is the distribution of the number of units in each firm, determined by the Bose–Einstein process or the Simon process. We must emphasize, that according to the GPG framework the stylized Fact II, i.e. the tent-shape distribution of growth rates, arises only in a large sample of firms as a convolution of distributions of the growth rates of firms with different number of units. Growth rates of individual firms are not sampled from their collective growth rate distribution. This consequence of the GPG framework is in line with (Lunardi et al. 2001).

It is more difficult to find the distribution of logarithmic growth rates $P_r(r|S)$, the mean $\langle r(S) \rangle$ and the variance $\sigma_r^2(S)$ as a function of the firm size S, which is the sum of the sizes of individual units. These quantities are available empirically in a larger number of databases and, moreover, are relevant from an economic point of view. If the distribution of unit sizes $P_\xi(\xi)$ is wide (V_ξ is large), the distribution of logarithmic growth rates for a given value of K strongly depends on the size of the firm, S:

$$P_r(r|K,S) \neq P_r(r|K). \tag{3.77}$$

The relationship between $P_r(r|K)$ and $P_r(r|S)$ is not easy to establish because the conditional probability $P(S|K)$, which is the convolution (3.70) of K distributions P_ξ, converges to a Gaussian distribution very slowly for large V_ξ, as shown in Figure 3.8. Through Bayes' Law, $P(S, K) = P(S|K)P_K = P(K|S)P(S)$, we find

$$P(r|S) = \sum_K P(r|S,K)P(K|S) = \sum_K P(r|S,K)P(S|K)P_K/P(S). \tag{3.78}$$

The distributions $P(r|S,K)$, $P(S|K)$, P_K and P_S can be derived from the parameters of the model. As we have seen in Figure 3.8, when $K > \exp(V_\xi)$, the distribution $P(S|K)$ develops a maximum near $S = S_K \equiv \mu_\xi K$, where $\mu_\xi = \exp(m_\xi + V_\xi/2)$ is the mean of the lognormal distribution of units. Conversely, $P(K|S)$, as a function of K, develops a maximum near $K_S = S/\mu_\xi$. For the values of S, such that $P_{K_S} > 0$, $P(r|S) \approx P(r|S,K_S) = P(r|K_S)$. We observe this behavior since $P(K|S)$ near its maximum serves as a Dirac function $\delta(K - K_S)$, so that only terms with $K \approx K_S$ make a dominant contribution to the sum of Equation (3.78). Accordingly, one can approximate $P(r|S)$ by $P(r|K_S)$ and $\sigma_r(S)$ by $\sigma_r(K_S)$ for a wide range of firm sizes. However, for exponential P_K and lognormal P_ξ, it might happen that $P_{K_S} < 1/N$, while $P_\xi(S) > 1/n$, where N is the total number of firms and $n = N\langle K\rangle$ is the total number of units. In this case, the largest firms would be large not because they own a large number of units, but because they are made of a single very large unit. Accordingly, for these firms, we can no longer use the approximation $P(r|S) \approx P(r|K_S)$. Hence, $\sigma_r(S)$ no longer follows $\sigma_r(K_S)$ and starts to increase with the size of the firm. We will explore this condition in detail (Figure 3.15). Keeping these limitations in mind, we will first explore the behavior of the growth rate as a function of K.

Dependence of the Growth Rate Distribution on the Number of Units

The closed form of the distribution $P(r|K)$ and its mean $m_r(K)$ and variance $\sigma_r^2(K)$ are not easy to obtain in the general case. We can derive them only in the limits $K \to 1$ and $K \to \infty$. On the basis of the central limit theorem, it is possible to prove that, in the limit of very large K, $P_r(r|K)$ converges to a Gaussian distribution (Appendix 7.2)

$$P_r(r|K) = \frac{\sqrt{K}}{\sqrt{2\pi V_r}} \exp\left(-\frac{(r-m_r)^2 K}{2V_r}\right), \tag{3.79}$$

where the mean logarithmic growth rate, m_r, is

$$m_r = m_\eta + V_\eta/2 + \ln(1 + \lambda\Delta t - \mu\Delta t), \tag{3.80}$$

and the normalized variance V_r is

$$V_r = \frac{(1 + \lambda\Delta t - \mu\Delta t)\exp(V_\xi)[\exp(V_\eta) - 1] + (\lambda\Delta t + \mu\Delta t)\exp(V_\xi)}{(1 + \lambda\Delta t - \mu\Delta t)^2} + \frac{(\lambda^2 - \mu^2)\Delta t^2[\exp(V_\xi) - 1]}{(1 + \lambda\Delta t - \mu\Delta t)^2}. \tag{3.81}$$

From Equations (3.79), (3.80), and (3.81), it follows that in the limit of $K \to \infty$, $\sigma_r^2(K) = V_r/K$ is inversely proportional to K, while the average growth rate converges for $K \to \infty$ to a finite limit $m_r(K) \to m_r$. These findings allow us to hypothesize that $\langle r(S)\rangle$ does not strongly depend on S, while $\sigma_r(S) \sim S^{-1/2}$, yields $\beta = 1/2$. However, these predictions are not accurate due to a very slow convergence of $P_r(r|K)$ to a Gaussian distribution when $K \to \infty$.

Figure 3.12 shows simulated distributions of $P_r(r|K)$ for several values of $K = 2^k$, using independent lognormally distributed unit sizes ξ_i and growth rates η_i with a realistic set of parameters obtained from the PHID database (see Chapter 4 and Fu et al. (2005)). In this figure, we can see that $P_r(r|K)$ starts as a Gaussian distribution that coincides with the distribution of $\ln \eta$ for $K = 1$, and then develops tent-shaped tails for intermediate values of K, but finally converges back to a Gaussian distribution for $K \to \infty$.[9] Accordingly, for small r, the shape of $P_r(r|K)$ resembles a Gaussian distribution for any K with different $V_r(K)$. Thus, Equation (3.79) provides a relatively good approximation for $P_r(r|K)$ if we use accurate values $\sigma_r^2(K)$ and $m_r(K)$, which we will attempt to obtain in the following subsection.

Dependence of the Growth Rate Mean and Variance on the Number of Units in the Absence of Entry and Exit of Units

As mentioned in the last section, the distribution of growth rates for small K is affected by large shocks due to the entry and exit of units, which happen at random time intervals with low probabilities $\lambda\Delta t$ and $\mu\Delta t$, respectively. The behavior of $m_r(K)$ and $\sigma_r^2(K)$ for small K is strongly affected by those shocks. In this subsection, we assume that $\lambda\Delta t$ and $\mu\Delta t$ are much smaller than m_η and V_η, so that

[9] Note that according to GPG framework growth rates of individual firms with given number of units are drawn from the distributions shown in Figure 3.12 if one neglects the entry and exit of units. One can see, that these distributions are different for the firms with different number of units. It would be interesting to repeat statistical tests of (Lunardi et al. 2001) against these distributions.

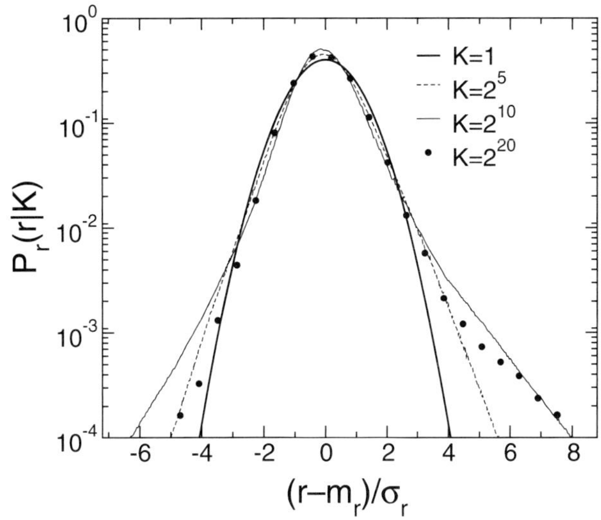

Figure 3.12 Normalized distribution $P(r|K)$ for different values of K when entry and exit of units is not considered ($\lambda = \mu = 0$). For $K = 1$, the distribution $P(r|K)$ coincides with the distribution of $\ln \eta_i$, which is Gaussian by our assumption. As K increases, the departure from the Gaussian increases and reaches its maximum for $K \approx 10^3$. At this value of K the distribution develops a tent shape. For $K = 10^6$ the distribution again slowly approaches a Gaussian distribution as predicted by the Central Limit Theorem. The parameters of the simulations $V_\xi = 5.13$, $m_\xi = 3.44$, $V_\eta = 0.36$ and $m_\eta = 0.016$ are taken from the PHID data base (see Chapter 4 and Riccaboni et al. 2008). We also assume that the change in the number of products in the firm during time interval Δt is negligible: $\Delta t(\lambda - \mu) \to 0$. The figure is reproduced from figure 4 in Buldyrev et al. (2007).

they can be neglected. In this case, the logarithmic growth rate for a firm consisting of one unit coincides with $\ln \eta$ and, thus, $m_r(1) = m_\eta$ and $V_r(1) = V_\eta$.

The convergence to a Gaussian distribution for $K \to \infty$ is very slow for large V_ξ and V_η, (Figure 3.12); therefore, for each finite K,

$$m_r(K) \equiv \mathrm{E}(r|K) \tag{3.82}$$

increases monotonically with K from m_η for $K = 1$ to m_r for $K \to \infty$, while

$$\sigma_r^2(K) \equiv \mathrm{Var}(r|K) < V_r/K \tag{3.83}$$

decreases monotonically from V_η for $K = 1$, approaching its asymptotic limit V_r/K from below (Figure 3.13).

The values of $m_r(K)$ and $V_r(K)$ cannot be obtained analytically. However, $\sigma_r(K)$ and $m_r(K)$ depend solely on V_ξ and V_η and do not depend on m_ξ and m_η, except for the leading asymptotic term in $m_r(K)$. Therefore, we rely on computer

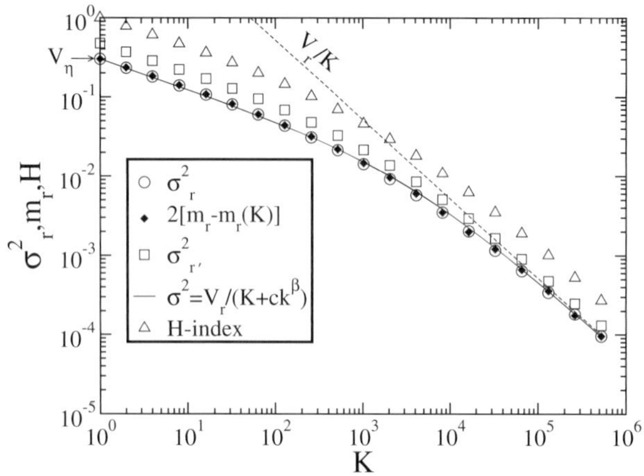

Figure 3.13 The behavior of the standard deviation of the growth rate $\sigma_r^2(K)$ as a function of K. Here, a crossover from approximate power law $\sigma_r^2(K) \sim K^{-0.38}$ for small K to a limiting behavior predicted by Equation (3.81), for which $\sigma_r^2(K) \sim K^{-1}$. Solid line shows fit $\sigma_r^2 = V_r/(K + cK^{2\beta})$, where $c = V_r(\exp(V_\eta) - 1)/V_\eta$, $\beta = 0.19$. Here, we use values $V_\xi = 5$ and $V_\eta = 0.3$, which are typical for empirical data bases, and $m_\eta = 0$. Also shown are $m_r - m_r(K)$, standard deviation for the nonlogarithmic growth rate $\sigma_{r'}^2$, and H-index, respectively.

simulations with a set of parameters analogous to the one used in Figure 3.12. The results of these simulations are presented in Figure 3.13. In particular, we compare the behavior of $\sigma_r^2(K)$ with $2(m_r - m_r(K))$. A nearly perfect coincidence of these values suggests that for $\lambda\Delta t = \mu\Delta t = 0$, lognormally distributed η_i and any ξ_i independent of η_i, the following approximation can be used:

$$m_r(K) \approx m_r - \frac{\sigma_r^2(K)}{2}. \tag{3.84}$$

The accuracy of this approximation depends on V_η: for $V_\eta < 0.5$ the approximation is almost perfect for all K. This equation yields a monotonic increase of $m_r(K)$ from $m_r(1) = m_\eta$ for $K = 1$ to $m_r(\infty) \equiv m_r = m_\eta + V_\eta/2$ for $K \to \infty$, but this increase is negligible if V_η is small.

The properties of the nonlogarithmic growth rate are simpler. We already saw in Section 3.4 that $m_r'(K) = (\lambda - \mu)\Delta t$ is independent of $K = S$ if all units are equal in size. The same is true if units differ in size ($V_\xi > 0$), but the instant probabilities of adding and losing units are negligible $[(\lambda - \mu)\Delta t \to 0]$. In this case, we have

$$m_r'(K) = \exp(m_\eta + V_\eta/2) - 1. \tag{3.85}$$

Also, as shown in Appendix 7.2, Equation (7.89), $\sigma_{r'}^2$ can be expressed in terms of the average H-index, $\langle H \rangle$, computed for a firm's portfolios of products or in terms of the average effective number of units, K_e,

$$\sigma_{r'}^2(K) = \mathrm{Var}(\eta)\langle H \rangle = \frac{\mathrm{Var}(\eta)}{K_e}. \tag{3.86}$$

This relationship is visible in Figure 3.13 as the parallel shift of the graphs of $\langle H(K) \rangle$ and $\sigma_{r'}^2(K)$ by a factor of $\mathrm{Var}(\eta)$. If η is a lognormal variable, $\mathrm{Var}(\eta) = [\exp(V_\eta) - 1]\exp(2m_\eta + V_\eta)$. For $V_\eta = 0.3$, $m_\eta = 0$ used in Figure 3.13, $\mathrm{Var}(\eta) = 0.472$, which is in perfect agreement with the simulation results in Figure 3.13. The behaviors of σ_r^2(K) and $\sigma_{r'}^2(K)$ are very similar to each other (see Figure 3.13) since the asymptotic behavior of the H-index for large K is

$$\langle H \rangle = \exp(V_\xi)/K + O(1/K^2). \tag{3.87}$$

Thus, for large $K \to \infty$, $\sigma_r^2/\sigma_{r'}^2 = \exp(2m_\eta + V_\eta)$, while for small $K \to 1$, $\sigma_r^2/\sigma_{r'}^2 = \exp(2m_\eta + V_\eta)(\exp(V_\eta) - 1)/V_\eta$.

Figure 3.13 shows that $\sigma_r(K)$ exhibits an interesting crossover from a slow decay characterized by a power law $K^{-\beta}$ with $\beta \approx 0.2$ to the behavior predicted by the central limit theorem $K^{-1/2}$. We observe a crossover since the behavior of a firm consisting of a small number of units is dominated by the fluctuation of the largest unit, which can be much greater than the rest of the units, i.e., such firms essentially fluctuate as firms consisting of a single unit. Accordingly, we can claim that the central limit theorem must be applied not to the real number of firms K, but to $K_e(K) = 1/H$. Numerical simulations show that the behavior of $\sigma_r(K)$, $m_r - m_r(K)$, $\sigma_{r'}(K)$, and $H(K)$ can be approximated as $A/(K + cK^{2\beta})$, where A is defined by the exact asymptotic behavior for $K \to \infty$, c, is derived from the values of the quantities of interest at $K = 1$, and $\beta = \beta(V_\xi)$ can be derived from the average value of the slope on the log–log plot for small K. A good fit can be obtained using $\beta(V_\xi) = 1/(2.5 + 0.46V_\xi)$ (see Apppendix 7.3).

Since for firms consisting of a sufficient number of units, the size of the firm S is proportional to the number of units K, we can conjecture that the power law size-variance relationship $\sigma_r(S) \sim S^{-\beta}$ found in various systems originates from the power law behavior of $\sigma_r(K)$. For values of V_ξ in the range between 1 and 10, the values of β are confined in the range between $1/10$ and $1/3$, which is indeed observed in a large variety of systems. We will return to this problem in greater detail later in this chapter.

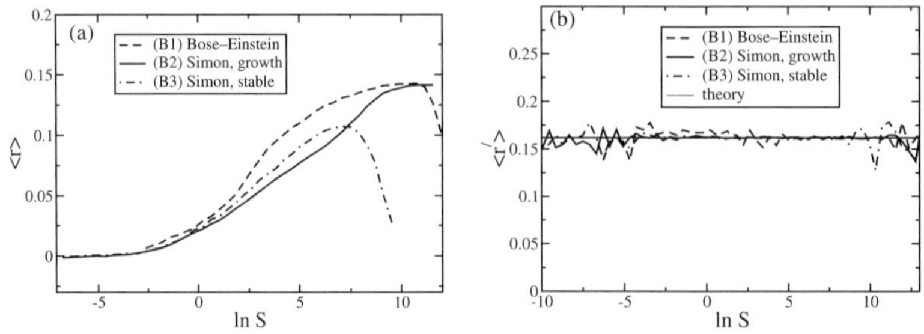

Figure 3.14 The dependence of the average growth rate on firm size for the cases of geometric (B1), power (B2), and logarithmic (B3) P_K for logarithmic (a) and nonlogarithmic (b) definitions. For the nonlogarithmic definition, all cases are in good agreement with the theoretical prediction $\exp(m_\eta + V_\eta/2) - 1$. Small irregularities of the graphs are due to statistical errors for finite number of realizations of the processes.

Dependence of the Mean Growth Rate on the Firm Size S in the Absence of Entry and Exit of Units ($\lambda\Delta t = \mu\Delta t = 0$)

If we neglect the change in the number of units, assuming that $\lambda\Delta t$ and $\mu\Delta t$ are very small compared to V_η, the average logarithmic growth rate $\langle r(S)\rangle \equiv m_r(S)$, as a function of the firm size S, closely follows the behavior of $m_r(K)$ with $K = K_S = S/\mu_\xi$. Thus, $m_r(S)$ increases monotonically from $m_r(1) = m_\eta$ for small firms to $\langle r(\infty)\rangle = m_r$ for large firms (Figure 3.14). The relation (3.84) is also valid as a function of S:

$$m_r(S) = m_r - \frac{\sigma_r^2}{2}(S). \tag{3.88}$$

We will understand the details of the behavior of $m_r(S)$ together with the behavior of $\sigma_r^2(S)$ in the next subsection. In contrast, the nonlogarithmic growth rate $\langle r'\rangle = \exp(m_\eta + V_\eta/2) - 1$ is constant for firms of all sizes (see Figure 3.14). This prediction contradicts the stylized Fact II, suggesting that, on average, small firms grow faster than large firms. This discrepancy emphasizes the importance of the arrival/launch of new units, which we neglect in this subsection.

Dependence of the Growth Rate Variance on the Firm Size S: Cases (B1), (B2), and (B3), $\lambda\Delta t = \mu\Delta t = 0$. Stylized Fact IV

Once we find the behavior of $\sigma_r(K)$, we rely on Riccaboni et al. (2008) to understand the behavior of $\sigma_r(S)$ by approximating it with $\sigma_r(K_S)$. However, it is reasonable to expect that most of the firms with $S < S_1 = \mu_\xi$ consist of one unit and thus,

$$\sigma_r^2(S) \approx V_\eta \tag{3.89}$$

for $S < \mu_\xi$. For large S, if $P(K_S) > 0$,

$$\sigma_r^2(S) \approx \sigma_r^2(K_S) \approx V_r/K_S \approx V_r\mu_\xi/S, \tag{3.90}$$

where m_η and V_η are the logarithmic mean and variance, respectively, of the unit growth distributions P_η, and V_r is given by Equation (3.81). We still assume that $\lambda\Delta t = \mu\Delta t = 0$. As a consequence,

$$V_r = \exp(V_\xi)[\exp(V_\eta) - 1]. \tag{3.91}$$

Hence, by using Equations (3.72) and (3.90), we obtain:

$$\sigma_r^2 = \frac{\exp(3V_\xi/2 + m_\xi)(\exp(V_\eta) - 1)}{S}. \tag{3.92}$$

We, therefore, expect a crossover from $\beta = 0$, for $S < \mu_\xi$, to $\beta = 1/2$, for $S \gg S^*$, where

$$S^* = \exp(3V_\xi/2 + m_\xi)(\exp(V_\eta) - 1)/V_\eta \tag{3.93}$$

is the value of S for which Equations (3.89) and (3.92) give the same value of $\sigma(S)$ (Figure 3.15). Note that for small $V_\eta < 1$, $S^* \approx \exp(3V_\xi/2 + m_\xi)$. The crossover range extends from $S_1 = \mu_\xi$ to S^*, with $S^*/S_1 = \exp(V_\xi) \to \infty$ for $V_\xi \to \infty$. Thus, in the double logarithmic plot of σ vs. S, one can find a wide region in which the slope β slowly varies from 0 to 1/2 ($\beta \approx 0.2$).

The crossover of β from 0 to $1/2$ is seen when $K^* = S^*/\mu_\xi = \exp(V_\xi)$ is such that $P_K(K > K^*)$ is significantly larger than zero. For the distribution P_K with a sharp exponential cutoff at $K = \kappa(t)$, the crossover is seen when $\kappa(t) \gg \exp(V_\xi)$ (Figure 3.15).

Suppose that the market is populated by N firms with $n = \langle K\rangle N$ products, where $\langle K\rangle = \sum_K P_K K$ is the average number of units in a firm. Two scenarios are possible for $S \gg S^*$. In the first scenario, no unit among all $N\langle K\rangle$ units of the system has $\xi_j \gg S^*$. In this scenario, we will observe a crossover to $\beta = 1/2$. In the second scenario, the distribution of the size of units P_ξ is so broad that there are units for which $\xi_j \gg S^*$. These exceptionally large units produce exceptionally large firms and the fluctuations of these units determine the fluctuations of the firms to which they belong. The H-index of these firms is close to unity and the effective number of units is very small. Accordingly, instead of decreasing inversely proportional to S, $\sigma_r^2(S)$ will start to increase for large S. These unstable large firms can produce large fluctuations that might negatively affect the entire system under investigation, being it a sector or the entire economy.

Whether the crossover to $\beta = 1/2$ is possible depends on the complex interplay between P_ξ and P_K. The crossover to $\beta = 1/2$ occurs only when $P_K(K > S/\mu_\xi) > 1/N$, but $P_\xi(\xi > S) < 1/(N\langle K\rangle)$ for $S > S^*$, which means

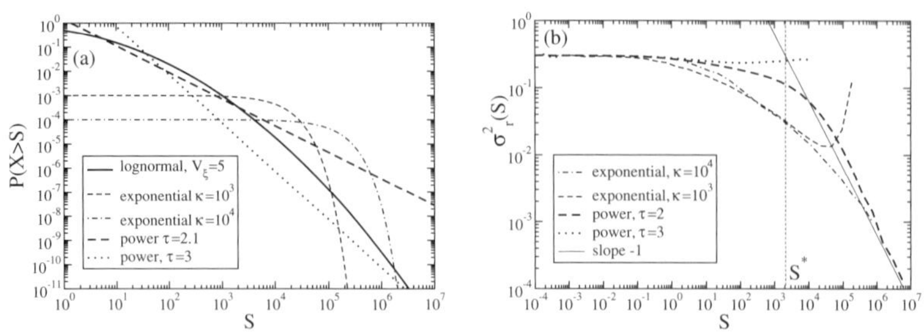

Figure 3.15 (a) A comparison of the decay of cumulative lognormal distribution of unit sizes $P_\xi(\xi > S)$ ($m_\xi = 0, V_\xi = 5$) with the decay of cumulative distributions of the number of units $P_K(K > K_S)/\langle K\rangle$, where $K_S = S/\mu_\xi$ and $\mu_\xi = \exp(V_\xi/2) \approx 12.2$. We use two exponential distributions with $\kappa = 10^4$ and $\kappa = 10^3$, and two power law distributions with $\tau = 2.1$ and $\tau = 3$. (b) Simulated behavior of $\sigma_r^2(S)$ for the four P_K distributions shown in panel (a) over a sample of N firms. For the exponential distributions $N = 10^5$ and for the power law $N = 10^7$. Panel (a) shows that for the exponential distribution with $\kappa = 10^3$, $P_K(K > K_S)/\langle K\rangle$ becomes smaller than $P_\xi(\xi > S)$ for $S = 114000$, $K_S = 9300$. The y coordinate of the crossing point gives $(\langle K\rangle N) = 10500$, which means that for any sample of firms with $N > 10500$ a spurious peak will be observed in the behavior of $\sigma_r^2(S)$ for $S > 114000$ shown in Panel (b). For $\kappa = 10^4$, the intersection occurs only at $S = S_\sigma = 1.8\times10^6$, $N = N_\sigma = 1.7\times10^6$. Since in our simulation shown in panel (b) N is also 10^5, we do not observe the increase of $\sigma_r^2(S)$ at large S but only a slow crossover to $1/S$ behavior, which for a wide range of S can be approximated by a power law $S^{-2\beta}$. Power law $P_K/\langle K\rangle$ for $\tau = 2.1$ is always greater than P_ξ for $S > S^*$ and, hence, $\sigma_r^2(S)$ must approach the asymptotic behavior $\sigma_r^2(S) \sim 1/S$ for large S. In contrast, power law $P_K\langle K\rangle$ with $\tau = 3$ becomes smaller than P_ξ for $S > 2000$, hence, no crossover is observed at $1/S$ behavior in panel (b) but rather a shallow minimum at $S \approx 100$.

that large firms predominantly consist of a large number of units. This case may be realized for distributions P_K with an exponential cutoff $\kappa \gg \exp(V_\xi)$ and power law distributions with small $\tau \approx 2$. If, on the contrary, $P_\xi(\xi > S) > 1/(N\langle K\rangle)$, but $P_K(K > S/\mu_\xi) < 1/N$, which takes place for small κ and large τ (Figure 3.15(a)), we observe a dramatic increase in $\sigma_r^2(S)$ for such S (Figure 3.15(b)). The values of $S = S_\sigma$ and $N = N_\sigma$, above which the increase in $\sigma_r^2(S)$ takes place, can be found from the intersection of the curves $P_\xi(\xi > S_\sigma) = P_K(K > S_\sigma/\mu_\xi)/\langle K\rangle = 1/(N_\sigma\langle K\rangle)$ (Figure 3.15(a)). The behavior of the H-index and $\sigma_{r'}^2(S)$ closely follows this pattern with a peak for large S. In fact Perline et al. (2006) found evidence of slight growth of $\sigma_r(S)$ for small US firms measured by the number of employees. These firms consist of a few units but the sales of these units may have various sizes; thus, we can expect the behavior shown on Figure 3.15(b) for $\tau = 3$.

The reason for an increase in $\sigma_r^2(S)$ for the exponential distribution P_K is that the lognormal distribution P_ξ of unit sizes decays slower than exponentially, and hence

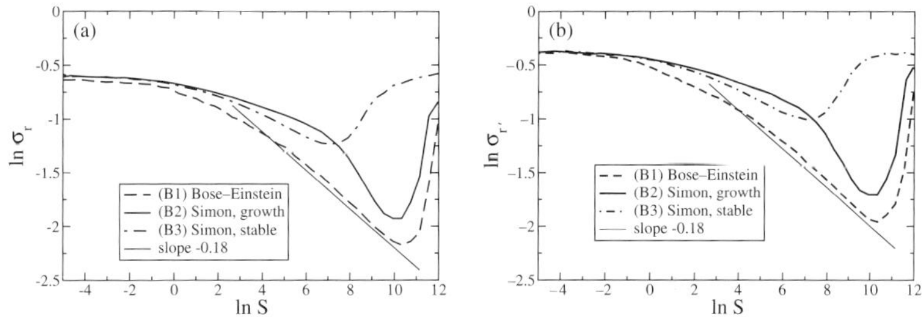

Figure 3.16 Size-variance relationship for the cases of exponential P_K ($\kappa = 1000$), power law P_K with exponential cutoff ($\tau = 2.1$) and logarithmic P_K $\alpha = 1.1$, for logarithmic (a) and nonlogarithmic (b) definitions. For all cases, $V_\xi = 5$ and $V_\eta = 0.3$.

for a sufficiently large sample of firms $N > N_\sigma$, we will always find undiversified extremely large firms that include a product significantly larger than the average unit size μ_ξ. For pure power law distributions with large τ, the initial decrease of P_K is faster than that of a lognormal distribution, so P_K quickly goes below $1/N$ for any reasonable sample of firms, while P_ξ remains large for a wide range of S (Figure 3.15).

The sharpness of the crossover depends on the type of P_K distribution. For power law distributions, we expect a sharper crossover than for exponential distributions, since most of the firms in a power law distribution have a small number of units K and, hence, the slope $\beta(S)$ stays approximately zero for $S < S^*$, the size at which the crossover is observed. For exponential distributions, we expect a slow crossover if $V_\xi < \ln \kappa$. For $S \gg S_1 = \mu_\xi$, the crossover is well represented by the behavior of $\sigma(K_S)$.

These heuristic arguments are confirmed by computer simulations presented in Figure 3.16, which shows typical examples of the size-variance relationship when we can neglect size fluctuations due to a change in the number of units. One can see that for the Bose–Einstein case there is an approximate power law regime with $\beta \approx 0.18$. For the Simon process, P_K is a power law with an exponential cutoff and, hence, σ_r^2 does not show any regime with an approximately constant slope.

In summary, the exponent β of the size-variance relationship within the outlined framework does not follow a genuine power law, but a crossover from $\beta = 0$ for small companies comprised of one unit to $\beta = 1/2$ for large firms consisting of many independent units. The addition of correlations between the growth of units by modeling a firm as a hierarchical tree leads to an exact power law size-variance relation with constant β at the expense of introducing additional assumptions and parameters. The interested reader is referred to Appendix 7.4. Another model leading to an exact value of $\beta = 0.25$ has been proposed by

Sutton (2002), who postulates that a firm consisting of K elementary units is split into integer partitions of K, where all partitions are selected with equal probabilities and their parts fluctuate according to the Gibrat's Law.[10]

Distribution of Growth Rates in the Gibrat–Bose–Einstein Case (B1)
$\lambda \Delta t = \mu \Delta t = 0$. *Stylized Fact III*

In order to find the distribution of growth rates $P_r(r)$ for a given distribution of the number of units P_K, we can use Equation (3.76), once the conditional distribution $P_r(r|K)$ is known. In order to find a closed form approximation for the Bose–Einstein case, characterized by the geometric P_K, we replace the summation in Equation (3.76) with integration, replace the distribution P_K with Equation (3.47), and replace the distribution $P(r|K)$ with Equation (3.79). Accordingly,

$$P_r(r) \approx \frac{1}{\sqrt{2\pi V_r}} \int_0^\infty \frac{1}{\kappa(t)} \exp\left(\frac{-K}{\kappa(t)}\right) \exp\left(-\frac{(r-m_r)^2 K}{2 V_r}\right) \sqrt{K}\, dK,$$
$$= \frac{\sqrt{\kappa(t)}}{2\sqrt{2 V_r}} \left(1 + \frac{\kappa(t)}{2V_r}(r-m_r)^2\right)^{-\frac{3}{2}}, \tag{3.94}$$

where $\kappa(t)$ is the average number of units given by Equation (3.45). The distribution of Equation (3.94) has the same tent shape as the distribution of the growth rates in the pure Bose–Einstein process given by Equation (3.54), but with a different parameter V_r. (Figure 3.17). This distribution for $|r - m_r| > \sqrt{2V_r/\kappa}$ decays asymptotically as $1/r^3$ and, thus, it does not have finite variance. The divergence of the variance is an artifact introduced by the replacement of summation by integration in Equation (3.76).

The summation of Equation (3.76) can be made explicit by using an exact geometric distribution for P_K given by Equation (3.44) and an approximate equation for $P(r|K)$ given by Equation (3.79),

$$P_r(r) \approx \frac{1}{\sqrt{2\pi V_r}(\kappa - 1)} \sum_{K=1}^{\infty} \left(1 - \frac{1}{\kappa}\right)^K \exp\left(-\frac{(r-m_r)^2 K}{2 V_r}\right) \sqrt{K}. \tag{3.95}$$

Since K in the exponential function can be taken out as a power, this complicated equation is reduced to a power series for the polylogarithm of order μ defined by:

$$\mathrm{Li}_\mu(x) = \sum_{n=1}^{\infty} \frac{x^n}{n^\mu}. \tag{3.96}$$

[10] See also Wyart and Bouchaud (2003).

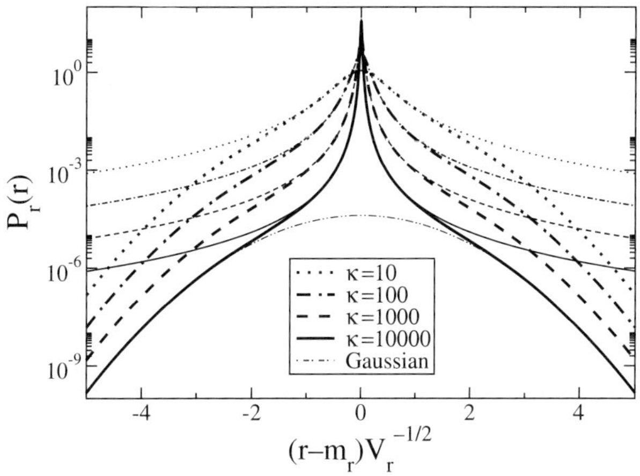

Figure 3.17 A comparison of two types of approximations for the growth rate distribution for the case of combined Bose–Einstein preferential attachment of units with the Gibrat growth of unit sizes, for various κ / V_r. Thin lines correspond to approximation (3.94), which predicts the infinite range of the power law behavior. Thick lines correspond to approximation (3.97), which predicts the crossover to a Gaussian behavior for $|r - m_r| > \sqrt{V_r}$.

with $\mu = -1/2$. Thus,

$$P_r(r) = \frac{\mathrm{Li}_{-1/2}[(1 - 1/\kappa)\exp(-(r - m_r)^2/(2V_r))]}{(\kappa - 1)\sqrt{2\pi V_r}}. \tag{3.97}$$

For $\kappa \to \infty$ and small r, the leading term of the asymptotic expansion of Equation (3.97) coincides with Equation (3.94), but, for $r \to \infty$, the main contribution is given by the first term of the Taylor expansion (3.96), which is a Gaussian distribution with variance V_r. A comparison between the polylogarithm of Equation (3.97) and the power law distribution of Equation (3.94) is shown in Figure 3.17. One can see that a region of approximately –3 power law behavior exists for $\sqrt{2V_r/\kappa} < |r - m_r| < \sqrt{V_r}$ which emerges for $\kappa > 100$.

However, the polylogarithm, which is the best closed form approximation of the growth rate distribution for the Bose–Einstein case, overestimates the range of the power law behavior because of the replacement of the $P_r(r|K)$ distributions presented in Figure 3.12 by the Gaussian distributions with variance V_r/K, which is correct only for very large K. For small K, $\sigma_r^2(K) \ll V_r/K$. In particular, $\sigma_r^2(1) = V_\eta \approx V_r/\exp(V_\xi)$. As a consequence, for very large r, the distribution is dominated by the fluctuation of the firms consisting of only one unit, which is a Gaussian distribution with variance V_η. Hence, for $r > V_\eta$, we expect a crossover from a power law behavior to a Gaussian cut-off with variance V_η. Note that the term with the slowest decay is the first term in the sum of Equation (3.76), which decays

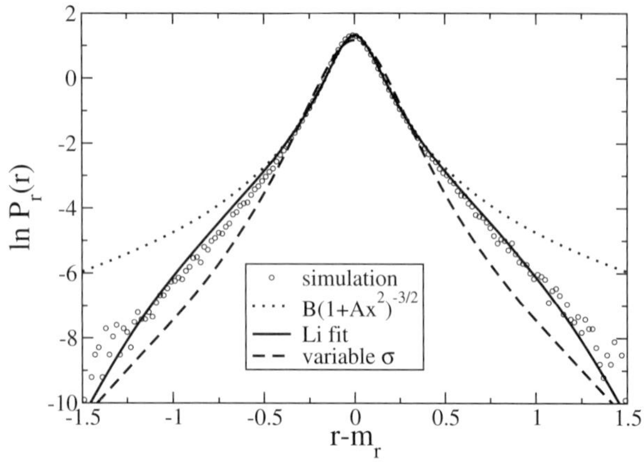

Figure 3.18 Simulation of the growth rate distribution for the case of Bose–Einstein proportional growth of number of units resulting in the geometric distribution $P_K(K)$ (3.44) with $\kappa = 1000$, combined with the Gibrat growth of unit sizes with $V_\eta = 0.3, V_\xi = 5$ (circles). Solid line represents poli-logarithmic fit with $\kappa = 16, V_r = 0.146$, while the dashed line represents the distribution, obtained by summation of Gaussians with variable $\sigma_r^2(K) = V_r(K + cK^{2\beta})$, where $V_r = \exp(V_\xi)(\exp(V_\eta) - 1)$, $c = V_r/V_\eta - 1$, $V_\xi = 5, V_\eta = 0.3$, and $\beta = 0.2$. The figure represents Case (B1).

as $\exp(-(r - r_m)^2/2V_\eta)$. Thus, the power law tails of the growth rate distribution can exist only if $\kappa \gg \exp(V_\xi)$. For $V_\xi = 5$, even for $\kappa = 1000$, the power law tails are not visible and the simulated distribution resembles a Laplace distribution (Figure 3.18).

Instead of using an asymptotic approximation for $\sigma_r^2(K) = V_r/K$ when summing up the terms $P(r|K)$ in Equation (3.76), we can use a numerical approximation $\sigma_r^2(K) < V_r/(K + cK^{2\beta})$, but still employ a Gaussian approximation for the shape of $P(r|K)$. The results have a similar tent shape but, in this case, the tails for $\kappa \to \infty$ have a power law regime $P_r(r) \sim r^{-1/\beta-1}$. This fact can be established by replacing the summation by integration and using the Laplace asymptotic method. However, even this approximation fails to correctly represent the simulated $P_r(r)$ if we use realistic values of the parameters, e.g., $V_\eta = 0.3$, $V_\xi = 5$ and $\kappa = 1000$ (Figure 3.18). The discrepancy is due to the approximation of $P_r(r|K)$ – which for intermediate K develops tent-shaped tails – with perfect Gaussian distributions. Nevertheless, a satisfactory fit can be achieved by using the polylogarithmic Li-distribution with parameters $\kappa = 16$ and $V_r = 0.15$, with both κ and V_r drastically reduced with respect to the values used in simulations.

In summary, the Bose–Einstein process combined with Gibrat process, successfully reproduces various tent shape distributions for $\kappa > \exp(V_\xi)$, with a range of power law tails decaying as $|r - m_r|^{-3}$ or faster.

Distribution of Growth Rates in the Simon Growth Process with $\lambda\Delta t = \mu\Delta t = 0$, Case (B2)

As we saw in Section 3.5, in the presence of entry of new firms ($\nu > 0$), the distribution P_K must be replaced by a power law with an exponential cutoff. The closed-form solution in this case cannot be obtained, but once again, by replacing the summation in Equation (3.76) by integration from 1 to infinity and using partial integration, we can express the integral via an incomplete gamma function, which, in the limit $b \to 0$, $t \to \infty$, becomes a complementary error function:

$$P_r(r) \approx \frac{1}{\sqrt{2\pi V_r}} \int_1^\infty \frac{1}{K^2} \exp\left(-\frac{(r-m_r)^2 K}{2V_r}\right) \sqrt{K} dK$$
$$= \sqrt{\frac{2}{\pi V_r}} \exp\left(-\frac{(r-m_r)^2}{2V_r}\right) - \frac{|r-m_r|}{V_r} \text{erfc}\left(\frac{|r-m_r|}{\sqrt{2V_r}}\right). \tag{3.98}$$

In this case, $P_r(r)$ has a Laplace cusp in the center and Gaussian tails. When $b > 0$, the graph shows almost no change, except that the sharp cusp in the center is replaced by a smooth algebraic function behaving as $C - |r - m_r|^{1+2b}$:

$$P_r(r) = \frac{1+b}{(b+1/2)\sqrt{2\pi}} \left[1 - \left(\frac{|r-m_r|}{\sqrt{2V_r}}\right)^{1+2b} \Gamma(1/2 - b)\right] + O(r^2). \tag{3.99}$$

Again, a more accurate approximation does not replace the summation in Equation (3.76) by integration but uses Equation (3.64) for P_K, which is exact in the limit $t \to \infty$ and $\alpha = 0$, i.e.,

$$P_r(r) \approx \frac{b+1}{\sqrt{2\pi V_r}} \sum_{K=1}^{\infty} \mathrm{B}(b+2, K) \exp\left(-\frac{(r-m_r)^2 K}{2 V_r}\right) \sqrt{K}$$
$$= \frac{1+b}{\sqrt{2\pi V_r}} \mathrm{Bs}_b \left[\exp\left(-\frac{(r-m_r)^2}{2V_r}\right)\right], \tag{3.100}$$

where B is the Euler beta function and

$$\mathrm{Bs}_b(x) = \sum_{n=1}^{\infty} \mathrm{B}(b+2, n)\sqrt{n} x^n \tag{3.101}$$

is an analytical function in the interval $x \in (0, 1)$, which can be expressed as an integral of poly-logarithm. The cases $b = 0$ (the Simon proportional growth model in the limit $t \to \infty$, $b \to 0$), and $b = 1$ (the Barabasi–Albert preferential attachment model of scale-free network growth in the limit $t \to 0$) are of particular interest. Figure 3.19 shows the graphs of $P_r(r)$ for these cases.

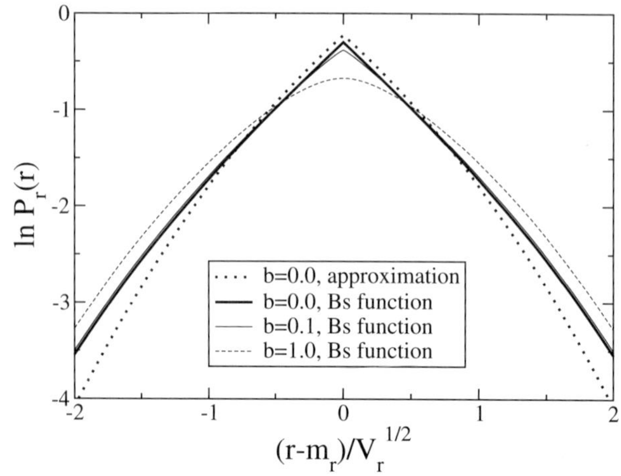

Figure 3.19 Approximation of the behavior of the growth rate distribution $P_r(r)$ for the case of new entries with $b = 1$, $b = 0.1$ and $b \to 0$, given by Equation (3.100) and the approximation of Equation (3.98). The figure represents Case (B2).

Growth Rate Distribution in the stable Simon process with $\lambda\Delta t = \mu\Delta t = 0$, *Case (B3)*

In order to find an approximation for the growth rate distribution in a stable economy with $\lambda - \mu + \nu = 0$, we use Equation (3.66) for P_K in the sum in Equation (3.76),

$$P_r(r) \approx \frac{1}{\sqrt{2\pi V_r}\ln[\alpha/(\alpha-1)]}\sum_{K=1}^{\infty}\frac{\alpha^K \exp\left(-\frac{K(r-m_r)^2}{2V_r}\right)}{\sqrt{K}}$$
$$= \frac{\mathrm{Li}_{1/2}\left[\alpha\exp\left(-\frac{(r-m_r)^2}{2V_r}\right)\right]}{\sqrt{2\pi V_r}\ln[\alpha/(\alpha-1)]}. \tag{3.102}$$

The asymptotic behavior of the central section for $\alpha \to 1$ and $(r-m_r)^2/(2V_r) \to 0$ can be obtained by replacing the summation by integration from 0 to ∞,

$$P_r(r) = \frac{1}{\sqrt{2V_r}\ln[\alpha/(\alpha-1)]}\left(\ln\alpha + \frac{(r-m_r)^2}{2V_r}\right)^{-\frac{1}{2}}. \tag{3.103}$$

This approximation has power law tails $P_r \sim (r-m_r)^{-1}$ for $(r-m_r)^2 \gg V_r \ln\alpha$, but when $(r-m_r)^2 \gg V_r$, the asymptotic distribution is a Gaussian distribution with mean m_η and variance V_r. Thus, $P_r(r)$ for $\alpha \to 1$ exhibits a classical tent-shaped distribution (Figure 3.20).

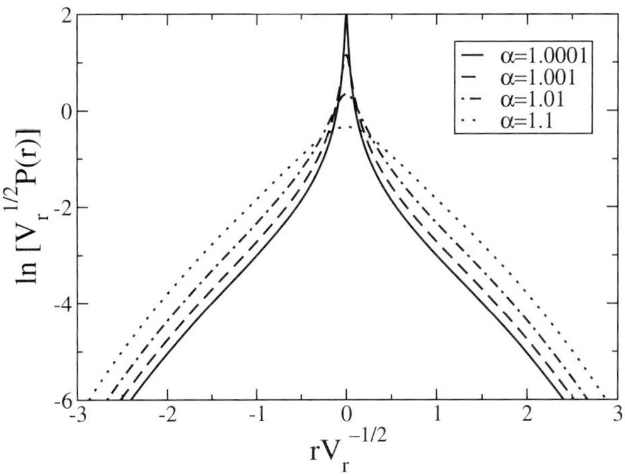

Figure 3.20 Approximation of the behavior of the growth rate distribution $P_r(r)$ for the case of stable economy $\nu+\lambda-\mu=0$ and several values of $\alpha=\mu/\lambda$ given by Equation (3.102). The figure represents Case (B3).

Again, the approximation in Equation (3.102) neglects the fact that $\sigma_r^2(K) \ll V_r/K$ for small K. In reality, the tails of the distribution $P_r(r)$ are dominated by the behavior of the first term in the sum (Equation 3.76), which is a Gaussian distribution with variance V_η. Hence, the distribution $P_r(r)$ converges to a Gaussian distribution with variance V_η for $(r-m_r)^2 > V_\eta$. Accordingly, the power law regime predicted by Equation (3.103) is valid only if $V_r \ln\alpha \ll (r-m_r)^2 \ll V_\eta$. For small V_η, $V_r/V_\eta \approx \exp(V_\xi)$, hence the power law can be observed only if $\ln(\alpha) \approx \alpha - 1 \ll \exp(-V_\xi)$, which for $V_\xi = 5$ is achieved when $1 < \alpha < 1.005$. It is difficult to expect that in real economic systems $\alpha = \mu/\lambda$ can remain constant within such a narrow interval. Accordingly, the tent shape distribution of the growth rates, although theoretically possible, is unlikely to be observed in the case of a stable economy. Figure 3.21 shows computer simulations of the growth rate distribution for various α and $V_\xi = 5$.

In general, if the distribution of number of units P_K behaves for small K as $P_K \sim K^{-\tau}$ with $\tau < 3/2$, then the approximation of summation by integration in Equation (3.76) in which $P_r(r|K)$ is given by Equation (3.79), predicts that the growth rate distribution of has a range of power law tails $P_r(r) \sim (r-m_r)^{-3+2\tau}$, and thus may, in principle, have a tent shape. But this prediction may not materialize if V_ξ is large enough and the convergence of $P_r(r|K)$ to the asymptotic form (3.79) is slow.

To summarize, when $\lambda\Delta t$ and $\mu\Delta t$ are negligible and V_ξ is large, a tent-shape distribution with a narrow maximum in the center and power law tails emerges only for the Bose–Einstein process, when the distribution P_K is geometric and,

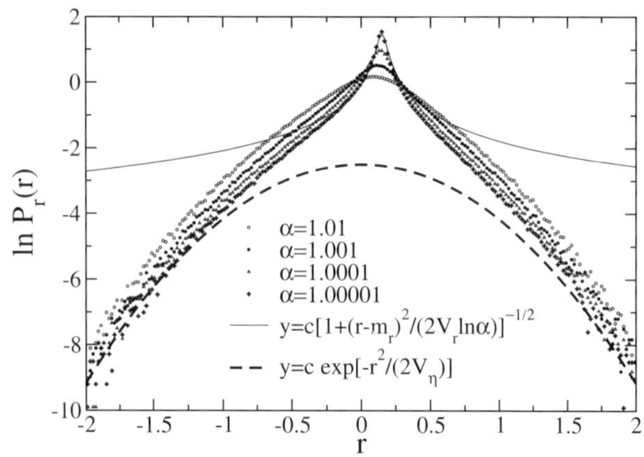

Figure 3.21 Simulation of the behavior of the growth rate distribution $P_r(r)$ for the case of a stable economy $\nu + \lambda - \mu = 0$ and several values of $\alpha = \mu/\lambda$ for $V_\xi = 5$ and $V_\eta = 0.3$. The figure represents Case (B3). The Gaussian asymptotic behavior for $r - m_r$ is shown by the dashed bold line. The power law behavior for $\alpha - 1 = 10^{-5}$ is shown by a thin solid line. The tent shape behavior of the simulated distribution starts to evolve when $\alpha \leq 1.001$.

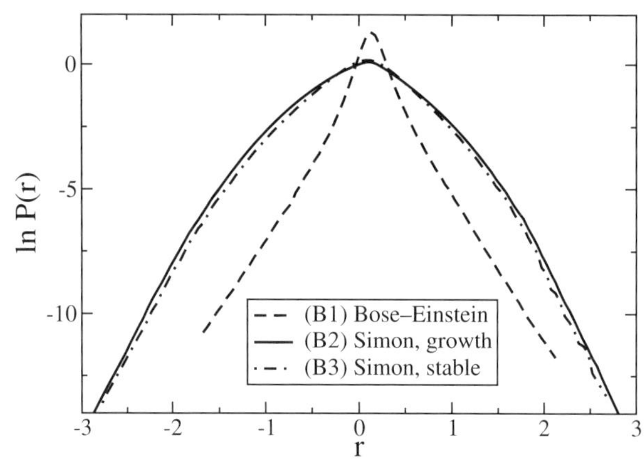

Figure 3.22 Simulated distribution of the firm growth rate for the three cases of P_K used in Figure 3.10 for $V_\xi = 5$, $V_\eta = 0.3$, $m_\eta = 0$, and $\lambda\Delta t = \mu\Delta t = 0$: the geometric P_K with $\kappa = 1000$, power law P_K with $\tau = 2.1$, and logarithmic P_K with $\alpha = 1.1$.

thus, is not dominated by firms consisting of a few units. In contrast, in the case of the Simon process, when the distribution P_K is a power law distribution and it is dominated by the small firms, the tent shaped tails do not develop. For small V_ξ, and $b \to 0$, we observe instead a sharp Laplace cusp near the center of the distribution due to the power law tails of P_K. For the logarithmic P_K, which exists in a stable

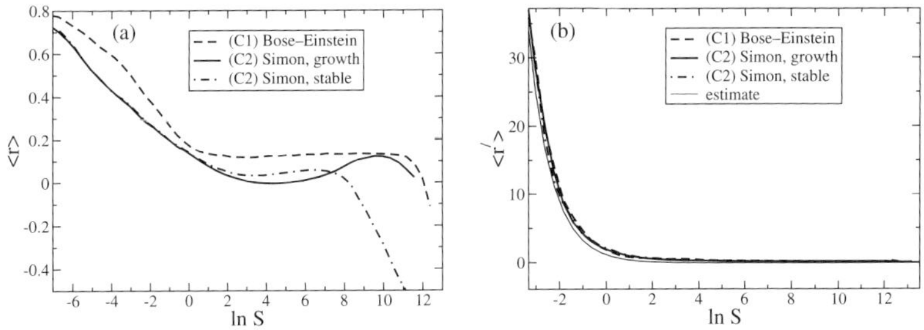

Figure 3.23 The dependence of the average growth rate on firm size for the three cases of $P_K(K)$ (C1: Bose-Einstein), (C2: Simon with overall growth, $\lambda - \mu > 0$) and (C3: stable Simon, $\lambda - \mu + \nu = 0$) used in Figure 3.10 when the change in the number of products in a firm cannot be neglected ($\lambda \Delta t = 0.1$ and $\lambda \Delta t = 0.09$) for logarithmic (a) and nonlogarithmic (b) definitions. We use $V_\xi = 5$, $m_\xi = 0$, $V_\eta = 0.3$, and $m_\eta = 0$. For the nonlogarithmic definition, the results diverge for small S because the smallest value of the nonlogarithmic growth rate for a firm consisting of a single small product is –1 when the firm loses this product, while the largest value has no bound because this firm can launch a second product that is significantly larger than the first one. The larger is V_ξ, the stronger is this effect. A thin smooth line gives a theoretical lower bound estimate $r = \lambda \exp(m_\xi + V_\xi/2)/S - \mu$.

economy with $\alpha - 1 > \exp(-V_\xi)$, the growth rate distribution is also dominated by firms with a small number of units and, hence, it has approximately a normal shape (Figure 3.22) with some sharpening in the center.

Growth Rates for the Case $\lambda \Delta t > 0$, $\mu \Delta t > 0$ (Cases (C1), (C2), and (C3))

In the analysis from the last section, we have neglected the effect of entry and exit of units on the growth rates of firms. However, if $\lambda \Delta t$ and $\mu \Delta t$ are not negligible, the nonlogarithmic average growth rate, $m_{r'}(S)$, increases dramatically for small, one-unit, firms (Figure 3.23). The second unit, added to these firms with probability λ, can be extremely large with an average size $\exp(m_\xi + V_\xi/2)$. The loss of a unit with a probability μ makes a limited negative contribution $\langle r' \rangle = -1$ (Mansfield 1962). Thus, we should expect, for small firms, that

$$m_{r'}(S) = \left(\lambda \frac{\exp(m_\xi + V_\xi/2)}{S} - \mu \right) \Delta t, \qquad (3.104)$$

which means that for small firms, the average growth rate is inversely proportional to the size of the firm. Once the term correspondent to the behavior of one-unit firms becomes insignificant for $S \gg \exp(m_\xi + V_\xi/2)$, we should observe constant growth rate $m_{r'} = \exp(m_\eta + V_\eta/2) + (\lambda - \mu)\Delta t$ as presented in Equations (3.50) and (3.85). The same phenomenon causes the decrease in logarithmic growth rates $m_r(S)$ with S. However, due to the asymmetry of $\ln(x)$ – which increases very slowly for

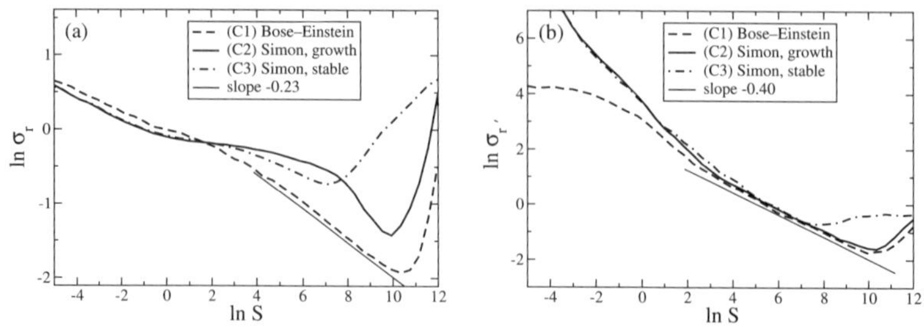

Figure 3.24 The size variance relationship for the three cases (C1), (C2), and (C3) described in Figure 3.23 for logarithmic (a) and nonlogarithmic (b) definitions.

$x \to \infty$ – the effect is less pronounced. We also see an increase of $m_r(S)$ for large S because, for $S \to \infty$, the addition and subtraction of units can be approximated by a Gaussian distribution and, therefore, the analysis of Equation (3.80) is valid again with $m_r(S) \to m_r = (\lambda - \mu)\Delta t + V_\eta/2 + m_\eta$.

To summarize, the GPG predicts the increase of the growth rates for small companies, in agreement with a well-established set of empirical evidences in industrial economics (stylized Fact II). Indeed, start-up companies whose initial sale is small can grow by orders of magnitude, if they launch a second, more successful product. The death of a small start-up company has no effect on the average logarithmic growth rate, $m_r(S)$, and it gives only a small contribution of -1 for the nonlogarithmic growth rate $m_{r'}(S)$.

By taking into account the effect of fluctuations of the number of units on the size-variance relationship (Figure 3.24), we observe an expansion of the region of power law behavior in the case of the Bose–Einstein process, while for the Simon growth process the size-variance relationship is still far from a power law in the case of logarithmic growth rates. For nonlogarithmic growth rates, the behaviors of all three cases become closer to the power law, but the value of the exponent β becomes unrealistically large (0.4). Since for $S \to 0$ nonlogarithmic growth rate of a small firm consisting of one unit can be approximated by $\lambda \Delta t \xi / S$ as in Equation (3.104) we can approximate

$$\sigma_{r'}^2 \approx \frac{\lambda^2 (\Delta t)^2 \mathrm{Var}(\xi)}{S^2}. \tag{3.105}$$

We expect $\beta \to 1$ for $S \to 0$ for nonlogarithmic growth rates, while for logarithmic growth rates $r \approx \ln(\lambda \Delta t \xi / S)$ and the dependence on S trivializes to an additive constant $-\ln(S)$. For logarithmic growth rates σ_r^2 converges for $S \to 0$ to a finite limit: $\sigma_r^2 \to V_\xi$ and $\beta(S) \to 0$.

For the fully developed case of the GPG framework, when $\lambda \Delta t > 0$, $\mu \Delta t > 0$, $V_\eta > 0$, and V_ξ is large, the distribution $P_r(r)$ develops fat tails even when P_K is

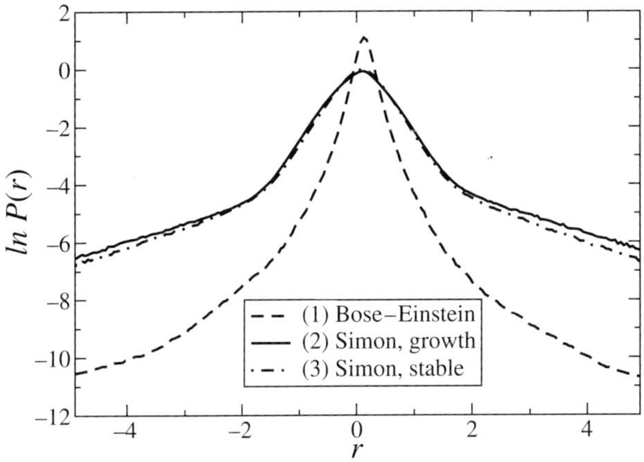

Figure 3.25 The distribution of firm growth rates for the three cases (C1), (C2), and (C3) described in Figure 3.23 for $V_\xi = 5, V_\eta = 0.3$, $m_\eta = 0$, and $\lambda = 0.1$, $\mu = 0.09$ in cases (C1) and (C2) and $\lambda = 0.1$, and $\mu = 0.1001$ in case (C3).

a power law. These tails occur when large products are added to firms with only a few small products (Figure 3.25) and thus they become especially pronounced in the case of power law P_K, which is dominated by firms with a small number of units.

Indeed, if a new unit ξ_2 is added to a firm with one unit ξ_1, the logarithmic growth rate is $r = \ln(1 + \xi_2/\xi_1)$. For small ξ_2/ξ_1, $r \approx \xi_2/\xi_1$ is a lognormal variable with zero mean and variance $2V_\xi$, and the distribution of the lognormal variable can be approximated by $1/r$ in a wide range of r. We can expect a wide range of $1/r$ decay for $P_r(r)$ when P_K is a power law, if $\lambda\Delta t, \mu\Delta t > 0$. The central section of the distribution is well approximated by Equation (3.100), but as demonstrated by the computer simulation results in Figure 3.26, the tails follow a power law distribution. Figure 3.26 suggests an important result regarding the growth rate distribution in the case (C2), which is the most general case of the GPG model with $\nu > 0$ and $V_\xi > 0$, $\Delta t\lambda > 0$, $\Delta t\mu > 0$. The central part of this distribution for small $r - m_r$ is governed by the behavior of case (B2) – in which we can neglect the effect of the addition of new units on the growth rates – and, thus, coincides with the dome-shaped profile displayed in Figures 3.16 and 3.19. In contrast, the behavior of the tails is governed by the addition of new units, has approximately $1/r$ behavior as discussed above and coincide with the results for the uniform Gibrat process of unit sizes with $V_\eta = 0$, for which the distribution of growth rates displays a nice tent shape. Accordingly the tent-shaped distribution of growth rates can be obtained for the case with new entries and unequal unit sizes (C2) if V_η is very small. But, in general, the GPG model with realistic parameters cannot reproduce all

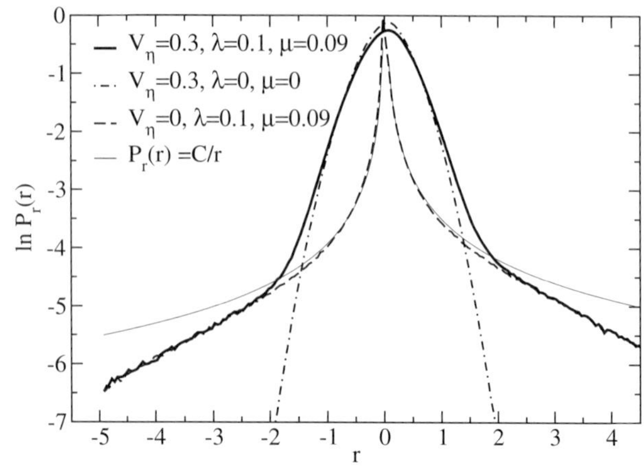

Figure 3.26 Computer simulations of P_r for power law $P_K = \mathrm{B}(2, K)$ for Case (C2). The distribution of units, P_ξ, and their growth rates, P_η, are lognormal with $V_\xi = 5$, $m_\xi = 0$, $V_\eta = 0.3$, and $m_\eta = 0$. The new units are drawn from the same lognormal distribution as the existing units with probability $\lambda\Delta t = 0.1$. The existing units are removed with probability $\mu\Delta t = 0.09$. The distribution in the central part can be well approximated by the distribution corresponding to $\lambda\Delta t = \mu\Delta t = 0$, which can be fitted by Equation (3.100), while the tails of the distribution can be well approximated by the pure Bose–Einstein process ($V_\eta = 0$) for nonequal units with $V_\xi = 5$, with $\lambda = 0.1$ and $\mu = 0.09$. For small r, this distribution can be approximated as $C_\pm/|r|$, where $C_\pm$ is some constant linearly depending on λ and μ with different proportionality coefficients for positive and negative r.

four stylized facts with good accuracy. The main reason for this is the divergent behavior of P_K for $K \to 0$ in the presence of entry.

A Model by John Sutton

John Sutton has introduced an original solution to reconcile the tent-shaped distribution of growth rates with Simon's assumption of new firm entries (Sutton 1997, 1998). As we have seen, the tent-shaped tails emerge if the distribution of $P(K)$ does not diverge when $K \to 0$. The Sutton model generalizes the Simon model by considering the case in which the probability that a currently active firm captures a new opportunity is nondecreasing with firm size. In fact, the growth rates λ and μ, defined in Assumptions (2) and (3) of the GPG framework, may depend on the number of units K in a given firm. As we will see in Chapter 4 and further discuss in Chapter 5, empirical data suggest that $\lambda(K)$ and $\mu(K)$ are decreasing functions of K. Sutton's assumption is equivalent to postulating that $\lambda(K)$ and $\mu(K)$ should not decrease faster than $1/K$. One possible way to model such relationships is by assuming that some finite fraction of the opportunities is not distributed in proportion to the number of units in a firm, but it is distributed

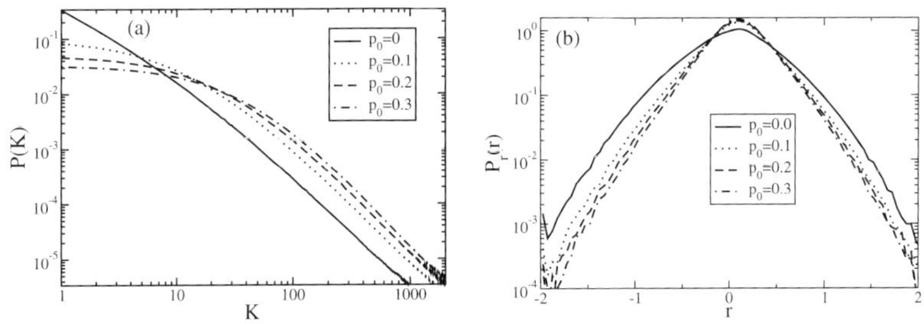

Figure 3.27 (a) The distribution of the number of units within firms obtained by simulating the Sutton process with $\lambda = 0.1$, $\mu = 0.1$, $\nu = \nu' = 0.001$, and $p_\lambda = p_\mu = 0.0$, 0.1, 0.2, and 0.3. In each simulation, $n_0 = N(0) = 10$ and $n_\lambda(t) = 10^5$. (b) The growth rate distribution for the system of firms with P_K distributions obtained in panel (a) and lognormal distributions P_ξ and P_η with $V_\xi = 5$, $\eta = 0.3$.

equally among the firms, small and large ones. The reason for this assumption is that usually firms are built by a relatively small number of leaders/innovators, who generate new ideas with a much higher rate than the rest of the employees. Accordingly, we can postulate that in Assumption (2) of the GPG framework, the probability p_i that firm i with K_i units captures a new opportunity is equal to $K_i(1 - p_\lambda)/n(t) + p_\lambda/N_a(t)$, where $N_a(t)$ is the number of currently active firms that have at least one active unit and p_λ is the probability that a unit will be captured by a firm directly, without taking into account its number of units. In this model, we can introduce $\lambda(K)$, defined as the ratio of the number of units, added to the firms with K units per unit time, to the total number of units:

$$\lambda(K) = \lambda\left(1 - p_\lambda + p_\lambda\frac{\langle K\rangle}{K}\right), \tag{3.106}$$

where $\langle K\rangle$ is the average number of units in active firms. Analogously, we can modify Assumption (3), postulating that the probability that a firm will lose one unit is $K_i(1 - p_\mu)/n(t) + p_\mu/N_a(t)$ and

$$\mu(K) = \mu\left(1 - p_\mu + p_\mu\frac{\langle K\rangle}{K}\right). \tag{3.107}$$

Simulations show that the distribution P_K – while retaining the power law tail for $K \to \infty$ – loses its divergence for $K \to 0$ and, instead, shows only a mild increase for $K \to 0$. Accordingly, the tent shape distribution of the growth rates is restored as in the Bose–Einstein process without firm entry. As an illustration, in Figure 3.27 we present (a) the results of simulations with $\lambda = 0.1$, $\mu = 0.1$, $\nu = \nu' = 0.001$, and $p_\lambda = p_\mu = 0.0$, 0.1, 0.2, and 0.3. In each simulation, we use $n_0 = N(0) = 10$ and $n_\lambda(t) = 10^5$. For sufficiently large p_λ and p_μ, the resulting P_K does not diverge for $K \to 0$ but continues to exhibit power law tail

$P_K \sim K^{-2-b}$ with $b = \nu/(\lambda - \mu)$ for $K \to \infty$. Consequently, the growth rate distribution for the GPG framework with large V_ξ restores the tent shape, which emerges when P_K follows the geometric distribution (Figure 3.27(b)). This result is consistent with the analytical solution obtained in Sutton (1997) who has shown that for the limiting case $p_\lambda = 1$, $\mu = 0$ the firm size distribution converges for $t \to \infty$ to a geometric distribution. In the general case studied here the distribution experiences a crossover from a geometric for small K to a power law for large K. This can be proven analytically using the scheme presented in Appendix 7.1.

In summary, Sutton model provides a relevant explanation of the emergence of the tent shape of the growth rate distribution in the Simon growth process. However, the model does not explain why the empirical growth rate distribution of units already displays the tent shape, as it has been shown in Fu et al. (2005).

3.7 Innovation and Multiple Levels of Aggregation

As we have shown in Fu et al. (2005), the tent-shaped distribution of growth rates is an ubiquitous feature of growth processes at different levels of aggregation. As we have discussed, the GPG framework produces the tent shape distribution only when the distribution of the number of units in the firms is not strongly dominated by firms with only a few units. When the distribution of the number of units is exponential, or, as in the Sutton model, does not diverge for $K \to 0$, we observe the tent-shaped distribution, but when it increases as $1/K^2$ or faster, as in the case of the Simon model with entry of new firm, the tent-shaped distribution cannot be observed. In fact, in this case, the behavior of $P_r(r)$ for large r is dominated by the distribution of growth rates $\ln \eta$ for the individual units, which we assume to be Gaussian. However, available empirical evidence suggests that this assumption is incorrect for the growth rates of products, which follow a markedly tent-shaped distribution (see Fu et al. 2005). Numerical studies show (Figure 3.28a) that, when $P_K(K) \sim K^{-2-b}$, the tail of the growth-rate distribution of firms coincides with the tail of the growth-rate distribution of units, i.e., Equation (3.76) guarantees the propagation of the tent shape distribution of the growth rates from units to firms. An interesting question is: How does this distribution emerge at the lowest level of aggregation?

A plausible explanation is that the distribution P_K at the lowest level of aggregation cannot be dominated by small K, because most products are mass produced and distributed through many selling units with fluctuating demand. As an example, we present an analytical solution for a two-step GPG framework in which the most elementary units have lognormal distributions $P_\xi(\xi)$ and $P_\eta(\eta)$. We assume that the units at the first observable level of aggregation (e.g., products) consist of L elementary constituent units, where L follows the geometric distribution $P_1(L)$, resulting from the Bose–Einstein process (see Equation (3.44)).

$$P_1(L) = 1/\kappa(1 - 1/\kappa)^{L-1} \tag{3.108}$$

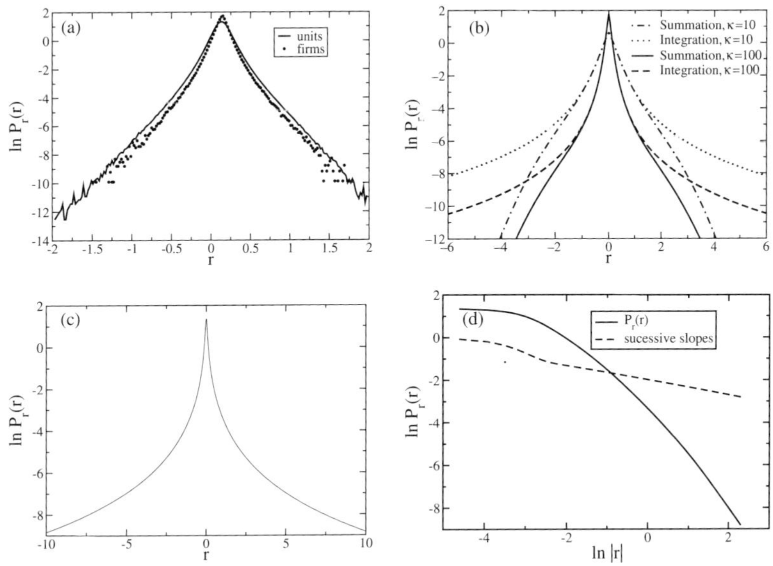

Figure 3.28 The growth rate distribution of firms for two-level aggregation models. (a) The Simon process has been used to generate the distribution of the number of composite units M in the firm $P_2(M) = 1/[M(M+1)]$, and the Bose–Einstein–Gibrat process to generate the growth rate distribution $P_{r,1}(r)$ of composite units with the geometric distribution $P_1(L)$ ($\kappa = 1000$) of the number of elementary units, L, and lognormal ξ ($V_\xi = 5$) and $\eta(V_\eta = 0.3)$ of elementary units. $P_{r,1}(r)$ of composite units develops a tent shape, as in Figure 3.18, while the second level of aggregation of composite units into firms with a power law distribution $P_2(M)$ transforms $P_{r,1}(r)$ into the distribution of the growth rates of firms, $P_{r,2}(r)$, leaving the tails of $P_{r,1}(r)$ unchanged, but creating a Laplacian cusp in the center of $P_{r,2}(r)$. (b) Analytical approximation of the growth rate distribution of firms in the two-step Simon–Bose–Einstein–Gibrat model, in which the firms consist of M composite units, where M has a power law distribution (see Equation (3.109)) and the composite units consist of L elementary units, where L has a geometric distribution, Equation (3.108), with $\kappa = 100$ (solid and dashed lines) and $\kappa = 10$ (dot-dashed and dotted). The growth rate distribution $P_r(r|K)$ is approximated by Equation (3.79) with $V_r = 1$. Solid and dot-dashed lines are the exact summations given by Equation (3.115). Dashed and dotted lines are continuous approximations given by Equation (3.114), in which summation from $K = 1$ to ∞ is replaced by integration from $K = 0$ to ∞. (c) Growth rate distribution of the firms when $P_2(M)$ is the same as in (a), but $P_1(L)$ is the discretized lognormal distribution given by Equation (3.116) with $V_L = 10$, $m_L = 2$, and $V_r = 100$. The shape of the graph does not strongly depend on the parameters. (d) is the same as in (c) but in double logarithmic scale. We also plot the derivative of $\ln P_r(r)$ vs. $\ln r$, which shows a continuous change of the slope from -1 to -3.

Finally, we assume that the classes of the second level of aggregation (e.g., firms) consist of M composite units, where M follows a Pareto-like distribution $P_2(M)$, resulting from the Simon process (see Equation (3.64)).

$$P_2(M) = \frac{1}{M(M+1)}. \tag{3.109}$$

Equation (3.109) is the result of the Simon model with new firms entry in the limit $t \to \infty$ and $b \to 0$. The class of the second level of aggregation (a firm) consists of M classes of the first level of aggregation (products) each of which consists of L_i elementary units, where $i = 1, 2, \ldots M$ is the product index. Thus, the total number K of elementary units in a firm is

$$K = \sum_{i=1}^{M} L_i, \tag{3.110}$$

where L_i have a geometric distribution. The distribution of the sum of the M geometrically distributed independent random variables can be expressed in terms of negative binomial distribution (Feller 1968)

$$P_M(K) = \frac{(1-1/\kappa)^{K-M}(K-1)!}{\kappa^M (M-1)!\,(K-M)!}, \quad (K \geq M). \tag{3.111}$$

Thus,

$$P_K(K) = \sum_{M=1}^{K} P_2(M) P_M(K) = \frac{\kappa - (1-1/\kappa)^K(\kappa + K)}{K(K+1)}. \tag{3.112}$$

The negative term in the numerator of the final expression of Equation (3.112) prevents P_K from the power law divergence for $K \to 0$, while vanishing for $K \to \infty$. Therefore, in the two-level aggregation model, P_K is almost constant at small K, while it decreases as a power law for $K \to \infty$, thus combining the features of the distributions emerging in Bose–Einstein process and the Simon process as in the Sutton model discussed in the previous subsection.

We can now compute the distribution of firm by sizes using Equation (3.69), assuming that the distribution of the sizes of elementary units is lognormal with a given V_ξ and m_ξ, which for small V_ξ is very similar to $P_K(K)$, but for large V_ξ can be found via computer simulations. The distribution of firm sizes in Figure 3.29(a) has a left tail resembling the size distribution of of the first-level aggregation units, which is the same as in the Bose–Einstein–Gibrat case shown in Figure 3.9(a), i.e., a power law with a positive exponent smaller than 1, which depends on V_ξ and κ of elementary constituent units. The right tail is a power law governed by the distribution of the number of composite units in the firm (Equation 3.109). The exponent characterizing the right tail has a negative value $-\tau + 1 \approx -1$.

We can obtain $P_r(r)$ by using a Gaussian approximation of Equation (3.79) for $P_r(r|K)$ and Equation (3.76). The summation can be done numerically or

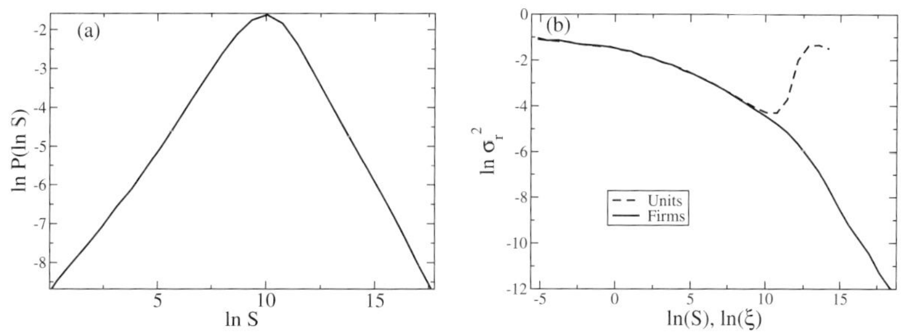

Figure 3.29 The two-level aggregation model. (a) Firm size distribution for the Simon–Bose–Einstein–Gibrat model with two levels of aggregation. The Simon growth process generates the distribution of the number of composite units in the firm $P_M(M) = 1/[M(M+1)]$, while the Bose–Einstein–Gibrat process generates the growth rate distribution $P_r(r)$ of composite units (e.g. products) with geometric $P_K(K)$ ($\kappa = 1000$) and lognormal ξ ($V_\xi = 5$) and η ($V_\eta = 0.3$). The same parameters as those in Figure 3.28(a) are used. (b) Size variance relationships in the two-level aggregation model for composite units and firms with the same set of parameters as in panel (a).

approximated analytically if we replace it with integration and we replace the discrete distribution $P_M(K)$ with the continuous gamma distribution (Feller 1968)

$$P_M(K) \approx \frac{\exp(-K/\kappa)K^{M-1}}{\kappa^M(M-1)!}. \tag{3.113}$$

The continuous approximation is given by an explicit formula

$$P_{rc}(r) = \frac{2\tilde{r}^2 + 1 - 2|\tilde{r}|\sqrt{\tilde{r}^2+1}}{\sqrt{\tilde{r}^2+1}\sqrt{2V_r/\kappa}}, \tag{3.114}$$

where $\tilde{r} = (r - m_r)\sqrt{\kappa/(2V_r)}$ is the scaled growth rate. Distribution (3.114) has a Laplace cusp in the center and power law tails $P_r(r) \sim r^{-3}$ for $r \to \infty$. If we do not replace summation by integration, we obtain

$$P_r(r) = \frac{1}{\sqrt{2\pi V_r}}\left[\kappa \mathrm{Bs}_0\left(e^{-\tilde{r}^2}\right) - (\kappa-1)\mathrm{Bs}_0\left(\theta e^{-\tilde{r}^2}\right) - \mathrm{Li}_{1/2}\left(\theta e^{-\tilde{r}^2}\right)\right], \tag{3.115}$$

where $\theta = 1 - 1/\kappa$. As in all earlier examples, the distribution P_r differs from P_{rc} due to replacement of summation by integration and the tail of P_r has a crossover from a power law to a Gaussian decay (Figure 3.28(b)).

The higher level units have a nontrivial size-variance relation $\sigma_r^2(\xi)$, which emerges because large units are likely to consist of many elementary units, which fluctuate independently. We can compute $\sigma_r^2(S)$ for the firms if we know $\sigma_r^2(\xi)$ (Figure 3.29(b)). The geometric $P_L(L)$ for composite units creates an approximate power law behavior of $\sigma_r^2(\xi)$ at the higher level of aggregation, while the power law distribution of the number of units in the firms eliminates a spurious increase of $\sigma_r^2(S)$ for large firms.

There is another possible explanation of the tent-shaped distribution of the growth rates. Empirical evidence suggests that the size distribution of products can be approximated by a lognormal distribution. The life cycle of products is not long enough for the Gibrat proportional growth process to produce this distribution, and the size distribution of new products is already very broad and approximately lognormal. As a consequence, one can hypothesize that for individual products that consist of many elementary units, the distribution of the number of these elementary units is lognormal. Therefore, we assume that the distribution $P_1(L)$ of the number of subunits is a discretized lognormal distribution,

$$P_1(L) = C \exp[-(\ln L - m_L)^2/(2V_L)]/L, \tag{3.116}$$

where C is the normalization constant such that $\sum P_1(L) = 1$, and that $P_2(M)$ is given by Equation (3.109). We still assume that the subunits engage in a Gibrat growth process with given V_η and V_ξ. Using Equations (3.79) and (3.76), we can calculate the growth rate distribution of the products (see Figure 3.28(c)). Here, the tails of the tent-shaped distribution do not follow an inverse cubic power law, but their slope on a log–log scale changes continuously in a wide range of r, from -1 to -3, which is often observed empirically.

3.8 Conclusions

In this chapter we have outlined the features and the predictions of our stochastic framework on size and growth of firms. According to our approach, firms consist of business units, i.e., products sold in independent submarkets, which can be added and deleted in proportion to the existing number of units with rates λ and μ, respectively, while new firms can be created with rate ν (see Assumptions (1–4) in Section 3.2). The first part of the model accounts for the distribution of the number of units P_K within firms. The second part of the model assumes that units can fluctuate in size according to a simple proportional growth mechanism, which leads to their size distribution $P_\xi(\xi)$ with logarithmic mean m_ξ and variance V_ξ, while their logarithmic growth rates obey distribution $P_\eta(\eta)$ with mean m_η and variance V_η (Assumptions (5)–(7) in Section 3.2). In the following subsections, we will summarize the predictions of the GPG framework for every relevant combination of parameters λ, μ, ν, t, V_ξ, m_η, and V_η studied in this chapter. We will begin our summary with the brief outline of all studied cases. Case (A0) is the pure Gibrat process in which each firm consists of a single unit. Cases (A1), (A2), and (A3) assume that the units in a firm do not change in size. Case (A1) is the pure

Bose–Einstein process with no new firm entry, resulting in a geometric distribution of P_K. Case (A2) is the pure Simon growth model with new firm entry, resulting in a power law distribution of P_K with exponential cutoff. Case (A3) is the pure Simon model of stable economy resulting in a logarithmic distribution of P_K. Cases (B1), (B2), and (B3) are the same as cases (A1), (A2), and (A3), but with units obeying Gibrat's Law. However, in cases (B1–B3) we neglect the change in the number of units in a firm during the observation period. Cases (C1), (C2), and (C3) are the same as cases (B1), (B2), and (B3), but here we do not neglect the change in the number of units in the firms. Thus, letters in the case identifier indicate the properties of firm growth, while digits indicate the properties of the distribution of the number of units. Finally, case (D) is the two-level GPG framework with entry, combining the Bose–Einstein, the Simon and the Gibrat processes. Altogether, we have studied 11 distinct cases:

(A0) *Gibrat process*: $\lambda = \mu = \nu = 0$, $V_\xi > 0$, $V_\eta > 0$, $m_\eta \neq 0$. Each firm consists of one unit, obeying the Gibrat proportional growth process.

(A1) *Bose–Einstein process*: $\lambda > \mu \geq 0$, $\nu = 0$, $V_\xi = V_\eta = m_\eta = 0$. The units can be added to and deleted from the firms, but no new firms can be created. The total number of units is growing, but the number of firms is stable. All units have the same size, which does not change in time.

(A2) *Simon growth process*: $\lambda > \mu \geq 0$, $\nu > 0$, $V_\xi = V_\eta = m_\eta = 0$. The units can be added to and deleted from the firms, and new firms can be created. The total number of units and firms is growing. All units have the same size, which does not change in time.

(A3) *Simon process in a stable economy*: $\mu > \lambda > 0$, $\nu = \mu - \lambda > 0$, $V_\xi - V_\eta = m_\eta = 0$. The units can be added to and deleted from the firms, and new firms can be created. The total number of units and active firms is stable. All units have the same size, which does not change in time.

(B1) *Gibrat–Bose–Einstein process without entry of new units*: $\lambda > \mu \geq 0$, $\nu = 0$, $V_\xi > 0$, $V_\eta > 0$, $m_\eta \neq 0$. Units can be added to and deleted from firms, but no new firms enter the industry. The total number of units is growing, while the number of firms is stable. The units can change their size, but the change in the number of units in any firm during observation period Δt is negligible: $\lambda\Delta t \to 0$, $\mu\Delta t \to 0$. The units have lognormal size distribution $P_\xi(\xi)$ and lognormal distribution of growth rates $P_\eta(\eta)$.

(B2) *Gibrat–Simon growth process without entry of new units*: $\mu > \lambda \geq 0$, $\nu > 0$, $V_\xi > 0$, $V_\eta > 0$, $m_\eta \neq 0$. Units can be added to and deleted from firms, and new firms can be created. The total number of units and firms is growing, the units can change their size, but the change in the number of units in any firm during observation period Δt is negligible: $\lambda\Delta t \to 0$, $\mu\Delta t \to 0$.

The units have lognormal size distribution $P_\xi(\xi)$ and lognormal distribution of their growth rates $P_\eta(\eta)$.

(B3) *Gibrat–Simon process for a stable economy without entry of new units.* $\mu > \lambda > 0$, $\nu = \mu - \lambda > 0$, $V_\xi > 0$, $V_\eta > 0$, $m_\eta \neq 0$. The units can be added to and deleted from the firms, and new firms can be created. The total number of units and active firms is stable. The units can change their size, but the change in the number of units in any firm during observation period Δt is negligible: $\lambda\Delta t \to 0$, $\mu\Delta t \to 0$. The units have lognormal size distribution $P_\xi(\xi)$ and lognormal distribution of growth rates $P_\eta(\eta)$.

(C1) *Gibrat–Bose Einstein process with entry of new units and exit of existing units*: $\lambda > \mu \geq 0$, $\nu = 0$, $V_\xi > 0$, $V_\eta > 0$, $m_\eta \neq 0$. The units can be added to and deleted from the firms. The total number of units is growing, but the number of firms is stable. The change in the number of units in any firm during Δt is not negligible: $\lambda\Delta t > 0$, $\mu\Delta t > 0$. The units have lognormal size distribution $P_\xi(\xi)$ and lognormal distribution of growth rates $P_\eta(\eta)$.

(C2) *Gibrat–Simon growth process with entry of new units and exit of existing units*: $\lambda > \mu \geq 0$, $\nu > 0$, $V_\xi > 0$, $V_\eta > 0$, $m_\eta \neq 0$. The units can be added to and deleted from the firms and new firms can be created. The total number of units and firms is growing and the change in the number of units in any firm during Δt is not negligible: $\lambda\Delta t > 0$, $\mu\Delta t > 0$. The units have lognormal size distribution $P_\xi(\xi)$ and lognormal distribution of growth rates $P_\eta(\eta)$.

(C3) *Gibrat–Simon stable process with entry of new units and exit of existing units*: $\mu > \lambda \geq 0$, $\nu = \mu - \lambda > 0$, $V_\xi > 0$, $V_\eta > 0$, $m_\eta \neq 0$. Units can be added to and deleted from firms, and new firms can be created. The total number of units and active firms is stable. The change in the number of units in any firm during Δt is not negligible: $\lambda\Delta t > 0$, $\mu\Delta t > 0$. The units have lognormal size distribution $P_\xi(\xi)$ and lognormal distribution of growth rates $P_\eta(\eta)$.

(D) *Simon–Bose–Einstein–Gibrat growth process with entry/innovation and two levels of aggregation*: $\lambda > \mu \geq 0$, $\nu > 0$, $V_\xi > 0$, $V_\eta > 0$, $m_\eta \neq 0$. The units can be added to and deleted from the firms, and new firms can be created. The total number of units and firms is growing. The units of the firms consist of many elementary units, the number of which changes according to the Bose–Einstein process. These elementary units have a lognormal size distribution $P_\xi(\xi)$ and lognormal distribution of growth rates $P_\eta(\eta)$.

The predictions for the variants of the framework are summarized in Table 3.1 and in the pages that follows.

Case (A0): Gibrat process ($\lambda = \mu = \nu = 0$, $V_\xi > 0$, $V_\eta > 0$, $m_\eta \neq 0$)

(1) Size distribution: lognormal (Equation (3.43)).

(2) Average logarithmic growth rate does not depend on size.

(3) Average growth rate does not depend on size.
(4) Size-variance relationship: $\beta = 0$.
(5) Growth rate distribution: lognormal. (Equation (3.40)).
(6) Comments: The variance of the size distribution grows with time. All the predictions on the growth process are falsified by empirical evidence.

Case (A1): Bose–Einstein process ($\lambda > \mu \geq 0$, $\nu = 0$, $V_\xi = V_\eta = m_\eta = 0$)

(1) Size distribution: exponential or gamma (Equation (3.48); Figure 3.2).
(2) Average logarithmic growth rate is large for very small firms and below average for intermediate firms (Figure 3.3(a)).
(3) Average growth rate does not depend on size (Equation (3.50); Figure 3.3(a)).
(4) Size-variance relationship: $\beta = 0.5$ (Equation (3.52); Figure 3.3(b)).
(5) Growth rate distribution: tent shape with rounded top and power law tails $P_r(r) \sim r^{-3}$ (Equation (3.54); Figure 3.4).
(6) Comments: The prediction on the size distribution, the size-variance relationship and the size-growth relationship are falsified by available empirical observations.

Case (A2): Simon growth process ($\lambda > \mu \geq 0$, $\nu > 0$, $V_\xi = V_\eta = m_\eta = 0$)

(1) Size distribution: power law for infinite evolution times, (Equation (3.58), Figure 3.5); power law with an exponential cutoff for finite times (Equation (3.60); Figure 3.5).
(2) Average logarithmic growth rate is large for very small firms and below average for intermediate firms (Figure 3.6a).
(3) Average growth rate does not depend on size (Equation (3.50); Figure 3.6a).
(4) Size-variance relationship: $\beta = 0.5$ (Equation (3.52); Figure 3.6b).
(5) Growth rate distribution: discontinuous distribution consisting of finite elementary units (Figure 3.7).
(6) Comments: The predictions on the size-variance and size-growth relationships and the growth rate distribution are falsified by available empirical observations.

Case (A3): Simon process in stable economy ($\mu > \lambda > 0$, $\nu = \mu - \lambda > 0$, $V_\xi = V_\eta = m_\eta = 0$)

(1) Size distribution: logarithmic distribution (Equation 3.66).
(2) Average logarithmic growth rate is large for very small firms and below average for intermediate firms (Figure 3.6a).
(3) Average growth rate does not depend on size (Figure 3.6a).
(4) Size-variance relationship: $\beta = 0.5$ (Figure 3.6b).

(5) Growth rate distribution: discontinuous distribution consisting of finite atoms (Figure 3.7).

(6) Comments: The predictions on the size distribution, size-variance, and size-growth relationships, and growth rate distribution are falsified by available empirical observations.

Case (B1): Gibrat–Bose–Einstein process without entry of new units
$(\mu \Delta t \to 0,\ \lambda \Delta t \to 0,\ \lambda > \mu \geq 0,\ \nu = 0,\ V_\xi > 0,\ V_\eta > 0,\ m_\eta \neq 0)$

(1) Size distribution: crossover from lognormal to exponential depending on V_ξ and the average number of units κ (Figures 3.9(a), 3.10).

(2) Average logarithmic growth rate increases with size (Equation (3.88); Figure 3.14a).

(3) Average growth rate does not depend on size (Figure 3.14b).

(4) Size-variance relationship: crossover from

$$\beta = \frac{1}{2.5 + 0.46 V_\xi} \tag{3.117}$$

for small S to $\beta = 0.5$ for large S. Spurious increase of $\sigma_r(S)$ for very large S (Figure 3.16).

(5) Growth rate distribution: tent shape distribution with a rounded top with developing power law tails for intermediate r and a lognormal cutoff for very large r (Equations (3.94), (3.97); Figures 3.18, 3.22).

(6) Comments: The predictions on the size distribution and the size-variance and size-growth relationships are falsified by available empirical observations.

Case (B2): Gibrat–Simon growth process without entry of new units
$(\mu \Delta t \to 0,\ \lambda \Delta t \to 0,\ \lambda > \mu \geq 0,\ \nu > 0,\ V_\xi > 0,\ V_\eta > 0,\ m_\eta \neq 0)$

(1) Size distribution: lognormal left tail and power law right tail, depending on V_ξ (Figures 3.9(b), 3.10).

(2) Average logarithmic growth rate increases with size (Equation (3.88); Figure 3.14a).

(3) Average growth rate does not depend on size (Figure 3.14b).

(4) Size-variance relationship: sharp crossover from $\beta < 0.1$ for small S to $\beta = 0.5$ for large S (Figure 3.16).

(5) Growth rate distribution: dome shaped distribution with a Laplacian cusp at the center for $t \to \infty$ and lognormal tails. For finite t the growth rate distribution is almost indistinguishable from lognormal. (Equations (3.98), (3.99), (3.100); Figures 3.19, 3.22).

(6) Comments: Predictions on size-variance and size-growth relationships and growth rate distribution are falsified by available empirical observations.

Case (B3): Gibrat–Simon stable process without entry of new units and exit of existing units ($\mu\Delta t \to 0$, $\lambda\Delta t \to 0$, $\mu > \lambda \geq 0$, $\nu = \mu - \lambda$, $V_\xi > 0$, $V_\eta > 0$, $m_\eta \neq 0$)

(1) Size distribution: distorted lognormal (Figure 3.10).
(2) Average logarithmic growth rate increases with size (Equation (3.88); Figure 3.14a).
(3) Average growth rate does not depend on size (Figure 3.14b).
(4) Size-variance relationship: crossover from $\beta \approx 0.1$ for small S to $\beta = 0.5$ for large S (Figure 3.16).
(5) Growth rate distribution: tent shaped distribution with a rounded top, developing power law tails with lognormal cutoffs (Equations (3.102), (3.103); Figures 3.20, 3.21, 3.22).
(6) Comments: The predictions on the size-variance and size-growth relationships are falsified by available empirical observations.

Case (C1): Gibrat–Bose Einstein process with entry of new units and exit of existing units ($\mu\Delta t > 0$, $\lambda\Delta t > 0$, $\lambda > \mu \geq 0$, $\nu = 0$, $V_\xi > 0$, $V_\eta > 0$, $m_\eta \neq 0$)

(1) Size distribution: crossover from lognormal to exponential depending on V_ξ and the average number of units κ (Figures 3.9(a), 3.10).
(2) Average logarithmic growth decreases with size (Figure 3.23a).
(3) Average nonlogarithmic growth rate dramatically increases for small firms $S \to 0$ (Equation (3.104); Figure 3.23b).
(4) Size-variance relationship displays approximately power law behavior with $0 < \beta < 0.5$ in a wide range of S with a spurious increase of $\sigma_r(S)$ for very large S (Figure 3.24).
(5) Growth rate distribution: tent shaped distribution with a rounded top and strong power law tails and a lognormal cutoff for very large r (Figure 3.25).
(6) Comments: The predictions on the size distribution are falsified by available empirical observations.

Case (C2): Gibrat–Simon growth process with entry of new units and exit of existing units ($\mu\Delta t > 0$, $\lambda\Delta t > 0$, $\lambda > \mu \geq 0$, $\nu > 0$, $V_\xi > 0$, $V_\eta > 0$, $m_\eta \neq 0$)

(1) Size distribution: lognormal left tail and power law right tail, depending on V_ξ (Figures 3.9(b), 3.10).
(2) Average logarithmic growth rate decreases with size for small firms (Figure 3.23a).
(3) Average nonlogarithmic growth rate dramatically increases for small firms when $S \to 0$ (Equation (3.104); Figure 3.23b).
(4) Spurious increase of $\sigma_r(S)$ for very large S (Figure 3.24).

(5) Growth rate distribution: lognormal distribution near the center and strong tails for very large r. (Figures 3.25, 3.26).
(6) Comments: the predictions on the growth rate distribution and size-variance relationship are falsified by available empirical observations.

Case (C3): Gibrat–Simon stable process with entry of new units and exit of existing units ($\mu\Delta t > 0,\ \lambda\Delta t > 0,\ \mu > \lambda \geq 0,\ \nu = \mu - \lambda,$ $V_\xi > 0, V_\eta > 0,\ m_\eta \neq 0$)

(1) Size distribution: distorted lognormal (Figure 3.10).
(2) Average logarithmic growth rate decreases with size (Figure 3.23).
(3) Average nonlogarithmic growth rate dramatically increases for small firms when $S \to 0$ (Equation (3.104); Figure 3.23).
(4) Size-variance relationship has a spurious increase for large S (Figure 3.24).
(5) Growth rate distribution has a rounded top and strong power law tails for very large r (Figure 3.25).
(6) Comments: The predictions on the size-variance relationship are falsified by available empirical observations. The predictions on the growth rate distribution are falsified by available empirical observations for realistic sets of parameters.

Case (D): Simon–Bose–Einstein–Gibrat growth process with entry/innovation and two levels of aggregation

(1) Size distribution: approximate power law with a positive exponent for the left tail, lognormal near the center and a region of power law decay for the right tail (Figure 3.29(a)).
(2) Average logarithmic growth rate decreases with size.
(3) Average nonlogarithmic growth rate dramatically decreases for small firms.
(4) Size-variance relationship obeys an approximate power law with $0 < \beta < 0.5$ in a wide range of S with a crossover to $\beta = 0.5$ for large S (Figure 3.29(b)).
(5) Growth rate distribution has a tent shape with a Laplace cusp at the center and power law tails (Equation (3.114) (3.115); Figure 3.28).
(6) Comments: The predictions on all the relevant distributions are not falsified by available empirical evidences, across a large number of different data sets.

Concluding Remarks

This chapter presented our framework for the analysis of the growth of business firms (GPG). In GPG, firms consist of units, which pursue different business opportunities based on different ideas and produce different products.

Our framework combines two elementary benchmarks.

First, the Simon model, which describes changes in the number of business units and elementary opportunities driven by innovation. Second, the Gibrat process, which describes the fluctuations of the size of individual units. We focus on six fundamental parameters: the innovation rate, λ, which represents the rate of arrival of new business units; the rate of destruction of business units, μ; the rate of entry of new firms, ν; the dispersion of the logarithmic growth rates of units, V_η; the logarithmic dispersion of the unit sizes, V_ξ; and the mean logarithmic growth rate, m_η. Another crucial parameter of the model is time, t, which allows us to describe the properties of a growing economy as well as the convergence to equilibrium for $t \to \infty$. Note that $\mu > 0$ sets the average life-time of units, $1/\mu$, and, thus, stabilizes the unit size distribution, justifying the independence from time Gibrat's parameter V_ξ, while $\nu > 0$ stabilizes the distribution of the number of units per firm for $t \to \infty$.

In this chapter, we have explored the parametric space generated by GPG (see Table 3.1) and found that it is impossible to accurately reproduce all four stylized facts presented in Chapter 1 unless a two-level aggregation model with entry (case D) is introduced, in which the units of the firms consist of smaller subunits. In Chapter 5, we will show that available empirical data strongly support this conclusion, documenting that the growth rate distribution for products has already a tent shape form and a nontrivial size-variance relationship with $0 < \beta < 1/2$. Once the tent-shaped distribution of the growth rates and the size-variance relationship originate at the lower level of aggregation, they are preserved, and become even more evident, at higher levels of aggregation.

Also, simulations of the GPG show that if $P_r(r)$ has a tent shape for the entire ensemble of firms in the model with large V_ξ, the tent shape is also observed for $P_r(r|S)$, i.e., for the subsets of firms with given S, as demonstarted by the empirical data of Figure 2.5. The width of the conditional growth rate distributions $P_r(r|S)$ decreses with S as the size-variance reationship predicts. The reason for the preservation of the tent shapes for the conditional distributions $P_r(r|S)$ is that, for large V_ξ, the subset of firms with given S has a very large spread of the number of units, so that even the subsets with very large S have nonzero probabiity to contain firms with a very few units. Hence, very large growth rates corresponding to the tails of the tent-shape distribution will be observed if the new units are added to or subtracted from the firms consiting of small number of units.

Even in the two levels of aggregation model, the size variance relationship cannot be described by an exact power law with fixed β. In fact, we do predict a crossover, in which different factors contribute to the empirically observed values of β, in the range of 0.1–0.3. The most important of these factors is the width of the size distribution of units, V_ξ, which determines the value of exponent β, Equation (3.117). Additional end deletion of units due to innovation and Schumpeterian creative destruction also play an important role, expanding the range of power law behavior (cf. Figures 3.16 and 3.24). Addition and deletion of units is also related to the decrease of the growth rates of firms with respect to firm size (Stylized Fact II).

The first set of assumptions of GPG is based on the Simon's proportional growth model and it determines the shape of the size distribution in terms of number of units $P_K(K)$. In the absence of new firms ($\nu = 0$) $P_K(K)$ is exponential. If there is an influx of new companies ($\nu > 0$), $P_K(K)$ becomes dominated by small firms with a few units and, for $K \to 0$, $P_K(K)$ resembles a power law $P_K(K) \sim K^{-\tau}$ with an exponential cutoff for larger K. As the time of innovation is growing $t \to \infty$, the cutoff shifts to larger K and P_K becomes power law for $K \to \infty$ as well.

The shape of $P_K(K)$ is important to account for Stylized Facts I and III. Together with the distribution of unit sizes $P_\xi(\xi)$ it shapes the distribution of firm sizes $P(S)$, which may vary significantly, depending on the parameters of the model, from a lognormal to a power law with an exponential cutoff in its right tail (Stylized Fact I). GPG predicts that the power law behavior of $P(S)$ is a consequence of the power law behavior of $P_K(K)$ and hence the parameters that account for the formation of the power law tail are the influx of new firms ($\nu > 0$) and large time of the innovation process $t \to \infty$.

The distribution of number of units, $P_K(K)$, drives the tent shape of the growth rate distribution, which is a combination of a Laplacian body and power law tails: if $P_K(K)$ is not dominated by small firms, i.e. it is a slow varying function for $K \to 0$, like an exponential distribution, the distribution of growth rates develops power law tails $P_r(r) \sim |r|^{-3}$ for $r \to \pm\infty$, while the power law tail for $P_K(K)$ for $K \to \infty$ is responsible for the formation of the Laplacian cusp in $P_r(r)$ for $r \to 0$. Interestingly enough, a slow varying behavior for $K \to 0$ can be observed only in the absence of the new firms, while the power-law tail for $K \to \infty$ emerges only in their presence. Thus, the one-level GPG model cannot account for the tent-shaped distribution of growth rates. This contradiction is overcomed by the two-level aggregation model: the tails of the tent shape are formed at a micro level of aggregation, on which the distribution of subunits is slow varying for $K \to 0$, while the Laplacian cusp forms on the second aggregation level for which the distribution of units follow a power law for $P(K) \to \infty$. Once the tails are formed, they propagate at higher levels of aggregation.

All in all, our results show that innovation and entry are key ingredients of industrial growth, and, moreover, that what we know about growth cannot be accounted for without considering them.

4

Testing Our Predictions

In this chapter, we test the propositions derived from our theoretical framework along four dimensions: the size distribution of firms, the growth rate distribution, the relationships between firm size, and both mean and the variance of the growth rates.

Along each dimension, we test the predictions derived from the stochastic framework described in Chapter 3 as a Simon–Bose–Einstein–Gibrat growth process (see Case D in Table 3.1). In this model specification, products can be added to and deleted from firms ($\lambda > 0$ and $\mu \geq 0$, respectively), while new firms can be created with probability $\nu > 0$. By assuming $\lambda > \mu \geq 0$, we consider the case in which both the number of products and firms are growing. Furthermore, in this specification of the model, we include two levels of aggregation. The number of units changes according to a Bose–Einstein process, while both their size distribution $(P(\xi)_\xi)$ and growth rate distribution $(P(\eta)_\eta)$ are lognormal.

Our framework has a multilevel structure, where a firm's growth is the outcome of dynamics at the level of units/products, which are driven by innovation and competition.

Here, in our empirical investigation of innovation through the launch of new products and firm growth, we rely on PHID, a unique dataset that decomposes firm sales figures into the number and the sales of constituent products. The version of PHID used for the preparation of this book covers sales figures of over 130,000 pharmaceutical products marketed by 4,921 companies in 21 countries between 1998 and 2008.

Within PHID, firms capture new business opportunities by launching new products, and the size of each firm is defined as the sum of the sales of its products: $S_\alpha(t) = \sum_{i=1}^{K_\alpha(t)} \xi_i(t) = \langle \xi_\alpha(t) \rangle K_\alpha(t)$, where $\langle \xi_\alpha(t) \rangle$ is the average size of products of firm α at time t and $K_\alpha(t)$ is the number of products belonging to firm α at time t.

This chapter has been coauthored with Andrea Morescalchi and Valentina Tortolini.

We treat each product as the elementary unit of analysis. Innovative companies develop new chemical or biological entities, which, after undergoing preclinical and clinical trials, can be approved as drugs for specific therapeutic indications. As a measure of the intensity of innovation within the industry, the number of new entities approved by the US Food and Drug Administration and equivalent agencies in other countries is often used (Sutton 1998; Pammolli et al. 2002, 2011).

Pharmaceutical products have specific therapeutic properties. This feature allows us to associate products and their indications to independent submarkets (Sutton 1998; Bottazzi et al. 2001).

In addition to PHID, we test the predictions of our framework for the general run of industries in the United States and Europe. We evaluate the robustness of results across industrial sectors and national economies: manufacturing firms in OECD countries[1] (ORBIS); publicly traded manufacturing firms in the United States (Compustat); the universe of French firms (FICUS); the gross domestic product (GDP) of 195 countries from 1960 to 2011 (World Bank).

According to the generalized proportional growth (GPG) model, the number of products within firms is expected to follow a Pareto distribution with an exponential cutoff, while the size distribution of firms, $P(S)$ is expected to be lognormal with a power law right tail. Regarding the growth rate of firms, the model predicts a tent-shaped distribution $P(r)$ with power law tails $P(r) \sim r^{-3}$. Finally, we expect that the mean growth rate decreases with firm size, while the variance of the growth rate obeys an approximate power law dependency on the firm size $\sigma_r \sim S^{-\beta}$, with $\beta \leq 0.5$ in a wide range of S.

We combine two different approaches, commonly used in the literature (Hall 1987), to challenge the consistency of the GPG model.

The first approach consists of a comparison between the distributions derived from a model and the data. The empirical distributions are fitted with the predictions of a stochastic model. For instance, predictions of Gibrat's Law can be falsified by evaluating the lognormality of the empirical size distribution. This control is often paired with the analysis of the tails of the distribution. The analysis of the distributional properties has a long tradition in physics, biology, population studies, and linguistics. Recently, rigorous tests have been introduced to properly ascertain the shape of empirically observed skewed distributions of size and growth.

The second approach focuses on the analysis of the determinants of firm growth, including size, age, innovation, diversification and so on. This analysis naturally involves the use of econometric techniques and has been widely used in economics. For instance, to asses the validity of Gibrat's hypothesis, one can test if growth rates are independent from size.

[1] The Organisation for Economic Co-operation and Development (OECD) was founded in 1961. For the list of the countries, see www.oecd.org.

In this chapter, we test the predictions of our stochastic framework, combining the econometric and the distributional approaches.

The chapter is structured as follows. Sections 4.1 and 4.2 focus on the analysis of size and growth of products and firms, respectively. The analysis of the size distribution is performed by means of the most common statistical tests used to detect the emergence of a Pareto tail. The analysis of the growth distribution is performed by comparing the coherence of different theoretical models with the empirical distribution of growth rates. In Section 4.3, we investigate the relationship between firm size and firm growth. A statistical appendix (Chapter 7, Appendix 7.5) describes the distributions and the statistical tests used in this chapter.

4.1 Size Distributions

Firm size has been measured in multiple ways, including annual sales, current employment, and occasionally, other measures like total assets. Some studies have investigated the size of establishments as constituent units of firms (Rossi-Hansberg and Wright 2007*b*; Henly and Sanchez 2009), whereas products are typically considered in the literature on international trade (Bernard et al. 2010; Arkolakis and Muendler 2010; Carsten and Neary 2010).

Here, we consider the size of products and firms in terms of annual sales across multiple industries, countries and data sources.

Candidate distributions are Zipf, Pareto or, less frequently, lognormal distributions.[2] A goodness of fit analysis is typically performed in the literature. The reproducibility of results has often been an issue because of the limitations in accessing official data. Moreover, only a few studies have investigated the universe of firms either in the United States (Axtell 2001; Rossi-Hansberg and Wright 2007*b*; Luttmer 2010) or in other countries (see Cabral and Mata 2003 for Portugal; Eaton et al. 2011; Garicano et al. 2013 for France).

The Size of Business Firms

In the literature, the distribution of firm size has been predicted to be either lognormal or power law or, most likely, a lognormal distribution with a power law right tail.[3] Our framework comes to a similar conclusion. Here, we first compare the empirical size distribution at both the product and firm level with a lognormal distribution using the Kolmogorov–Smirnov (KS) test (Chakravarti et al. 1967). Then, we test the emergence of a Pareto tail for firm sizes.

[2] Some recent contributions in the field of international economics took a similar approach (Di Giovanni et al. 2011; Keith et al. 2014).

[3] The lognormal and power law distributions are described in the Statistical Appendix 7.5, Chapter 7.

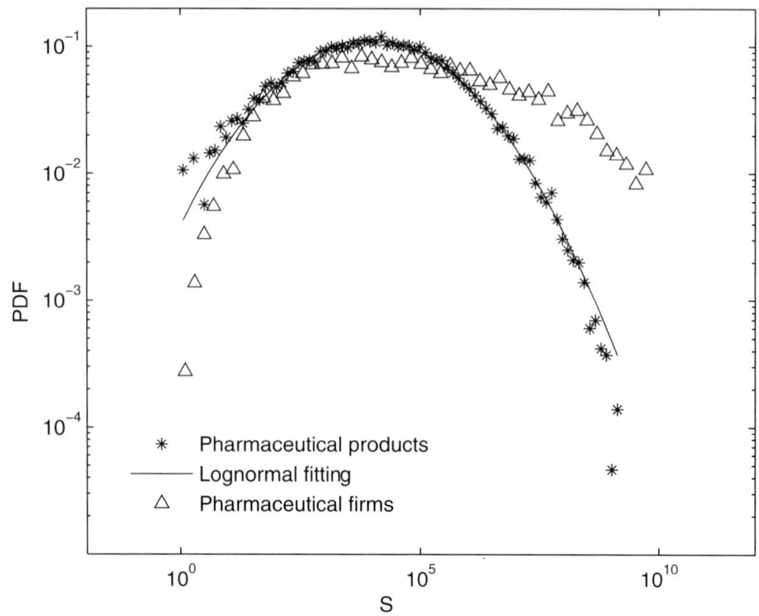

Figure 4.1 Product size distribution (⋆) and firm size distribution (△) fitted by a lognormal model. Data source: PHID

The analysis of firm size distribution is characterized by some difficult issues, i.e. (a) the power of goodness of fit tests, which may be unreliable in case of small sample sizes; (b) if it exists, the determination of the starting point of the power law behavior for large firms (Malevergne et al. 2009; Bee et al. 2011).

We now study the relationship between the shape of the size distribution at the product and firm level. Figure 4.1 shows that the distribution of product sizes looks approximately lognormal, whereas the size distribution of firms shows a departure in the upper tail. The sum of lognormally distributed random variables does not have a closed form solution, and several approximations involving series evaluations have been proposed for the shape of the resulting distribution (De Fabritiis et al. 2003).[4] Moreover, a lognormal distribution $P(S)$ with parameters μ and σ behaves as a power law between S^{-1} and S^{-2} for a wide range of its support $S_0 < S < S_0 e^2 \sigma^2$, where S_0 is a characteristic scale, corresponding to the median value (Sornette 2000; De Fabritiis et al. 2003).

[4] The problem of approximating the distribution of a sum of i.i.d. lognormals has a long history. As mentioned, the classical approach is to approximate the distribution of a sum of lognormals with another lognormal distribution. This approach was used by Wilkinson (1934) and later also by Fenton (1960). The Fenton–Wilkinson method, a central limit-type result, can deliver inaccurate approximations of the distribution of the lognormal sum when the number of summands is small or the dispersion parameter is high, in particular in the tail regions. Another more recent approach is based on approximation and simulation algorithms. For a survey, see Gulisashvili and Tankov (2013).

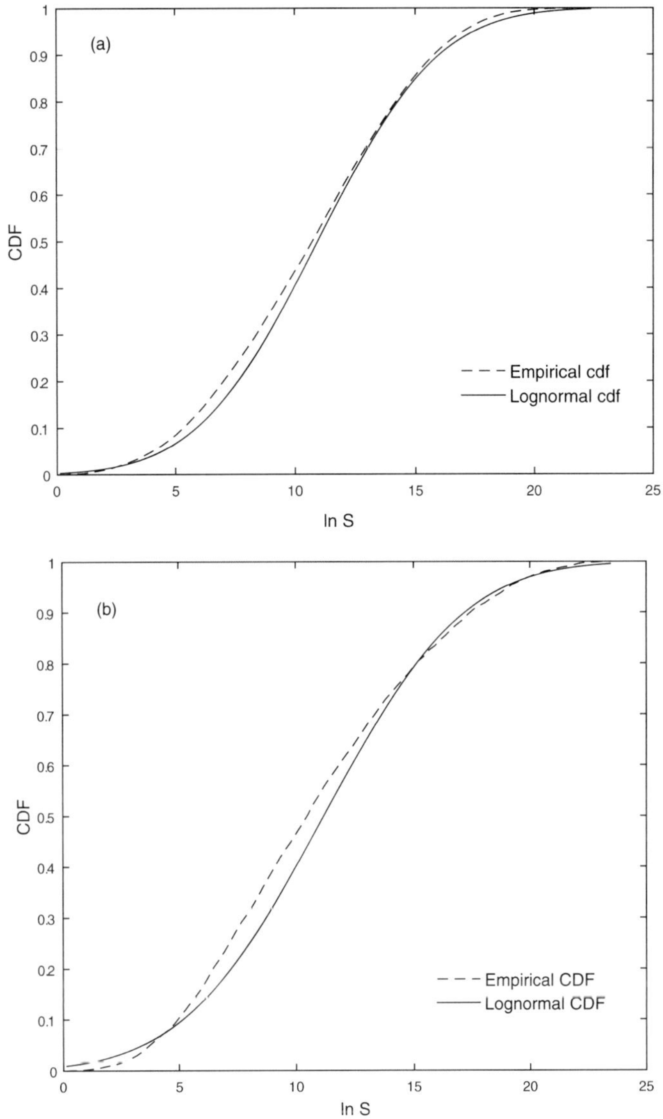

Figure 4.2 Empirical and lognormal CDF for the size of pharmaceutical (a) products and (b) firms. Data source: PHID

Figure 4.2 shows the cumulative density function (CDF) of the size distribution at the product and firm level. The visual inspection is confirmed by the KS statistics.[5] Here, we report only the expression of the KS statistics D_n, given $X_1, \ldots X_n$ i.i.d. observations,

[5] A detailed description of the KS test (together with other nonparametric tests of goodness of fit) is provided in Chapter 7, Appendix 7.5.

Table 4.1 *KS test results for product size distribution and firm size distribution. We reject the null hypothesis of a lognormal distribution ($p < 0.001$). Data source: PHID*

Products		Firms	
D_n*statistics*	*p-value*	D_n*statistics*	*p-value*
0.0280	$p < 0.001$	0.0456	$p < 0.001$

$$D_n = \sup_{-\infty<t<\infty} |F_n(t) - F_0(t)|, \tag{4.1}$$

where $F_n(t)$ and $F_0(t)$ are the CDF of the empirical and theoretical distributions, respectively. The test is performed under the null hypothesis:

$$H_0 : F(t) = F_0(t), \forall t. \tag{4.2}$$

The value of the KS statistics D_n and the associated p-value are reported in Table 4.1.[6] The value of D_n is 0.028 for the product size distribution and 0.046 for the firm size distribution. In both cases, the null hypothesis of lognormality is rejected ($p < 0.001$).

Given the KS test results, we move on and test the hypothesis of the emergence of a power law (Pareto) tail.

The lognormal distribution and the power law are mathematically different but they can be statistically distinguished only in the limit for $n \to \infty$ (Perline 2005), so that in a finite sample size the tests often have low power.

We follow Bee et al. (2013) and run several tests: the Uniformly Most Powerful Unbiased (UMPU) test developed by Del Castillo and Puig (1999) and used by Malevergne et al. (2009), the Maximum Entropy (ME) test by Bee et al. (2011), the test proposed by Gabaix and Ibragimov (2011) (henceforth, GI), and finally, the test proposed by Clauset et al. (2009). All tests are described in Chapter 7, Appendix 7.5.

First, we inspect the size distributions through the UMPU, ME, and GI tests. According to the results reported in Table 4.2, the size distribution at the level of products does not have a Pareto tail, since the number of observervation in the Pareto tail is lower than 1% for all the tests.

As a further assesment of the robustness of our results, we apply, both at the firm and at the product level, the method proposed by Clauset and colleagues (hereafter, CSN), to detect if the power law is a plausible model for the data (Clauset et al. 2009). We first estimate with the maximum likelihood method (ML) the scaling parameter (γ, see Equation 6.129 for the definition of the power law) and the

[6] The p-value, p, is defined as the probability of obtaining a result equal to or larger in absolute value than what is actually observed when the null hypothesis is true.

Table 4.2 *Pareto tail test results for two significance levels* ($\alpha = 0.05$ *and* $\alpha = 0.01$)*. The* α*-value is the predefined value of the false positive, i.e., it represents the probability of mistakenly identifying the presence of Pareto tail when the real distribution is lognormal. Smaller value of* $\alpha = 0.01$ *implies less probability of the lognormal distribution, and hence longer Pareto tails (Malevergne et al. 2009). For each test the table reports, the number (integer number) and the percent of observations in the Pareto tail (in brackets). The total number of observations n, is reported for products and firms. Data source: PHID*

	Firms $n = 4921$		Products $n = 60352$	
	$\alpha = .05$	$\alpha = .01$	$\alpha = .05$	$\alpha = .01$
ME	900 (18.29%)	950 (19.30%)	310 (0.51%)	320 (0.53%)
UMPU	450 (9.14%)	650 (13.21%)	80 (0.13%)	130 (0.22%)
GI	301 (6.12%)	406 (8.25%)	102 (0.17%)	139 (0.23%)

lower bound (S_{min}) of the power law behavior. Then, by using these estimates, we generate $N = 100$ samples of different sizes n, with $10 \leq n \leq 1000$, from a power law distribution. For each synthetic sample, we test the plausibility of the hypothesis of the power law tail.

As before, the observed data and the synthetic samples are compared by means of KS. The power law is a plausible hypothesis for the data if the resulting p-value of the goodness of fit test is greater than a given significance level (usually 0.05 or 0.01), while it is rejected otherwise.

Figure 4.3 shows the average p-value of the maximum likelihood power law model for samples extracted from the firm size distribution as a function of n. We do not report results for products, since, in this case, the average p-values are always smaller than 0.001. Therefore, we can conclude that the test rejects the power law hypothesis at the product level, while the hypothesis is not rejected for the firm size distribution (see also Figure 4.4).

These results are in agreement with the predictions of GPG for the size distributions. The methodology proposed by Clauset and coauthors is more conservative than the ME test regarding the length of the Pareto tail for the size distribution of firms. In all years, we find that about 11% of the largest firms follow a power law distribution and account for about 98% of the market (see Table 4.3).

In synthesis, in line with the predictions of our framework, the tests do not detect any power law behavior for the size distribution of products (Table 4.2). Incidentally, we observe that this finding seems to contradict the model developed

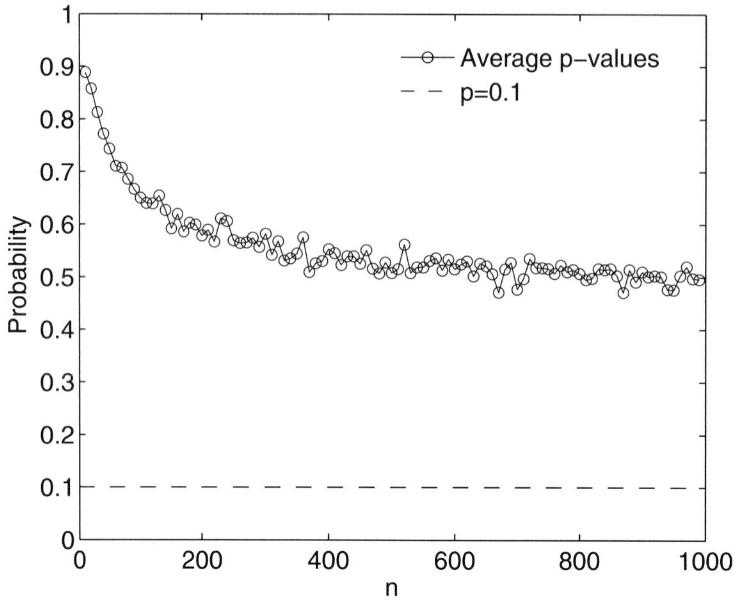

Figure 4.3 Average p-value for the maximum likelihood power law model for samples extracted from the firms' size distribution as a function of n. Data source: PHID

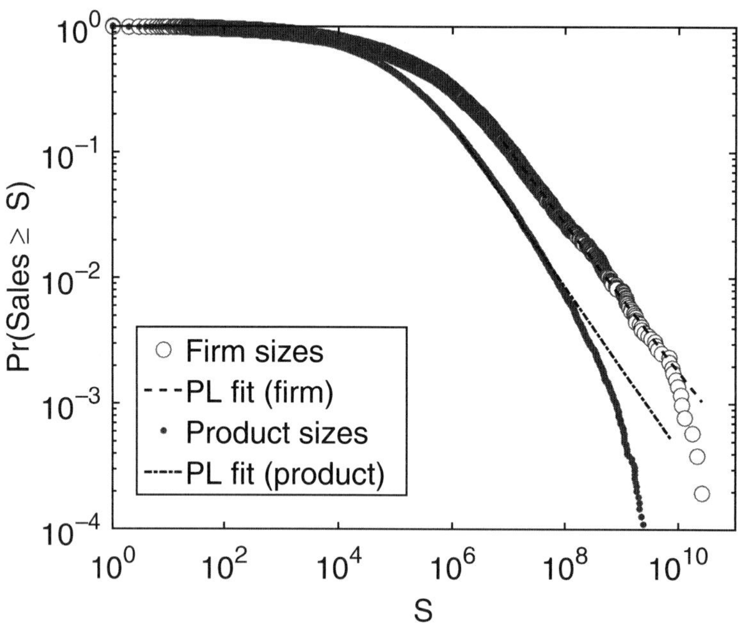

Figure 4.4 The countercumulative distribution functions $P(S)$ and their maximum likelihood power law fits for size distributions of pharmaceutical firms and products in the year 2003, for the firms the value of the slope parameter is $\gamma = 0.59$. Data source: PHID

Table 4.3 *Basic parameters of the Pharmaceutical Industry Data set (PHID), along with their power law fits and the corresponding p-value (p), for the size of firms ($P(S)$), for the years 1994–2003. In the table, n is the number of firms in the sample; $\langle S \rangle$ is the average natural logarithm of the sales for firms in the tail; $\sigma(S)$ is the standard deviation of the logarithm of the sales for firms in the tail; $\hat{S}_{max}$ e $\hat{S}_{min}$ are the natural logarithms of the upper and lower boundaries of the tail; $\tau = 1 + \gamma$ is the exponent characterizing the PDF of the size distribution (see Equation 3.58); the percentage of observations and the percentage of total sales for the firms belonging to the tail are reported in column "% in the tail." ML estimates as in (Clauset et al. 2009). Nonstatistically significant values, >.05, are denoted in bold. Data source: PHID*

Year	n	$\langle S \rangle$	$\sigma(S)$	$\hat{S}_{max}$	$\hat{S}_{min}$	$\hat{\tau}$	% in the tail	p
1994	3 326	17.12	19.43	22.85	15.81	1.58	11.24 (98.22)	**0.43**
1995	3 242	17.23	19.52	22.89	15.85	1.58	11.81 (98.30)	**0.36**
1996	3 160	17.33	19.62	22.94	16.03	1.58	11.30 (98.18)	**0.41**
1997	3 342	17.37	19.70	23.00	16.26	1.62	10.74 (97.71)	**0.57**
1998	3 452	17.50	19.89	23.26	16.33	1.60	10.31 (97.92)	**0.43**
1999	4 961	17.30	19.88	23.48	16.24	1.61	8.35 (97.65)	**0.69**
2000	5 010	17.40	20.00	23.60	15.78	1.61	11.20 (98.43)	**0.75**
2001	5 139	17.51	20.14	23.74	15.80	1.59	11.23 (98.53)	**0.64**
2002	5 166	17.60	20.25	23.86	16.11	1.59	9.74 (98.25)	**0.26**
2003	5 139	17.70	20.32	23.94	15.85	1.59	12.14 (97.11)	**0.58**

by Takayasu et al. (2014), which suggests that unit sizes follow a power law distribution. Conversely, we find a significant power law tail for the size of firms, while the length of the tail varies across the different tests and seems to be associated with a reduction of the sample size (see Malevergne et al. 2009; Bee et al. 2013).

The Number of Units per Firm

We now study the distribution of the number of units in a firm, $P(K)$. Here, we identify units with products. When we consider the entry of new firms, GPG predicts that $P(K)$ is Pareto with an exponential cutoff.[7]

Again, we refer to PHID to test this hypothesis. As predicted, $P(K)$ shows a power law behavior in its central part with an exponential cutoff in the upper tail (see Figure 4.5). The entry of new firms is the main driver of the emergence of the Pareto tail. Table 4.4 shows that the distribution of the number of products is Pareto

[7] The power law distribution, the Pareto distribution and the exponential distribution are briefly described in Chapter 7, Appendix 7.5.

Table 4.4 *Basic parameters of the Pharmaceutical Industry Data set (PHID), along with their power law fits and the corresponding p-value, for the number of products by firm ($P(K)$), for the years 1994–2003. In the table, n is the number of firms in the sample; $\langle S \rangle$ is the average natural logarithm of the sales for products in the tail; $\sigma(S)$ is the standard deviation of the logarithm of the sales for products in the tail; $\hat{S}_{\max}$ and $\hat{S}_{\min}$ are the natural logarithms of the upper and lower boundaries of the tail; $\tau = 1 + \gamma$ is the exponent characterizing the PDF of the size distribution (see Equation 3.58); the percentage of observations and the percentage of total sales for the products belonging to the tail are reported in column "%* in the tail.*" ML estimates as in (Clauset et al. 2009). Nonstatistically significant values, >.05, are denoted in bold. Data source: PHID*

year	n	$\langle K \rangle$	$\sigma(K)$	$\hat{K}_{\max}$	$\hat{K}_{\min}$	$\hat{\tau}$	% $n(S)$tail	p
1994	3 326	15.73	65.57	1 443	17	1.97	16.15(81.08)	**0.12**
1995	3 242	16.17	66.31	1 427	19	1.97	13.76(79.90)	0.02
1996	3 160	16.60	66.21	1 422	19	1.97	14.15(80.03)	0.03
1997	3 342	17.56	65.56	1 442	28	2.11	16.70(80.47)	**0.11**
1998	3 452	17.67	64.51	1 435	32	2.17	10.78(71.38)	**0.25**
1999	4 961	14.36	54.07	1 402	26	2.23	11.19(71.06)	**0.56**
2000	5 010	14.44	52.67	1 378	27	2.26	11.26(70.74)	**0.90**
2001	5 139	14.64	52.60	1 393	28	2.27	11.03(70.22)	**0.94**
2002	5 166	14.90	52.88	1 395	33	2.27	9.43(67.03)	**0.82**
2003	5 139	15.10	52.79	1 366	30	2.27	10.61(69.56)	**0.72**

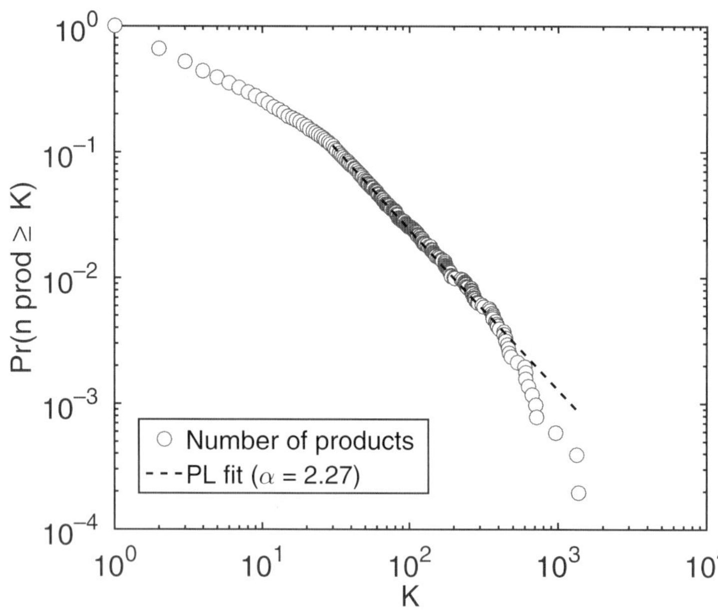

Figure 4.5 The countercumulative distribution function, $P(K)$, and their maximum likelihood power law fits for the distributions of the number of products by pharmaceutical firms for the year 2003.

in all years of our sample, except for 1995 and 1996. Across all years, we notice that the fraction of products in the Pareto tail ranges from 9.43% (2002) to 16.70% (1997), and these products account for a market share that varies from about 67% in 2002 up to more than 80% in 1997. Overall, in agreement with our predictions, the number of products per firm is approximately Pareto distributed, with some departures in the lower and upper tails.[8]

Firm Sizes across Industries and Countries

Industry concentration and turnover vary significantly across sectors and countries (Sutton 1997). In this section, we test the predictions of our framework for a broad range of industries and countries. First, we use the Compustat data, where large companies are overrepresented (Hall 1987; Axtell 2001). Second, we employ the FICUS database (*Fichier complet de Système Unifié de Statistique d'Entreprises*), maintained by the French National Statistical Office (INSEE), which covers the entire population of French firms.[9] We use total revenues to measure firm size and we focus on a sample of more than 2 million firms in the year 2003 (results are not sensitive to the choice of year). Finally, we analyze the size of manufacturing firms in the OECD countries in the year 2010 using sales data from ORBIS–Bureau Van Dick.

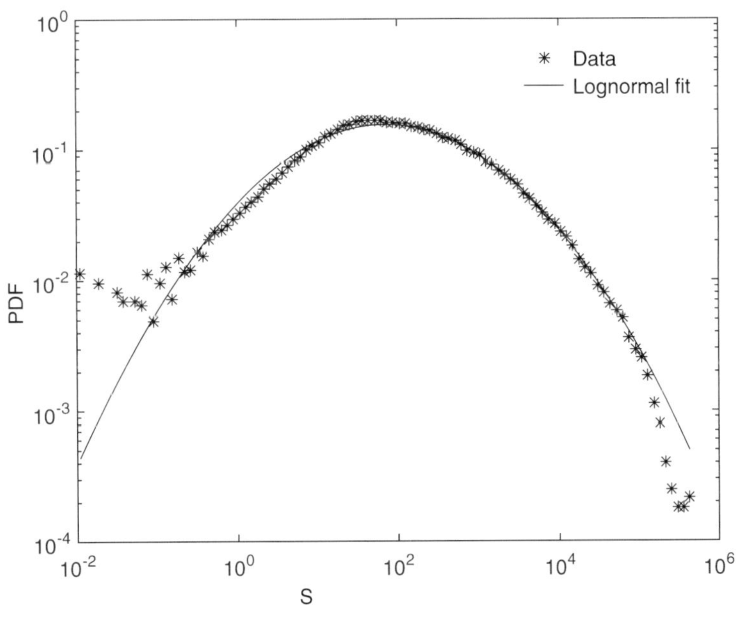

Figure 4.6 Firm size distribution and lognormal fitting for the year 2010. Data source: Compustat

[8] A more detailed analysis of the $P(K)$ distribution is performed in Chapter 5.

[9] The data are analogous to those used by Eaton et al. (2011) and have been used elsewhere as well (Bee et al. 2017; Garicano et al. 2013).

Table 4.5 *Pareto tail test results for two significance levels ($\alpha = .05$ and $\alpha = .01$). For each test the table reports, the number (integer number) and the percent of observations in the Pareto tail (in brackets). The total number of observations, n, is reported for each dataset. Data sources: COMPUSTAT (year 2000 and year 2010), FICUS, ORBIS*

	COMPUSTAT, 2000		COMPUSTAT, 2010	
	n = 6 647		n = 9 027	
	p = 0.05	p = 0.01	p = 0.05	p = 0.01
ME	200 (3.01%)	210 (3.16%)	210 (2.33%)	230 (2.55%)
UMPU	100 (1.15%)	140 (2.11%)	170 (1.88%)	180 (1.99%)
GI	114 (1.72%)	146 (2.22%)	135 (1.5%)	203 (2.25%)
	French firms		ORBIS	
	n = 2 247 547		n = 386 945	
	p = 0.05	p = 0.01	p = 0.05	p = 0.01
ME	1 750 (0.08%)	2 150 (0.1%)	310 (0.08%)	360 (0.09%)
UMPU	1 600 (0.17%)	1 650 (0.07%)	110 (0.02%)	180 (0.05%)
GI	2 400 (0.11%)	3 480 (0.15%)	67 (0.02%)	70 (0.02%)

Figure 4.6 shows that the lognormal fits quite well the size distribution of Compustat companies in the body, but not in the tails. The lognormality hypothesis is rejected by the CSN test.

The departure from lognormality in the right tail of the size distribution has been assessed through the UMPU, GI, and ME tests. The results of the three tests are reported in Table 4.5. The three tests convey similar results for each distribution of firm size: the distributions do not follow a power law, not even in the tails. Moreover, none of the aggregate distributions passes the goodness of fit KS test between the data and the power law using the CSN approach ($p < .0001$).

When we consider size distributions for specific industries, we find that in some cases a power law emerges in the right tails. Table 4.6 shows the results of the tests for four industrial sectors: pharmaceuticals; textile; motor vehicles; trailers and semitrailers (cars); computers, electronic and optical products, electrical equipment (computers). The sales data are extracted from ORBIS for the year 2010. In interpreting the results, one should keep in mind that the emergence of a power law tail is influenced by industry-specific characteristics, such as the distribution of

Table 4.6 *Pareto tail test results for two significance levels ($\alpha = 0.05$ and $\alpha = 0.01$). For each test the table reports, the number (integer number) and the percent of observations in the Pareto tail (in brackets). The total number of Observations, n, is reported for each industrial sector. Data source: ORBIS, year 2010*

	Pharmaceutical industry		Textile industry	
	n = 1 648		n = 14 573	
	$\alpha = 0.05$	$\alpha = 0.01$	$\alpha = 0.05$	$\alpha = 0.01$
ME	600 (36.41%)	610 (37.01%)	1400 (9.61%)	1450 (9.95%)
UMPU	540 (32.77%)	560 (33.98%)	1150 (7.89%)	1350 (9.26%)
GI	500 (30.34%)	520 (31.55%)	1300 (8.92%)	1600 (10.98%)
	Car industry		Computer industry	
	n = 5 845		n = 28 509	
	$\alpha = 0.05$	$\alpha = 0.01$	$\alpha = 0.05$	$\alpha = 0.01$
ME	350 (5.99%)	350 (5.99%)	800 (2.81%)	900 (3.16%)
UMPU	200 (3.42%)	250 (4.28%)	100 (0.35%)	180 (0.63%)
GI	– 0%	– 0%	– 0%	– 0%

the number of products $P(K)$, the variance of the product sizes and the existence of independent submarkets. The correspondent size distributions are presented in Figure 4.7.

Strong evidence for the emergence of the power law tail was also found for the size distribution of the French firms (see Bottazzi et al. 2011; Bee et al. 2017).

4.2 The Distribution of Growth Rates

In this section, we focus on the growth rate distribution. The following cases are compared:

a) Gibrat's process, which predicts a normal distribution for the (log) growth rates;
b) Laplace (symmetric exponential) distribution;
c) Bose–Einstein process, which predicts a probability density function for the growth rate with power law tails $P(r) \sim r^{-3}$ (see Equation (3.54));
d) The distribution summarized in Equation (3.114) that predicts a tent shape probability density function for the growth rate with power law tails $P(r) \sim r^{-3}$.

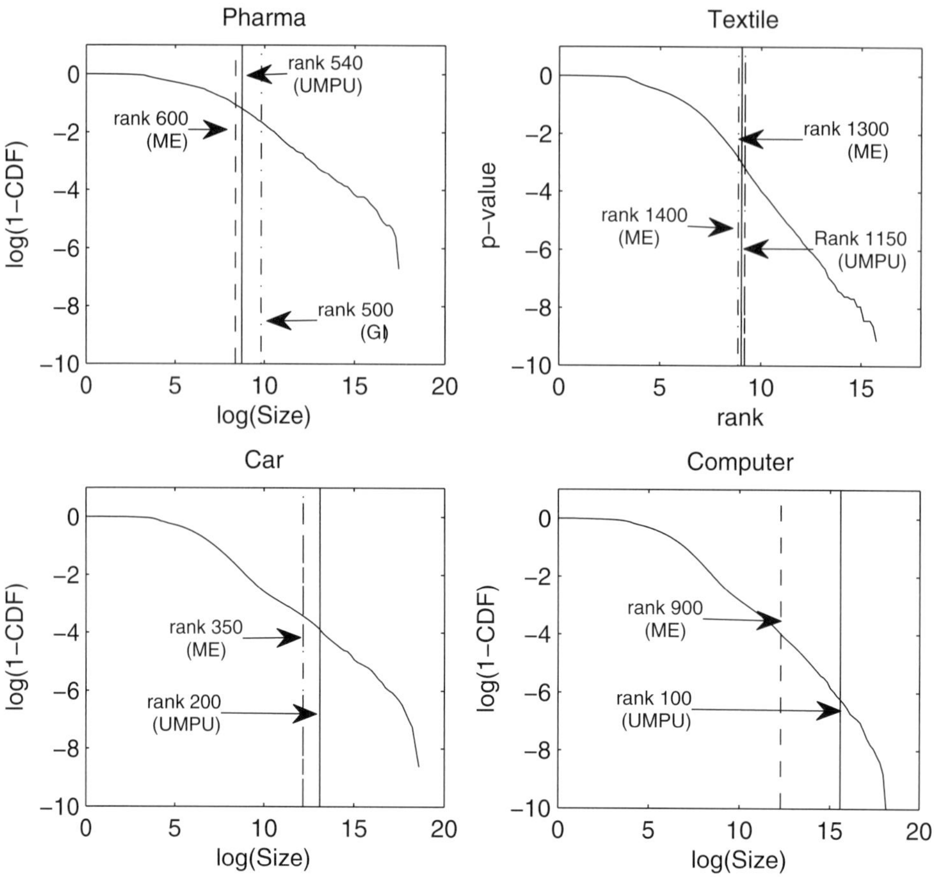

Figure 4.7 Complementary cumulative distribution of firm size. The vertical lines mark the power law cut-off identified by the GI, the ME, and the UMPU tests. Data source: Compustat, year 2010

Growth Rate at Different Levels of Aggregation

As shown in Figure 4.8, the theoretical distribution summarized in Equation (3.114) performs very well for product growth rates and firm growth rates in the pharmaceutical industry. Annual growth rates are defined as the log-difference between sales in two consecutive years (see Equation 2.4). Marked departures from the Gaussian model can be detected. This finding is consistent with the predictions of the GPG model with two levels of aggregation, which posits the emergence of a tent shape distribution with power law tails also at the product level. The growth distribution is stable upon aggregation from products to firms, while our framework provides a good fit (see Table 4.9) also for the growth distributions at the industry level and for country GDP (Fu et al. 2005).

Table 4.7 *Maximum Likelihood Estimates (MLE) of the yearly firm growth distribution: μ and σ are the parameters of Gaussian, Laplace, and exponential power distribution; while $K/2V_r$ is the parameter of Bose–Einstein model (Equation (3.54)) and GPG with two levels of aggregation (Equation (3.114)). KS and AD columns contain the value of D_n and A_n respectively (see Equation (6.171)). Data source: PHID*

Distribution	μ	σ	β	$K/2V_r$	KS	AD
Gaussian	−0.0564	1	–	–	20.75	n.a.
Laplace	0.007	0.488	–	–	8.26	58.59
Bose–Einstein	–	–	–	6.32	3.81	0.24
exponential power	0.0203	0.0696	0.4858	–	4.08	0.11
GPG	–	–	–	2.45	2.62	0.16

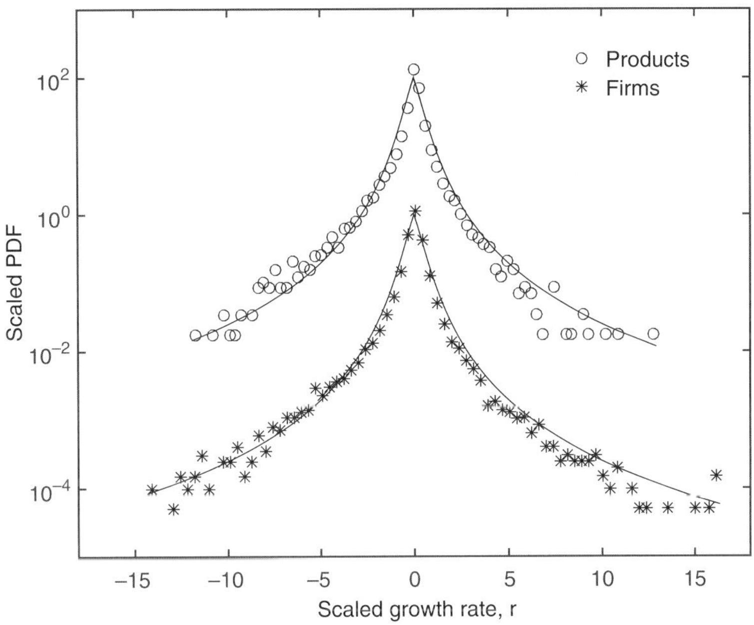

Figure 4.8 Yearly growth distributions of firms (stars) and stable products (circles). Empirical fit of Equation (3.114). For clarity, the growth distribution of firms is offset by a factor of 10^2. Data source: PHID

Table 4.7 shows the results of the KS and the Anderson–Darling (AD) goodness of fit tests for the candidate distributions listed above. Like the KS test, the AD test quantifies the agreement of data with a given probability distribution. As compared to the KS test, the AD test gives more weight to observations in the tails of the distribution (see Chapter 7, Appendix 7.5 for a detailed

Table 4.8 *Tail behavior of the firm growth distribution (Hill estimator)* $P(r) \sim r^{-3}$, *where* $x = ln|r|$, $x_m in$ *is the starting point of the tail and KS is the value of* D_n *for KS test. Data source: PHID*

Tail	Slope	$x_m in$	KS	% in the tail
Positive	3.0255	2.1632	0.0644	3.3934
Negative	3.0903	0.9302	0.0494	3.2975

description of the tests). Two level aggregation GPG framework (Equation (3.114)) is compared, at the firm level, with the Gaussian distribution, the Laplace distribution, the Bose–Einstein model (Equation (3.54)) and the exponential power distribution (see Buldyrev et al. 2007). The exponential power distribution, also known as the generalized Gaussian distribution, is a parametric family of distributions, including the normal distribution and the Laplace distribution as particular cases (see Kotz et al. 2001). For each of these models, the theoretical CDF (obtained by estimating the unknown parameters of the model with the maximum likelihood method) is compared with the empirical cumulative ditribution function through the KS and AD tests.

Table 4.7 shows, for each model, the values of the estimated parameters and the results of the KS and AD tests. Overall, the GPG outperforms the Gaussian, the Laplace, and the Bose–Einstein fits. Furthermore, the GPG framework performs better than the exponential power distribution regarding the whole distribution (as shown by the results of the KS test), while the AD test reveals that the exponential power distribution provides a slightly better fit in the tails.

We use the Hill estimator to investigate the tail behavior of the growth distribution (Embrechts et al. 1997). Table 4.8 shows that the growth distribution has power law tails: about 6.7% of the total growth events are power law distributed, $P(r) \sim r^{-3}$, in accordance with our predictions.

In summary, GPG provides a better fit to our data than alternative candidate distributions. Moreover, the shape of the growth distribution is stable upon aggregation. In order to test if our results also hold at the aggregate level of national economies, we measure the growth rate of the gross domestic product (GDP) of 195 countries from 1960 to 2011 (World Bank data: http://data.worldbank.org).

Figure 4.9 shows that the growth distribution in Equation (3.114) works well for country GDP as well as for the collection of publicly traded firms from multiple industries (Compustat). This must be surprising, since Compustat reports only on publicly traded firms while the naive explanation of the leptokurtic tails of the growth rate distribution is that they are created by small undiversified firms. Marked departures from a Gaussian shape are found at all levels of aggregation.

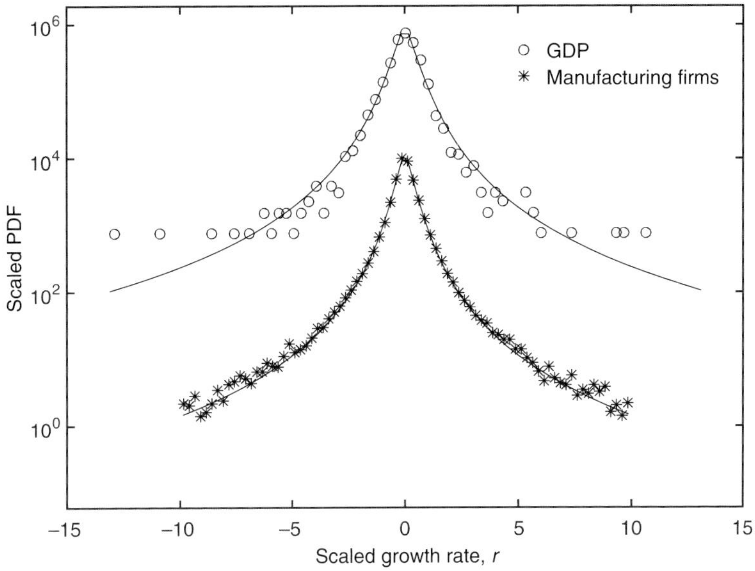

Figure 4.9 Empirical tests for the probability density function (PDF) $P_g(g)$ of growth rates rescaled by $\sqrt{V_r/2K}$ (see Equation (3.114)). Country GDP (◯) and all manufacturing firms in Compustat ($*$) are shown. The shapes of $P_r(r)$ for the two levels of aggregation are well approximated by the PDF predicted by the model (lines). Lines are obtained based on Equation (3.114). After rescaling, the two PDFs can be fitted by the same function. For clarity, the manufacturing firms are offset by a factor of 10^4 and the GDP data are offset by a factor of 10^6. Data source: World Bank, Compustat

Furthermore, while $P_r(r)$ can be reasonably well approximated by a Laplace distribution for country GDP, ignoring the few points in the tails as outliers, the distribution for firms is clearly more leptokurtic than a Laplace distribution. Therefore, we can conclude that, as predicted by our framework, the growth distribution has a Laplace body and power law tails across different levels of aggregation within the economy.

Firm Growth Across Sectors

We now present an additional investigation on the stability of the firm growth distribution across industries. We rely on Compustat data to compare the prediction of the GPG with alternative distributions (Gaussian, Laplace, and exponential power distributions).

In Figure 4.10, the growth distribution calculated on the Compustat data is compared with four maximum likelihood distributions: a Gaussian distribution with $\mu = 0.0844$ and $\sigma = 0.3702$, a Laplace distribution with $\mu = 0.0844$ and $\sigma = 0.1854$, a distribution with power law wings $\sim r^{-3}$ summarized in

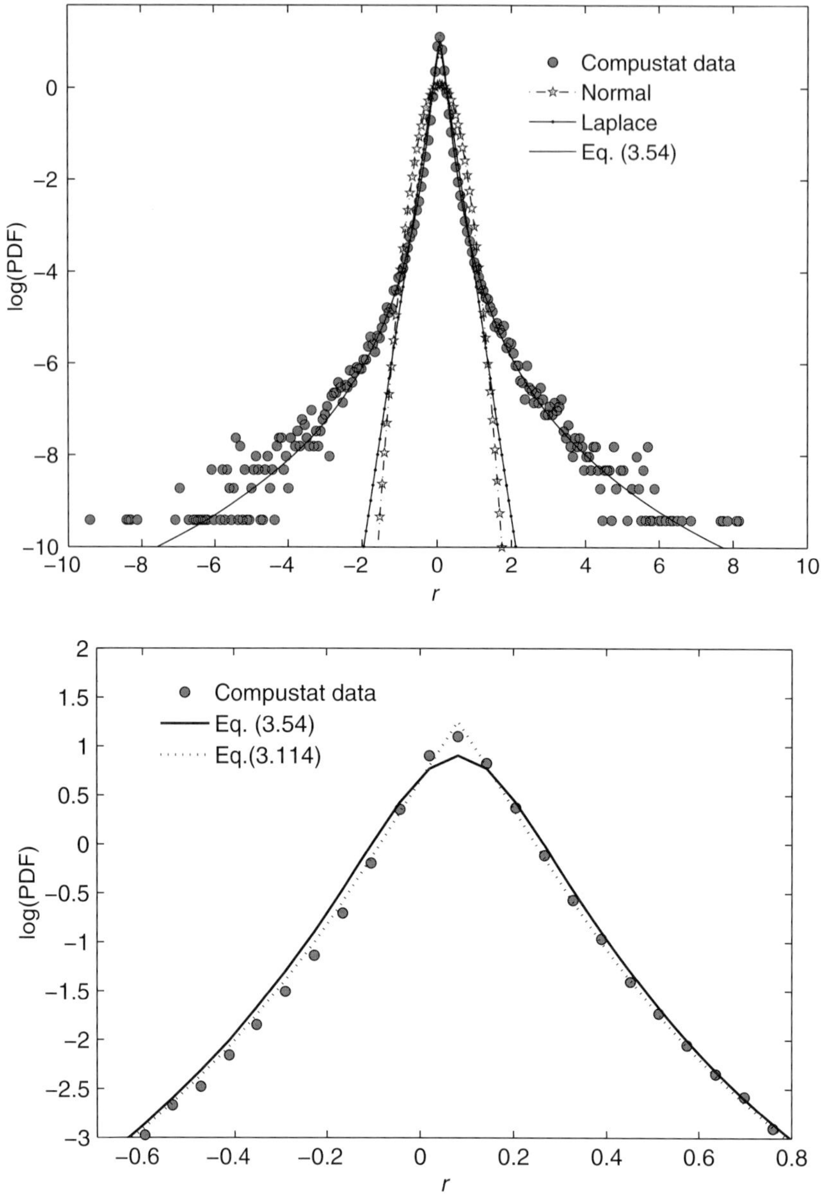

Figure 4.10 The growth distribution of firms (Compustat data). In the top panel, dots represent the empirical growth rate distribution. This distribution is compared with a Normal distribution ($\mu = 0.0844$ and $\sigma = 0.3702$); a Laplace distribution $\mu = 0.0844$ and $\sigma = 0.1854$ with power law tails $\sim r^{-3}$ summarized in Equation (3.54) with parameter $\frac{\kappa}{2V_r} = 24.5$; a tent-shaped distribution with power law tails $\sim r^{-3}$ summarized in Equation (3.114) with parameter $\frac{\kappa}{2V_r} = 12.25$. The bottom panel shows the fitting of the central part of the growth rate distribution, where the differences between fittings by Equations (3.54) and (3.114) are visible. Data source: Compustat

Table 4.9 *Maximum Likelihood Estimates (MLE) of the yearly firm growth distribution: μ and σ are the parameters of Gaussian, Laplace, and exponential power distribution; while $K/2V_r$ is the parameter of Bose–Einstein model (Equation (3.54)) and GPG with two levels of aggregation (Equation (3.114)). KS and AD columns contain the value of D_n and A_n respectively (see Equation (6.171)). Data source: Compustat*

Distribution	μ	σ	$K/2V_r$	KS	AD
Gaussian	0.0844	0.3702	–	17.1173	2.29E+79
Laplace	0.0844	0.1854	–	5.0453	1.10E+07
Bose–Einstein	–	–	31.55	3.7989	0.0837
GPG	–	–	12.65	1.6734	0.0343

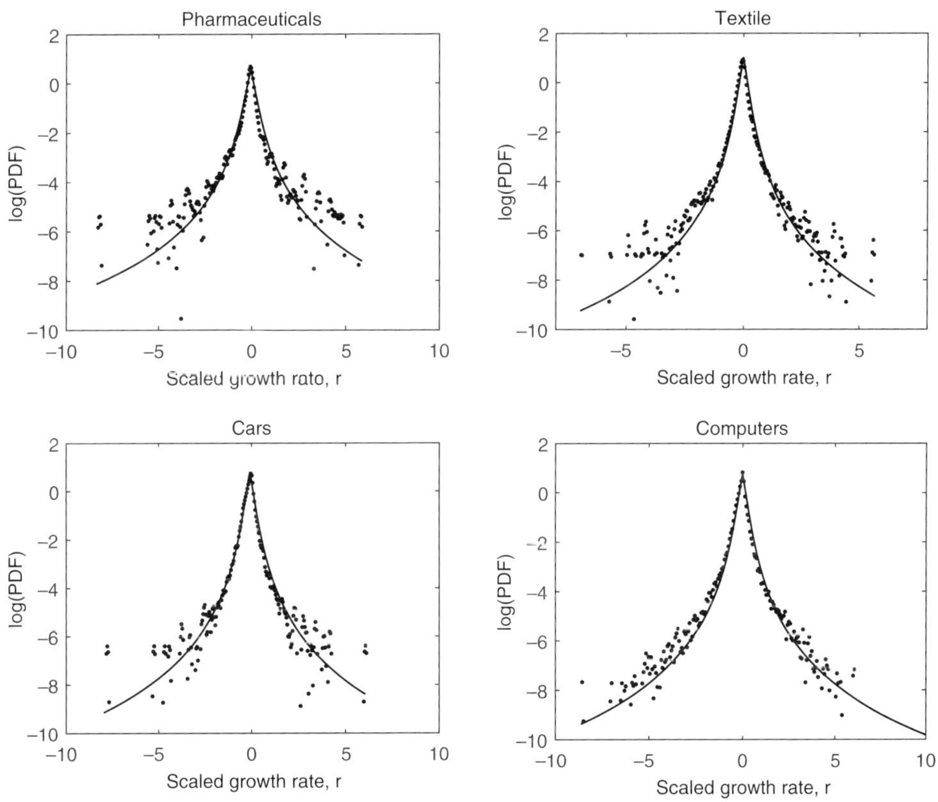

Figure 4.11 Growth rate distributions for different industrial sectors. The parameter $\alpha_{GPG} = \frac{K}{2V}$ is estimated with the Maximum Likelihood Estimation (MLE) method. For pharmaceutical $\alpha_{GPG} = 6.27$, for textile $\alpha_{GPG} = 9.27$, for the car industry $\alpha_{GPG} = 18.88$, and for computers $\alpha_{GPG} = 15.11$. Data source: Compustat

Equation (3.54) with parameter $\frac{\kappa(t)}{2V_r} = 31.55$ and a tent shape distribution with power-law wings $\sim r^{-3}$ summarized in Equation (3.114) with parameter $\frac{\kappa}{2V} = 12.65$.

Figure 4.10(a) clearly shows that the Bose–Einstein model and the framework summarized in Equation (3.114) outperform other distributional models, whereas they perform similarly. Therefore, as in the previous subsection, we performed KS and AD tests in order to compare the goodness of fit in the two cases. The KS and AD statistics are reported in Table 4.9. The tent-shaped distribution with a Laplacian cusp and power law tails $P(r) \sim r^{-3}$ described in Equation (3.114) outperforms all the other distributions. The results of the KS test are confirmed also by a visual inspection of the fit of the central part of the distribution (Figure 4.10, bottom panel).

Interestingly enough, the same tent shape emerges also at the level of individual sectors. Figure 4.11 reports the empirical distributions of four industrial sectors (cars, computers, pharmaceuticals and textiles) together with the theoretical distribution derived from our framework. These densities are well described by Equation (3.114).

4.3 The Relationship between Size, Age, Diversification, and Growth

The Size–Growth Relationship

In this section, we study the relationship between growth and some of the main characteristics of firms, such as size, age, innovation, and diversification. As discussed in the previous Chapters, the growth of firms depends on their size: smaller firms have a lower survival probability, but those firms that survive tend to grow faster than larger firms (Mansfield 1962; Evans 1987b; Hall 1987; Dunne et al. 1989; De Wit 2005; Rossi-Hansberg and Wright 2007*b*; Growiec et al. 2018). The negative relationship between size and growth does not hold for larger firms, whose growth rates tend to be unrelated to past growth or to firm size.

We refer here to the nonlogarithmic measure of the growth rate, r'. In order to visually inspect the relationship between growth and size we first refer to PHID, grouping firms into consecutive size (S) bins containing the same number of companies. Figure 4.12 shows the negative relationship between size and average growth. A negative dependence is observed for almost all size bins with the notable exception of large companies ($S > \$10^6$).

In order to better investigate the effect of product diversification on firm growth rates, Growiec et al. (2018) have taken a closer look at firm growth, survival probability and changes in the number of products for monoproduct and multiproduct

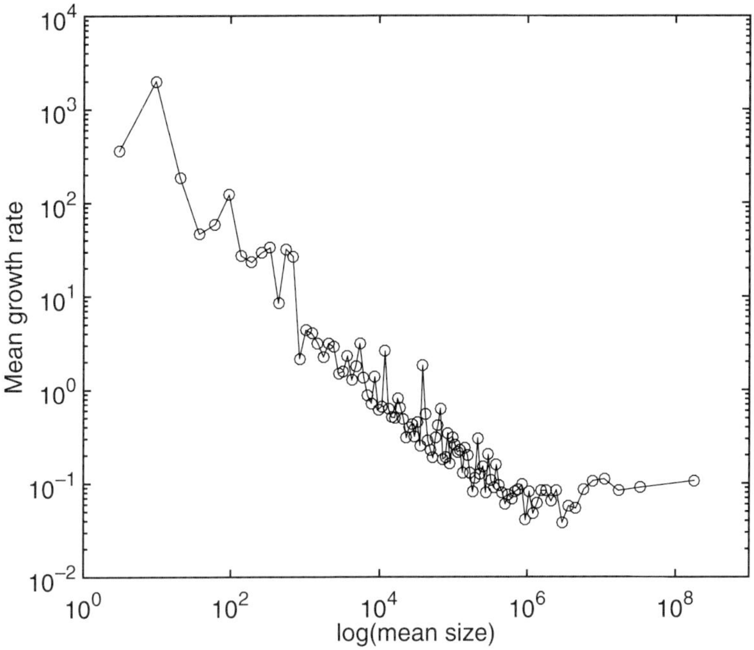

Figure 4.12 The relationship between the logarithm of firm sales measured in dollars (S) and its mean growth rate (r') for pharmaceutical companies. Data source: PHID

firms ($K = 1, 2, 3$ and $K > 3$). They have shown that in the pharmaceutical industry, the average growth rate of a firm with a single unit is almost fifty times larger than the average growth rate of a company with more than three units. Furthermore, among companies with one unit, companies that capture new business opportunities grow a hundred times faster than others.

In the pharmaceutical industry, this can happen for instance in the case of new blockbuster drugs launched by biotech start-up companies with one product serving a restricted segment of the market. Therefore, rare spurs of growth seem to correspond to innovation-driven growth.[10]

Survival Probability

The number of products K also affects the survival probability of firms. Growiec and coauthors found that companies with one unit have a higher exit probability than companies with more than one unit (13.17% versus 0.20% for companies with $K > 3$, see Growiec et al. 2018). Qualitatively, GPG predicts this effect but

[10] When the median growth rate is considered instead of the mean, the relationship is flat for all K.

underestimates it by a factor of three (Figure 5.3). Moreover, in Growiec et al. (2018), authors investigate the survival probability of firms conditional on some of the firm specific variables, such as the number of products at time t, $K(t)$, the age of the firm T, and the average unit size $\langle \xi \rangle$. The analysis confirms that firms with more units have a lower probability to exit and that the average unit size has also a positive effect on the survival probability. Conversely, a firm's age is far less significant, in accordance with the GPG framework, in which the exit probability μ is independent of the product age and size. Though preliminary, this result suggests that the age effect on firm survival could be mediated by the innovation process and the capture of new business opportunities, as shown by Klette and Kortum (2004).

All in all, we find that the downward sloping relationship between firm growth and size among small firms is driven primarily by innovation and selection (Mansfield 1962). Therefore, we must take into account the extensive margin of growth (i.e., variations in the number of products) and selection when studying the relationship between firm size and its growth rate.

The Variance of Firm Growth Rates

We now move on to the analysis of the size-variance relationship. Our framework predicts that the relationship between size and variance crucially depends on the partition of firm sales into units. The negative relation between the standard deviation of the growth rate σ_r and sizes of industrial firms, S, is well documented (see e.g. Hall 1987; Bottazzi et al. 2001; Sutton 2002; Koren and Tenreyro 2013) with a notable exception of Perline et al. (2006). However, the specific dependence of $\sigma_r(S)$ on S is still debated. As was proposed in Stanley et al. (1996) and Amaral et al. (1998) the variance of the growth rate of firms obeys the universal scaling relationship with the firm size $\sigma_r(S) \sim S^{-\beta}$, where $\beta \approx 0.2$ is a constant. During the last 20 years, this "scaling puzzle" has been at the core of a lively debate in the literature. These observations were made for the logarithmic growth rates (Figure 2.8). However, the GPG framework predicts that in the presence of innovation, i.e. when new units can be created, there is a dramatic difference between $\sigma_{r'}(S)$ for nonlogarithmic growth rates and $\sigma_r(S)$ for logarithmic growth rates and $\beta = \beta(S)$ is not constant for either measures, but a slow varying function of S, with different asymptotic behaviors. For nonlogarithmic growth rate, $\beta(S)$ is a decreasing function of S changing from 1, for $S \to 0$, to some value $\beta(\infty) \leq 1/2$. For some variants of the model, β can become even negative, while for logarithmic growth rates $\beta(S)$ is a decreasing function of S, changing in the range from 0 for small S to a larger value $\beta_{\max} \leq 1/2$ for larger S, but then can decrease again and become even negative, coinciding for large S with the behavior of nonlogarithmic β. This behavior is caused by the complex interplay between the distribution of unit sizes P_ξ, which is assumed to be lognormal with large logarithmic variance V_ξ and the distribution of number of units P_K, which can have a complex shape from an exponential distribution to a Pareto one.

Using PHID, we have tested the predictions of the GPG at the level of firms and at the level of products. If the behavior of $\sigma_r(S)$ for the products is similar to that for firms, it can be regarded as an evidence in favor of the two-level aggregation model, suggesting that products are complex entities, consisting of several units. Figure 4.13 shows the relationship between the average size and the variance of the logarithmic growth rates for firms (panel a) and for products (panel b) in the pharmaceutical industry. Note that, by definition, $\sigma_r(S)$ is not a property which can be defined for single firm. It is an ensemble average defined for many firms whose sizes belong to an interval between $S - \Delta S/2$ and $S + \Delta S/2$, where ΔS is the bin size. Since S spans many orders of magnitude, we work with logarithmic sales $s = \ln(S)$ and logarithmic bins $[s - \Delta s/2, s + \Delta s/2]$ and compute the variance $\sigma_r^2(s)$ of the sample of annual growth rates of firms collected over the entire period of PHID (10 years) of all firms, whose size at the beginning of each year belonged to this bin. For investigation of products we define $s = \ln \xi$ and use the same technique as for firms. Obviously, this procedure should dramatically depend on the bin size. For small bin sizes each bin will consist of a very few observations N_s, and we can expect some noise in the data, since the standard error analysis shows that the statistical variance of the value $\ln[\sigma_r(s)]$ – which we report on the graph – is $1/[2(N_s - 1)]$. On the other hand, if bins were too large the data would be smooth but we would lose the resolution necessary to determine variation in $\beta(S)$, which is the local slope on the graph of $\ln[\sigma_r(s)]$ versus s. We will determine $\beta(S)$ by the least square linear fit for the bins between $s_{\min}$ and $s_{\max}$. To take into account the accuracy of $\sigma_r(s)$ for different bins, we minimize the sum of the squares of the residuals normalized by the statistical variance $1/[2(N_s - 1)]$ of each observation. This method is identical to the ordinary least square fit in which we assume that each bin yields $N_s - 1$ identical observations. The error bar of the observed slope β can be obtained by the standard error analysis, which assumes that the residuals are normally distributed. The scaling hypothesis of a power law with a fixed β is rejected if the fitted line does not fall within the given confidence intervals determined by the error bars of certain bins. We repeat this procedure for different bin sizes to verify if our results are stable with respect to the bin size.

Visual inspection of the data in Figure 4.13(a) shows that, as predicted by GPG, in the presence of innovation we see a dramatic difference in the behavior of the nonlogarithmic and logarithmic growth rates for small S, with nonlogarithmic growth rates skyrocketing to infinity. In order to provide a better visualization of the data, in the nonlogarithmic case we do not plot large values of σ. This data is

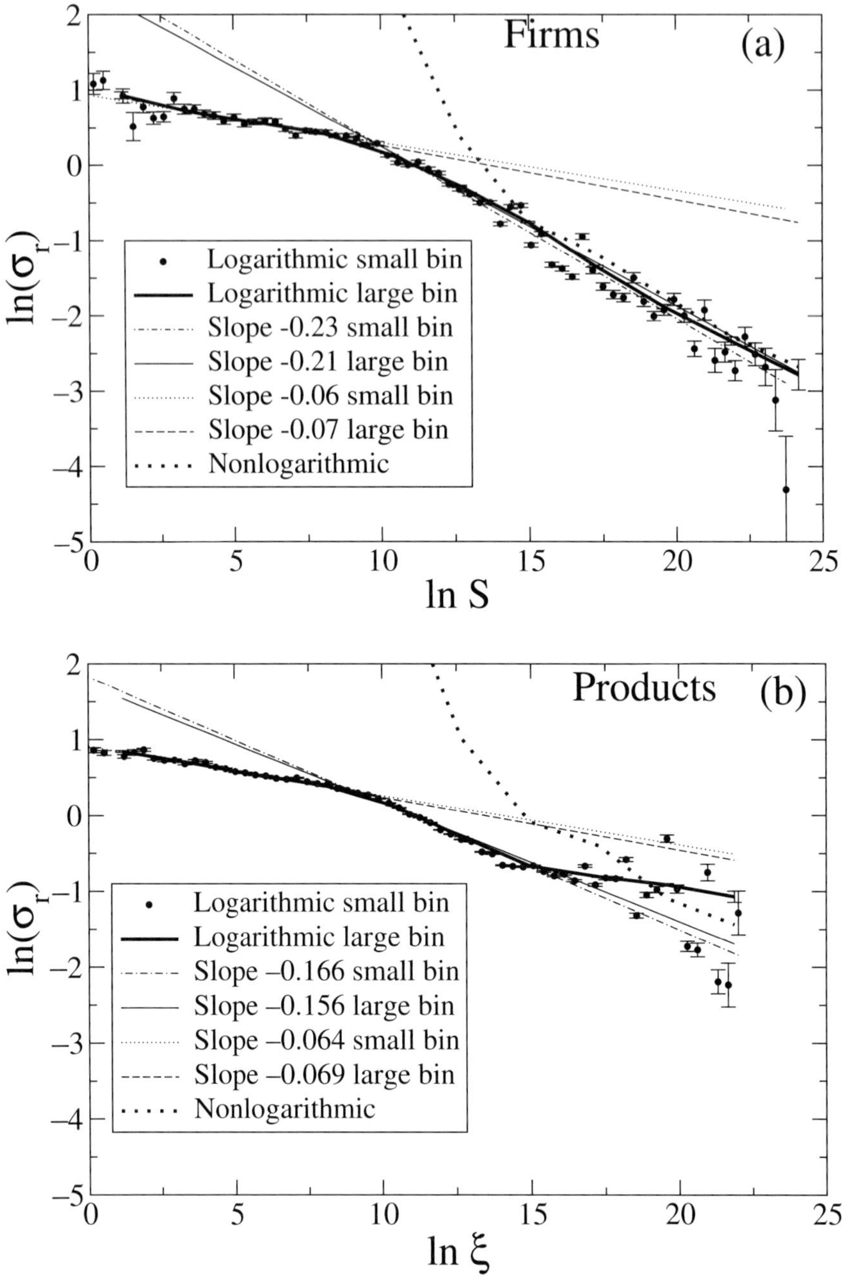

Figure 4.13 The relationship between the average size and the variance of the logarithmic and nonlogarithmic growth rates for of firms (a) and products (b) in pharmaceutical industry. For estimation of the scaling exponent β we use different fitting ranges and different bin sizes (Table 4.10). Data source: PHID

Table 4.10 *Least square estimation of β for products and firms as in Figure 4.13 for different fitting ranges $[s_{\min}, s_{\max}]$ and bin sizes Δs. (For products $s = \ln \xi$). The linearity hypothesis is rejected if for any bin the data is three standard error away from the fit. (99.7% confidence level), and accepted otherwise. Data source: PHID*

Data	$s_{\min}$	$s_{\max}$	Δs	β	Linearity
Firms	0	10	$\ln 2/2 = 0.35$	0.06 ± 0.02	Accepted
Firms	0	10	$\ln 10 = 2.3$	0.06 ± 0.02	Accepted
Firms	10	25	$\ln 2/2 = 0.35$	0.23 ± 0.03	Accepted
Firms	10	25	$\ln 10 = 2.3$	0.21 ± 0.02	Accepted
Products	0	10	$\ln 2/2 = 0.35$	0.06 ± 0.02	Accepted
Products	0	10	$\ln 10 = 2.3$	0.06 ± 0.02	Accepted
Products	10	25	$\ln 2/2 = 0.35$	0.16 ± 0.02	Rejected
Products	10	25	$\ln 10 = 2.3$	0.17 ± 0.02	Rejected

presented in Chapter 5 (Figure 5.25(a)). For large S both methods produce similar values as predicted by GPG. Furthermore, the nonlogarithmic growth rates cannot be fitted by a single power law and we observe a relatively sharp crossover at $s = s^* \approx 10$ ($S \approx$\$20,000) from a small $\beta \approx 0.06$ to large $\beta \approx 0.2$ for $s > 10$. In Table 4.10 we present the values of beta and the error analysis for bins of various sizes. We can see that the scaling hypothesis is not rejected for $s > 10$. Moreover, the values of β observed for different bin sizes are within the correspondent error bars. However, the scaling hypothesis for the entire range of firm sizes is rejected. Still, the constancy of β from very small firms $S \approx 20,000$ to the largest $S \approx \$30,000,000,000$, i.e, over six orders of magnitude, is even better than the GPG predicts for the reasonable values of the parameters. We will provide a possible explanation of constancy of $\beta(S)$ in Chapter 5.

To test the two-level aggregation hypothesis we investigate the behavior of $\sigma_r(\xi)$ for products. In the case of products the difference between the logarithmic and nonlogarithmic growth rates is even larger than in the case of firms. This suggests that if products consist of many units, these units are of larger sizes comparatively to the total than in the firms. For small products with sales $\xi < \$20,000$ the behavior of $\sigma_r(\xi)$ coincides with the behavior of $\sigma_r(S)$ for firms, which is expected because these firms consist of essentially one product. However, for larger products the behavior is very different and the universal scaling hypothesis is rejected. We see a short region with the slope $\beta \approx -0.16$, but for larger products the variance of growth rates stays almost constant. This behavior is very similar to the one predicted by GPG with a single aggregation level for a distribution of number of units $P(K)$ with small exponential cutoff and large V_ξ, as seen in Figure 3.24(a). An interpretation is that products consist of multiple fluctuating units, while the exponential cutoff, κ, of the distribution of their number is small comparatively to the logarithmic variance of their sizes: $\kappa < \exp(V_\xi)$.

Overall, we find that the data are in good agreement with the predictions of GPG.

Further Tests on the Size–Growth Relationship

As shown in the previous sections, selection and innovation both affect the size–growth relationship. Therefore, in this subsection, we study the relationship between size and growth, taking into account other relevant factors.

The relationship between firm size and growth performence has been extensively investigated in the literature (De Wit 2005; Coad 2009). In a nutshell, there is a general agreement on a negative size–growth relationship. Moreover, this relationship is not observed in samples of large firms. The predictions of GPG are consistent with these empirical findings.

In GPG, the expected growth rate for small sizes is computed as Equation (3.92):

$$m_{r'}(S) = \left(\lambda \frac{\exp(m_\xi + V_\xi/2)}{S} - \mu\right)\Delta t. \tag{4.3}$$

The results of the simulations presented in Figure 3.23(b) show significant departures from the generic flat relationship predicted by the *proportional* growth model. These departures are especially pronounced when K and S are small, since the increase in firm size due to innovation (i.e., the launch of new products) is clearly visible.

We use dynamic panel data estimation methods to test the dependence between growth and size in the PHID dataset (Wooldridge 2010; Greene 2012).[11] The test is carried out by estimating the parameters of the following equation:

$$\ln(S_{i,t}) - \ln(S_{i,t-1}) = g\ln(S_{i,t-1}) + \sum_{j=1}^{r} \alpha_j x_{j,i,t} + \mu_i + u_{i,t}, \tag{4.4}$$

where $S_{i,t}$ are firm annual sales, $x_{1,i,t} \ldots x_{r,i,t}$ is a set of explanatory variables, μ_i is a time-constant, firm-specific unobserved component, and $u_{i,t}$ is an idiosyncratic error. The coefficient g is the "Gibrat's coefficient": testing $g = 0$ corresponds to test independence between growth and size. Equation (4.4) can be rewritten as:

$$s_{i,t} = \tilde{g}s_{i,t-1} + \sum_{j=1}^{r} \alpha_j x_{j,i,t} + \mu_i + u_{i,t}, \tag{4.5}$$

where $\tilde{g} = 1 + g$, and $s_{i,t} = ln(S_{i,t})$. Equation (4.5) is equivalent to Equation (4.4), as well as testing for $\tilde{g} = 1$ is equivalent to testing for $g = 0$. The vector $x_{j,i,t}$

[11] See Morescalchi et al. (2019) for a more detailed description of the estimation methods employed here.

contains the following control variables: *age*, *entry*, *exit*, *molecule*, *diversification*, and *year dummies*. *Age* is calculated as the age of the firm's oldest product. *Entry* is defined as $k_{i,t}^{in}/k_{i,t-1}$, where $k_{i,t}^{in}$ is the number of new products marketed by the ith firm in year t; *exit* is defined as $k_{i,t}^{out}/k_{i,t-1}$, where $k_{i,t}^{out}$ is thc number of products lost in year t; *molecule* is a binary variable identifying firms that introduce new entities (innovative products based on new molecules) in their portfolio; *diversification* is the share of firm sales associated to the firm principal Anatomical Therapeutic Chemical (ATC) Classification[12] class.

We estimate Equation (4.5) by employing a first-difference generalized method of moments (Arellano and Bond 1991) to account for endogeneity.

Endogeneity arises when one or more explanatory variables are related to the error term, which in this case comprises a time-fixed effect (μ_i) and an idyosincratic component ($u_{i,t}$). Possible endogeneity arising by correlation with μ_i can be accommodated by removing μ_i from the estimand equation with an ad-hoc transformation of the data, such as the first-difference (FD). FD transformation is implemented by subtracting from both sides of Equation (4.5) the same components expressed in one-year lag, generating the following estimand equation:

$$\Delta s_{i,t} = \tilde{g}\Delta s_{i,t-1} + \sum_{j=1}^{r} \alpha_j \Delta x_{j,i,t} + \Delta u_{i,t}, \tag{4.6}$$

where μ_i is subtracted away. However, $\Delta s_{i,t-1}$ is necessarily correlated with $\Delta u_{i,t}$ and, hence, ordinary least square (OLS)[13] estimates of Equation (4.6) are biased. Equation (4.6) can be consistently estimated by a GMM model with instrumental variables (IV). IVs can identify the relation between $\Delta s_{i,t}$ and $\Delta s_{i,t-1}$ by capturing variation in $\Delta s_{i,t-1}$ that is unrelated to $\Delta u_{i,t}$. Natural IV candidates for $\Delta s_{i,t-1}$ are $\Delta s_{i,t-2}$, $\Delta x_{i,j,t-1}$ and further lags.[14]

Interactions between year dummies[15] and the inverse Mills ratio (IMR) are also included in $x_{j,i,t}$ to control for selection. The IMR is computed after estimating year-by-year probit models for firm selection (see Wooldridge 2010 for discussion a of selection and methods to correct for it).

In Table 4.11, we report FD-GMM estimates of the size–growth equation, either controlling or non-controlling for selection (see Moreschalchi et al. 2019 for additional evidence). We insert as explanatory variables: *age*, *entry*, *exit*,

[12] In the pharmaceutical industry, the ATC System is used for the classification of drug active ingredients. We construct the ATC-based explanatory variable considering the first four digits of the ATC code, which correspond to the third level of the classification and indicate the pharmacological subgroup of the drug.

[13] See Wooldridge (2010) and Greene (2012) for exhaustive explanation.

[14] The FD transformation is generally preferred in this set-up since longer lags of the transformed regressors remain orthogonal to the transformed error and hence they can be used as valid IVs.

[15] A dummy, also called indicator, is a variable that can assume value 1 or 0.

Table 4.11 *The relationship between firm size and growth. FD-2GMM estimates with correction for selection. Age is calculated as the age of the oldest product; $entry$ is the number of new products marketed by the $i-th$ firm in year t; $exit$ is the number of products lost in year t; $molecule$ is a binary variable identifying firms that introduce new molecules in its portfolio; diversification is the share of firm sales associated to the firm principal ATC class. Lags of explanatory variables are denoted with a numerical subscript reflecting the number of years ahead of the current year t. For each explanatory variable and for each model we report in the columun "Coeff" the estimated coefficient (** = Significant at 1%, * = significant at 5%) and the associated standard error computed by panel bootstrap (in brackets). The column "95% C.I." reports the lower bound and the upper bound of the 95% confidence interval for each estimated coefficient. Data source: PHID*

	FD-GMM			FD-GMM Attrition		
$\ln(sales)$	Coeff	95% C.I.		Coeff	95% C.I.	
$\ln(sales)_{-1}$	0.887** (0.045)	0.799	0.975	0.790** (0.068)	0.657	0.923
$\ln(age)$	−0.273** (0.070)	−0.410	−0.137	−0.155 (0.085)	−0.322	0.011
entry	0.146** (0.043)	0.062	0.230	0.148** (0.045)	0.059	0.236
$entry_{-1}$	0.081** (0.029)	0.025	0.138	0.075* (0.029)	0.017	0.132
exit	−0.270** (0.057)	−0.381	−0.158	−0.302** (0.054)	−0.408	−0.197
molecule	0.031** (0.011)	0.009	0.054	0.031* (0.013)	0.006	0.056
$molecule_{-1}$	0.066** (0.010)	0.046	0.087	0.061** (0.011)	0.039	0.083
$molecule_{-2}$	0.039** (0.009)	0.022	0.057	0.035** (0.010)	0.016	0.055
diversification	0.342** (0.106)	0.134	0.550	0.333** (0.111)	0.115	0.552
year dummies × IMR				✓		
year dummies	✓			✓		
Firms	2,262			2,262		
Observations	11,922			11,922		

molecule, *diversification*, and year dummies. Interactions between year dummies and the IMR are also included to control for selection (see Wooldridge 2010, for discussion on selection and methods to correct for it). Lags of explanatory variables are also included in $x_{j,i,t}$ if significant. They are denoted in Table 4.11 with a numerical subscript reflecting the number of years ahead of the current year t. Both FD-GMM models suggest that the Gibrat coefficient $\tilde{g}$ is significantly lower than 1, as indicated by the 95% confidence interval. This is equivalent to a significantly negative size effect in Equation (4.4), as captured by the coefficient g. The Gibrat hypothesis is, hence, rejected, supporting earlier evidence that small firms grow faster than large firms. Point estimates of the two models reported in Table 4.11 suggest that the departure from the Gibrat law becomes stronger when selection is controlled for. A test for the presence of a selection effect can be carried out by testing joint significance of coefficients of the interactions between year dummies and the IMR (see Wooldridge 2010). Since these coefficients turn out to be jointly significant, we can reject the null hypothesis that selection is absent. This implies that correction for selection is necessary and hence we select the FD-GMM model correcting for it as our best model. In this model, estimate of $\tilde{g}$ is equal to 0.79, corresponding to $g = -0.21$. This estimate implies that, ceteris paribus, if a firm is larger than another one by one percent sales, we expect that its logarithmic growth rate next year will be 0.21 percentage points smaller than the logarithmic growth rate of the smaller firm.

Coefficients of the other regressors used in our best model are plausible in sign and magnitude. Younger firms grow faster than old ones but the age coefficient is only close to significance, which is in line with GPG predictions. We note that the effect of age loses significance only after correcting for selection, consistently with the correlation between firm age and survival. The launch of new innovative products has a long-lasting positive effect on firm growth, with the strongest impact one year after launch. Furthermore, the rates of product inflow and outflow have a strong positive and negative impact on growth, respectively. The impact of inflows persists up to the first lag (year) though it becames smaller. Therefore, the negative growth-size relationship holds after controlling for selection bias.[16]

We now perform additional estimates to test the role of innovation in the size–growth relationship. Specifically, we apply our best model to the following three cases: (i) we remove the sales generated by new products entering the market in t; (ii) we consider the sample of firms that keep a constant number of products in the time frame; and (iii) we keep the complementary sample of dynamic firms that change their number of products in at least one year.

Table 4.12 reports estimates for the three cases. The FD-GMM estimates of $\tilde{g}$ after controlling for selection are 0.95, 0.95, and 0.73, respectively. Interestingly, we note that while the departure from Gibrat's law is even more remarkable for firms that do change their product portfolio, Gibrat's law does hold true for firms

[16] Several tests have been carried out to asses the validity of these results. Overall, the validity is supported (see Morescalchi et al. 2019).

Table 4.12 *The size–growth relationship for three groups of firms: all firms, but no new products; only firms with the same product portfolio; only firms with product turnover. Age is calculated as the age of the oldest product; entry is the number of new products marketed by the $i - th$ firm in year t; exit is the number of products lost in year t; molecule is a binary variable identifying firms that introduce new molecules in its portfolio; diversification is the share of firm sales associated to the firm principal ATC class. Lags of explanatory variables are denoted with a numerical subscript reflecting the number of years ahead of the current year t. For each explanatory variable and for each model we report in the columun "Coeff" the estimated coefficient (** = Significant at 1%, * = significant at 5%) and the associated standard error computed by panel bootstrap (in brackets). The column "95% C.I." reports the lower bound and the upper bound of the 95% confidence interval for each estimated coefficient. Data source: PHID*

	All Firms but no new products			Only firms without product flow			Only firm with product flow		
	FD-GMM Selection			FD-GMM Selection			FD-GMM Selection		
ln(sales)	Coeff	95% C.I.		Coeff	95% C.I.		Coeff	95% C.I.	
$ln(sales)_{-1}$	0.942***	0.737	1.147	0.947**	0.661	1.234	0.725**	0.583	0.867
	(0.105)			(0.146)			(0.072)		
ln(age)	−0.541***	−0.874	−0.205	−0.307	−0.658	0.045	0.045	−0.160	0.250
	(0.102)			(0.179)			(0.104)		
entry	0.106	−0.029	0.051				0.147**	0.048	0.245
	(0.021)						(0.050)		
$entry_{-1}$	−0.015	−0.059	0.276				0.060*	0.007	0.113
	(0.022)						(0.027)		
exit	−0.062	−0.185	0.060				−0.275**	−0.385	−0.165
	(0.063)						(0.056)		
molecule	−0.011	−0.033	0.010				0.026*	0.001	0.052
	(0.011)						(0.013)		
$molecule_{-1}$	−0.009	−0.033	0.0.16				0.066**	0.043	0.088
	(0.012)						(0.011)		
$molecule_{-2}$	−0.003	−0.033	0.016				0.035**	0.015	0.055
	(−0.003)						(0.010)		
diversification	0.512***	0.2157	0.808	0.589	−0.138	1.316	0.269*	0.042	0.495
	(0.151)			(0.371)			(0.116)		
year dummies × IMR		✓			✓			✓	
year dummies		✓			✓			✓	
firms		1,598			600			1,662	
observations		7,707			2,951			8,821	

with a stable number of products as $\tilde{g}$ is not statistically different from 1.[17] The main message we can draw from our estimates is that changes in the number of products is the main driver of the observed departures from Gibrat's law to hold. The law holds once we remove the contribution of product turnover, in line with the predictions of our framework.

4.4 Conclusions

In this chapter, we have tested the predictions of GPG with respect to the Stylized Facts (I–IV) presented in Chapter 1.

The hypothesis that the distribution of firm sizes is lognormal is rejected for all the datasets that we have analyzed. We have found size distributions with different ranges of a power law behavior, with exponents τ in agreement with GPG, which predicts that the range of a power law behavior for firm size distributions increases over time, while its slope depends on the rate of entry of new firms.

We then compared the shape of the growth rate distribution of firms against several theoretical predictions, such as normal, Laplace, and several alternatives proposed in Chapter 3. Our empirical tests have shown that the best fit for the distribution of growth rates is achieved in the case described by Equation (3.114), which was derived for the GPG with two levels of aggregation.

Our findings do not falsify the proposition according to which the standard deviation of growth rates $\sigma_r(S)$ decreases with S slower than $S^{-1/2}$, being approximated by a power law dependence $\sigma_r(S) \sim S^{-\beta(S)}$ where $\beta(S)$ exhibits a crossover from a small value $\beta(S) \approx -0.06$ for small S to $\beta(S) \approx -0.24$ for large S, in agreement with GPG predictions.

Finally, we have shown that the average growth rate decreases with firm size, after having controlled for the sample bias associated with the lower survival rate of small firms. We also found that innovation is crucial to explain departures from Gibrat's Law.

[17] Diagnostic tests support the validity of the three econometric models (see Morescalchi et al. 2019).

5

Testing Our Assumptions

In this chapter, we test the realism of the assumptions of our framework. We exploit the features of PHID, which decomposes the size of business firms into the number and the sizes of their products, considered here as the constituent units of the firm. The notion of units is the key ingredient of the GPG model, which is embedded in Assumptions (1–7) introduced in Chapter 3. In PHID, products are drugs that we treat as independent business opportunities within firms. PHID also contains information on the sales of packs which are the subunits of products.

5.1 Testing Assumptions (1–4)

The two key sets of assumptions of our framework (see Section 3.2) imply that the number of units in a firm grows in proportion to the existing number of units (Assumptions (1–4)), while the size of each unit fluctuates in proportion to its size (Assumptions (5–7)). In particular, Assumption (1) postulates that firms consist of units. Here, we assume that products in PHID correspond to the units of GPG introduced by Assumption (1). Since Assumption (1) is postulated, we first study the validity of Assumptions (2) and (3).

Time Dependence of λ and μ

Figure 5.1 shows how the total number of firms, $N(t)$, the total number of products, $n(t)$, and total sales, $S(t)$, evolved over a period of 10 years.[1] One can see that the number of firms slightly decreases over time, and that the total number of products is almost constant, while the total sales grow at an accelerating rate. In principle, the fluctuations in the number of products observed in Figure 5.1 can be consistent

[1] Here, we count only the products and firms that have positive sales, ignoring all negative database entries, which occasionally occur in the database.

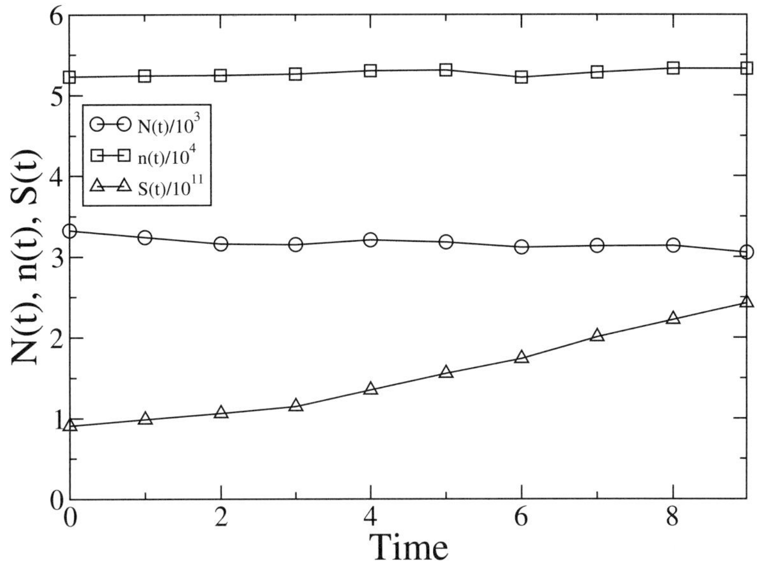

Figure 5.1 The behavior of the total number of firms $N(t)$, the total number of products $n(t)$ and the total sales $S(t)$ in US dollars at the industry level for the pharmaceutical industry as a function of time, measured in years. The average number of products produced by a firm, $\langle K \rangle$, is approximately 17 and does not significantly change with time. Data source: PHID

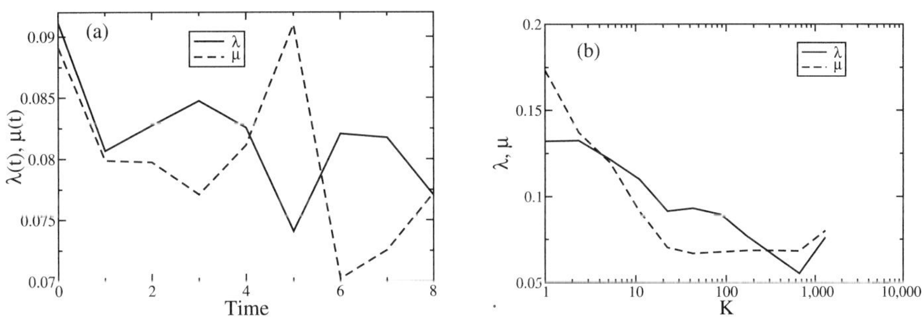

Figure 5.2 (a) The behavior of λ and μ as a function of time. (b) The behavior of λ and μ as functions of the number of products, K, in a firm. The average values are $\langle \lambda \rangle = 0.82$, $\langle \mu \rangle = 0.78$. Data source: PHID

with Assumptions (2) and (3); therefore, the data must be explored in greater detail in order to detect possible violations of the assumptions.

Figure 5.2(a) shows the dependence of the birth rate of products, λ, and the death rate of products, μ, on time. One can see that the average value of $\langle \lambda \rangle = 0.082$ is slightly greater than that of $\langle \mu \rangle = 0.078$, contradicting the equilibrium assumption of Klette and Kortum (2004) that $\mu > \lambda$. By using the elementary statistical error theory regarding the standard deviation of the average of n independent random variables (Feller 1968), given that $n(t) \approx 5.3 \times 10^5$, one can expect that relative fluctuations of the annual estimates of λ and μ are of the order $1/\sqrt{n\lambda} \approx 1/\sqrt{n\mu} \approx 0.015$, if λ and μ are time independent. In PHID, relative fluctuations are about 0.06 for λ and 0.09 for μ, showing that λ and μ are not time-independent. Nevertheless, these departures do not alter significantly the predictions of the GPG, since the parameter α can be expressed in terms of the total number of new products, n_λ, and total number of products, n_μ, which exited, as shown in Equation (3.15). Simulations with λ and μ confirm this theoretical conclusion. In order to model a system with variable λ, μ and ν, we assume that $\lambda = \lambda_0 + \Delta_\lambda(t)$, $\mu = \mu_0 + \Delta_\mu(t)$ and $\nu = \nu_0 + \Delta_\nu(t)$, where $\Delta_\lambda(t)$, $\Delta_\mu(t)$ and $\Delta_\nu(t)$ are arbitrary functions of time, such that their time averages over the growth period are equal to zero. As an example, we perform simulations with harmonic functions $\Delta_x(t) = a_x \cos(\omega_x t + \phi_x)$, where $x = \lambda, \mu, \nu$ with different amplitudes, a_x, frequencies, ω_x, and phases, ϕ_x, as explained by Darwin (1953). We find that if these amplitudes are less than, or equal to the average values of the corresponding parameters and $\lambda_0 + \nu_0 > \mu_0$, then the results of the simulations with variable parameters are within the error bars expected from the simulations with static parameters, in which $a_x = 0$ (Figure 5.3).

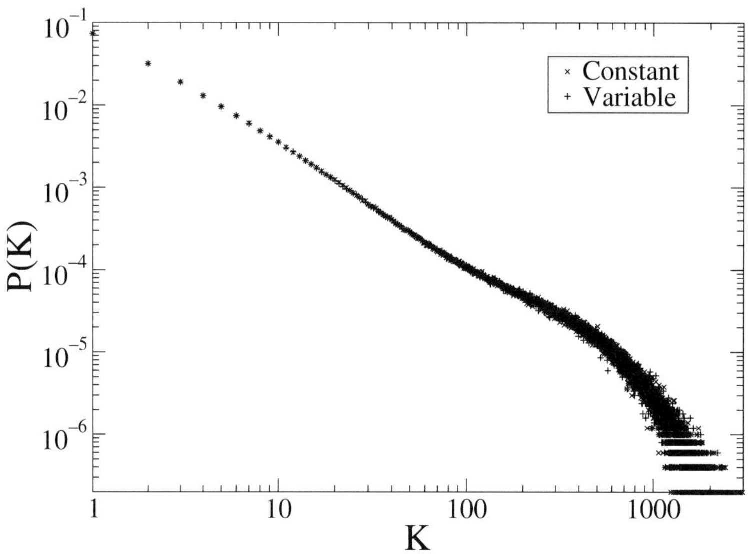

Figure 5.3 Comparison of a simulated distribution of the number of products in a firm with constants $\lambda = 0.1$, $\mu = 0.09$, and $\nu = 0.001$, and a simulated distribution with variable $\lambda(t) = 0.1[1 + \cos(2\pi t/10{,}000)]$, $\mu(t) = 0.09[1 - \cos(2\pi t/10{,}000)]$ and $\nu(t) = 0.001[1 + \cos(2\pi t/1000)]$. In both simulations, $n_\lambda(t) = 400{,}000$, $n_\mu = 360{,}000$, $n_0 = 1{,}000$, and $N_0 = 1{,}000$. Initially, all firms consist of one product, while all the new firms sell one product. Data source: simulations

Dependence of λ and μ on K

Figure 5.2(b) shows the dependence of λ and μ on the number of products in a firm, K. Again, the assumption of independence of λ and μ from K is not supported by empirical evidence. As mentioned in Section 3.6, these departures can be taken into account theoretically by the Sutton model and via simulation. If, according to Equations (3.106) and (3.107), $\lambda(K) = \lambda(1 - p_\lambda + p_\lambda\langle K\rangle/K)$ and $\mu(K) = \mu(1 - p_\mu + p_\mu\langle K\rangle/K)$, then large p_λ and p_μ reduce the number of firms with a small number of products and, consequently, improve the tent-shaped form of the growth rate distribution. However, fitting the observed dependence of $\lambda(K)$ and $\mu(K)$ (Figure 5.2(b)), using Equations (3.106) and (3.107), yields p_λ and p_μ to be less than 0.01. This small number is due to the large average number of products in a firm, $\langle K\rangle \approx 17$. Hence, the observed dependency of λ and μ on K is not sufficient to produce any observable change in the shape of the distribution of the number of products in a firm, P_K.

Testing Assumption (4)

We now test the validity of Assumption (4) on entry of new firms and on the absence of a similar assumption on exit. Figure 5.4 shows the dependence of ν and ν' on time. We find that, on average, new firms consist of $\langle k'\rangle = 1.68$ products. Our assumptions do not include the exit of firms with a large number of products. To characterize this departure, we compute χ as the number of products, Δ_χ, per unit of time, Δt, in the firms which exit from t to $t+\Delta t$ divided by the total number of products $n(t)$ at time t. We also calculate χ', which represents the number of firms, Δ'_χ, per unit of time, which disappear during the same time interval, divided by $n(t)$:

$$\chi = \frac{\Delta_\chi}{n(t)\Delta t}, \tag{5.1}$$

$$\chi' = \frac{\Delta'_\chi}{n(t)\Delta t}. \tag{5.2}$$

Figure 5.4 shows that we cannot neglect the possibility of the firm exit, since the parameters χ' and χ are comparable in order of magnitude with ν and ν'. Obviously, $\chi = \langle k'\rangle_\chi \chi'$, where $\langle k'\rangle_\chi \approx 1.3$ is the average number of products in the exiting firm. If firm exit is solely due to the loss of all the products via Assumption (3), $\chi \approx \chi' \approx \mu P_1 N(t)/n(t) \approx 0.0019$, where $P_1 = 0.3788$ is the fraction of firms with one product, while in reality $\chi = 1.3\chi' \approx 0.0063$, i.e., three times greater than expected.

Note that new as well as dying firms do not always consist of one product, but have a power law distribution of products $P(K) \sim K^{-\gamma}$ with $\gamma = 3$ (Figure 5.5).

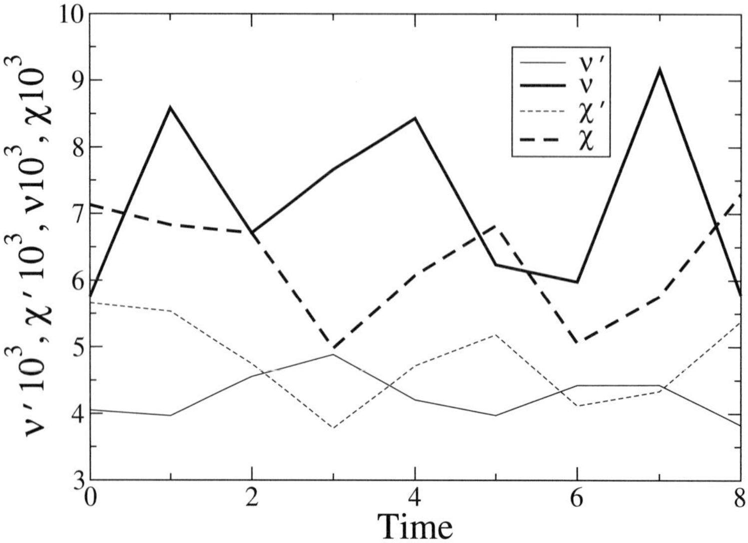

Figure 5.4 The dependence of ν and ν', as well as χ and χ', on time. Data source: PHID

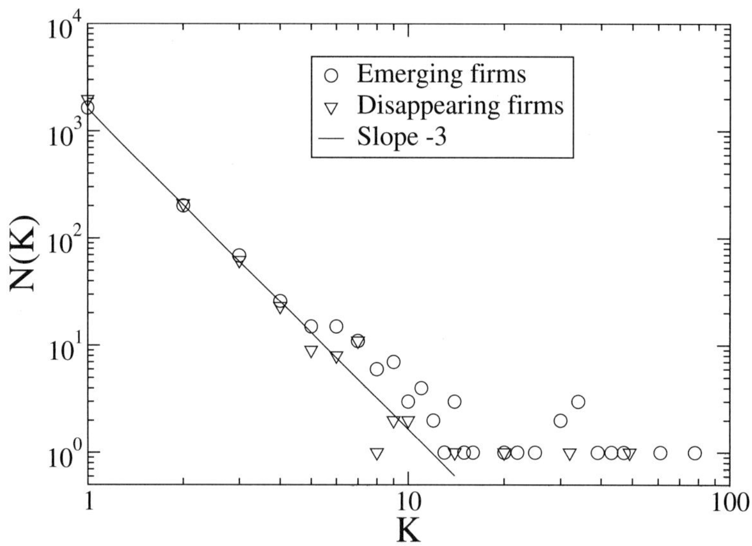

Figure 5.5 Distributions of the number of products in new and exiting firms. Data source: PHID

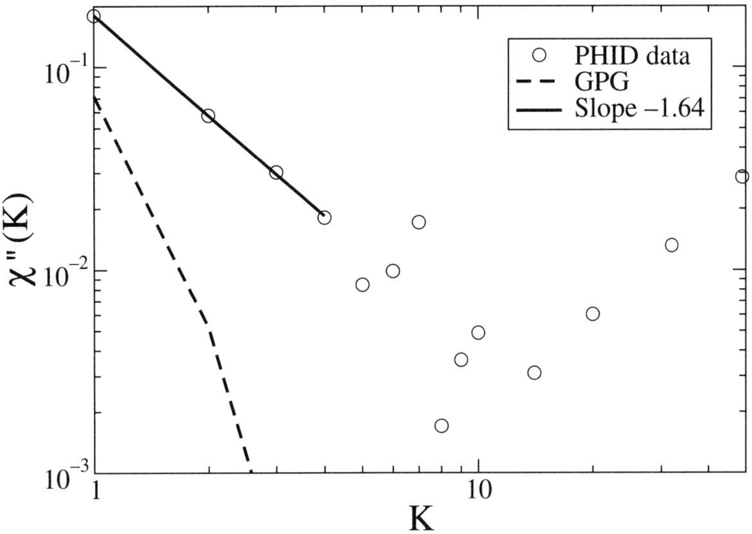

Figure 5.6 Comparison of the empirical exit probability of a firm with K products with the predictions of the GPG. Data source: PHID

We can also consider the probability $\chi''(K)$ of a firm with K products at time t exiting at time $t + 1$. Our framework predicts that

$$\chi''(K) = \left(\frac{(R-1)\alpha}{R-\alpha} \right)^K, \tag{5.3}$$

where $R = \exp[(\lambda - \mu)\Delta t]$ is the growth of the number of products in a time period Δt. Thus, for $\Delta t = 1$, $\chi''(K)$ must decrease exponentially with the number of products as 0.072^K. However, our empirical analysis (Figure 5.6) suggests that $\chi''(K)$ decreases as a power law, with rare events corresponding to the death of firms with more than one product.

In principle, we can explicitly simulate the exit of firms by adding to our framework the deletion of randomly selected firms with a probability depending on the number of products. This complication would make the model too complex to be solved analytically. The question is, then, can we implicitly take into account the exit of firms within our framework? Interestingly, the number of firms created per time unit, and the number of firms deleted from the market per time unit are almost exactly the same. This case can be modeled assuming that some of the new firms are continuations, under a new name, of firms which existed in the industry. To take this into account within the GPG framework, we can decrease the rate of introduction of new firms ν and ν'. We should also alternate the distribution of the number of products in the new firms, P'_K, and adjust the values of λ and μ,

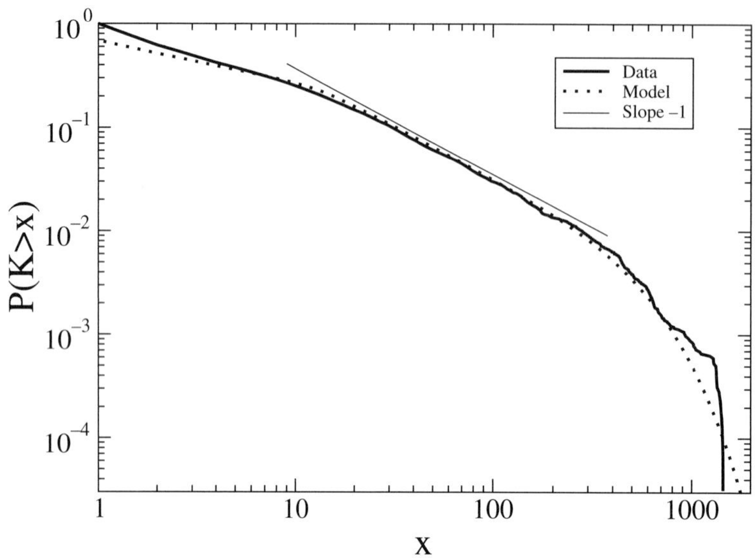

Figure 5.7 Fitting the cumulative distribution of the number of products in pharmaceutical firms with the prediction of the GPG, assuming that λ and μ are independent of K. The justification of the parameters is presented in the main text: $\lambda = 0.0793$, $\mu = 0.0739$, $\nu' = 0.00112$, $P_1(0) = 1$, $N(0) = 20$, $P_1' = 10/11$, $P_{15}' = 1/11$ and $t = 200,000$. Data source: PHID

to keep the overall growth of the industry unchanged. Indeed, the detailed analysis of the databases show that we can take into account the death of large firms by selecting $\mu = 0.0739$, $\lambda = 0.0793$, $\nu' = 0.00112$, $\nu = 0.00254$, $P_1' = 0.9094$, and $P_{15}' = 0.0906$.

If we want to compute P_K for the model, we must know the initial number of units in firms and their evolution in time. These numbers cannot be found in our data, but they can be assumed such that they would result in a certain number of products at the present day. Figure 5.7 shows the fit of the cumulative distribution of the number of products in firms, using the parameters discussed earlier in the chapter. We use $t = 200,000$, and we assume that in the beginning there were 20 "firms," each producing one product. Although these numbers are, to a certain extent, arbitrary, they are consistent with the fact that the industry existed since many decades. Also, in simuations we use the avarage values of λ, μ, and ν corresponding to the time period covered by PHID. In the past, those values could be much higher. To take this into account we can use instead the total numbers of products added and deleted since the start of the industry: $n_\lambda(t)$, $n_\nu(t)$, and $n_\mu(t)$, and the true evolution time t as in Equations (3.19)–(3.28), which can be much smaller than the simulation time, τ, obtained by fitting based on constant values of λ, μ, and ν.

The right tail of the graph of P_K in Fig. (5.7) is well reproduced by fit. However, we can see that the model underestimates the number of firms with a few products. This departure cannot be accounted for by the fact that λ and μ depend on K, because, as we have shown in the previous subsection, this dependence is not sufficient to explain a significant departure in P_K. Moreover, such a dependence would only further reduce the number of small firms with a few products. Thus, the departure is more likely to be accounted for by the excessive simplification[2] according to which $P'_K = 0$ for $1 < K < 15$, which we introduce when we simulate P_K in Figure 5.7.

In conclusion, Assumptions (1–4), although not entirely realistic, account for the observed P_K with reasonable accuracy. Modifications to GPG can be introduced to adjust for the dependence of the parameters λ, μ, and ν on t and K, as well as by taking into account the fact that firms with many products can exit due to mergers or bankruptcy.

5.2 Testing Assumptions (5) and (7)

We now turn to Assumptions (5–7), integrating the statistical analysis already performed in Chapter 4. Although in Assumption (5) we do not explicitly state the functional form of the distribution of unit sizes, P_ξ, our analytical calculations in Chapter 3 are made for a lognormal P_ξ. The theoretical plausibility of the lognormality of P_ξ stems from Assumption (6), which states that unit sizes change over time according to Gibrat's Law.

Figure 5.8 shows the distribution of the logarithm of sales of products and firms. At a visual inspection, the distribution of product sizes does not look like a lognormal distribution, but rather like an exponential mixture of log-normal distributions, given by Equation (3.69), which is characterized by a lognormal right tail fit with $m_\xi = 11.05$ and $V_\xi = 7.17$, while $\mathrm{E}(\xi) = 10.26$, $\mathrm{Var}(\xi) = 11.10$. The right tail of the firm size distribution can be approximated by a power law $P(S) \sim S^{-1.53}$, with an exponential cutoff.

To further test the behavior of the right tail of the distribution of product sizes, we compute the cumulative distribution of product sizes and attempt to fit it with the lognormal distribution:

$$P(\ln(\xi) > x) = \frac{1}{2}\mathrm{erfc}\left[\frac{(x - m_\xi)}{\sqrt{2V_\xi}}\right], \tag{5.4}$$

where $\mathrm{erfc}(x)$ is the complementary error function (Figure 5.9). It is clear that the right tail is poorly fitted by the lognormal distribution with $m_\xi = 10.28$, $V_\xi = 11.1$

[2] We use this simplified assumption due to the impracticability of fitting the data using 15 arbitrary parameters for P'_K.

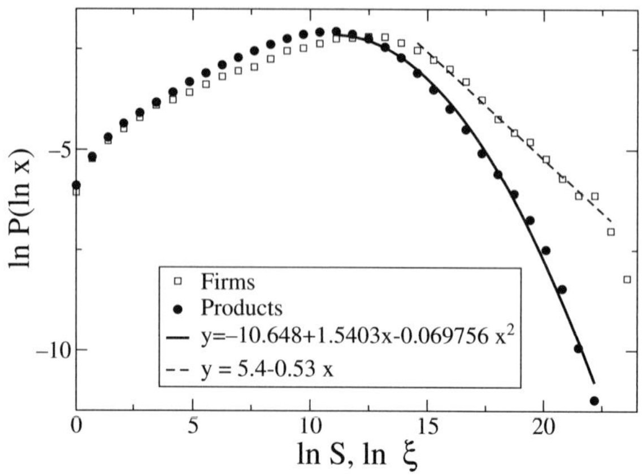

Figure 5.8 The distributions of the logarithm of products and firm sizes. Data source: PHID

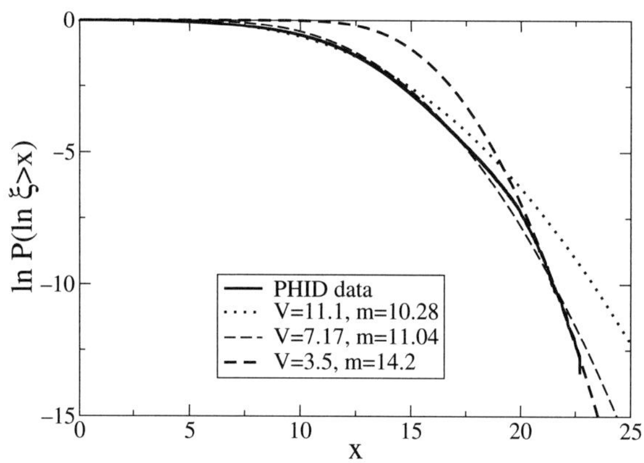

Figure 5.9 The cumulative distribution of products sales in a double logarithmic scale together with lognormal fits with various parameters. Data source: PHID

taken from averaging $\ln \xi$. The fit improves when the parameters are taken from the Gaussian fit $m_\xi = 11.05$, $V_\xi = 7.17$ obtained from Figure 5.8, but, still, the number of large products is overestimated. The best fit for the right tail can be obtained with $V_\xi = 3.0$, $m_\xi = 14.2$. This very small value of V_ξ for the right tail accounts for the observed behavior of the H-index. As a consequence, simulations of the size-variance relationship with the empirical P_ξ show a much better agreement with the data. In particular, these simulations do not suffer from the spurious increase of σ_r for large firms, which has been shown in Figure 3.15(b).

In conclusion, the product size distribution cannot be represented by a lognormal distribution. In fact, the right tail of the distribution decreases faster than the right

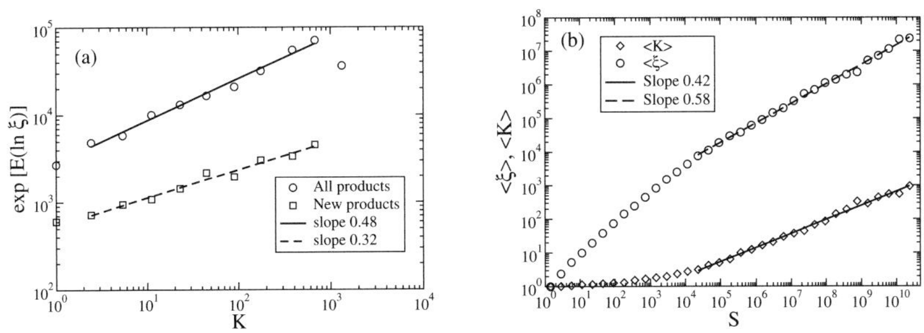

Figure 5.10 (a) The dependence of the average logarithmic product size on the number of products in a firm. Also shown, the average logarithmic size of a new product, added to a firm with K products. (b) The dependence of average number of products $\langle K \rangle(S)$ and the product size $\langle \xi \rangle(S)$ on the firm size, S. The product of these two quantities is exactly S. Data source: PHID

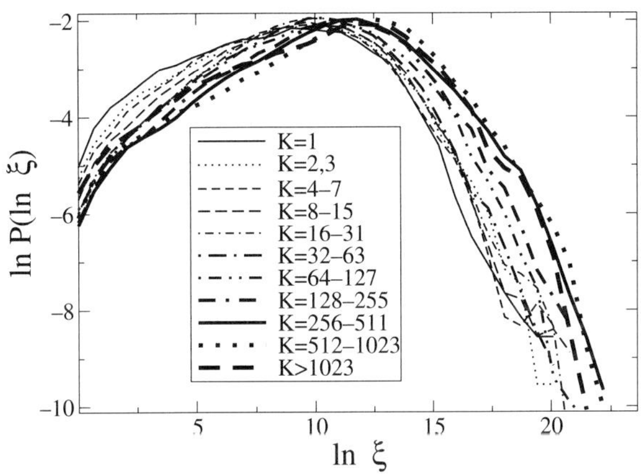

Figure 5.11 The distributions of product sizes for companies with a different number of products. Data source: PHID

tail of the lognormal distribution obtained using the same logarithmic mean and variance. We can expect that simulations of firm growth with observed P_ξ would produce a much better agreement with empirical data.

Another important part of Assumption (5) is the independence of P_ξ from the number of products per firm. Figure 5.10(a) shows the behavior of the average logarithm of product size with respect to the number of products in a firm which violates the assumption of the independence of ξ and K. Moreover, the distribution of product sizes for firms with K products (Figure 5.11) becomes broader and its maximum shifts to the right, in violation of Assumption (5) of the model. This behavior may have an important implication on the emergence of the size-variance relationship. Indeed, since there are positive correlations between $\langle \xi \rangle$ and the number of units K, which can be approximated by a power law (Fig. 5.10 (a)), we can expect that, both the average size of a product and the average number of products must depend as power laws on firm size:[3]

$$\langle \xi \rangle \sim S^{\delta}, \quad (5.5)$$

$$\langle K \rangle \sim S^{1-\delta} \quad (5.6)$$

Indeed, as we can see from Figure 5.10(b) for large S >\$22,000, $\delta \approx 0.58$. The relations of Equation (5.5) and Equation (5.6) were first proposed in (Amaral et al. 1998). Since, for independent growth rates of products, one would expect $\sigma_r \sim K^{-1/2}$ for $K \to \infty$. using Equation (5.6) we get

$$\sigma_r \sim S^{(1-\delta)/2} = S^{-0.21} \quad (5.7)$$

for $S \to \infty$ in perfect agreement with the results of Chapter 4. Also, this behavior partially explains the difference in the exponents characterizing the distribution of firms in terms of number of products (Figure 5.7), which yields $P(K > k) \sim k^{-\tau_K+1}$ in the intermediate range of K and sales (Figure 5.8), which predicts $\ln[P(\ln(S))] \sim \ln(S)(-\tau_S + 1)$ for large S, where $\tau_K \approx 2$, while $\tau_S \approx 1.53$. Using Equation (5.6) we can employ the relationship between the PDFs of two variables $P(S)ds = P(K)dK$ to relate τ_S and τ_K

$$\tau_S = \tau_K(1 - \delta) + \delta \approx 1.42, \quad (5.8)$$

which coincides with the observed value 1.53 within 10%. This discrepancy can be attributed to deviations of observed relationships from exact power laws.

The dependence of product size on the number of units in a firm might provide an example of nontrivial decision-making processes by company management, which is not captured by our simplified stochastic framework. Indeed, this departure deserves a detailed investigation that is beyond the scope of this book.

Assumption (7) states that the sizes of new products are drawn from a distribution that is identical to the distribution of already existing products. Analogously, in our simulations, we assume the independence of the rate of product removal from product size. Figure 5.12 shows the distribution of the logarithm of sales of all products; stable products (existing during all years covered in the database; new products; and exiting products. New products tend to be smaller than stable products, while exiting products are even smaller. Moreover, the distribution of stable products lacks the fat left tail of small products observed in the distribution of all products.

[3] The exponents describing the behavior of $\langle \xi \rangle | K$ and $\langle K \rangle | S$ do not obey standard algebra, because K and ξ are both random variables with some joint distribution $P(K, \xi)$. For example, if $P(X, Y)$ is a double lognormal distribution, defined by the exponent of the quadratic form $A \ln^2 X + 2B \ln X \ln Y + C \ln^2 Y$, then $\langle Y \rangle | X \sim X^p$, and $\langle X \rangle | Y \sim Y^q$, where $p = -B/C$ while $q = -B/A$, which obey standard relation $pq = 1$ only if $AC = B^2$, i.e. when the quadratic form degenerates into a complete square $(\sqrt{A} \ln X \pm \sqrt{C} \ln Y)^2$.

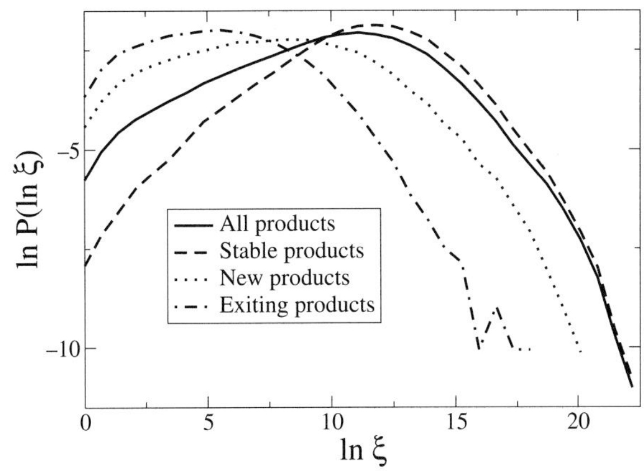

Figure 5.12 The distribution of the logarithms of product sales with different history: all products, new products, exiting products, and stable products. Data source: PHID

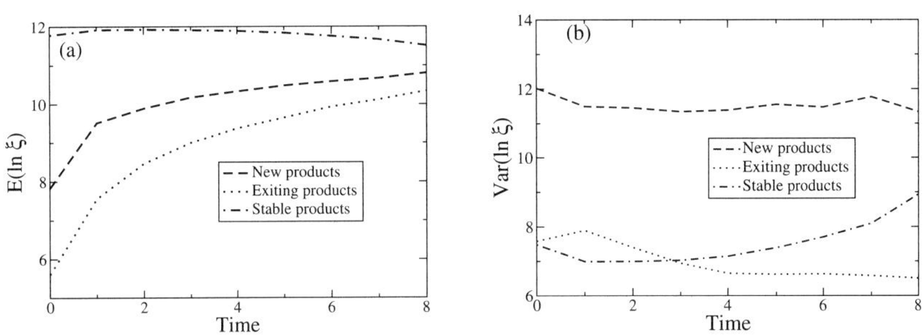

Figure 5.13 (a) The dependence of the mean logarithm of new and exiting products on time from their launch or exit in comparison to stable products. (b) The time-dependence of the variance of the same quantities. Data source: PHID

This finding is confirmed by the study of $\mathbb{E}[\ln \xi(t)]$ and $\mathrm{Var}[\ln \xi(t)]$ as a function of the age of a new product and the number of years before its exit from the market. Figure 5.13, shows that new products, indeed, have a tendency to grow. In contrast, products, that will exit from the market have a tendency to shrink long before their last year of life. Thus, the probability of product exit is obviously not independent of the sales of the product, as postulated in Assumption (3). Figure 5.14(a) shows the probability that a product or a firm survives for more than t years from launch. According to Assumption (3), this probability should be linear on a semi logarithmic scale, with an average slope of approximately $\mu = -0.08$. Indeed, the graph is almost linear but the average slope is -0.1, confirming that young products are less stable than old ones.

It is interesting to note that the probability to exit during the first year after launch is higher than in subsequent years. It is also remarkable that new firms, in the time frame covered by the database, are less stable than products launched by large firms. This findings is not surprising, since the majority of new entrant firms rely on a single product, which tends to be smaller than the new products launched by large and established companies. The slope of the survival probability for firms is -0.15. If we assume that all firms die with equal probability, independently of their age, this slope must be $-\langle K \rangle \chi' \approx -0.08$, which is approximately two times smaller. This fact confirms that established firms are much more stable than new ones. GPG supports this prediction since, in the model, the firms that survive longer, on average, have more products and, hence, they are less likely to exit. Within the GPG framework, it can be shown analytically that in the simplest case, when each new firm has a single product, the survival probability of firms (see Chapter 7, Appendix 7.1) is

$$P_s(t) = \frac{\exp[(\lambda - \mu)t](1 - \alpha)}{\exp[(\lambda - \mu)t] - \alpha}. \tag{5.9}$$

The derivative of the logarithm of this function monotonically approaches zero for $t \to \infty$. Of course, this simple formula does not take into account neither the dependence of λ and μ on K, nor the fact that new firms may have more than one product. However, the function qualitatively captures the behavior of the survival probability of firms. The fact that the survival probability of the products follows the same pattern suggests that products are also complex objects consisting of elementary units.

The entry of new products and the exit of old products are governed by different rules (Figure 5.14(b)). The products launched during the first year covered in the database and that survive for the next nine years reach their limiting average size within the first two years after their launch. In contrast, the average logarithmic size of the products that exit during the last year covered by the database begin to shrink long before their exit. Obviously here we observe a violation of Assumption (6), namely the independence of growth rates on product age. Another problem is the violation of Assumption (7), which postulates that the average size of a new product is equal to the average size of products already in the market. These violations are caused by the fact that in our parsimonious framework, we did not control for product life cycles. Nevertheless, the quick growth of new products to reach their stable size suggests that the launch of new products is adequately taken into account by GPG. In contrast, product exit is a gradual process.

It is interesting to compute the dependence of the rate of product removal, μ, on product size, ξ, (Figure 5.15). Assumption (3) implies that μ is independent of product size and that each product exit with equal probability. In reality, the

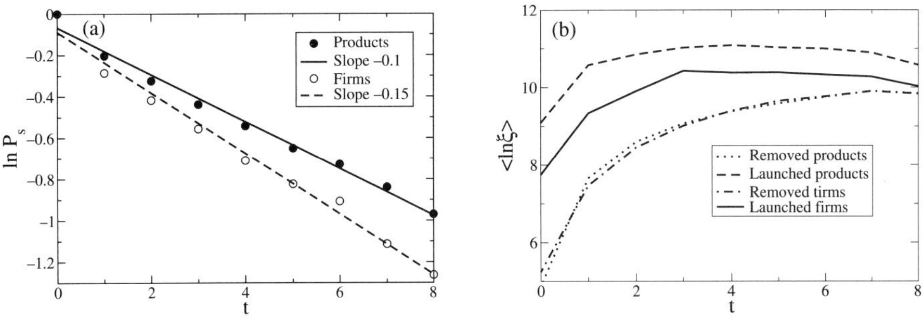

Figure 5.14 (a) The dependence of the logarithm of the survival probability of products and firms as a function of time elapsed since their entry. (b) The average logarithmic product/firm size as function of time after their entry in comparison to the average logarithmic product size of the product/firm removed from the market as a function of time prior to its removal. Here, we take into account only the long-standing products/firms which survive for nine years after entry or nine years prior to exit. Data source: PHID

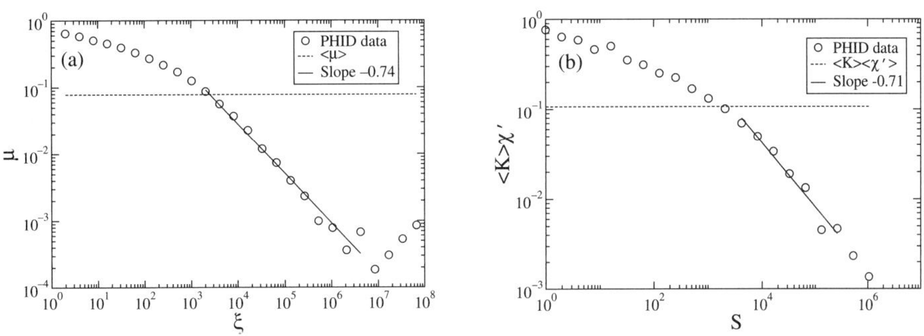

Figure 5.15 (a) The dependence of the probability of a product of size ξ to exit during the following year. (b) The dependence of the probability of a firm with sales S to exit during the following year. This probability is related to the rate of the firm exit, χ', presented in Figure 5.4. Since χ' is normalized by the total number of products, $n(t)$, but the probability of firm exit is normalized by the number of firms, $N(t)$, the probability of firm exit is equal to $\chi'\langle K\rangle$, where $\langle K\rangle$ is the average number of products in a firm. Data source: PHID

probability for a product to exit dramatically decreases with the product sales. For large sales it can be approximated by an negative power law.

The behavior of new and exiting firms follows a process analogous to the one observed for products. The behavior of exiting firms closely follows the behavior of the exiting products. This result is not surprising, given the structure of our data base, which does not consider mergers and acquisitions, reporting both firms before a merger under the name acquired at merger. Figure 5.15, which does not consider mergers and acquisitions, indicates that the sales of exiting firms never

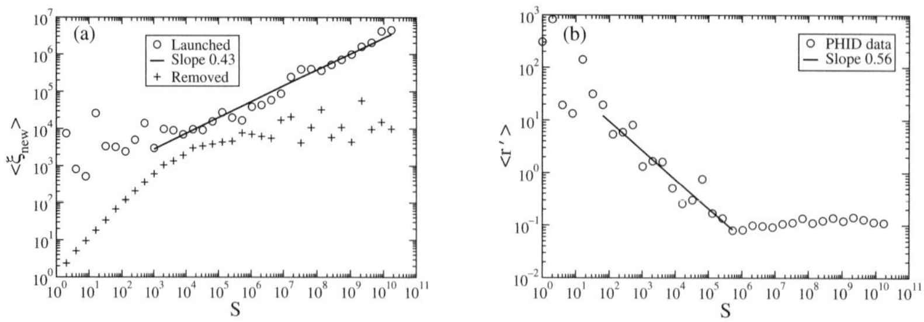

Figure 5.16 (a) The dependence of the average sales of new products and the exit products on firm size. The averages size of products that exit is always much smaller than the average size of new products. The slope on the graph indicates exponent δ' of Equation (5.10). (b) The average non-logarithmic growth rate of firms as a function of their sales. The slope of the graph, –0.56, coincides with $\delta' - 1$. A crossover point, $S = S_M \approx 10^6$, above which the average growth rate is almost constant, is clearly visible. Data source: PHID

exceed 2 million dollars. In a nutshell, the absence of a random deletion of firms in GPG, symmetric to Assumption (4), is not falsified by the data.

Another important component of Assumption (7) is the independence of the new products from firm size. Figure 5.16(a) shows the dependence of the average sales of the new products on the total sales of the firm. This figure also shows the average size of the products that exited as a function of firm sales. The sales of a new product depend on the sales of the firm as a power law with an exponent $\delta' = 0.43$:

$$\langle \xi_{new} \rangle = aS^{\delta'}, \tag{5.10}$$

where $a \approx 146$. This behavior only weakly violates Assumption (7), but it has important implications for the dependence of the average growth rate on the size of the firm due to the entry of new products. Indeed, if we neglect the effect of deleting the products (their average sales are much smaller than the average sales of the new products [Figure 5.16(a)]) the average firm size at time $t+1$ is given by $S(t+1) = S(t)\eta + \lambda\langle \xi_{new} \rangle$, where η is the average Gibrat variable of Assumption (6). Hence, the average non-logarithmic growth rate $r'(S) = S(t+1)/S(t) - 1 = a\lambda S^{\delta'-1} + \eta - 1$. Thus, if $S < S_M \equiv [(\eta - 1)/(a\lambda)]^{1/(\delta'-1)}$, then the average growth rate for small $S < S_M$

$$\langle r' \rangle(S) \sim S^{\delta'-1} \sim S^{-0.58}. \tag{5.11}$$

For $S > S_M$, we have $\langle r' \rangle(S) = \eta - 1$ (see Figure 5.16(b)). Considerations analogous to those leading to Equation (3.105) show that for $S \to 0$

$$\sigma_{r'} \approx S^{\delta'-1}. \tag{5.12}$$

Note that these findings differ from the predictions of the GPG which assumes independence of ξ_{new} and S, and thus predict $\langle r' \rangle(S) \sim S^{-1}$ and $\sigma_{r'} \approx S^{-1}$ for $S \to 0$.

Unfortunately, the duration of our records (10 years) does not allow us to fully investigate the life cycle of products. Moreover, the features of the distribution of new, exiting, and stable products are industry specific (Argente et al. 2018). However, GPG reproduces very well the dependence of the average growth rate of firms on their size and other stylized facts related to the growth rates of the firm. Further investigations can show how the life cycle of business units and products affects the rise and fall of the firms.

We now analyze the concentration and inequality of products and firms. We compute the Gini index for PHID (Figure 5.17). Based on the number of products in a firm, K, $G_K = 0.81$, while based on the total sales of a firm $G_S = 0.98$. The Gini coefficient based on product sales, ξ, is $G_\xi = 0.96$, increasing from 0.949 in year zero to 0.966 in year nine. If we consider the Gini index for the lognormal distribution, we conclude that effective V_ξ increases from roughly 7.5 in year zero to 9.0 in year nine. This means that products size concentration grows in time. Competition and the high number of independent submarkets, that characterize the pharmaceutical industry, act as a stabilizing factor so that concentration among firms remains almost constant in time, while being dominated by product size concentration (see also Sutton 1998).

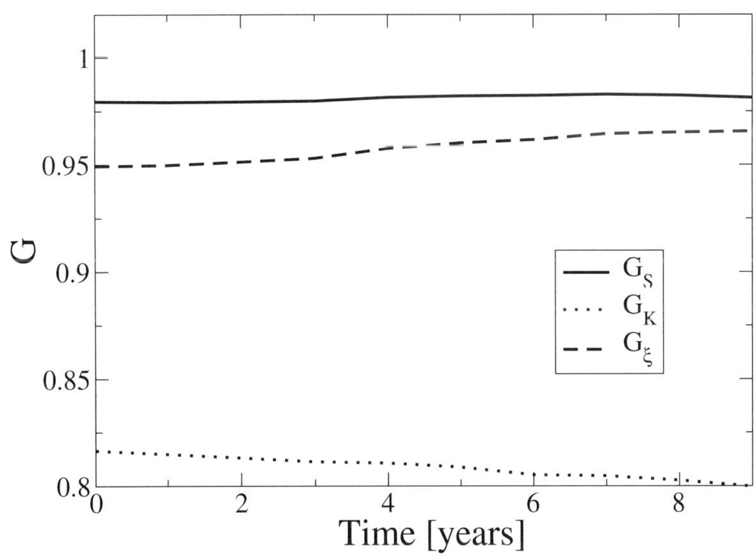

Figure 5.17 The dependence of the Gini index of firms and products on time for the pharmaceutical industry. Data source: PHID

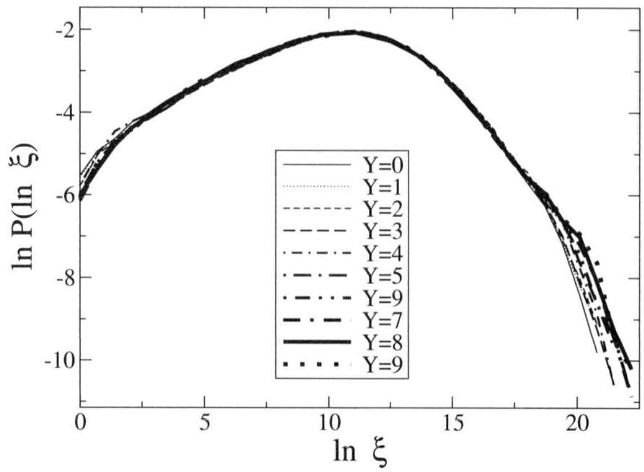

Figure 5.18 The distributions of product sizes for pharmaceuticals for different years. Data source: PHID

5.3 Testing Assumption (6)

Assumption (6) postulates Gibrat's hypothesis. Accordingly, the variance of the product size distribution should grow linearly over time. In order to test this prediction, we plot the product size distributions for the 10 years covered by our database (Figure 5.18). Contrary to Gibrat's Law predictions, the distributions are identical in the center and, hence, the variance does not depend on time. The only systematic changes that can be observed are an increase in the number of the larger products and a decrease in the number of the smaller products. Thus, the growth of the industry (Figure 5.1) is driven by the growth of the largest products. This departure from Gibrat's Law is related to the finite life time of products, which – in agreement with Assumption (3) – have an average life time of $1/\mu \approx 10$ years (Figure 5.14). In other words, product exit acts as a stabilizing factor for the variance of size distributions.

Testing the Functional Form of Product Growth Rates

Gibrat's Law would imply the emergence of the lognormality of product growth rates, r, at least for sufficiently long Δt. Figure 5.19 shows the growth rates distribution, of packs, products, and firms, as well as stable packs, products, and firms (which exist for more than three years and that will continue to exist for at least another three years). All three distributions are described by the tent-shaped curves. The distributions of packs and products show a bump in a left tail associated with the packs and products in the last years of their life. Indeed, Figures 5.13 and 5.14 show a much faster decline at the end of the product life cycle than the growth of products at the beginning of their life cycle. The bump becomes

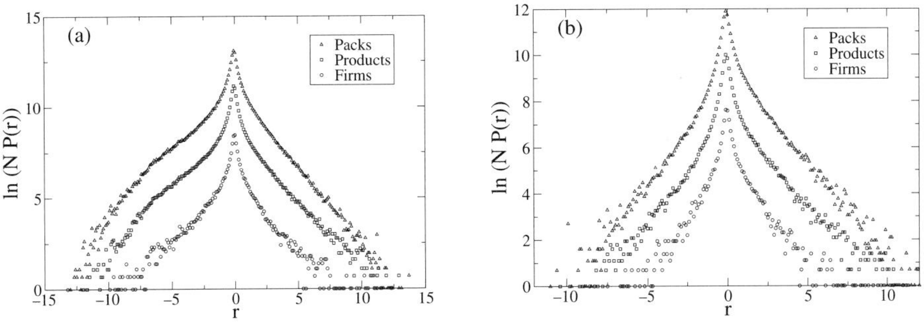

Figure 5.19 (a) The distribution of the growth rates of all packs, products, and firms. (b) The distribution of the growth rates of stable packs, products, and firms. Data source: PHID

smaller when stable products are considered. The tent shape of the distribution of product growth rates contradicts the hypothesis that this distribution emerges due to Gibrat's Law. In contrast, the tent shape of the distribution suggests that the products are not elementary units and that they consist of smaller units, which are added and removed according to the proportional growth process described in Assumptions (2) and (3). Consistent with this idea is the fact that the growth rates distribution for firms closely follows that of the products, but it is more symmetric. As the multilevel GPG suggests, once the tent shape of the growth rate distribution emerges at a low aggregation level, it is inherited at higher aggregation levels and becomes more pronounced. Figure 5.19 shows that it emerges already at the level of packs, suggesting that the packs being subunits of products are not the elementary units of the pharmaceutical industry.

According to GPG, the tails of the growth rate distribution obey the power law behavior $P_r(r) \sim r^{-\tau_r}$, where τ_r, depending on the parameters of GPG, assumes different values between 1 and 3. In order to test this prediction, we plot the data of Figure 5.19 versus $\ln |r|$ (Figure 5.20). One can see regions of the power law behavior in the tails with slopes varying from –1.5 to –3, in agreement with GPG.

Figure 5.21 shows the fitting of the growth rates distribution of stable products by two equations predicted by GPG. One equation is based on the assumption of exponential P_K with $\langle K \rangle \equiv \kappa$ and the Gaussian distribution of the growth rates for a product consisting of K units with the variance V_r/K, obtained from Equation (3.53) with replacement of summation by integration,

$$P(r) = \frac{1}{2}\sqrt{\frac{\kappa}{2V_r}}\left(1 + \frac{\kappa r^2}{2V_r}\right)^{-3/2}. \tag{5.13}$$

Another fit is based on the two-level aggregation assumption that composite units consist of elementary units distributed exponentially, and that in the second

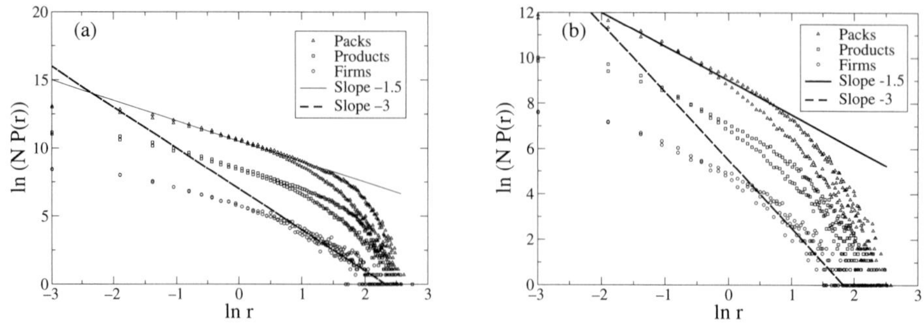

Figure 5.20 (a) The distribution of the growth rates of all packs, products and firms versus $\ln|r|$. (b) Distribution of the growth rates of stable packs, products and firms versus $\ln|r|$. Data source: PHID

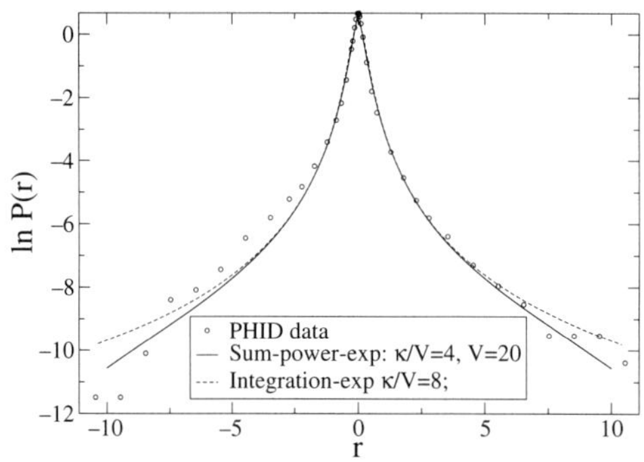

Figure 5.21 The distribution of the growth rates of stable products with fits predicted by GPG. Data source: PHID

level of aggregation the units are distributed as a power law and no replacement of summation by integration is performed, resulting in Equation (3.115):

$$P(r) = \frac{1}{\sqrt{2\pi V_r}} \left\{ \kappa \mathrm{Bs}_0 \left[\exp\left(\frac{r^2}{2V_r} \right) \right] \right. \\ \left. - (\kappa - 1)\mathrm{Bs}_0 \left[\theta \exp\left(\frac{r^2}{2V_r} \right) \right] - \mathrm{Li}_{1/2} \left[\theta \exp\left(\frac{r^2}{2V_r} \right) \right] \right\}, \tag{5.14}$$

where $\theta = 1 - 1/\kappa$, and special functions $\mathrm{Li}_{1/2}(x)$ and $\mathrm{Bs}_0(x)$ are given by Equation (3.96) and Equation (3.101), respectively. One can see that both equations fit the positive part of the distribution quite well, while they both fail to reproduce the shoulder on the negative side of the distribution. This shoulder may be related to factors that are industry-specific, in particular, patent expiry and generics entry (Pammolli et al. 2002; Magazzini et al. 2004).

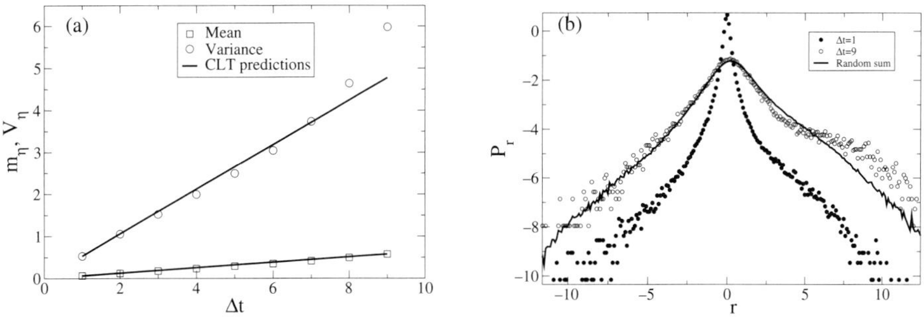

Figure 5.22 (a) The dependence of the mean and variance of the growth rates of the products that survived for 10 years as a function of the time interval Δt versus $\ln|r|$, plotted against the predictions of the Central Limit Theorem. (b) The distribution of the growth rates of these products for $\Delta t = 1$ and $\Delta t = 9$ compared with the distribution of the sum of nine randomly selected annual growth rates. Data source: PHID

Testing the Predictions of the Central Limit Theorem

Gibrat's Law implies the independence of the growth rates of the same product at different times. Hence, the Central Limit Theorem predicts that the variance of the logarithmic growth rates $r_{\Delta t} = \ln[\xi(t + \Delta t)/\xi(t)]$ must grow linearly with the time interval Δt and the distribution of the logarithmic growth rates must converge to a normal distribution as $\Delta t \to \infty$. Indeed, Figure 5.22(a) shows an almost linear dependence of both the variance and the average logarithmic growth rates of products, which survive for the entire 10 years covered in our database. Small deviations, observed for very large observation periods, are related to the fact that some of the products studied are approaching the beginning or the end of their existence at the beginning or at the end of the time frame covered by the database. In addition, the distributions of the logarithmic growth rates $r_{\Delta t}$ must approach the normal distribution for $\Delta t \to \infty$. Indeed, Figure 5.22(b), shows that the central part of the distribution approaches a Gaussian distribution, but the tails remain prominent. In order to test the convergence of the growth rate distribution to the Gaussian as required by the Central Limit Theorem, which assumes the absence of autocorrelations, we compute the distribution of the sum of nine randomly selected annual growth rates and compare it with the actual growth rates distribution of stable products for $\Delta t = 9$. The central part and the left tail of the actual and artificial distribution almost perfectly coincide, but in the left tail, the departure is quite dramatic. This test also demonstrates that the tent shape distribution is very robust against summation and still remains a tent shape for the sum of nine terms. The convergence to the Gaussian distribution is visible only in the central part.

Interestingly, in the case of long-living products, the peak on the left tail of the growth rate distribution disappears, but it is replaced by the peak on the right side. Products that survive longer tend to be the most succesful ones.

In conclusion, we note that the Central Limit Theorem predictions work to some extent, but some effects of the products' life cycles and small positive autocorrelation of products' growth rates are present.

Dependence of Growth Rates on Size

Gibrat's Assumption (6) implies that the average growth rates and their standard deviations are independent of product sizes. Figure 5.23 shows the behavior of the average nonlogarithmic product growth rates and its standard deviation versus the size of the products and packs. In violation of Gibrat's Law, the growth rate decreases monotonically with product size. The standard deviation shows a power law behavior with an exponent $\beta = 0.21$.

Figure 5.24 shows the analogous behavior for the logarithmic product growth rate and its standard deviation versus the size of the product. The growth rate strongly depends on the product size but shows a region of negative values associated with the logarithm asymmetry. The standard deviation markedly decreases as the product's size decreases but it cannot be fitted with a power law over a large interval. The smaller slope of the log–log plot of the size-variance relationship for packs than for products is consistent with the fact that packs are more elementary units than products.

In Chapter 4, we tested the predictions of GPG on the relationship between firm growth rate and size. Here, we present a brief analysis of this relationship at the firm level to visually compare them with growth rates at the product and pack levels. Figure 5.25(a) shows the behavior of the non-logarithmic firm growth rate

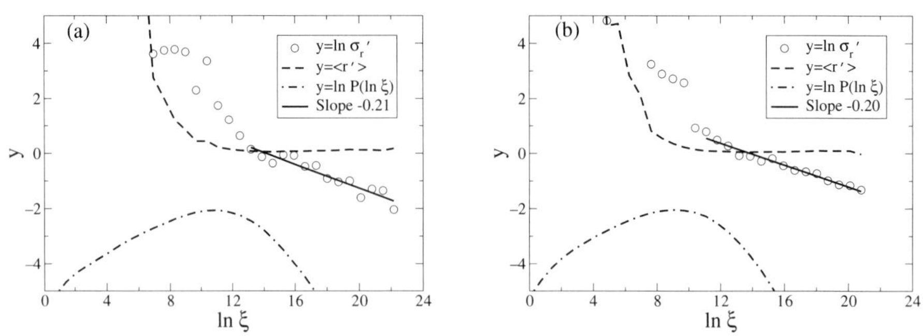

Figure 5.23 (a) The dependence of the average nonlogarithmic growth rate of the products and its standard deviation on the product sales. The PDF of the logarithmic product sizes is also shown. (b) The same analysis as in panel (a), performed for packs. Data source: PHID

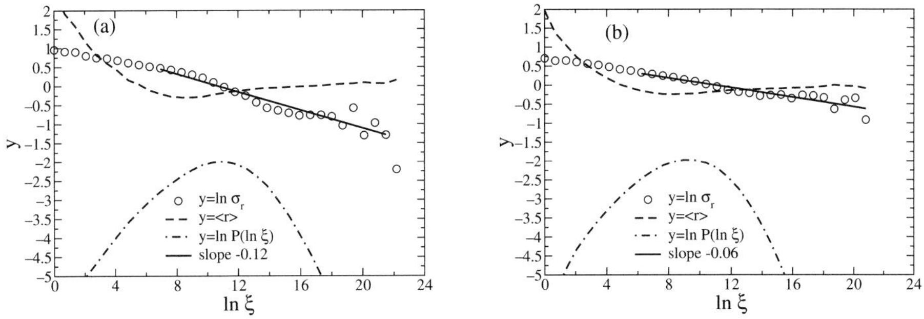

Figure 5.24 (a) The dependence of the average logarithmic growth rate of the products and its standard deviation on the product sales. The PDF of the logarithmic product sizes is also shown. (b) The same analysis as in panel (a), performed for packs. Data source: PHID

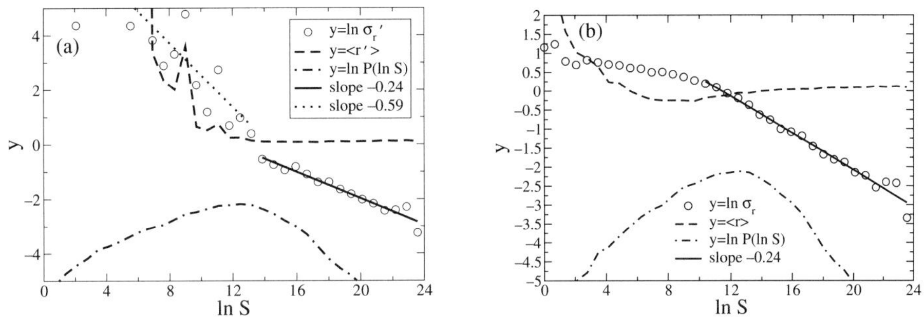

Figure 5.25 (a) The dependence of the non-logarithmic growth rate of the firms and its standard deviation on the firm sales. The PDF of the logarithmic firm sales is also shown. (b) The same analysis as in panel (a), performed for logarithmic growth rates. Data source: PHID

and its standard deviation versus the size of the firm. The growth rate monotonically decreases as the firm size decreases for $S < S_M \approx 10^6$, but, for $S > S_M \approx 10^6$, it stays almost constant. The standard deviation shows a broad region of a power law behavior with an exponent $\beta = 0.24$, corresponding to the right tail of the firm size distribution for $S > S_M$ and another region of the power law behavior for $S < S_M$ with the exponent $1 - \delta' \approx 0.6$ described by Equation (5.12).

Figure 5.25(b) shows the behavior of the average logarithmic firm growth rate and its standard deviation versus the size of the firm. The growth rate strongly depends on the firm size. The standard deviation shows a broader region of power law behavior with an exponent $\beta = 0.24$, corresponding to the entire right tail and the central part of the firms' size distribution as was already shown in Chapter 4.

As shown in Chapter 3, the H-index must be directly proportional to $\sigma_{r'}^2(S)$ if the growth rates of individual products belonging to the same firm are independent

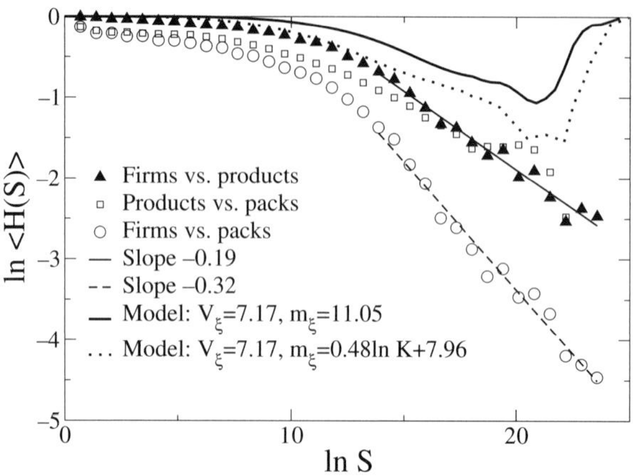

Figure 5.26 The dependence of the H-index, at the level of individual firm, computed using sales of products or packs, on the firm sales. We also show a result of computer simulations of the GPG model for the lognormal distribution of the product sizes with $V_\xi = 7.2$, which is obtained from the fit of the right tail of the product size distribution and the empirical distribution of number of products P_K. Data source: PHID

from each others, as GPG assumes. The comparison of the size dependence of the H-index, calculated for products and packs within firms, with the size-variance relationship of firms' growth rate provides a test of Assumptions (6) of the GPG framework which assumes the independence of η_j for different products in the same firm.

Figure 5.26 shows the behavior of the average H-index for individual firms, computed considering products and packs, showing a region of the power law behavior with $2\beta_H = 0.19$ in terms of products and $2\beta'_H = 0.31$ in terms of packs. Accordingly, the H-index alone cannot fully explain the size-variance relationship of the firm displayed in Figure 5.25, which show much larger values of β. The fact that the slopes of the H-index for products and packs within firm, are not coherent with the value for 2β from Figure 5.25 may indicate that growth rates of packs and products belonging to the same firms tend to be cross-correlated. A more compelling reason is that Var[η] in Equation (3.86) as we see it in Figure 5.23, depends on product size, with the exponent $\beta_p = 0.21$. Taking into account from Figure 5.26: $\langle H \rangle \sim S^{2\beta_H}$, with $2\beta_H = 0.19$, and from Equation (5.5): $\langle \xi \rangle \sim S^\delta$ with $\delta = 0.58$, we obtain from Equation (3.86): $\beta = \beta_p\delta + \beta_H = 0.22$ in a perfect agreement with our results from Chapter 4.

Figure 5.26 also shows that GPG does not reproduce the behavior of the H-index, generating values that tend to be higher than the real ones, especially for large values of S. This deviation can be partially ascribed to the dependence of products' size distribution on the number of products K. In our data, we find that the largest products of large firms, in terms of K, are larger, by two orders of magnitude, than the largest products of firms with a small number of products. As a consequence, firms with a small number of products and a high H-index are small in size. Thus, these firms cannot contribute to the bins of large firms and cannot increase the average H-index for these bins. In contrast, in the model, the product sizes are drawn, independently of the number of products K in a firm, from the same lognormal distribution. As a consequence, in our simulations, it is much more probable to observe an extremely large product in a firm with a small number of products. Such a firm would have an H-index for product, close to unity, and would contribute to the bin of the largest firms. In the model, we observe an increase of the H-index computed for products within large firms, which cannot be observed in our data. Furthermore, the assumption that the products of all firms are drawn from the same lognormal distribution accounts for the peak visible in Figure 5.26.

In order to test this conjecture, we consider a model in which $V_\xi = 7.17$, taken from the behavior of the right tail of the distribution, is constant, while m_ξ depends on K as in Figure 5.10: $m_\xi = 0.48 \ln K + 7.96$. Although the model with variable m_ξ is closer to real world data in terms of reproducing the H-index, it still generates a peak for large S. This departure is related to the fact that the right tail of the product size distribution decreases faster than a lognormal distribution, as shown in Figure 5.8. If we replace, in the simulations, the lognormal distribution of product sizes with the empirical distribution, then the agreement between the simulated and the real H-indices computed for products within firms becomes extremely good.

The Magnitude of Growth Events

Our framework sheds light on another relevant feature of processes of the industrial and economic growth: the size distribution of growth events that can be measured as changes of the sales of products and firms. It can be shown that GPG predicts, in some regions of the parameter space, the possibility that the tails of this distribution obey power laws. GPG predicts that, in the case of firm entry and in the presence of a sufficiently long-time evolution, the distribution of the number of units per firm develop a power law $P(K) \sim K^{-\tau}$, where $\tau = \tau_K \approx 2$, with an exponential cutoff (Figure 5.8). If the sizes of units have a distribution with V_ξ not very high and are independent of the number of units in the firm, the size distribution of firms retains a power law behavior in a certain range of sizes with the same τ. However, as we have seen in this chapter, the empirical evidence suggests that, at least in PHID, the average number of units $\langle K \rangle \sim S^{1-\delta}$ and, therefore, according to Equation (5.8), $\tau_S = \tau_K(1 - \delta) + \delta < \tau_K$. Since the standard deviation of the growth rates $[S(t+1) - S(t)]/S(t)$ scales as $S^{-\beta}$, the standard deviation of the sizes of growth events $S(t + 1) - S(t)$ scales as $S^{1-\beta}$. The empirical evidence suggests

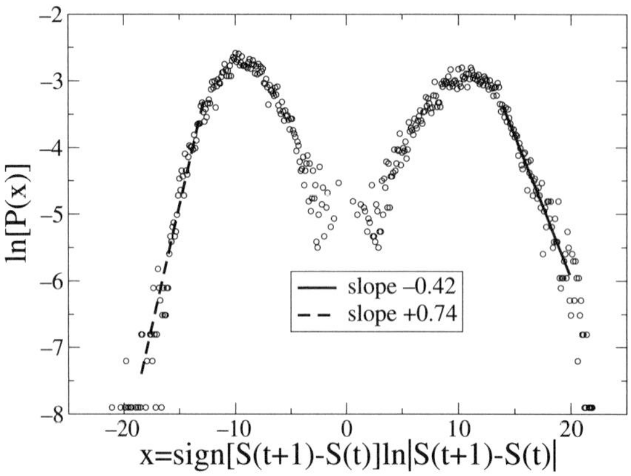

Figure 5.27 The PDF of the logarithm of the annual growth events at the firm level over 10 years covered by PHID. To analyze separately positive and negative events we compute the value $x = \text{sign}[S(t+1) - S(t)] \ln(|S(t+1) - S(t)|)$. One can see that both negative and parts resemble the distribution of the firm sizes (Figure 5.8) reflected with respect to $x = 0$, but with slightly different slopes. The negative part has a slope 0.74, while the positive part has a slope –0.42. Data source: PHID

that the standard deviation of growth rates is much larger than the average growth rate. Therefore, the average absolute value of the changes ΔS scales as $S^{1-\beta}$. By equating the PDFs of S and ΔS, $P(S)dS = P(\Delta S)d\Delta S$, and taking into account $P(S) \sim S^{-\tau_S}$, we obtain $P(\Delta S) \sim (\Delta S)^{-\tau_\Delta}$, where

$$\tau_\Delta = (\tau_S - \beta)/(1 - \beta) > \tau_S. \tag{5.15}$$

For example, for PHID, $\tau_S \approx 1.53$ (Figure 5.8), and $\beta \approx 0.23$. Therefore, we can expect $\tau_\Delta \approx 1.7$. In practice, due to a complex interplay of the power law cutoffs, the broadness of the unit size distribution, and a relationship between σ_r and $\langle r \rangle$, we can expect a significant deviation of τ_Δ from the predicted value. In order to test the validity of this prediction, we compute a histogram of the logarithm of the magnitude of the annual growth events at the firm level, separately analyzing positive and negative events (Figure 5.27). The slope of the negative part is coherent with the prediction,[4] while the value of the slope for the positive part is by 20% smaller. This discrepancy can be explained by the fact that, for positive shocks, $\langle r \rangle$ is comparable to σ_r and, hence, we can approximate $\Delta S \sim S$, and then $\tau_\Delta = \tau_S$, which would yield a better agreement. The growth events of products have a similar behavior, but give slightly different exponents for the tails. In conclusion, we can expect that the Zipf's law of the size distribution and the power law

[4] Since we plot the histogram of the logarithm, $\tau_\Delta = 1 + \gamma$, where γ is the observed slope.

size-variance relationship of economic entities at different levels of aggregation should be observed together with the emergence of power law tails in the distribution of the magnitude of the growth events. This finding seems to confirm the granularity hypotheses formulated by Gabaix to account for aggregate fluctuations (Gabaix 2011). However, as we have shown, the range of the power laws and their exponents can vary significantly for different data sets. In order to perform a direct test of the granularity hypothesis from products to firms, we compute the average contribution of the highest change of a single product to the total change of the sales of the firm, for 1% of the largest growth events at the firm level. We find that for positive variations of firm sales, the average contribution of the highest change of product sales accounts for 48%, while for negative variations it accounts for 83%. These contributions for the top 10% of firm growth events are equal to 68%and 94%, respectively, while for the top 0.1% they are 39% and 90%, respectively. These numbers strongly support the existence of a granularity property at the firm level. The contribution of the largest variation in firm sales to the total variation in sales at the level of the industry is not as strong, as it account for approximately 14%. This suggests that the aggregate volatility is not always caused by idiosyncratic shocks in a particular firm or sector. As Acemoglu et al. propose (2012), this may happen due to an intersectorial network of interactions in which a shock to one firm or sector may produce a cascading effect and affect the aggregate.

Correlations of the Growth Rates of Different Products

The deviation of the H-index from the $\sigma_{r'}^2(S)$ reported in Figure 5.26 suggests the existence of some correlation between the growth rates of products belonging to the same firm. In this section, we compute the correlation coefficients for each couple of products i and j in a firm, ω, according to the following formula:

$$C_{\omega,i,j} = \frac{\mathrm{Cov}(\eta_i - 1, \eta_j - 1)}{\sqrt{\mathrm{Var}(\eta_i - 1)\mathrm{Var}(\eta_j - 1)}}, \tag{5.16}$$

where

$$\eta_i(t) = \xi_i(t+1)/\xi_i(t), \tag{5.17}$$

$$\mathrm{Cov}(\eta_i - 1, \eta_j - 1) = \langle(\eta_i - 1)(\eta_j - 1)\rangle_{ij} - \langle\eta_i - 1\rangle_{ij}\langle\eta_j - 1\rangle_{ij}, \tag{5.18}$$

and

$$\mathrm{Var}(\eta_i - 1) = \langle(\eta_i - 1)^2\rangle_{ii} - \langle\eta_i - 1\rangle_{ii}^2. \tag{5.19}$$

The angle brackets indicate the weighted average of a quantity x over time, which is defined as

$$\langle x\rangle_{ij} = \sum_{t=1}^{9} x(t)\xi_i(t)\xi_j(t)/s_{ij}, \tag{5.20}$$

where

$$s_{ij} = \sum_{t=1}^{9} \xi_i(t)\xi_j(t). \tag{5.21}$$

Finally, we compute the weighted average of the correlation coefficients for a company

$$\langle C_\omega\rangle = \sum_{i=2}^{K_\omega}\sum_{j=1}^{i} C_{\omega,i,j}s_{ij}/s_\omega, \tag{5.22}$$

where K_ω is the number of products in a company ω, active during a period of 10 years, and

$$s_\omega = \sum_{i=2}^{K_\omega}\sum_{j=1}^{i} s_{ij}. \tag{5.23}$$

We compute the weighted average of C_ω for a group of companies within a certain bin Ω of annual sales during a period of activity of the firm:

$$\langle C\rangle_\Omega = \sum_{\omega\in\Omega} C_\omega s_\omega / \sum_{\omega\in\Omega} s_\omega. \tag{5.24}$$

Figure 5.28 shows the average correlation coefficient, $\langle C\rangle_S$, versus the average annual sales of a company, S, showing an increase of correlations with firm sales.

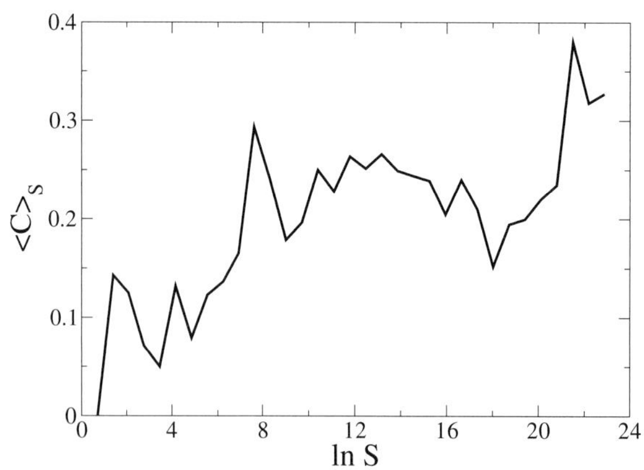

Figure 5.28 The dependence of the weighted average correlation coefficient of the product growth rates on the average annual sales at the firm level. Data source: PHID

Are these correlations statically significant, given the size of the overall market? In order to answer this question, we compute the expected standard deviation for the correlation coefficient of lognormally distributed, uncorrelated, and randomly generated growth rates over the time period covered by our data. We found a value of 0.353, which is of the order of the largest average $\langle C \rangle_{\Omega}$ observed in PHID. As a consequence, it is unlikely that correlations between products' growth rates can explain the difference between the size-variance relationship and the H-index behavior. The most plausible explanation is thus the existence of the size-variance relationship for products, which stems from the fact that products are not elementary units. Hence, the two-level aggregation GPG is the most likely candidate to account for the size-variance relationship observed in Chapters 2 and 4.

5.4 Conclusions

In this chapter, we have summarized our findings regarding the validity of the assumptions of the GPG framework and characterized the most significant departures of these assumptions from empirical data. Whether these departures are universal and how they depend on the features of the industry that we have investigated is a promising research field that, we hope, will originate from this book.

Overall, our study confirms the validity of our first set of Assumptions (1–4) regarding entry and exit of individual products, which we identify as firm units. Regarding Assumptions (2) and (3), we find that the rate of entry of new products λ is slightly larger than the rate of exit μ[5] and only weakly depends on time and on the number of products in a firm. We do observe a systematic decrease of μ and λ with the number of the existing products in the firm. However, this decrease is not very strong in the case of the pharmaceutical industry. Investigation of this dependence in other industries appears of significant interest.

We find a departure from the asymmetry outlined by Assumption (4). Indeed, we observe a significant flow, not only of entering firms, but also of exiting firms. Our assumptions do not include a specific rule for the exit of large firms except for the gradual loss of all of their products. An interesting new observation is the power law dependence of the distribution P'_k, the number of products in both new firms and exiting firms (Figure 5.5). The exit of firms might be implicitly taken into account by GPG by reducing the number of entering firms. Overall, the simulations of the distribution of the number of products in all firms, based on measured parameters λ, μ, ν, and P', resulted in a very good fit with the empirical distribution (Figure 5.7).

[5] Contradicting the equilibrium assumption (Klette and Kortum 2004).

As per Assumptions (5)–(7), we have confirmed the findings of our statistical tests in Chapter 4. In particular, Assumption (6) on the lognormality of product size distributions: the right tail of the distribution decreases faster than the lognormal distribution when the parameters are based on the fit near the central part (Figure 5.9).

The most interesting departure is violation of Assumption (5), regarding the independence of product sizes from the number of products in a firm. We find a robust correlation between average product size and number of products (Figure 5.10). This departure was predicted by Amaral and colleagues, who modelled the dynamics of products' number and size within a firm (Amaral et al. 1998). This power law relationship contributes to generate the stylized fact IV, which is: the size-variance relationship with exponent $\beta \approx 0.24$ observed in the data (Figure 5.25). Elementary scaling arguments predict $\beta = (1-\delta)/2 = 0.21$, but the discrepancy can be easily related to other effects. Moreover, if the assumption of the independence of product size and the number of products in the firm would have been true, GPG would predict a spurious increase in the H-index for the largest firms, as well as an increase in their volatility (Figure 5.26). Verifying or falsifying this prediction for other industries is an interesting future line of research.

Second, an important departure is the violation of Assumption (7), which states that the sizes of newly launched products are drawn from the overall distribution of product sizes. We find that, on average, the size of a new product is by two orders of magnitude smaller than the size of a stable product (Figure 5.12). Moreover, new products grow very fast during the first two years of their existence. The average size of new products depends, as a power law, on the firm size S: $\langle \xi_{\text{new}} \rangle \sim S^{\delta'}$, with $\delta' = 0.43$. This law explains the stylized fact II on the decreasing growth rates of firms with their size, which indicates that the $\langle r' \rangle \sim S^{\delta'-1}$ (Figure 5.16).

Moreover, as soon as a growth rate caused by innovative launch of new products becomes smaller than m_η, the average growth rate of products from Assumption (6) abruptly stops to decrease: in this case, large firms grow not because of innovation but because of the growth of their existing products.

Third, Assumptions (5) and (6), stating the independence of V_ξ, m_ξ and V_η, m_η from launching and exiting of products is violated. Products have characteristic life cycles: newly launched products grow quickly, with huge growth rate variances, while old products experience a slow decay prior to their exit from the market (Figure 5.13). This feature, again, is in part industry-specific, and future investigations in other sectors represent an interesting research trajectory (Argente et al. 2018).

Fourth, as already shown extensively in Chapter 4, in a striking departure from Gibrat's Assumption (6), the distribution of the growth rates of products is not lognormal but tent-shaped as for the firms (Figure 5.19). This is a strong evidence of the multilevel structure of firms, suggesting that products themselves consist of a large number of fluctuating units. Regarding the assumption of the independence of annual growth rates of different products from each other, the distribution of growth rates over longer periods of time almost perfectly coincides with the simulated distribution with shuffled annual growth rates (Figure 5.22). Thus, Assumption (6), which states the independence of growth rates is not falsified. Interestingly, the tent-shaped distribution of growth rates is robust against summation. The central limit theorem predicts the convergence of the growth rate distribution over long time intervals to a Gaussian distribution. However, in practice, the tent shape is preserved for a 10-year period and the convergence is visible only near the center of the distribution.

Fifth, Assumption (6), which states the independence of the growth rates variance V_η from product size, is violated. In fact, products experience almost the same size-variance relationship as firms, with a smaller $\beta \approx 0.1$ (Figure 5.24), which reveals the presence of a multilevel aggregation process. Further studies of this multilevel structure are important for the understanding of the rise and fall of firms, as well as to study the impact of processes of innovation and competition at higher levels of aggregation.

Finally, fine-grained investigations of the structure of both temporal and cross-sectional correlations must be performed in order to capture specific features of the industrial dynamics in different sectors, which can be characterized based on our stochastic benchmark. As databases on the fine grained structure of firms are becoming available (see, e.g., Argente et al. 2018), investigating the growth of products and units will be possible. At this stage we hypothesize that the observed tent-shaped distribution of the growth rates of products are caused by aggregation of smaller subunits, due to a Bose–Einstein process. What mechanisms lead to its formation, being a Bose–Einstein process, a Sutton process (Sutton 1997), or a manifestation of the submarket size, is an open question for future research.

6

Conclusions

In this book, we have developed and tested a stochastic framework, which aims to account for a set of empirical regularities on the size and growth of business firms and on the relationship between firm growth, size, age, innovation, and diversification.

We are aware of the limitations to our own approach to law discovery, which focuses on a rarefied representation of casual relationships (Pearl 2000) and then revolves around finding regularities and patterns in data (see Petroni 1992, 1993). However, it is our belief that any suitable benchmark on the growth of firms should account for multiple stylized facts with a minimal set of plausible assumptions.

In the spirit of Ijiri and Simon (1964) and Sutton (1997, 1998), we have introduced a stochastic framework to be enriched with context specific elements, strategic interactions, production networks, the nature of demand, the role of regulation, and institutions.

Our model is based on three essential ingredients.

A first ingredient is innovation, which we describe as the arrival, capture, and loss of novel business opportunities. Business opportunities are of different sizes, and firms grow thanks to the growth of existing activities and to the capture of new opportunities. In fact, we can say that the regularities that we have decribed about growth can be justified only when we do consider innovation.

The second key ingredient is proportional growth, which we introduce as a benchmark data generating process. We consider both Gibrat's and Simon's points of view and we focus on the number and the size of elementary business units. The number of units in a firm evolves in proportion to the number of preexisting units, while each unit grows proportionally to its size following a geometric random walk.

A third important ingredient of our model is that firms are diversified across products, markets, and technologies. Diversified multiproduct firms dominate international markets. By considering firms as portfolios of products of different sizes sold in different markets, we reveal some fundamental mechanisms that rule the dependency of the variance of firm growth on size. Even more importantly, our framework sheds light on the mechanisms that drive the contribution of the rise and fall of business firms to growth at higher levels of aggregation within the economy. In fact, the properties of growth are preserved upon aggregation. Therefore, national economies exhibit size and growth distributions analogous to the ones that we observe for firms and products, while macroeconomic instability can be driven by granular effects, which are persistent across multiple scales of economic systems.

Despite the success of our model to reproduce some general properties of growth processes across industries and levels of aggregation, we are aware of its limitations.

First, the partition of firm size into constituent units reveals a dependency between size and the number of the units, which is not explained by our model. Further research is needed to account for this crucial relationship. Second, fine-grained investigations of the structure of both temporal and cross-sectional correlations must be performed in order to capture specific features of industrial dynamics for products and firms in different sectors. As detailed databases on the fine-grained structure of firms are becoming available, novel investigations on growth at the microlevel of products define a new research frontier. At present, the tent-shaped distribution of growth rates at the microlevel of products is far from being fully explained, and this is an open question for future research. Third, beyond our simplified representation of interdependence, products and firms are not independent entities, but they do interact in multiple complex networks.

We are fully aware of these limitations, which we discuss in the book. However, our aim was to identify a minimal set of plausible assumptions that account for general patterns of growth across multiple domains.

In the future, our benchmark can be expanded to interpret real-world dynamics in different settings. Perhaps, someone will find a more parsimonious model, which can account for a broader set of stylized facts.

7

Appendices

7.1 A Model of Proportional Growth

Introduction

The Simon model of proportional growth in terms of number of units defined in Assumptions (1–4) in Chapter 3 describes not only the growth of firms but also a wide range of social and ecological phenomena in which units aggregate into classes. Hence, in this section, we will refer to a firm as a class. We illustrate an idea of the derivation of the distribution $P_k(t)$ of the number of units in a class at time t, leaving the details of the derivation for the latter subsections.

Assumptions (1–4) specify a stochastic process in which the number of units in each class and the number of classes can randomly change at each time step. The distribution of the number of units in a class at time t can be analytically determined, using the generating function approach (Cox and Miller 1968). The generating function of the distribution $P_k(t)$ is defined as

$$G(z,t) = \sum_{k=0}^{\infty} P_k(t) z^k. \tag{7.1}$$

If we know the generating function at time t, we can find $P_k(t)$ as its Taylor expansion with respect to z. Although the coefficients $P_k(t)$ do not give us an exact $N_k(t)/N(t)$ at a given time for each realization of a stochastic process, they do provide the mathematical expectation of $N_k(t)/N(t)$ in an infinite ensemble of realizations: $P_k(t) = \langle N_k(t)/N(t) \rangle$, where $\langle \dots \rangle$ denotes an ensemble average, i.e., for each realization of the stochastic process, N_k/N is a random variable with the known mean and a certain variance, the determination of which is beyond the scope of this study.

The term $P_0(t)$ corresponds to the empty classes that have lost all their units in the process of evolution. These classes are not removed from the list of classes and are kept there for historic reasons, i.e., most economic databases retain the names of firms that disappear due to bankruptcy or a merger. In our model, $P_0(t) > 0$ only if $\mu > 0$. An important parameter affecting the state of an economy is the death–birth ratio $\alpha = \mu/\lambda$ introduced in Equation (3.15).

We will show that if $\alpha \geq 1$, then $P_0(t) \to 1$ for $t \to \infty$, and if the entry of new classes is not sufficient: $\nu < \mu - \lambda$, the system dies out. Thus, in our analysis, we first focus on the case: $\alpha < 1$. However, we will also solve the case of a stable economy: $\alpha > 1$, $\nu + \lambda - \mu = 0$.

Another important parameter is the modified growth factor of the economy, defined in Equation (3.18)

$$R(t) = \left(\frac{n(t)}{n_0}\right)^{1/(1+b)} = \exp[(\lambda - \mu)t], \tag{7.2}$$

where $b = \nu/(\lambda - \mu)$ is the firm-unit birth ratio. We will show that the generating function of $P_k(t)$ can be expressed only in terms of R, α, and b

$$G(z,t) = \frac{1}{R_c(t)} G_{\text{old}}(z, R(t)) + \left(1 - \frac{1}{R_c(t)}\right) G_{\text{new}}(z, R(t)), \tag{7.3}$$

where

$$R_c(t) \equiv \frac{N(t)}{N(0)} = \frac{\langle k\rangle b}{\langle k\rangle'(1+b)}(R^{b+1} - 1) + 1 \tag{7.4}$$

is the growth factor of classes,

$$G_{\text{old}}(z, R) = \sum_{m-0}^{\infty} P_m(0) \left(\frac{z(1 - R\alpha) + (R-1)\alpha}{R - \alpha - (R-1)z}\right)^m \tag{7.5}$$

is the generating function of the old classes that existed at time $t = 0$,

$$G_{\text{new}}(z, R) = \frac{R^{1+b}(1+b)}{R^{1+b} - 1} \int_1^R G'(z, \mathcal{R})\mathcal{R}^{-2-b} d\mathcal{R}, \tag{7.6}$$

is the generating function of the new classes created during the entire process, and $G'(z, R)$ is the samc as $G_{\text{old}}(z, R)$, in which the initial distribution of units, $P_m(0)$, is replaced by the distribution of units in the new classes, $P'_m(0)$:

$$G'(z, R) = \sum_{m=0}^{\infty} P'_m(0) \left(\frac{z(1 - R\alpha) + (R-1)\alpha}{R - \alpha - (R-1)z}\right)^m. \tag{7.7}$$

The expressions for $G_{\text{old}}(z, R)$ and $G_{\text{new}}(z, R)$ can be readily expanded in powers of z, using binomial expansions, and the latter can be integrated over $\mathcal{R}$:

$$G_{\text{old}}(z, R) = \sum_k P_k^o(R) z^k \tag{7.8}$$

and

$$G_{\text{new}}(z,R) \propto \int_1^R G'(z,\mathcal{R})\mathcal{R}^{-2-b}d\mathcal{R} \propto \sum_k \int_1^R P_k'(\mathcal{R})\mathcal{R}^{-2-b}d\mathcal{R}z^k = \sum_k P_k'(R)z^k \tag{7.9}$$

The coefficients in front of the powers of z yield the expressions for the distribution of the number of units $P_k(t)$ in terms of growth parameters $R = R(t)$ and $R_c = R_c(t)$,

$$P_k(t) = \frac{1}{R_c}P_k^o(R) + \left(1 - \frac{1}{R_c}\right)\frac{R^{1+b}(1+b)}{R^{1+b}-1}P_k'(R). \tag{7.10}$$

Here, $P_k^o(R)$ depends only on the initial distribution of units in the preexisted classes $P_k(0)$, while $P_k'(R)$ depends only on the initial distribution of units in the newly created classes $P_k'(0)$. Note that, from the structure of $G_{\text{old}}(z,R)$ and $G'(z,R)$, it follows that, if $k \gg R$ is sufficiently large, then $P_k(R)$ decays exponentially as θ^k, where

$$\theta = \frac{R-1}{R-\alpha} < 1. \tag{7.11}$$

Elementary algebra shows that from the expressions for R in Equation (7.2) with $b = 0$ and α Equation (3.15),

$$\theta = \frac{n_\lambda(t)}{n_\lambda(t) + n_0} = 1 - \frac{1}{\kappa}, \tag{7.12}$$

where $n_\lambda(t)$ is the number of units added to the existing classes in the time interval from 0 to t. Thus, θ is related to the innovation factor, κ, defined in Equation (3.45).

Due to integration, the coefficients for $P_k'(R)$, when $k \ll R$, behave as a power law $\sim k^{-2-b}$, followed by an exponential cutoff θ^k for $k \gg R$. The expressions for $P_k(R)$ and $P_k'(R)$ can be presented in terms of a rapidly converging series of α^j and θ^j and computed for $k \sim 10^5$. The analytical results are in excellent agreement with the simulations, in which we perform 10^6 independent realizations of the stochastic process defined by Assumptions (1–4) and average the $N_k(t)/N(t)$ obtained in each individual realization (Figure 7.1). The details of the derivation of the analytical expressions and the asymptotic behavior of $P_k(t)$ are presented here.

Preferential Attachment with No New Firm Entry

First, we find an analytical expression for $P_k(t)$ when $\nu = 0$. An analytical expression for the more complex case $\nu > 0$ can be found by integrating the expressions obtained for $\nu = 0$ over time.

Suppose that we initially have $N_k(0)$ classes with k units. In each time step, a randomly selected unit dies with probability μ, and a new unit emerges with probability λ and is added to a class with k units with a probability proportional to k.

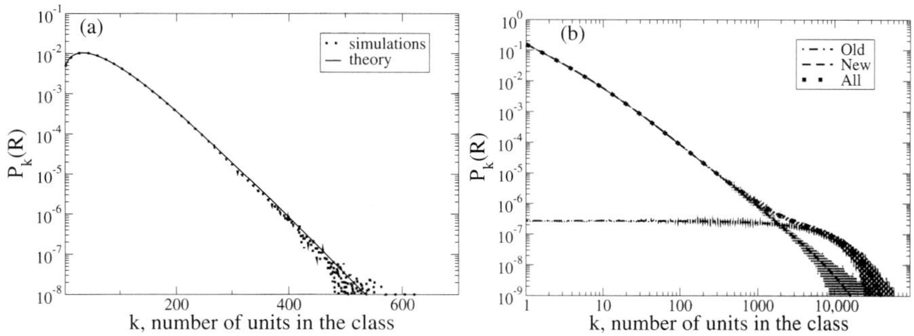

Figure 7.1 (a) The distribution $P_k(R)$ for the case $\nu = 0$ (no new classes), $\alpha = 0.25$, $R = n(t)/n_0 = 21$ for the case when initially all classes have exactly 3 units: $N = N_3 = 100$, $n_0 = 300$. The exponential decay with a slope $\ln\theta = \ln[(R-1)/(R-\alpha)] = -0.037$ is preceded by a power law increase. The simulations are averaged over 10^6 realizations of the stochastic process. (b) The distribution $P_k(R)$ for the case $b = 0.05$ (new classes are created), $\alpha = 0.8$, $R = (n(t)/n_0)^{1/(1+b)} = 1458$, for the case when all of the initial classes have exactly one unit $N = N_1 = 100$ and all of the newly created classes also have only one unit $P_1' = 1$. Due to the magnitude of statistical noise, the results of simulations averaged over 10^5 realizations are shown not by individual points but by hatched areas, where the points are located. The simulation results for old (verticaly hatched area) and new classes (horizontally hatched area) to the total $P_k(t)$ (diagonally hatched area) are shown separately. The theoretical results for different types of classes are shown by different line styles: old (dot-dashed), new (dashed), and all (dotted). The slope of the straight line behavior for the new classes gives an exponent $2 + b = 2.05$. As $k \to \infty$, the distribution is dominated by the exponential distribution of the old classes: θ^k, where $\theta = (R-1)/(R-\alpha) = 0.99986284$.

In this case, the total number of units at time t is

$$n(t) = n_0 e^{t(\lambda - \mu)}. \tag{7.13}$$

Because there is no entry, the total number of classes is constant,

$$N(t) = N(0).$$

Following the work of Kendall (1948), Cox and Miller (1968), and Luttmer (2012), we will derive a system of equations for the time evolution of the number of classes with exactly k units, $N_k = N_k(t)$. At each time step, we take out one unit from a class with k units with probability

$$\mu k N_k$$

and we add one unit to a class with k units with probability

$$\lambda k N_k.$$

Thus, N_k decreases by one unit in one time step with probability

$$(\mu + \lambda)kN_k.$$

The number N_k increases by 1 if the unit is added to the classes with $k - 1$ units, or if a unit is subtracted from the classes with $k + 1$ units. The probabilities of such events are:

$$\lambda(k-1)N_{k-1}$$

and

$$\mu(k+1)N_{k+1},$$

respectively. Thus, the mathematical expectation of the change of N_k in a small time interval Δt is

$$N_k(t+\Delta t) - N_k(t) = [\lambda(k-1)N_{k-1} + \mu(k+1)N_{k+1} - (\mu+\lambda)kN_k]\Delta t.$$

Since $N(0)$ is constant, in the limit of $\Delta t \to 0$, the probabilities $P_k(t) = N_k(t)/N(0)$ satisfy a differential equation:

$$\frac{dP_k(t)}{dt} = [\lambda(k-1)P_{k-1}(t) + \mu(k+1)P_{k+1}(t) - (\mu+\lambda)kP_k(t)]. \quad (7.14)$$

This system of an infinite number of differential equations can be solved by using generating functions. We multiply each equation by z^k and sum them up as follows:

$$\sum_{k=0}^{\infty} z^k \frac{dP_k(t)}{dt} = \left[\lambda \sum_k z^k (k-1)P_{k-1}(t) + \mu \sum_k z^k (k+1)P_{k+1}(t) - (\mu+\lambda)\sum_k z^k k P_k(t)\right]. \quad (7.15)$$

If we introduce a generating function

$$G(z,t) = \sum_k z^k P_k(t), \quad (7.16)$$

then the left side of Equation (7.16) is

$$\sum_{k=0}^{\infty} z^k \frac{dP_k(t)}{dt} = \frac{\partial G(z,t)}{\partial t} \quad (7.17)$$

and

$$\sum_{k=0} z^k (k+1)P_{k+1}(t) = \frac{\partial G(z,t)}{\partial z},$$

while

$$\sum_{k=0} z^k k P_k(t) = z\frac{\partial G(z,t)}{\partial z}$$

and

$$\sum_{k=0} z^k (k-1) P_{k-1}(t) = z^2 \frac{\partial G(z,t)}{\partial z}.$$

Hence, the generating function $G(z,t)$ satisfies the equation:

$$\frac{\partial G(z,t)}{\partial t} - \frac{\partial G(z,t)}{\partial z}[\mu - (\lambda+\mu)z + \lambda z^2] = 0. \tag{7.18}$$

This is a first-order linear partial differential equation, known as a transport equation, the theory of which is well developed in mechanics. The geometric meaning of the transport equation is that the gradient of $G(z,t)$ is orthogonal to a vector (dt, dz), where

$$dz = [-\mu + (\lambda+\mu)z - \lambda z^2]dt,$$

which means that along this vector $G(z,t)$ is constant, since

$$dG = \frac{\partial G}{\partial z} dz + \frac{\partial G}{\partial t} dt = 0.$$

Thus, the line satisfying the differential equation

$$\frac{dz}{dt} = -\mu + (\lambda+\mu)z - \lambda z^2 \tag{7.19}$$

lies on the surface $G(z,t) = C$, where C is a constant. This line is called a characteristic curve. The equation of this line is easy to find. Separation of variables gives

$$dt = \frac{dz}{-\mu + (\lambda+\mu)z - \lambda z^2}. \tag{7.20}$$

In order to integrate the right side of Equation (7.20), we express it as a sum of simple fractions,

$$\frac{1}{-\mu + (\lambda+\mu)z - \lambda z^2} = \frac{A}{z - z_1} + \frac{B}{z - z_2},$$

where A and B are undefined coefficients, and z_1 and z_2 satisfy the quadratic equation,

$$\lambda z^2 - (\lambda+\mu)z + \mu = 0.$$

Note that

$$z_1 = 1$$

and

$$z_2 = \alpha \equiv \frac{\mu}{\lambda}.$$

By reducing the right side of Equation (7.20) to a common denominator,

$$-\frac{1}{\lambda} = A(z - \alpha) + B(z - 1).$$

Thus,

$$B + A = 0, \quad A\lambda\alpha + B\lambda = 1 \text{ and } A = -B = -1/(\lambda - \mu).$$

Finally, multiplying both sides of the differential equation (7.20) by $\lambda - \mu$,

$$dt(\lambda - \mu) = -\frac{dz}{z-1} + \frac{dz}{z-\alpha}$$

and integrating, we obtain:

$$t(\lambda - \mu) = -\ln(1 - z) + \ln(z - \alpha) + C,$$

or, by using Equation (7.13), we obtain:

$$n(t) = C\frac{z-\alpha}{1-z}.$$

The constant C plays the role of the integral of the differential Equation (7.19). Since C stays constant on the characteristic curve, it satisfies its equation for $t = 0$, when $n(t) = n_0$:

$$C = n(t)\frac{1-z}{z-\alpha} = n_0\frac{1-z}{z-\alpha}. \tag{7.21}$$

Since G must also be a constant on this curve, C should be an arbitrary function of G: $C = \Phi(G)$, which can be found from the initial condition at $t = 0$, because at this point the generating function is known from the initial distribution $P_m \equiv P_m(0)$ of class sizes m:

$$G(z, 0) = \sum_{m=0}^{\infty} P_m z^m. \tag{7.22}$$

We can solve z from Equation (7.22) because $G(z, 0)$ is a continuous monotonic function of z for $z \in [0, 1)$:

$$z = f(G), \tag{7.23}$$

where $f(G)$ is the inverse function of $G(z,0)$. Now, by substituting $z = f(G)$ into the right side of Equation (7.21) we obtain $C = \Phi(G) = n_0[1-f(G)]/[f(G)-\alpha]$, and rearranging it we obtain:

$$\frac{n(t)}{n_0} = \frac{(z-\alpha)}{(1-z)}\frac{[1-f(G)]}{(f(G)-\alpha)}. \tag{7.24}$$

Thus, $G(z,t)$ can be found by solving the algebraic Equation (7.24). We then notice that the left side of Equation (7.24) is nothing but a modified growth factor defined in Equation (3.18), which is reduced for the case $\nu = 0$ to

$$R \equiv \frac{n(t)}{n_0}. \tag{7.25}$$

This important parameter captures the relative increase in the number of units over time t. The rate of growth can change with time, but in the final answer only the relative increase of the number of units is important. By replacing $n(t)/n_0$ with R in Equation (7.24), we obtain:

$$R(1-z)[f(G)-\alpha] = (z-\alpha)[1-f(G)],$$

or

$$f(G)[R(1-z)+z-\alpha] = R(1-z)\alpha + (z-\alpha)$$

and

$$f(G) = \frac{z(1-R\alpha)+(R-1)\alpha}{R-\alpha-(R-1)z}.$$

If we take into account Equations (7.22) and (7.23), and the fact that G is constant on the characteristic curve, we obtain:

$$G = G(f(G),0) = \sum_{m=0}^{\infty} P_m[f(G)]^m.$$

Finally, by using Equations (7.24) and (7.25), we find the generating function G as a function of z and R:

$$G(z,R) = \sum_{m=0}^{\infty} P_m \left(\frac{z(1-R\alpha)+(R-1)\alpha}{R-\alpha-(R-1)z}\right)^m. \tag{7.26}$$

In order to confirm Equation (7.26), we verify that $G(z,R)$ satisfies the fundamental property of the generating functions $G(z,R)|_{z=1} = 1$. Indeed,

$$G(1,R) = \sum_{m=0}^{\infty} P_m \left(\frac{(1-R\alpha)+(R-1)\alpha}{R-\alpha-(R-1)}\right)^m,$$

or

$$G(1,R)=\sum_{m=0}^{\infty}P_m\left(\frac{1-\alpha}{1-\alpha}\right)^m=\sum_{m=0}^{\infty}P_m=1.$$

When the expression on the right side of Equation (7.26) is expanded in powers of z, the coefficients give us $P_k(t)$.

When $\alpha=0$ and when all classes initially have only one unit ($P_1=1$, $P_k=0$ if $k\neq 1$), then

$$G(z,R)=\frac{z}{R(1-\frac{R-1}{R}z)},$$

or, considering that for $\alpha=0$, we get

$$\theta\equiv\frac{R-1}{R}<1,$$

$$G(z,R)=\sum_{k=1}^{\infty}\frac{1}{R}\theta^{k-1}z^k.$$

Thus,

$$P_k(t)=P_k(R)=\theta^{k-1}/R=\theta^{k-1}-\theta^k,$$

which is a geometric distribution. As expected, the average number of units in a class at time t is given by

$$\langle k\rangle(t)=1/(1-\theta)=R=\frac{n(t)}{n_0}=\frac{n(t)}{N(0)}.$$

In this simple case, $n_0=N(0)$, because each class initially has only one unit.

In order to determine the relationship when $\alpha>0$, we divide the numerator and the denominator of Equation (7.26) by $R-\alpha$:

$$G(z,R)=\sum_{m=0}^{\infty}P_m\left(\frac{\alpha\theta+\zeta z}{1-\theta z}\right)^m, \tag{7.27}$$

where

$$\zeta=\frac{1-\alpha R}{R-\alpha}=1-(1+\alpha)\theta. \tag{7.28}$$

We can expand the right side of Equation (7.27) in powers of z by expanding its numerator and denominator separately:

$$G(z,R)=\sum_{m}P_m\left(\sum_{k=0}^{m}\frac{m!}{k!\,(m-k)!}(\alpha\theta)^{m-k}\zeta^k z^k\right)\left(\sum_{k=0}^{\infty}\frac{(m+k-1)!}{k!\,(m-1)!}\theta^k z^k\right). \tag{7.29}$$

In particular,

$$P_0(R) = \sum_m P_m(0)(\alpha\theta)^m = G(\alpha\theta, 0),$$

meaning that a fraction of classes $P_0(R)$ have lost all their units and exited, so that they cannot attract any further unit.

If $R \to \infty$, then $\theta \to 1$. Thus,

$$P_0(\infty) = G(\alpha, 0).$$

If $\alpha \to 1$, then $\mu \to \lambda$ and, thus, $P_0(\infty) \to 1$, which means that all the classes will die out. Our formalism is nevertheless applicable when $\alpha \geq 1$, i.e., when the number of deleted units, $n_\mu(t)$, is greater than the number of added units, $n_\lambda(t)$. Obviously, the system will eventually collapse when $n(t) = n_0 + n_\lambda(t) - n_\mu(t) = 0$, but if n_0 is infinitely large, this will take an infinitely long time. In fact, θ, in powers of which all the distributions are expressed, depends only on factor $n_\lambda(t)/n_0$, and thus, due to Equation (7.12), always remains in the interval $(0, 1)$, for which these distributions exist. Moreover, the term $\alpha\theta$, which defines the fraction of inactive firms, remains less than 1, for any value of $R > 0$. Since for $\alpha > 1$, R decreases exponentially with time, this will happen only when $t \to \infty$.[1]

In the real life, the functions $n_\mu(t)$ and $n_\lambda(t)$ can be oscillating, due to periods of contraction and growth, but innovation incorporates all the uncertainties and allows us to present all of the probability distributions in terms of the innovation factor.

In the simple case of $P_1 = 1$, the distribution of $P_k(R)$ is geometric with the fraction of dead firms:

$$P_0(R) = \alpha\theta$$

and

$$P_k(R) = (\zeta + \alpha\theta^2)\theta^{k-1} = (1 - P_0)(1 - \theta)\theta^{k-1} \qquad k > 0. \tag{7.30}$$

If the initial $P_k(0) = \theta_0^{k-1}(1 - \theta_0)$ is geometric, with a certain parameter θ_0, then Equation (7.27) predicts that $P_k(t)$ will remain geometric at any time. In fact, the sum in Equation (7.27) can be rewritten as the sum of an infinite geometric series that still has the form $G(z, R) = (P_0 + \zeta_1 z)/(1 - \theta_1 z)$ but with new parameters

$$\theta_1 = 1 - \frac{(1 - \theta)(1 - \theta_0)}{1 - \alpha\theta\theta_0}, \tag{7.31}$$

$$\zeta_1 = \frac{\zeta(1 - \theta_0)}{1 - \alpha\theta\theta_0}, \tag{7.32}$$

[1] For the finite system, this will happen at a finite time. Its mathematical expectation can be estimated as the time when only one unit is left. By using Equation (7.25) this time can be approximated as $\ln n_0/(\mu - \lambda)$.

and the new fraction of dead firms

$$P_0 = \frac{\alpha\theta(1-\theta_0)}{1-\alpha\theta\theta_0}. \tag{7.33}$$

After some algebra, we find that for $k > 0$

$$P_k = (1-P_0)(1-\theta_1)\theta_1^{k-1}, \tag{7.34}$$

which is again the geometric distribution, but with a new fraction of dead firms.

When at $t = 0$ ($R = 1$) all classes consist on m units, i.e., when $P_m = 1$, we can multiply the polynomials in Equation (7.29) and obtain a coefficient of z^k for $k > 0$,

$$P_k^m(R) = \frac{\theta^{k-m}}{(m-1)!}\sum_{j=0}^{\min(k,m)} \frac{m!}{j!\,(m-j)!}\zeta^j(\alpha\theta^2)^{m-j}\frac{(k+m-j-1)!}{(k-j)!}. \tag{7.35}$$

For the special case of $k = 0$, we obtain that

$$P_0^m(R) = (\alpha\theta)^m \tag{7.36}$$

by placing $z = 0$ in the m-th term of Equation (7.27). Note that Equation (7.35) is a binomial expansion of $(\alpha\theta^2 + \zeta)^m = (1-\theta)^m(1-\alpha\theta)^m$, in which each term is multiplied by $(k+m-j-1)!\,/((k-j)!\,)$, which is the product of $m-1$ successive integers $(k-j+m-1)\ldots(k-j+1)$. Accordingly, we rewrite Equation (7.35) as a derivative of order $(m-1)$ with respect to a dummy variable x,

$$P_k^m(R) = \frac{\theta^{k-m}}{(m-1)!}\frac{d^{m-1}}{dx^{m-1}}[x^{k-1}(x\alpha\theta^2+\zeta)^m]|_{x=1}. \tag{7.37}$$

By using the general Leibniz rule for the m-th derivative,

$$P_k^m(R) = \sum_{j=1}^{\min(m,k)} \frac{(k-1)!}{(k-j)!}\alpha^{m-j}\theta^{k+m-2j}(1-\theta)^j(1-\alpha\theta)^j\frac{m!}{j!\,(m-j)!\,(j-1)!}. \tag{7.38}$$

This equation can be derived in a much simpler way by using elementary probabilistic arguments. A class initially consisting of m units can be regarded as a sum of m classes, each consisting of one unit. In the proportional growth model, each of these classes will evolve independently and at a certain R will survive with probability $P_s = 1-\alpha\theta$. If a class survives, units will be distributed according to a geometric distribution. The probability that j out of m classes will survive is given by the binomial formula

$$P_s(j,m) = (1-P_s)^j(P_s)^{m-j}\binom{m}{j}, \tag{7.39}$$

while the distribution of the number of units in j survived classes is given by the sum of independent random variables distributed geometrically. The sum of j geometric distributions is the negative binomial distribution $f(k-j; j, 1-\theta)$, with an argument shifted by j, where $f(K; r, p) = \binom{K+r-1}{K} p^r (1-p)^K$ is a negative binomial distribution with r degrees of freedom (Feller, 1968). The shift by j is due to the fact that j survived classes have at least j units. By combining a binomial and a negative binomial distribution we arrive we arrive at

$$P_k^m = \sum_{j=1}^{m} (1-P_s)^j (P_s)^{m-j} \binom{m}{j} f(k-j; j, 1-\theta), \tag{7.40}$$

which is equivalent to Equation (7.38). When we compare the analytical calculations using Equation (7.38) and simulations, we find that they are in perfect agreement with each other (Figure 7.1(a)).

The goal of the following paragraph is to analyze Equation (7.38) for $k \to \infty$ and to show that the maximum of P_k^m as a function of k disappears when $\alpha > (m-1)/(m+1)$. When $k \to \infty$, then the term with $j = m$ in Equation (7.38) is the leading term, because it grows as k^{m-1} due to the product of $m-1$ integers $(k-1)!/(k-m)! = (k-1)\ldots(k-m+1)$. Thus, for fixed R, the leading term in $P_k^m(R)$ for $k \to \infty$ is proportional to $\theta^k k^{m-1}$, which decreases slower than exponentially. In fact, this term can be approximated by the gamma distribution with the shape parameter m and the rate parameter $-\ln(\theta) \approx 1-\theta$. To see how the other terms behave for large R, we introduce a scaled continuous variable $x = k(1-\theta) = k/\kappa$, where $\kappa - 1$ is the innovation factor, and replace all terms in which the power of $(1-\theta)$ exceeds the power of k by zero, since they will die out for $R \to \infty$ and fixed x. In this limit, the distribution will scale with κ without changing its shape. All other remaining instances of θ can be replaced by 1. Thus, Equation (7.38) can be simplified as the probability density of x:

$$P^m(x) = \sum_{j=0}^{m} \exp(-x) \frac{x^{j-1}}{(j-1)!} (1-\alpha)^j \alpha^{m-j} \binom{m}{j}. \tag{7.41}$$

In order to find the maximum of $P^m(x)$, we differentiate it with respect to x and equate it to zero. By cancelling all unnecessary terms we obtain a polynomial equation for the position of a maximum:

$$\frac{x^{m-1}}{(m-1)!} + \sum_{r=0}^{m-2} x^r (1-\alpha)^r \alpha^{m-r-2} \binom{m+1}{r+2} \left(\alpha - \frac{m-r-1}{m+1}\right) = 0. \tag{7.42}$$

If all of the expressions in the parentheses are positive, then all coefficients are positive, and the equation does not have positive roots. If at least one coefficient is negative, then there is a positive root. The smallest coefficient is for $r = 0$, which becomes positive for $\alpha > (m-1)/(m+1)$ and the maximum disappears at $x = 0$; QED.

We compute the derivatives of the generating function (7.26) with respect to z at $z = 1$ and find the moments of the distribution (7.38). Simple algebra reveals that when all classes initially have exactly m units, the average number of units in the classes at time t is

$$\langle k \rangle_m = Rm, \tag{7.43}$$

and the variance is

$$\sigma_m^2 = mR(R-1)\frac{1+\alpha}{1-\alpha}. \tag{7.44}$$

Since the generating function of the distribution (7.38) is the power m of the generating function for the geometrical distribution (7.30), the random variable k which obeys distribution (7.38) coincides with the distribution of the sum of m independent random variables distributed geometrically. Hence, according to the central limit theorem, the distribution (7.38) converges to a Gaussian when $m \to \infty$ with the mean and variance given by Equations (7.43) and (7.44).

Proportional Growth with Entry

We now discuss the case in which some old classes exist, but new classes of average size ν/ν' are being created at a rate $\nu' > 0$ in proportion to the number of alredy existing units $n(t)$. Units can be deleted at rate μ from the existing classes and added at rate λ to the existing classes in proportion to the number of units in a class. According to Equation (3.5) in Section 3.2, the mathematical expectation of the change in the number of units during an infinitesimally small interval of time Δt is given by:

$$\Delta n(t) = (\nu + \lambda - \mu)n(t)\Delta t. \tag{7.45}$$

We now introduce the number of classes $n_{\text{old}}(t,\tau)$, which existed at time τ. For $t > \tau$, these classes do not receive the contribution $\nu n \Delta t$, because this contribution goes to the new classes that enter for $t > \tau$. However, all classes still receive their share in the number of added and deleted units, which is proportional to $n_{\text{old}}(t,\tau)$:

$$\Delta n_{\text{old}}(t,\tau) = (\lambda - \mu)n_{\text{old}}(t,\tau)\Delta t. \tag{7.46}$$

By sending Δt to zero, these two equations can be rewritten as differential equations:

$$\frac{dn}{dt} = (\nu + \lambda - \mu)n(t). \tag{7.47}$$

and

$$\frac{dn_{\text{old}}(\tau,t)}{dt} = (\lambda - \mu)n_{\text{old}}(\tau,t).$$

By solving the equations with the initial conditions $n(0) = n_0$ and $n_{\text{old}}(\tau,\tau) = n(\tau)$, we obtain

$$n_{\text{old}}(\tau,t) = [n(\tau)]^{\frac{\nu}{\lambda-\mu+\nu}}[n(t)]^{\frac{\lambda-\mu}{\lambda-\mu+\nu}}, \tag{7.48}$$

which we differentiate with respect to τ and obtain the number of units in the classes created from time τ to $\tau + \Delta\tau$,

$$\Delta n_{\text{new}}(\tau,t) = \Delta\tau \frac{\nu}{\lambda - \mu + \nu}\frac{dn(\tau)}{d\tau}\left(\frac{n(t)}{n(\tau)}\right)^{\frac{\lambda-\mu}{\lambda-\mu+\nu}}. \tag{7.49}$$

Before starting the rigorous derivation of the distributions, we will show by heuristic arguments that Equation (7.49) is the basis of Zipf's law, according to which the number of units in a class K is approximately inversely proportional to its rank $\mathcal{R}$ in the list of classes, generated in the descending order of the number of units. By taking into account Assumption (4), the number of new classes, created during the time interval from τ is $\tau + \Delta\tau$, is

$$\Delta N(\tau,t) = \Delta\tau\nu' n(\tau). \tag{7.50}$$

Since $dn(\tau)/d\tau = (\lambda - \mu + \nu)n(\tau)$, the average number of units in the class created at time τ is

$$\langle k(\tau,t)\rangle \equiv \frac{\Delta n_{\text{new}}(\tau,t)}{\Delta N(\tau,t)} = \frac{\nu}{\nu'}\left(\frac{n(t)}{n(\tau)}\right)^{\frac{\lambda-\mu}{\lambda-\mu+\nu}}. \tag{7.51}$$

Hence, neglecting statistical fluctuations, the number of units in a class $K \approx \langle k(\tau,t)\rangle$ is a monotonically decreasing function of the number of units $n(\tau)$ existing at the time of its introduction.[2] Thus, the rank of the class is $\mathcal{R} \approx n(\tau)$ and $K \sim \mathcal{R}^{-1/(1+b)}$, where $b = \nu/(\lambda - \mu)$. If $b \ll 1$, this approximate relation is equivalent to the Zipf's law.

For the rigorous derivation of P_K which does not imply any approximation, except the infinitely large number of units in the system, we will use the already introduced modified growth factor $R(t)$ that turns out to be the scaled ratio of the number of units existing in the old classes at time t and at time 0, which defines the evolution of the old classes,

$$R(t) = \left(\frac{n(t)}{n_0}\right)^{\frac{\lambda-\mu}{\lambda-\mu+\nu}} \tag{7.52}$$

[2] The assumption of monotonicity is the only heuristic assumption we make.

and introduce the scaled ratio of the number of units in the classes, existing at time t and at time τ, which defines the evolution of the new classes,

$$R(t,\tau) = \left(\frac{n(t)}{n(\tau)}\right)^{\frac{\lambda-\mu}{\lambda-\mu+\nu}}.$$

The distribution of units in the old classes is then defined by the generating function given by Equation (7.27), in which $R = R(t)$, while the distribution of units in the classes created between τ and $\tau + \Delta\tau$ is defined by Equation (7.27), in which $P_k = P'_k$ and $R = R(t,\tau)$. The generating function of the entire distribution will be the sum of the generating functions of the old classes, multiplied by the fraction of the old classes at the end of the process

$$N(0)/N(t)$$

and all of the generating functions of the new classes, created in the intervals $\Delta\tau$, $2\Delta\tau, \ldots t$, multiplied by the fractions of these classes among all the classes $N(t)$,

$$\nu'\Delta\tau n(\tau)/N(t).$$

The latter sum will converge in the limit $\Delta\tau \to 0$ to the integral

$$I(z,t) = \frac{\nu'}{N(t)} \int_0^t G'[z, R(t,\tau)]n(\tau)d\tau, \tag{7.53}$$

where $G'(z, R)$ is the generating function given by Equation (7.27), in which $P_m = P'_m$ is the initial distribution of units in the newly created classes. The total number the new classes is $N(t) - N(0)$. Therefore, for correct normalization, the generating function of the new classes is

$$G_{\text{new}}(z,t) = \frac{N(t)}{N(t) - N(0)} I(z,t) = \frac{\nu'}{N(t) - N(0)} \int_0^t G'[z, R(t,\tau)]n(\tau)d\tau, \tag{7.54}$$

Thus, the generating function of the entire distribution can be written as

$$G_{all}(z,t) = \frac{N(0)}{N(t)} G_{\text{old}}(z, R(t)) + \frac{N(t) - N(0)}{N(t)} G_{\text{new}}(z,t),$$

where $G_{\text{old}}(z, R) = \sum P_k^o(R)z^k$ is given by Equation (7.27), in which P_m is the initial distribution of units in the preexisting classes. The generating function of the new classes, $G_{\text{new}}(z,t)$, can be simplified by changing the integration variable from τ to $R(t,\tau)$,

$$G_{\text{new}}(z,t) = \frac{\nu' n(t)}{(\lambda - \mu)(N(t) - N(0))} \int_1^{R(t)} G'(z, R)R^{-2-b}dR, \tag{7.55}$$

where[3] $b = \frac{\nu}{\lambda-\mu}$.

Simple algebra shows that Equation (7.55) coincides with Equation (7.6) because the normalization factors before the integrals are, in fact, identical. The integral in Equation (7.55) is useful to present in terms of already introduced quantities:

$$\theta = \frac{R-1}{R-\alpha}, \quad R = \frac{1-\alpha\theta}{1-\theta},$$
$$dR = \frac{1-\alpha}{(1-\theta)^2}d\theta.$$

Thus,

$$\int_1^{R(t)} G'(z,R)R^{-2-b}dR = (1-\alpha)\int_0^{\frac{R(t)-1}{R(t)-\alpha}} d\theta \frac{(1-\theta)^b}{(1-\alpha\theta)^{b+2}} G'\left(z, \frac{1-\alpha\theta}{1-\theta}\right). \tag{7.56}$$

In the simplest case, in which all new classes consist of only one unit, we obtain $\nu' = \nu$, and we must use the equation for $G'(z,\theta)$ with $P_1'(0) = 1$. By using the expansion of the generating function for $P_1(0) = 1$ given by Equation (7.30), after some algebra, we find that

$$\int_1^{R(t)} G'(z,R)R^{-2-b}dR$$
$$= (1-\alpha)\int_0^{\frac{R(t)-1}{R(t)-\alpha}} d\theta \left(\frac{1-\theta}{1-\alpha\theta}\right)^{1+b} \left(\frac{\alpha\theta}{(1-\theta)(1-\alpha\theta)} + \sum_{k=1}^{\infty} \theta^{k-1} z^k\right). \tag{7.57}$$

The denominator can be expanded,

$$(1-\alpha\theta)^{-b-1} = 1 + (b+1)\alpha\theta + \frac{(b+1)(b+2)}{2!}(\alpha\theta)^2 \ldots .$$

Thus, the entire integral can be expressed as the sum of incomplete Beta functions

$$B(x, b+2, m+1) = \int_0^x (1-\theta)^{b+1}\theta^m d\theta, \quad x = \frac{R(t)-1}{R(t)-\alpha} < 1,$$

which, in turn, can be expressed by partial integration as the sum

$$B(x, b+2, m+1) = \frac{m!}{\prod_{i=0}^m (b+2+i)} - (1-x)^{b+2}x^m \frac{1}{b+2}$$
$$-(1-x)^{b+3}x^{m-1}\frac{m}{(b+2)(b+3)} - \ldots - (1-x)^{b+2+m}x^0 \frac{m!}{\prod_{i=0}^m (b+2+i)}.$$

[3] Note that the factor R^{-2-b} in Equation (7.55) is crucial for the emergence of the power law exponent $\tau = 2 + b$ in the P_K distribution for the Simon model. This factor appears only because of our assumption, that the new firms form in proportion to the total number of units in the system, $n(t)$. If we assume that the new firms form in proportion to the number of existing firms: $\Delta N = \nu N(t)\Delta t$, we obtain $\tau = 1 + b$.

The comparison with simulation gives excellent agreement [Figure 7.1(b)].

In the general case of arbitrary $P'_k(0)$, using Equation (7.38), for $k > 0$, we find that

$$P'_k(R) = \frac{R^{1+b}(1+b)(1-\alpha)}{R^{1+b}-1}\sum_{m=1}^{\infty} P'_m \sum_{j=1}^{m} \frac{\alpha^{m-j} I_{k+m,j}(\frac{R-1}{R-\alpha},\alpha,b)(k-1)!\,m!}{(k-j)!\,j!\,(m-j)!\,(j-1)!}, \tag{7.58}$$

and, for $k = 0$,

$$P'_0(R) = \frac{R^{1+b}(1+b)(1-\alpha)}{R^{1+b}-1}\sum_{m=1}^{\infty} P'_m \alpha^m I_{m,0}\left(\frac{R-1}{R-\alpha},\alpha,b\right), \tag{7.59}$$

where

$$I_{h,j}(x,\alpha,b) = \int_0^x \frac{\theta^{h-2j}(1-\theta)^{j+b}}{(1-\alpha\theta)^{b+2-j}} d\theta. \tag{7.60}$$

Due to the presence of a k-dependent prefactor $(k-1)!/(k-j)! = (k-1)\dots(k-j+1) \sim k^{j-1}$, all of the terms in this sum behave, for $k \to \infty$, as $k^{j-1} I_{k+m,j}$. In the subsection *Laplace Method for Integral Evaluation*, we will show that all these terms behave as a power law k^{-2-b} with an exponential cutoff $\exp[-k(1-\alpha)/R]$, which increases as $R \to \infty$. In simple terms, as $R \to \infty$, the upper limit of the integral in Equation (7.60) converges to 1: $x = (R-1)/(R-\alpha) \to 1$. Thus, the leading k-dependent term in Equation (7.58), $k^{j-1} I_{k+m,j}$, can be approximated by $k^{j-1} B(k+m-2j+1, j+b+1)/(1-\alpha)^{b+2+j}$, where $B(p,q)$ is a complete Beta-function. By using an approximation for the Beta-function for the case when one argument, $p = k+m-2j+1 \to \infty$, is large, and another, $q = j+b+1$, is finite, we have

$$k^{j-1} I_{k+m,j} \sim \Gamma(j+b+1)(1-\alpha)^{j-b-2}(k+m-2j+1)^{-j-b-1}k^{j-1} \sim \Gamma(j+b+1)(1-\alpha)^{j-b-2}k^{-b-2}.$$

This approximation leads to an important result: for an arbitrary distribution of units in the new classes, the distribution of the units in all the classes, in the infinite time limit, converges to a power law distribution. Numerically, one can compute $I_{h,j}$ by expanding $(1-\alpha\theta)^{j-b-2}$ in a series of θ,

$$I_{h,j}(x,\alpha,b) = \sum_{\ell=0}^{\infty} B(x, h+\ell-2j+1, j+b+1)\alpha^{\ell} \frac{(b-j+\ell+1)!}{(b-j+1)!\,\ell!}. \tag{7.61}$$

A Case of Shrinking or Stable Economy

The formalism described in the last subsection is applicable even when $\mu \geq \lambda$ and, thus, $\alpha > 1$. If $\nu' = 0$, and we must use Equation (7.27) with θ given by Equation (7.12) $\theta = n_\lambda(t)/(n_0 + n_\lambda)$, where $n_\lambda(t)$ is the number of new units launched in the system during the time interval from 0 to t. When $\nu' > 0$ and $\nu > \mu - \lambda$, we still use Equations (7.58) and (7.59), but $1/(b+1) < 0$ and, hence, $R \rightarrow 0$ for $t \rightarrow \infty$. Thus, $\theta \rightarrow 1/\alpha$, and, when computing integrals $I_{h,j}(x,\alpha,b)$, it is useful to change the integration variable to $\theta' = \alpha\theta$. Then, $I_{h,j}(x,\alpha,b) = \alpha^{2j-h-1} I_{h,j}(\alpha x, \alpha^{-1}, -2-b)$. The later integral can be approximated using the Laplace method or expanded in terms of incomplete Beta functions following the above procedure. The distribution P_k will have the power law behavior $P_k \sim k^{-b-2}$, with $b < 0$ but because of the prefactor $\alpha^{2j-h-1} \sim \alpha^{-k}$, the exponential cutoff is present even for $t \rightarrow \infty$ and, therefore, the power law tail does not play a significant role.

Finally, when the economy is stable, $\nu = \mu - \lambda$, we take the limit for $\lambda - \mu + \nu \rightarrow 0$ in Equation (7.52) and obtain $R(t) = \exp(-n_\nu(t)/n_0)$, where $n_\nu(t)$ is the total number of units launched together with new classes, which is equal to the net number of units deleted from the existing classes. In this case, the prefactor and the integral in Equation (7.58) can be simplified as

$$\frac{R^{1+b}(1+b)}{R^{1+b}-1} = -\frac{n_0}{n_\nu(t)}$$

and

$$I_{h,j}(x,\alpha,b) = \int_0^x \theta^{h-2j}(1-\theta)^{j-1}(1-\alpha\theta)^{j-1}d\theta.$$

For example, when all classes start with one unit ($N(0) = n_0$, $P_1(0) = 1$ and $P_1'(0) = 1$), the generating function is given by Equation (7.57), integrating which, we obtain,

$$P_0'(t) = 1 - \frac{n_0}{n_\nu(t)}(1-\alpha)\ln(1-\theta)$$

where $\theta = (1-R)/(\alpha - R)$ and

$$P_k'(t) = \frac{n_0\theta^k}{n_\nu(t)k}(\alpha - 1),$$

for $k > 0$. As $t \rightarrow \infty$, the number of active classes converges to $N(0)(\alpha - 1)\ln[\alpha/(\alpha-1)]$ and the distribution of units in the active classes converges to

$$P_k = \frac{1}{k\alpha^k \ln[\alpha/(\alpha-1)]}. \tag{7.62}$$

Thus, when $\alpha \rightarrow 1$, the distribution P_k becomes inversely proportional to k for a wide range of k.

Laplace Method for Integral Evaluation

The integrand in Equation (7.60) has a maximum at $\theta_{max} \in (0,1)$, and as $h \to \infty$, the maximum shifts toward 1 and eventually goes above the upper limit of the integration limit given by

$$x = \frac{R-1}{R-\alpha}.$$

Note that, as $h \to \infty$, the function under the integral becomes increasingly narrow around its maximum and becomes approximately zero for $\theta < x$. Thus, the integral begins to decay much faster when $\theta_{max} > x$. The condition $\theta_{max} = x$ defines the position of the crossover in the behavior of the distribution of new classes from a power law to an exponential distribution.

Integrals with this kind of sharp maximum can be evaluated using the Laplace method, i.e.,

$$\int_a^b \exp(f(x))dx,$$

where $f(x)$ is the logarithm of the integrand, which has a maximum at $x_0 \in (a,b)$ and $f''(x_0) \to -\infty$ when a parameter, such as h, goes to infinity: $h \to \infty$. If higher derivatives grow slower than the second derivative, then the graph of $f(x)$, near x_0, exhibits a nearly perfect parabola,

$$f(x) = f_0(x_0) + \frac{f''(x_0)(x-x_0)^2}{2}.$$

We know that the normal probability density is

$$\mathcal{N} = \frac{e^{-\frac{(x-\mu)^2}{2\sigma^2}}}{\sqrt{2\pi\sigma^2}}.$$

Thus we can see that in our integral f'' assumes the role of $1/\sigma^2$ and x_0 the role of μ, since the integral of the normal density from $-\infty$ to $+\infty$ is 1, our integral must asymptotically (when $f''(x_0) \to -\infty$) behave as

$$\int_a^b \exp(f(x))dx \sim \frac{\sqrt{2\pi}}{\sqrt{-f''(x_0)}} \exp[f(x_0)].$$

The symbol $\sim$ means that the limit of the ratio of the left side of the integral and the right side is 1 when $f''(x_0) \to -\infty$.

When $f(x)$ does not have a maximum inside the interval but reaches its maximal value at $x = b$ and has a finite derivative $f'(b) > 0$ at this point, which also goes to infinity as $h \to \infty$, then the integrand can be approximated as an exponent

$$e^{f(b)}e^{-f'(b)(b-x)},$$

and the integral behaves as

$$\int_a^b \exp(f(x))dx \sim \frac{1}{f'(b)} \exp[f(b)].$$

In the case of Equation (7.60), the higher derivatives of $f(x)$ near its maximum grow even faster than the second derivative and hence the classical Laplace method is not applicable. However, we can still follow the Laplace prescription and present our integral as

$$\int_0^x \exp[(b+j)\ln(1-\theta) - (b+2-j)\ln(1-\theta\alpha) + (h-2j)\ln\theta]d\theta.$$

The middle term is a finite analytical function in the interval [0, 1] and is, therefore, irrelevant for the calculation of the position of the maximum for $h \to \infty$. Thus, the maximum is defined by the two remaining competing terms, which can be infinitely large:

$$f(\theta) \approx (b+j)\ln(1-\theta) + (h-2j)\ln\theta.$$

The maximum of this function is reached at

$$\theta_{\max} = 1 - \frac{b+j}{b+h-j} = 1 - \frac{b+j}{h} + o(1/h). \tag{7.63}$$

By using Equation (7.63), the crossover condition, $\theta_{\max} < (R-1)/(R-\alpha)$, can be simplified for large R as

$$h < \frac{(b+j)R}{1-\alpha}.$$

Thus, for small h, the maximum is inside the domain of integration and the decay of the integral must be slow, while for large h, the decay must be fast. By computing $f'(x) \sim h$ for $h \gg R$ and large R, we obtain:

$$I_{h,j}(x,\alpha,b) \sim \frac{(1-\alpha)^{2j-2}}{hR^{b+j}} \exp\left(-\frac{h(1-\alpha)}{R}\right), \tag{7.64}$$

which decreases faster than exponential. In the case of $h \ll \frac{(b+j)R}{1-\alpha}$, we can approximate the integral in Equation (7.60) by

$$I_{h,j}(x,\alpha,b) = \int_0^x d\theta \frac{(1-\theta)^{b+j}}{(1-\alpha\theta)^{b-j+2}} \theta^{h-2j} \approx (1-\alpha)^{j-b-2} B(b+j+1, h-2j+1) \tag{7.65}$$

because the value of the integrand is exponentially small everywhere except in an infinitesimally narrow vicinity of the point $\theta_{\max} = 1 - (b+j)/h$, and for large enough h, one can approximate the slowly varying function $(1-\alpha\theta_{\max})^{j-b-2}$ by $(1-\alpha)^{j-b-2}$. Finally, by using Euler's formula

$$B(b+j+1,\, h-2j+1) = \Gamma(h-2j+1)\Gamma(b+1+j)/\Gamma(h-j+b+2)$$

and the Stirling approximation, we obtain

$$I_{h,j} \sim (1-\alpha)^{j-b-2}\Gamma(b+1+j)(h)^{-b-1-j} + o(h^{-b-1-j}).$$

Recalling that each term in Equation (7.58) is proportional to $k^{j-1}I_{k+m,j}$, we can conclude that for any initial distribution of units in the new classes, such that $P_k'(0) = 0$ for $k > m$, the resulting distribution $P_k'(R)$ decreases as a power law k^{-b-2} for $1 \ll k \ll \frac{(b+m)R}{1-\alpha}$, followed by the exponential decay given by Equation (7.64).

7.2 The Growth Rate Distribution

Once P_K, the distribution of the number of units in the classes, is known, the distribution of the growth rates $P_r(r)$ can be found as a convolution of P_K and a conditional distribution of growth rates $P_r(r|K)$ for classes consisting of exactly K units:

$$P_r(r) = \sum_{K=1}^{\infty} P_K P_r(r|K). \tag{7.66}$$

It would be desirable to derive an exact analytical expression for the probability density $P_r(r|K)$ or at least its mean $m_r(K)$ and variance $\sigma_r^2(K)$ for a general case of arbitrary distributions of unit sizes P_ξ and unit growth rates P_η, as well as for the arbitrary parameters λ, μ and ν characterizing the birth and death rates of the units.

Bose–Einstein Process

First, for simplicity, we focus on the Bose–Einstein process, assuming that all units have the same size, which does not change over time. In this case,

$$r(K) = \ln\left(\frac{K'}{K}\right), \tag{7.67}$$

where K' is the number of units at time $t+\Delta t$, provided that K is the number of units at time t. Since both K and K' are integers, $P_r(r|K)$ is a discrete distribution, consisting of discrete atoms, corresponding to the logarithms of rational numbers. Equation (7.38) gives us the conditional distribution $P(K'|K)$ of $K' = k$ for $K = m$, $R = \exp[(\lambda-\mu)\Delta t]$. Note that when a class loses all its units $K' = 0$, r is not defined. Thus, we must restrict ourselves to the case $K' > 0$ and renormalize the distribution (7.38) by dividing it by $1 - P(K' = 0)$, given by Equation (7.36). Hence, for the Bose–Einstein process the problem is solved: $r = \ln(K'/K)$, where

$$P(K'|K) = \frac{\sum_{j=1}^{K} \frac{(K'-1)!}{(K'-j)!} \alpha^{K-j} \theta^{K'+K-2j} (1-\theta)^j (1-\alpha\theta)^j \frac{K!}{j!(K-j)!(j-1)!}}{1-(\alpha\theta)^K}, \quad (7.68)$$

and $\theta = (R-1)/(R-\alpha)$. By using this equation, one can readily compute $m_r(K)$ and $\sigma_r^2(K)$, for any λ, μ and Δt (Figure 7.2).

Since for $K \to \infty$, the distribution $P(K'|K)$ converges to a Gaussian distribution, the distribution $P(r|K)$ also converges to a Gaussian. Indeed, by using Equations (7.43) and (7.44), we can present

$$K' = KR + \nu_K \sqrt{R(R-1)K(1+\alpha)/(1-\alpha)}, \quad (7.69)$$

where ν_K is the random variable with zero mean and unity variance, which converges to the normal distribution for $K \to \infty$. By expanding the logarithm, we obtain

$$r = \ln(R) + \ln\left(1 + \nu_k \sqrt{\frac{(R-1)(1+\alpha)}{RK(1-\alpha)}}\right)$$

$$= \ln(R) + \nu_K \sqrt{\frac{(R-1)(1+\alpha)}{RK(1-\alpha)}} \quad (7.70)$$

$$- \nu_K^2 \frac{(R-1)(1+\alpha)}{2RK(1-\alpha)} + O(K^{-3/2}). \quad (7.71)$$

Hence, for $K \to \infty$, $P_r(r|K)$ converges to a Gaussian distribution with mean

$$m_r(K) = \ln(R) \quad \frac{(R-1)(1+\alpha)}{2RK(1-\alpha)} + O(K^{-2}) \quad (7.72)$$

and variance

$$\sigma_r^2(K) = \frac{R-1}{RK}\frac{1+\alpha}{1-\alpha}. \quad (7.73)$$

The numerical calculations (Figure 7.2) agree well with the analytical results presented here.

When $\Delta t \to 0$, Equations (7.43) and (7.44) give

$$E(K') = K[1 + (\lambda - \mu)\Delta t] \quad (7.74)$$

and

$$\mathrm{Var}(K') = K(\lambda + \mu)\Delta t. \quad (7.75)$$

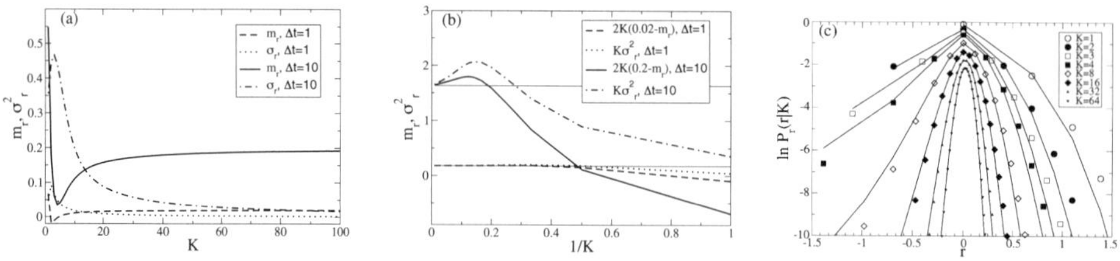

Figure 7.2 (a) The behavior of the average logarithmic growth rates $m_r(K)$ and their standard deviations $\sigma_r^2(K)$ as a function of K for $\lambda = 0.1$, $\mu = 0.08$, $\Delta t = 1$ and $\Delta t = 10$. One can see a nonmonotonic behavior of m_r caused by renormalization of the distribution by $1 - (\alpha\theta)^m$ and by the asymmetry of the logarithm, which decreases much faster for $K' < K$ than it increases for $K' > K$. A similar behavior is observed for actual firms. (b) Same graphs as in (a), but versus $1/K$, which test the limiting behavior of $m_r(K)$ and $\sigma_r(K)$ for $K \to \infty$ according to Equations (7.72) and (7.73). The horizontal lines show the limiting values $[(R-1)(1+\alpha)][R(1-\alpha)]$ for both $\Delta t = 1$ (small value) and $\Delta t = 10$ (large value). (c) The distribution $P_r(r|K)$ for $\lambda = 0.1$, $\mu = 0.08$, $\Delta t = 1$ and several values of K (symbols). The lines show the Skellam distribution which agrees well with the exact distribution for large K.

Accordingly, the random variable K' for sufficiently large K can be interpreted as

$$K' = K + K_\lambda - K_\mu, \tag{7.76}$$

where K_λ is the number of new units gained in the time interval Δt and K_μ is the number of units lost in time the interval Δt. From Assumptions (2) and (3) of the GPGM, it is clear that for short time periods the birth and death of units are described by two independent Poisson processes. Hence, K_λ is the Poisson random variable with mathematical expectation and variance $\lambda \Delta t K$ and K_μ is a Poisson random variable with mathematical expectation and variance $\mu \Delta t K$. In order to make the notations simple, we use renormalized birth and death rates $\lambda' = \lambda \Delta t$ and $\mu' = \mu \Delta t$, respectively. The distribution of the difference between two Poisson random variables $\Delta K = K' - K = K_\lambda - K_\mu$ is the well known Skellam distribution with mean

$$\mu_\Delta(K) = K(\lambda' - \mu') \tag{7.77}$$

and variance

$$\sigma^2_{\Delta K}(K) = K(\lambda' + \mu'). \tag{7.78}$$

For $\Delta K \geq 0$ the distribution is given by

$$P_K(\Delta K) = e^{-K(\lambda'+\mu')} \sum_{j=\Delta K}^{\infty} \frac{(K\mu')^j (K\lambda')^{j+\Delta K}}{j!\,(j+\Delta K)!}. \tag{7.79}$$

The values for negative ΔK can be obtained by using an obvious identity

$$P_K(-\Delta K) = P_K(\Delta K)\left(\frac{\mu}{\lambda}\right)^{\Delta K}. \tag{7.80}$$

Thus, for small Δt and large K, the distribution $P_r(r|K)$ can be well approximated by the Skellam distribution (Figure 7.2).

Gibrat Process

Now we follow our own work in Riccaboni et al. (2008) to derive an exact analytical expression for $P(r|K)$, $m_r(K)$, and $\sigma_r(K)$ for the case of a Gibrat process of unit sizes (lognormal and independent P_ξ and P_η), when the number of units, K, in the class cannot change ($\lambda = \mu = 0$).

By making the substitution $y = \ln x$ in the integrals, it is straightforward to show that for the n-th moment of the lognormal distribution

$$P_x(x) = \frac{1}{\sqrt{2\pi V_x}}\,\frac{1}{x}\,\exp\left(-(\ln x_i - m_x)^2/2V_x\right) \tag{7.81}$$

is equal to

$$\mu_{n,x} \equiv \langle x^n \rangle = \exp(nm_x + n^2 V_x/2). \tag{7.82}$$

Then, we can make an expansion of a logarithmic growth rate in inverse powers of K:

$$\begin{aligned}
r &= \ln \frac{\sum_{i=1}^K \xi_i \eta_i}{\sum_{i=1}^K \xi_i} \\
&= \ln \mu_{1,\eta} + \ln\left(\frac{1 + A/K + B/K}{K(1 + B/K)}\right) \\
&= m_\eta + \frac{V_\eta}{2} + \frac{A+B}{K} - \frac{(A+B)^2}{2K^2} + \frac{(A+B)^3}{3K^3} - \frac{B}{K} + \frac{B^2}{2K^2} - \frac{B^3}{3K^3} + \dots. \\
&= m_\eta + \frac{V_\eta}{2} + \frac{A}{K} - \frac{2AB + A^2}{2K^2} + \frac{A^3 + 3A^2B + 3AB^2}{3K^3} + O(K^{-4}),
\end{aligned}$$

where

$$A = \frac{\sum_{i=1}^K \xi_i(\eta_i - \mu_{1,\eta})}{\mu_{1,\eta}\mu_{1,\xi}} \tag{7.83}$$

$$B = \frac{\sum_{i=1}^K \xi_i - \mu_{1,\xi}}{\mu_{1,\xi}}, \tag{7.84}$$

are sums of centered random variables, which due to the central limit theorem converge as $K \to \infty$ to normal distributions with standard deviations growing as $\sqrt{K}$. Hence, the expansion (7.83) is valid with the leading term $A/K \sim 1/\sqrt{K}$

converging to a normal distribution. By using the assumptions that ξ_i, and η_i are independent: $\langle \xi_i \eta_i \rangle = \langle \xi_i \rangle \langle \eta_i \rangle$, $\langle \eta_i \eta_j \rangle = \langle \eta_i \rangle \langle \eta_j \rangle$, and $\langle \xi_i \xi_j \rangle = \langle \xi_i \rangle \langle \xi_j \rangle$ for $i \neq j$, we find that $\langle A \rangle = 0$, $\langle AB \rangle = 0$, and $\langle A^2 \rangle = V_r K$, where $V_r = a(b-1)$ with $a = \exp(V_\xi)$ and $b = \exp(V_\eta)$. Thus m_r and σ_r^2 can be formally expanded in inverse powers of K:

$$m_r = \langle r \rangle = \sum_{n=0}^{\infty} \frac{m_n}{K^n}$$

$$\sigma_r^2 = \langle r^2 \rangle - m_r^2 = \sum_{n=1}^{\infty} \frac{V_n}{K^n}, \tag{7.85}$$

where

$$\begin{aligned} m_0 &= m_\eta + V_\eta/2 \\ m_1 &= -V_r/2, V_1 = V_r, \\ V_2 &= V_r[a(5b+1)/2 - 1 - a^2 b(b+1)]. \end{aligned} \tag{7.86}$$

In order to find the remaining terms, we must open the parentheses in the expression for

$$\langle (r - m_r)^2 \rangle = \left\langle \left(\frac{A}{K} - \frac{2AB + A^2}{2K^2} + \frac{A^3 + 3A^2B + 3AB^2}{3K^3} + \frac{\langle A^2 \rangle}{2K^2} + O(K^{-2})^2 \right) \right\rangle, \tag{7.87}$$

keeping all of the terms, which give the values of the order of $(1/K^2)$. This expansion will include the terms $\langle A^2 \rangle / K^2$, $\langle A^2 B \rangle / K^3$, $\langle A^3 \rangle / K^3$, $\langle A^4 \rangle / K^4$, $\langle A^2 B^2 \rangle / K^4$, $\langle A^2 \rangle^2 / K^4$, and $\langle A^3 B \rangle / K^3$. Each of these terms has a structure of

$$\langle A^n B^m \rangle = \sum_{i_1, i_2, \ldots i_n, j_i, j_2, \ldots j_m} \langle \xi_{i_1} \tilde{\eta}_{i_1} \xi_{i_2} \tilde{\eta}_{i_2} \ldots \xi_{i_n} \tilde{\eta}_{i_n} \tilde{\xi}_{j_1} \tilde{\xi}_{j_2} \tilde{\xi}_{j_m} \rangle, \tag{7.88}$$

where $\tilde{\eta}_i = \eta_i - \mu_{\eta,1}$ $\tilde{\xi}_j = \xi_j - \mu_{\xi,1}$ are independent centered random variables, therefore $\langle \tilde{\eta}_i \rangle$=0; $\langle \tilde{\xi}_j \rangle$=0, $\langle \tilde{\eta}_i \xi_i \rangle = 0$, $\langle \xi_i \tilde{\eta}_i \xi_j \tilde{\eta}_j \rangle = 0$, and $\langle \tilde{\xi}_i \tilde{\xi}_j \rangle = 0$, for $i \neq j$. Thus, in these sums, the only nonzero contribution is given by the terms, which involve units with $i_k = i_\ell$, $j_k = j_\ell$, or $i_k = i_\ell = j_s$, or an even larger number of coinciding indices. Thus, for example, $\langle A^4 \rangle / K^4 = (3K^{-2} \langle \tilde{\eta}^2 \rangle^2 \langle \xi^2 \rangle^2 + K^{-3} \langle \tilde{\eta}^4 \rangle \langle \xi^4 \rangle) / (\mu_{\xi,1} \mu_{\eta,1})^4$. Since we are interested only in the terms behaving as $1/K^2$, the last term is irrelevant and can be neglected. Analogously, $\langle A^3 B \rangle / K^4 = K^{-3} \langle \tilde{\eta}^3 \rangle (\langle \xi^4 \rangle - \langle \xi^3 \rangle \mu_{\xi,1}) / (\mu_{\xi,1} \mu_{\eta,1})^4$ can also be neglected. Grouping all the terms of the same order in K in Equation (7.87) is a lengthy but straightforward task, which yields Equations (7.86).

The higher order terms involve terms like $\langle A^n \rangle / K^n$, which will become sums of various units $\langle \xi_i^k (\eta_i - \mu_{1,\eta})^k \rangle$, where $2 \leq k \leq n$ (Riccaboni et al., 2008). The contribution from $k = n$ has exactly K terms

$$\mu_{n,\xi}\mu_{1,\xi}^{-n}\sum_{j=0}^{n}\mu_{j,\eta}\mu_{1,\eta}^{-j}(-1)^{n-j}\binom{j}{n}$$

with $\mu_{j,x}\mu_{1,x}^{-j} = \exp(V_x j(j-1)/2)$. Thus, there are contributions to m_n and V_n that grow as $(ab)^{n(n+1)/2}$ with $ab > 1$, which is faster than the n-th power of any $\lambda > 0$. Thus, the radius of convergence of the expansions (7.85) is equal to zero, and these expansions have only a formal asymptotic meaning for $K \to \infty$. For small V_ξ, the approximation improves with n, but it is still impractical to use more than a few first terms.[4] However, these expansions are useful, since they demonstrate that μ and σ do not depend on m_η and m_ξ, respectively, except for the leading term in μ: $m_0 = m_\eta + V_\eta/2$.

Since our analytical approach cannot find exact analytical expressions for $\sigma_r(K)$ and m_r, except in the limit of very large K, we performed extensive computer simulations of the growth rates presented in Section 7.3.

A simpler expression can be derived for the standard deviation of the nonlogarithmic growth rate if we assume independence of all growth rates η_i and unit sizes ξ_i:

$$\sigma_{r'}^2 = \mathrm{Var}(\eta)\langle H(\xi, K)\rangle, \tag{7.89}$$

where $H(\xi, K)$ is the H-index:

$$H(\xi, K) = \frac{\sum_{i=1}^{K}\xi_i^2}{\left(\sum_{i=1}^{K}\xi_i\right)^2}. \tag{7.90}$$

Indeed,

$$\mathrm{E}(r') = \left\langle \frac{\sum^K \xi_i\eta_i}{\sum^K \xi_i}\right\rangle - 1 =$$

$$\sum^K \left\langle \frac{\xi_i}{\sum^K \xi_i}\eta_i\right\rangle - 1 =$$

$$\sum^K \left\langle \frac{\xi_i}{\sum^K \xi_i}\right\rangle \langle\eta_i\rangle - 1 =$$

$$\mathrm{E}(\eta)\left\langle \frac{\sum^K \xi_i}{\sum_K \xi_i}\right\rangle - 1 = \mathrm{E}(\eta) - 1.$$

By introducing the centered growth factor $\tilde{\eta}_i = \eta_i - \mathrm{E}(\eta)$, for which (due to independence of $\tilde{\eta}_i$) $\mathrm{E}(\tilde{\eta}_i\tilde{\eta}_j) = \mathrm{Var}(\eta)\delta_{ij}$, we obtain:

[4] Formal asymptotic expansion $\sum_{n=0} f_n/K^n$ of a function $f(K)$ means that for any N there exists a constant C_N, such that $|f(K) - \sum_{n=0}^{N} f_n/K^n| < C_N/N^{K+1}$, but $C_N \to \infty$ for $N \to \infty$.

$$\mathrm{Var}(r') = \left\langle \frac{\left(\sum_{i=1}^{K} \xi_i \tilde{\eta}_i\right)^2}{\left(\sum_{i=1}^{K} \xi_i\right)^2} \right\rangle =$$

$$\sum_{i=1,\, j=1}^{K} \left\langle \frac{\xi_i \xi_j \tilde{\eta}_i \tilde{\eta}_j}{\left(\sum_{i=1}^{K} \xi_i\right)^2} \right\rangle =$$

$$\sum_{i=1,\, j=1}^{K} \mathrm{E}(\tilde{\eta}_i \tilde{\eta}_j) \left\langle \frac{\xi_i \xi_j}{\left(\sum_{i=1}^{K} \xi_i\right)^2} \right\rangle =$$

$$\mathrm{Var}(\eta)\langle H(\xi, K)\rangle. \tag{7.91}$$

For lognormally distributed η_i and ξ_i, transformations, similar to those leading to Equation (7.86), yield

$$\sigma_{r'}^2(K) = \exp(2m_\eta + V_\eta)[\exp(V_\eta) - 1]\frac{\exp(V_\xi)}{K} \times \left(1 - \frac{2\exp(2V_\xi) - 3\exp(V_\xi) + 1)}{K} + \mathrm{O}(K^{-2})\right). \tag{7.92}$$

As in the previous case, the asymptotic expansion for the H-index does not converge for any K and can be used only for a relatively small V_ξ.

Combined Gibrat and Bose–Einstein process

In this section, we aim to find the leading terms in $P_r(r|K)$ when both $\lambda' = \lambda\Delta t > 0$, $\mu' = \mu\Delta t > 0$, $V_\xi > 0$ and $V_\eta > 0$. By combining the schemes of the two previous subsections, we can express r as

$$r = \ln \frac{\sum_{i=1}^{K'} \xi_i \eta_i}{\sum_{i=1}^{K} \xi_i}, \tag{7.93}$$

where for large K, $K' = K + K_\lambda - K_\mu$ with K_λ and K_μ being independent Poisson random variables with means $K\lambda'$ and $K\mu'$, respectively. Moreover, we can introduce centered random variables $\tilde{K}_\lambda = K_\lambda - K\lambda'$ and $\tilde{K}_\mu = K_\mu - K\mu'$ with variances $K\lambda'$ and $K\mu'$, respectively. Thus,

$$r = \ln \mu_{\eta,1} + \ln \frac{1 + \lambda' - \mu' + \frac{\tilde{K}_\lambda}{K} - \frac{\tilde{K}_\mu}{K} + \frac{A'}{K} + \frac{B'}{K}}{1 + \frac{B}{K}}, \tag{7.94}$$

where

$$A' = \frac{\sum_{i=1}^{K'} \xi_i (\eta_i - \mu_{1,\eta})}{\mu_{1,\eta}\mu_{1,\xi}} \tag{7.95}$$

$$B' = \frac{\sum_{i=1}^{K'} \xi_i - \mu_{1,\xi}}{\mu_{1,\xi}}. \tag{7.96}$$

By expanding the logarithm in inverse powers of K, we obtain

$$\begin{aligned} r = \ln \mu_{\eta,1} + \ln(1 + \lambda' - \mu') + \frac{1}{K(1 + \lambda' - \mu')} \\ \times (\tilde{K}_\lambda - \tilde{K}_\mu + A' + (B' - B) - (\lambda' - \mu')B). \end{aligned} \tag{7.97}$$

All of the random variables in this expression are centered and, hence, the average growth rate is

$$m_r = V_\eta/2 + m_\eta + \ln(1 + \lambda' - \mu') + O(1/K). \tag{7.98}$$

Next, we compute the variance of r, σ_r^2. Since $\tilde{\eta}_i \equiv \eta_i - \mu_{1,\eta}$ is independent of ξ_i, K_λ and K_μ, the covariance of A' with the rest of the terms is zero. The covariance of $\tilde{K}_\mu$ and $\tilde{K}_\lambda$ with B and B' is also zero, because $\tilde{\xi}_i \equiv \xi_i - \mu_{1,\xi}$ is centered. We can rewrite

$$B' - B = B_\lambda - B_\mu \equiv \frac{\sum^{K_\lambda} \tilde{\xi}'_i - \sum^{K_\mu} \tilde{\xi}''_i}{\mu_{1,\xi}}, \tag{7.99}$$

where $\tilde{\xi}'_i$ are the sizes of the new units, created at this time step, and $\tilde{\xi}''_i$ are the sizes of the old units, deleted at this time step. Note that all deleted units are present in the sum B and, hence, the covariance of B_μ and $(\lambda' - \mu')B$ is not zero, but is equal to $\text{Var}(B_\mu)(\lambda' - \mu')$. By using the formula for the variance of the sum of M independent random variables x_i, where M is a random variable, independent of x_i,

$$\text{Var}\left(\sum^{M} x_i\right) = \text{Var}(M)\text{E}^2(x_i) + \text{E}(M)\text{Var}(x_i),$$

we can obtain the variances of all of the terms in Equation (7.97):

$$\begin{aligned} \text{Var}(\tilde{K}_\lambda) &= \lambda' K \\ \text{Var}(\tilde{K}_\mu) &= \mu K \\ \text{Var}(A') &= K(1 + \lambda' - \mu')\text{Var}(\xi_i \tilde{\eta}_i)/(\mu_{1,\xi}\mu_{1,\eta})^2 \\ &= K(1 + \lambda' - \mu') \exp(V_\xi)[\exp(V_\eta) - 1] \\ \text{Var}(B_\lambda) &= K\lambda'\text{Var}(\xi) = K\lambda'[\exp(V_\xi) - 1] \\ \text{Var}(B_\mu) &= K\mu'\text{Var}(\xi) = K\mu'[\exp(V_\xi) - 1] \\ \text{Var}[(\lambda' - \mu')B] &= (\lambda' - \mu')^2 K[\exp(V_\xi) - 1]. \end{aligned} \tag{7.100}$$

By summing all terms and adding $2\text{Cov}(BB_\mu)(\lambda' - \mu') = 2(\lambda' - \mu')\text{Var}(B_\mu)$, we obtain:

$$\sigma_r^2(K) = \frac{(1+\lambda'-\mu')\exp(V_\xi)[\exp(V_\eta)-1]}{(1+\lambda'-\mu')^2 K} + \\ + \frac{(\lambda'+\mu')\exp(V_\xi) + (\lambda'^2 - \mu'^2)[\exp(V_\xi)-1]}{(1+\lambda'-\mu')^2 K}, \tag{7.101}$$

from which we obtain Equation (3.81). Note that the approximation $K' = K + K_\lambda - K_\mu$, where K_λ and K_μ are Poisson random variables, is valid only when λ' and μ' are small. Thus, to be mathematically consistent, we should expand Equation (7.101) in powers of λ' and μ' and drop all the nonlinear terms. However, the resulting equation will lose physical meaning and symmetry, without much gain in simplicity. Therefore, in our simulations, we refer to Equation (7.101).

7.3 Computer Simulations of Growth

Simulations of the Size-Variance Relationship as a Function of K

Since we cannot derive close-form expressions for $\sigma_r(K)$, we follow our own work (Riccaboni et al. 2008) and perform extensive computer simulations, where ξ and η are independent random variables taken from lognormal distributions P_ξ and P_η with different V_ξ and V_η, respectively.

First, we study the simple case of a nonlogarithmic growth rate, for which, according to Equation (7.89), the variance $\sigma_{r'}^2(K)$ can be expressed as a product of the variance of η and H-index of ξ. Hence, in order to study the dependence of $\sigma_{r'}^2$ on K, it is sufficient to study the dependence of $H(K)$. As shown in the last subsection, for small K and large V_ξ, $H(K) \approx 1$, while for $K > \exp(V_\xi)$, $H(K) \approx \exp(V_\xi)/K$. The results of our computer simulations reveal that for intermediate values of K, $1 \ll K \ll \exp(V_\xi)$, the behavior of $H(K)$ can be well approximated by a power law $H(K) \sim K^{-2\beta}$, where $0 < \beta < 1/2$. Indeed, Figure 7.3(a) shows that the curves $H(K)$ in a double logarithmic scale have a widening regime of a straight line behavior as V_ξ increases. The successive slopes of these approximately straight lines give the effective value of the power law exponent $\beta(K)$ (Figure 7.3(a)). One can see that for $V_\xi > 5$, the successive slopes, $\beta(K)$, develop a broad maximum, near which $\beta(K) \approx \beta_{\min}(V_\xi)$ is almost constant.

Interestingly, the inverse of $\beta_{\min}(V_\xi)$ is perfectly approximated for $V_\xi > 5$ by a straight line (Figure 7.4 (a)). Thus,

$$\beta_{\min} = \frac{1}{2(pV_\xi + q)}, \tag{7.102}$$

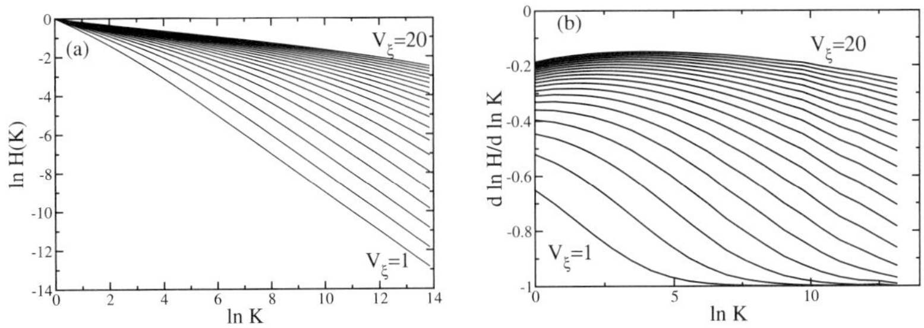

Figure 7.3 (a) Simulation results for $H(K)$, in the case of lognormal P_ξ with different V_ξ plotted against K in a double logarithmic scale. One can see that for large V_ξ, $\ln H(\ln K)$ can be well approximated by straight lines. (b) Successive slopes of the lines, plotted in panel (a), reveal a broad maximum, which gives an approximate value of the power law dependence $H(K) \sim K^{-2\beta_{\min}}$.

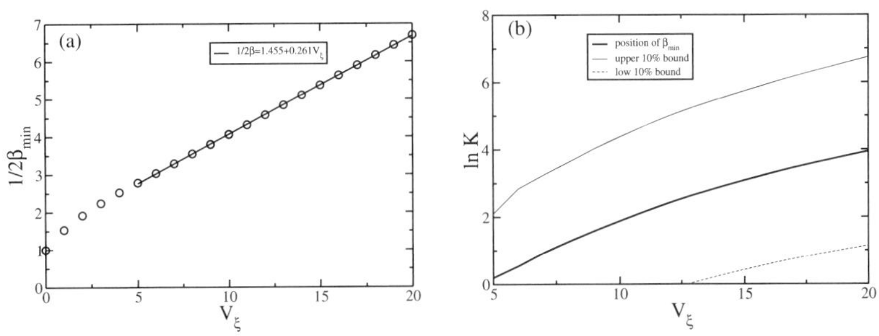

Figure 7.4 (a) The dependence of the inverse minimal value of $\beta(K)$ on V_ξ can be well approximated by a linear function. (b) The range of K, for which $\beta(K)$ is within 10% of its minimal value, increases with V_ξ.

where $p = 0.261$ and $q = 1.455$. The absolute value of the second derivative near this maximum decreases for $V_\xi \to \infty$, which causes the range of the approximate constancy of $\beta(K) \approx \beta_{\min}$ to increase with V_ξ (Figure 7.4(b)). Since in many natural systems $5 < V_\xi < 10$, our finding explains the abundance of an approximately power law size-variance relationship with $\beta \approx 0.18$.

As we suggested in Riccaboni et al. (2008), in the case of the logarithmic growth rate, σ_r^2, can be approximated as a product of a function of V_η and a function of V_ξ. The numerical results, presented in Figure 7.5, suggest that

$$\ln[\sigma^2(K)K/V_r] \approx F_\sigma\left[\ln(K) - f(V_\xi, V_\eta)\right], \tag{7.103}$$

where $F_\sigma(z)$ is a universal scaling function, describing a crossover from $F_\sigma(z) \to 0$ for $z \to \infty$ to $F_\sigma(z)/z \to 1$ for $z \to -\infty$, while $f(V_\xi, V_\eta) \approx f_\xi(V_\xi) + f_\eta(V_\eta)$ are functions of V_ξ and V_η, which have linear asymptotes for $V_\xi \to \infty$ and $V_\eta \to \infty$ (Figure 7.5(b)).

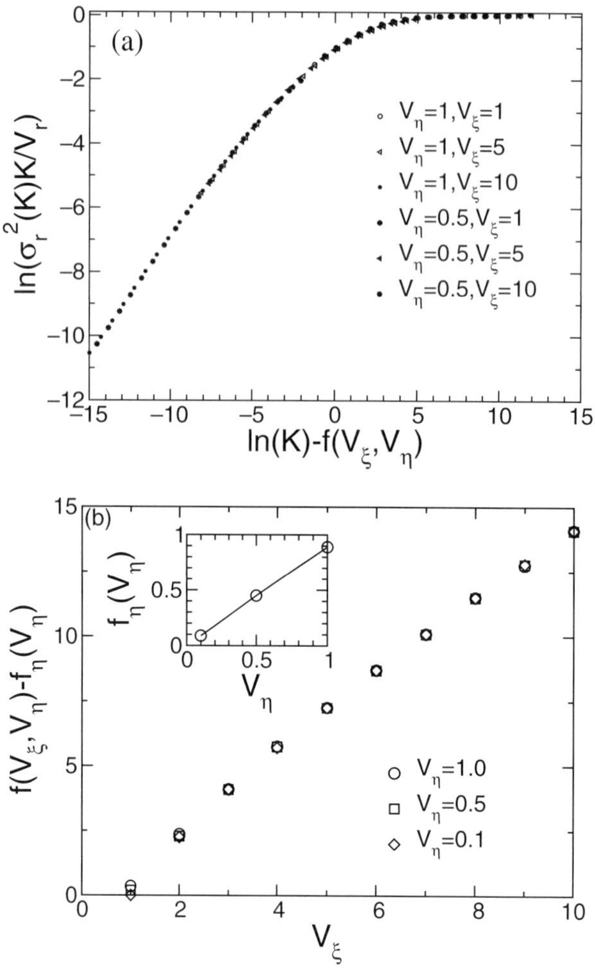

Figure 7.5 (a) Simulation results for $\sigma^2(K)$ in the case of lognormal P_ξ and P_η and different V_ξ and V_η, plotted on a universal scaling plot as a function of a scaling variable $z = \ln(K) - f(V_\xi, V_\eta)$. (b) The shift function $f(V_\xi, V_\eta)$. The graph shows that $f(V_\xi, V_\eta) \approx f_\xi(V_\xi) + f_\eta(V_\eta)$. Both $f_\xi(V_\xi)$ and $f_\eta(V_\eta)$ (inset) are approximately linear functions. The figure is reproduced from figure 4 in Riccaboni et al. (2008).

Accordingly, we can try to define $\beta(z) = (1 - dF_\sigma/dz)/2$ (Figure 7.6(a)). The main curve $\beta(z)$ can be approximated by an inversly linear function of z, when $z \to -\infty$, and by a stretched exponential as it approaches the asymptotic value 1/2 for $z \to +\infty$. The particular analytical shapes for these asymptotes are not known and are derived solely from the least square fitting of the numerical data. The scaling for $\beta(z)$ is an approximation with significant deviations from a universal curve for small K. For each V_ξ and V_η, $\beta(z)$ develops a minimum for a specific value of K, near which it is practically constant. The minimal value for β does not practically

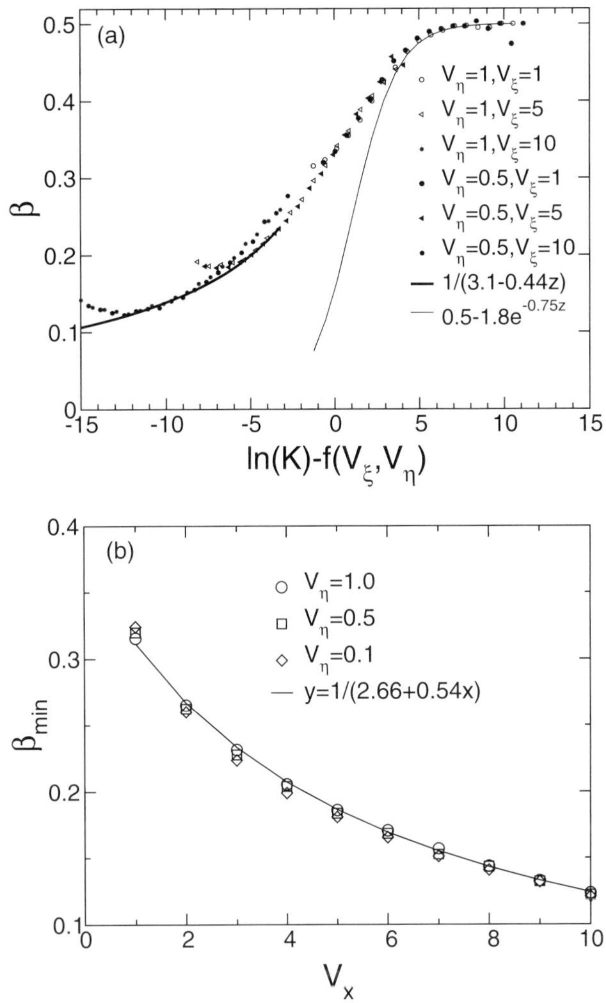

Figure 7.6 (a) The effective exponent $\beta(z)$, obtained by the differentiation of $\sigma^2(z)$, plotted in Figure 7.5(a). Solid lines indicate the least square fits for the left and right asymptotes. The graph shows significant deviations of $\beta(K, V_\xi, V_\eta)$ from a universal function $\beta(z)$ for small K, where $\beta(K)$ develops minima. (b) The dependence of the minimal value of $\beta_{\min}$ on V_ξ. One can see that this value practically does not depend on V_η and is inversly proportional to the linear function of V_ξ. The Figure reproduced from figure 5 in Riccaboni et al. (2008)

depend on V_η and is approximately inverse proportional to a linear function of V_ξ, as in Equation (7.102), with $p \approx 0.27$ and $q \approx 1.33$ in good agreement with the behavior of the nonlogarithmic growth rates (Figure 7.6(b)). This finding is significant for our study, since it indicates that near its minimum, $\beta(K)$ has a region of approximate constancy with the value $\beta_{\min}$ between 0.14 and 0.2 for V_ξ between 4 and 8, respectively. These values of V_ξ are quite realistic and correspond to the distribution of unit sizes, spanning over roughly two to three orders of magnitude (68% of all units), which is the case in the majority of economic and ecological systems. Thus, our study provides a reasonable explanation for the abundance of the value $\beta \approx 0.2$.

7.4 A Hierarchical Model and the Size-Variance Relationship

As we saw in Section 3.6, the GPG predicts that the variance of the growth rate undergoes a crossover from $\sigma_r(S) \sim S^{-\beta}$ for small S, with $\beta \approx 0$, as one expects for a class consisting of a single unit, to $\sigma_r(S) \sim S^{-1/2}$ for large S, as one expects for a class consisting of $K(S) = S/\mu_{1,\xi}$ units, due to the central limit theorem. Thus, within a GPG framework, the size-variance relationship cannot follow a simple power law with a fixed exponent $\beta < 1/2$, as the empirical data suggest. Assumption (6) of GPG postulates the absence of correlations between growth rates of different units of business firms. In this section, we will present a simple model of correlations between the units of the firm, which can be incorporated into the expanded version of the GPG benchmark. Throughout this section we closely follow the derivations presented in (Buldyrev et al. 1997).

Indeed, a long time ago, Hymer, Pashigian, and Mansfield (Hymer and Pashigian 1962; Mansfield 1962) noticed that the relationship between the variance of the growth rate and the size of business firms is not null but decreases with the increase in the size of a firm by a factor less than $1/K$, which we would expect if firms were a collection of K independent subunits of approximately equal size. In a lively debate in the mid-sixties, Simon and Mansfield (Ijiri and Simon 1964) argued that this was probably due to common managerial influences and other similarities of firm units, which imply that the growth rate of such components is positively correlated. This argument has been formalized (Stanley et al. 1996; Buldyrev et al. 1997).

In the following we refer to Buldyrev et al. (1997), and we reproduce the description of the hierarchical model that the authors have introduded. Let us assume that every company, regardless of its size, is made up of similarly sized units. (This can be assumed if the number of units in the company is much greater than $\exp(V_\xi)$.) Thus, a company of size $S(t)$ is, on average, made up of $K = S(t)/\mu_{1,\xi}$ units. We saw that if all the units change with the same growth rate η, then the growth rate of a company is the same as the growth rate of the units. Thus, $\sigma_r^2(S) = V_\eta$ is independent of the system size and, hence, $\beta = 0$. If, in contrast, all the units have independent growth rates η_i, then $\sigma_r^2 = V_r/K = V_r\mu_{1,\xi}/S$, and $\sigma_r(S) \sim S^{-\beta}$ with $\beta = 1/2$. In reality, η_i for different units may be correlated and this may lead to the intermediate value of $0 < \beta < 1/2$.

The much smaller value of β than 1/2 indicates the presence of strong positive correlations among a company's units. We can understand this result by considering

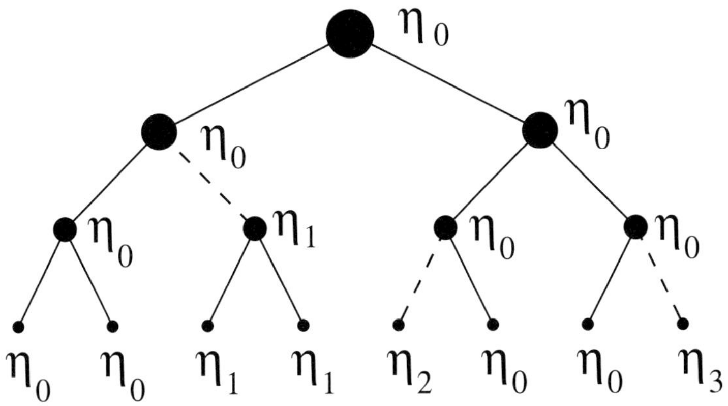

Figure 7.7 The hierarchical-tree model of a company. As an example, we represent a company as a branching tree with a branching factor $z = 2$. Here, the head of the company makes a decision about the change in the size of the lowest level units by a factor η_0. This decision is propagated through the tree, however, it is only followed with a probability Π, pictured in the figure as a full link. With probability $(1 - \Pi)$ a new growth rate η_i taken from the same distribution is defined, pictured as a slashed link. We see that at the lowest level, there are clusters of values η_i for the changes in size. The number of links connecting the nodes in a real company may vary from level to level and from node to node. We assume, however, that the results of our simple model are still valid if z represents some "typical" numbers of links. The figure is reproduced from figure 1 in Buldyrev et al. (1997)

the tree-like hierarchical organization of a typical company described by (Radner 1993). The head of the tree represents the head of the company, whose policy is passed on to the level beneath, and so on, until the units in the lowest level take action. As before, we assume that at time t the units have sizes $\xi_i(t)$ with $i = 1, 2, \ldots, K$, while their sizes at time $t + \Delta t$ are equal to $\xi_i(t + \Delta t) = \eta_i \xi_i(t)$. We also assume that at every level, except the lower one, each node is connected to h units in the following lower level, where h is a random variable with mean z and variance Z. Finally, we assume that only the units at the lowest level are production units and thus $S(t) = K\mu_{1,\xi}$, where K is the number of units at the lowest level of the tree (see Figure 7.7).

What are the consequences of this simple model? Let us first assume that the head of the company suggests a policy that could result in changing the size of each unit in the lowest level by a factor η_0. If this policy is propagated through the hierarchy without any modifications, then it is the same as assuming that all $\eta_i = \eta_0$ are identical, implying as we have seen before, that $\beta = 0$.

Of course, it is not realistic to expect that all decisions in an organization would be perfectly coordinated, as if they were all dictated by a single "boss." Hierarchies might be designed to take advantage of the information at different levels; and mid-level managers might even be instructed to deviate from decisions made at a higher levels, if they have information that strongly suggests that an alternative decision would be superior. Another possible explanation for some independence in the decision-making process is organizational failure due to either poor communication or disobedience.

In order to model the intermediate case between $\beta = 0$ and $\beta = 1/2$, let us assume that the head of a company makes a decision to change the size of the units in a company by a factor η_0. Furthermore, we consider that each manager at the nodes of the hierarchical tree follows his supervisor's policy with a probability Π, while he/she imposes a new *independent* policy with a probability $(1 - \Pi)$. The latter case corresponds to the manager, acting as the head of a smaller company made up of the units under his supervision. Hence, the size of the company becomes a random variable with a standard deviation that can be computed either with numerical simulations or using recursion relations among the levels of the tree.

Let $S(t + \Delta t)$, as before, represent the final size of a company with an initial size $S(t)$ and assume that the company has ℓ levels in its hierarchical tree. According to the rules of the model, the decision of the head of the company will only be followed by the units at the bottom level that are connected to the top by a chain of managers with "obeying links." Thus, the number of units, T_ℓ, in the company that follow the policy of the company head can be related to the problem of the number of male descendents of a family after ℓ generations (Harris 1989). The solution is that, for a ℓ-level tree with an average branching factor z, the average number of units at the end is given by:

$$\langle T_\ell \rangle = (z\Pi)^\ell. \tag{7.104}$$

We can see that the bottom, the ℓ-th, level of the tree is now divided into M_ℓ different clusters of size κ_i, each corresponding to a different independent value of η_i:

$$\sum_{i=0}^{M_\ell} \kappa_i = K_\ell, \tag{7.105}$$

where K_ℓ is the number of units at ℓ-th level of the tree. The size of the firm at time $t + \Delta t$ is then

$$S(t + \Delta t) = \sum_{i=0}^{M_\ell} \eta_i \sum_{j=1}^{\kappa_i} \xi_j, \tag{7.106}$$

where η_i and ξ_j are independent random variables. The new size for each cluster can be represented as a product of two independent random variables $y_i = \eta_i$ and

$$x_i = \sum_{j=0}^{\kappa_i} \xi_j, \tag{7.107}$$

so that

$$S(t + \Delta t) = \sum_{i=0}^{M_\ell} y_i x_i. \tag{7.108}$$

Now we present a brief heuristic derivation of the value of β, based on the fact that x_i has a power law distribution $P(x_i > x) \sim x^{1-\tau}$. Indeed, the average size of the cluster that originates at level n of the tree is equal to $(z\Pi)^{\ell-n}$. The average number of such clusters is equal to $(1 - \Pi)z^n$. By constructing a Zipf plot based on this information, we see that

$$\tau - 1 = \frac{\ln z}{\ln(z\Pi)}.$$

If the second moment of the distribution $P(x_i)$ exists ($\tau > 3$), then the H-index of a collection of M_ℓ variables x_i scales inverse proportionally to M_ℓ, while for $2 < \tau < 3$, when the second moment diverges,

$$H \sim M_\ell^{\frac{2}{\tau-1}-2}.$$

The total number of clusters M_ℓ is proportional to the total number of units in the tree, $K = z^\ell$, because for $\tau > 2$ the distribution $P(x_i)$ has a finite first moment. But K is proportional to the total size of the firm, S, because the units have average size $\langle\xi\rangle$. Hence, $H \sim S^{\frac{2}{\tau-1}-2}$. Using Equation (7.89), we see that for $\tau > 3$, $\beta = 1/2$, while for $2 < \tau < 3$,

$$\beta = \frac{\tau - 2}{\tau - 1} = -\frac{\ln \Pi}{\ln z}, \tag{7.109}$$

exactly as in the Takayasu model (Takayasu et al., 2014) with the difference that in their model, the distribution of unit sizes follows a power law, while in the hierarchical model the distribution of correlated clusters of units follows a power law.

In the following we will present a rigorous derivation of Equation (7.109). We can present the logarithmic growth rate of the firm, as in the pure Gibrat process, using Equation (7.83):

$$r = \ln(\mu_{1,\eta}) + \ln \frac{1 + (A + B)/K}{1 + B/K} = \ln(\mu_{1,\eta}) + \frac{A}{K}[1 + o(1)], \tag{7.110}$$

where $o(1) \to 0$ for $K \to \infty$ and

$$A = \frac{\sum_{i=1}^{M_\ell} x_i(\eta_i - \mu_{1,\eta})}{\mu_{1,\eta}\mu_{1,\xi}} \tag{7.111}$$

$$B = \frac{\sum_{i=1}^{K} \xi_i - \mu_{1,\xi}}{\mu_{1,\xi}}. \tag{7.112}$$

Since η_i and x_i are independent, $\langle A \rangle = 0$,

$$m_r = \ln(\mu_{1,\eta})[1 + o(1)]$$

and

$$\sigma_r^2 = \frac{\langle A^2 \rangle}{K^2}. \tag{7.113}$$

For any particular configuration of the obeying links, the average of A^2, taken over the distribution of η and ξ, is given by the diagonal terms:

$$\langle A^2 \rangle_{\eta,\xi} = \sum_{i=0}^{M_\ell} \mathrm{Var}(\eta_i) \langle x_i^2 \rangle_\xi / (\mu_{1,\eta}\mu_{1,\xi})^2. \tag{7.114}$$

By taking into account Equation (7.107), one can see that

$$\langle x_i^2 \rangle_\xi = \kappa_i(\mu_{2,\xi} - \mu_{1,\xi}^2) + \kappa_i^2 \mu_{1,x}^2. \tag{7.115}$$

Finally, by using Equation (7.105), we arrive at

$$\langle A^2 \rangle = \mathrm{Var}(\eta_i)/\mu_{1,\eta}^2 \left[K \mathrm{Var}(\xi_i)/\mu_{1,\xi}^2 + \left\langle \sum_{i=0}^{M_\ell} \kappa_i^2 \right\rangle_\Pi \right], \tag{7.116}$$

where $\langle \ldots \rangle_\Pi$ denotes the average over all configurations of the disobeying links. When we find this average as a function of K, we will find β. Let us introduce a random variable m_ℓ:

$$m_\ell = \sum_{i=0}^{M_\ell} \kappa_i^2. \tag{7.117}$$

In order to calculate $\langle m_\ell \rangle_\Pi$, we start by computing the conditional average value $\langle m_\ell \rangle |_{m_{\ell-1}}$, where $m_{\ell-1}$ refers to the previous level on the tree. A cluster of size κ_i, in the $(\ell - 1)$ level, is connected to χ_i nodes at the ℓ-th level:

$$\chi_i = \sum_{j=1}^{\kappa_i} h_j, \tag{7.118}$$

where h_j is the number of branches of the jth node connecting it to the units in the ℓ-level; κ_i' of the links are obeying, while $(\chi_i - \kappa_i')$ are disobeying. The obeying links will give rise to a cluster of size κ_i' in level ℓ, while the disobeying links give rise to $(\chi_i - \kappa_i')$ clusters of size one. Thus, we obtain

$$m_\ell = \sum_{i=0}^{M_{\ell-1}} \left(\kappa_i'^2 + (\chi_i - \kappa_i')\right)$$
$$= \sum_{i=1}^{M_{\ell-1}} (\kappa_i'^2 - \kappa_i') + \sum_{i=0}^{M_{\ell-1}} \chi_i.$$

The probability of a configuration with a κ_i' obeying links is

$$\binom{\chi_i}{\kappa_i'} \Pi^{\kappa_i'}(1-\Pi)^{\chi_i-\kappa_i'}. \tag{7.119}$$

Averaging over all possible configurations of links, we obtain

$$\langle m_\ell \rangle|_{m_{\ell-1}} = \sum_{i=1}^{M_{\ell-1}} \left\{ \sum_{\kappa_i'=0}^{\chi_i} \binom{\chi_i}{\kappa_i'} \Pi^{\kappa_i'}(1-\Pi)^{\chi_i-\kappa_i'}(\kappa_i'^2 - \kappa_i') \right\} + \sum_{i=1}^{M_{\ell-1}} \chi_i. \tag{7.120}$$

The series in Equation (7.120) can be calculated through combinatorics. By defining $q = 1 - \Pi$, $k = \chi_i$, and $j = \kappa_i'$, we obtain

$$\sum_{j=0}^{k} \binom{k}{j} (j^2 - j)\Pi^j (1-\Pi)^{k-j} = \Pi^2 \frac{\partial^2}{\partial \Pi^2} (\Pi + q)^s|_{\Pi+q=1}$$
$$= k(k-1)\Pi^2. \tag{7.121}$$

By replacing this result into Equation (7.120), we obtain

$$\langle m_k \rangle|_{m_{\ell-1}} = (\Pi)^2 \sum_{i=1}^{M_{\ell-1}} \chi_i^2 \tag{7.122}$$
$$- \Pi^2 \sum_{i=1}^{M_{\ell-1}} \chi_i + \sum_{i=1}^{M_{\ell-1}} \chi_i. \tag{7.123}$$

Now we can average this equation over all realizations of the tree. Note that $\sum_{i-1}^{M_{\ell-1}} \chi_i = K_\ell$, $\langle K_\ell \rangle = z^\ell$ and $\langle \chi_i^2 \rangle = \kappa_i^2 z^2 + \kappa_i Z$. Hence, $\langle m_\ell \rangle_\Pi$ satisfies the recursion relation:

$$\langle m_\ell \rangle_\Pi = (z\Pi)^2 \langle m_{\ell-1} \rangle_\Pi + ((1-\Pi^2)z + \Pi^2 Z)z^{\ell-1}, \qquad \langle m_0 \rangle_\Pi = 1. \tag{7.124}$$

By writing the first few terms in succession and using induction shows that

$$\langle m_\ell \rangle_\Pi = (z\Pi)^{2\ell} + [(1 + \Pi(^2 Z/z - 1)]z^\ell \sum_{i=0}^{\ell-1} (z\Pi^2)^i. \tag{7.125}$$

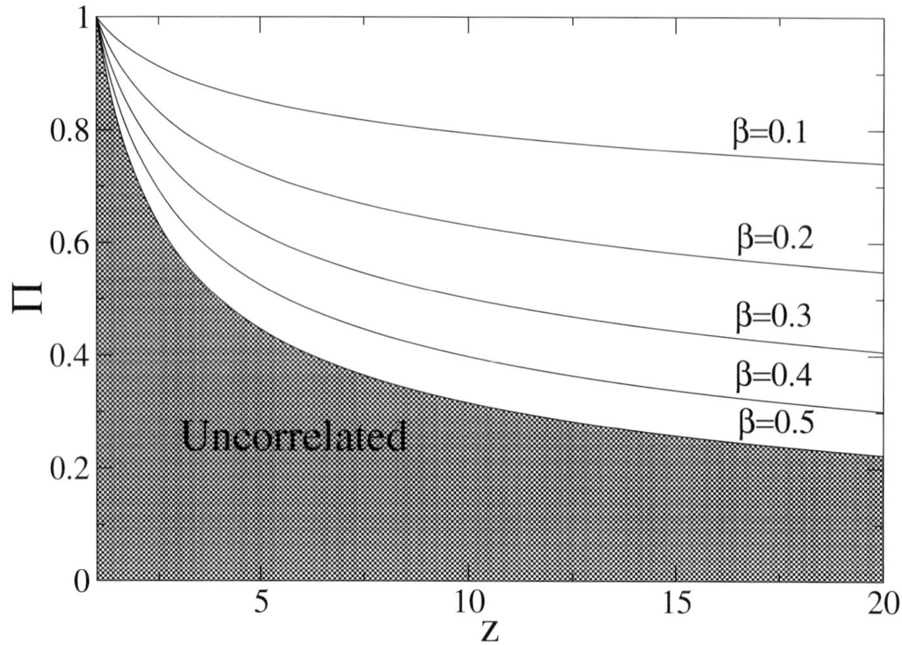

Figure 7.8 A phase diagram of the hierarchical tree model. Each pair of values of (Π, z) specifies a value of β. The plotted isolines correspond to several values of β. In the shaded area, marked "Uncorrelated," the model predicts that $\beta = 1/2$, i.e., the units of the company are uncorrelated. Our empirical data suggests that most companies have values of Π and z, close to the curve for $\beta = 0.2$. The figure is reproduced from figure 2 in Buldyrev et al. (1997)

Replacement of the geometric series by its value and simple calculations lead to

$$\langle m_\ell \rangle_\Pi = \left[(\Pi z)^{2\ell} (\Pi^2 (z - 1 + Z/z) - z^\ell (\Pi^2 (Z/z - 1) + 1) \right] / (z\Pi^2 - 1). \tag{7.126}$$

By combining this result with Equations (7.113) and (7.116) and using $\ell = \ln K / \ln z$, we obtain

$$\sigma_r^2(K) = \frac{\mathrm{Var}(\eta)}{\mu_{1,\eta}^2} \left[\left(\frac{\mathrm{Var}\xi}{\mu_{1,\xi}^2} - \frac{1 + \Pi^2(Z/z - 1)}{\Pi^2 z - 1} \right) K^{-1} + \frac{\Pi^2(z - 1 + Z/z)}{\Pi^2 z - 1} K^{-2\beta} \right], \tag{7.127}$$

where

$$\beta = -\frac{\ln \Pi}{\ln z}. \tag{7.128}$$

If $\Pi^2 z > 1$, then $\beta < 1/2$ and the second term in Equation (7.127) dominates and, thus, $\sigma_r(K) \sim K^\beta$ for $K \to \infty$. On the other hand, if $\Pi^2 z < 1$, then the first term in (7.127) dominates and $\sigma_r(K) \sim K^{-1/2}$ for $K \to \infty$, which implies that $\beta = 1/2$.

Since for $K \to \infty$, $S \sim K$, using the same arguments as in Section 3.6, we can conclude that, for $S \to \infty$, the hierarchical model leads to $\sigma_r(S) \sim S^{-\beta}$, where

$$\beta = \begin{cases} -\ln \Pi / \ln z & \text{if} \quad \Pi > z^{-1/2}, \\ 1/2 & \text{if} \quad \Pi < z^{-1/2}. \end{cases} \tag{7.129}$$

For finite S, one expects a crossover from a smaller values of β to the asymptotic value given by Equation (7.129).

Equation (7.129) is confirmed in the two limiting cases. When $\Pi = 1$ (absolute control), then $\beta = 0$. In contrast, if $\Pi < 1/z^{1/2}$, then decisions at the upper levels of management have no statistical effect on decisions made at the lower levels, and $\beta = 1/2$. Moreover, for a given value of $\beta < 1/2$, the control level Π will be a decreasing function of z: $\Pi = z^{-\beta}$, cf. Figure 7.8. For example, if we choose the empirical value $\beta \approx 0.15$, then Equation (7.129) predicts the plausible result $0.9 \geq \Pi \geq 0.7$ for a range of z in the interval $2 \leq z \leq 10$.

7.5 Statistical Appendix

In this section, we provide a brief description of some statistical distributions used to describe size and growth distributions. An extensive survey of parametric statistical distributions of economic size phenomena is provided by Kleiber and Kotz (2003).

Size and Growth Distributions

Power Law and Zipf's Law

The power law distribution has been used to describe a large number of empirical regularities in economics and finance (Gabaix 2009), computer science (Mitzenmacher 2003), physics, biology and social systems (Newman 2005). A random variable X, for $X \geq x_0 > 0$ follows a power law distribution if its complementary cumulative distribution function[5] (CCDF) is a power function of the form:

$$P(X > x) = Cx^{-\gamma}, \tag{7.130}$$

where $\gamma > 0$, $C > 0$. If both x and bx are larger than x_0, then a power law distribution satisfies $p(bx) = g(b)p(x)$, where $g(b) = b^{-\gamma}$, i.e., it is a *scale free* distribution if we ignore the cutoff x_0.

[5] The complementary cumulative distribution function is given by $1 - P(X \leq x)$.

A graphical inspection to see if an empirical distribution can follow a power law behavior consists of plotting the empirical CCDF in log–log scale. Indeed, since

$$\log[P(X > x)] = \log(Cx^{-\gamma}) = \log(C) - \gamma \log(x), \tag{7.131}$$

the CCDF of a power law distribution with exponent γ can be approximated with a straight line with slope = $-\gamma$ (Mitzenmacher 2003).

Among the most widespread names for the power law distributions are the Pareto distribution and Zipf's law (Pareto 1896; Zipf 1949).

Zipf's law states that the size y of the r-th largest occurrence of an event is inversely proportional to its rank r:

$$y \sim r^{-b}. \tag{7.132}$$

For example, if y is a certain income then Equation (7.132) means that the r-th richest person has an income r^b times smaller than the income of the richest person. Remember that if Equation (7.132) holds, then:

$$r \sim y^{-1/b}, \tag{7.133}$$

the probability that the variable Y will be equal to y is:

$$P(Y = y) = \frac{dr}{dy} \sim y^{-(1+1/b)}. \tag{7.134}$$

As we will see below, the expression in Equation (7.134) represents the PDF of a Pareto distribution.

Pareto Distribution

Italian civil engineer, economist and sociologist, Vilfredo Pareto, was the pioneer among scholars who, over time, devoted themselves to the study of size distributions. Pareto, in his *Cours d'économie politique* (Pareto 1896), showed that the number of taxpayers (in logarithmic scale) with an income higher than a certain threshold x and the value x (also in logarithmic scale) were related by a relationship almost linear with a slope = $-\gamma$ for some $\gamma > 0$.

Formally:

$$\ln(N_x) = A + \ln(x^{-\gamma}), \tag{7.135}$$

where $A, \gamma > 0$.

The cumulative distribution function (CDF) of a Pareto distribution is defined as:

$$F(x) = 1 - \left(\frac{x}{x_0}\right)^{-\gamma}, \quad x \geq x_0 > 0, \tag{7.136}$$

where γ is the shape parameter and x_0 is the scale parameter, while the density function is given by

$$f(x) = \frac{\gamma x_0^{\gamma}}{x^{\gamma+1}}, \quad x \geq x_0 > 0. \tag{7.137}$$

In Equation (7.137), γ is the parameter associated with the heaviness of the distribution tail: the tail is heavier if γ is smaller. Furthermore, $\gamma = \alpha - 1$, where α is the power-law slope.

The raw k-th moment[6] μ'_k is given by

$$\mu'_k = \frac{\gamma x_0^k}{\gamma - k}, \tag{7.138}$$

and exists only if $k < \gamma$.

The mean and variance expressions for a Pareto distribution are derived from the raw moment (Equation 7.138). The expected value is given by:

$$E(X) = \frac{\gamma x_0}{\gamma - 1}, \tag{7.139}$$

and exists only if $\gamma > 1$[7]. The variance is given by:

$$var(X) = \frac{\gamma x_0^2}{(\gamma - 1)^2(\gamma - 2)}, \tag{7.140}$$

and exists only if $\gamma > 2$. However, there is a variety of distributions for which Equation (6.123) holds asymptotically for large enough x. These distributions are said to have a power law or a Pareto tail but, technically, they are not Pareto distributions.

If a random variable Y follows an exponential distribution, for $Y > y_0$, then the random variable $X = \exp(Y)$ follows a Pareto distribution. Indeed, if

$$P(Y > y) = \begin{cases} e^{-(y-y_0)\gamma} & \text{if} \quad y > y_0, \\ 1 & \text{if} \quad y \leq y_0. \end{cases} \tag{7.141}$$

By introducing $x = \exp(y)$, $x_0 = \exp(y_0)$,

$$P(Y > y) = P(\ln(X) > \ln(x)) = P(X > x) = \begin{cases} e^{-(y-y_0)\gamma} = \left(\frac{x_0}{x}\right)^{\gamma} & \text{if} \quad x > x_0, \\ 1 & \text{if} \quad x \leq x_0, \end{cases} \tag{7.142}$$

which coincides with the definition of a Pareto distribution.

[6] The k-th raw moment of a distribution with continuous pdf $f(x)$ is defined as $\mu'_k = \int_{-\infty}^{+\infty} x^k f(x)dx$.

[7] For extremely heavy-tailed distributions of this class, other measures of location must be used (Kleiber and Kotz 2003).

Generalized Pareto Distribution

The generalized Pareto distribution (GPD) is a family of continuous probability distributions with three parameters: μ is the location parameter, σ is the scale parameter and ξ is the shape parameter. The GPD probability density function is given by:

$$f(x) = \frac{1}{\sigma}\left(1 + \xi\frac{x-\mu}{\sigma}\right)^{\left(-\frac{1}{\xi}-1\right)}, \tag{7.143}$$

for $x \geqslant \mu$ when $\xi \geqslant 0$, and for $\mu \leqslant x \leqslant \mu - \sigma/\xi$ when $\xi < 0$, where $\mu \in \mathbb{R}$, $\sigma > 0$, and $\xi \in \mathbb{R}$. The GPD with shape $\xi > 0$ and location $\mu = \sigma/\xi$ is equivalent to the Pareto distribution with scale $x_0 = \sigma/\xi$ and shape $\gamma = 1/\xi$, while if the shape ξ and location μ are both zero, the shape of the GPD is equivalent to the exponential distribution.

The shape GPD defines three classes of models nested in the GPD family

- when the shape parameter is equal to zero, we obtain a class of distributions characterized by a tail that decreases exponentially;
- when the shape parameter is positive, we obtain a class of distributions characterized by a tail that decreases as a polynomial, such as the Student's t distribution;
- distributions whose tails are finite, such as a beta-distribution, lead to a negative shape parameter.

Lognormal Distribution

The initial use of a lognormal distribution as size distribution is attributed to Robert Gibrat, who observed that the size distribution of French firms followed a lognormal distribution (Gibrat 1931).

Formally, a random variable X has a lognormal distribution if $\ln(X)$ has a normal distribution.

The PDF of a lognormal distribution can therefore be easily derived from the expression of the PDF of a normal distribution. In particular, remembering that in the case of a normal distribution the PDF is:

$$N(y) = \frac{1}{\sqrt{2\pi}\sigma}e^{-\frac{(y-\mu)^2}{2\sigma^2}}, \tag{7.144}$$

then, the PDF of a lognormal distribution is given by:

$$LN(x) = \frac{1}{x\sqrt{2\pi}\sigma}e^{-\frac{1}{2\sigma^2}(\ln x-\mu)^2}, \quad x > 0, \mu \in \mathbb{R}, \sigma > 0 \tag{7.145}$$

where μ is the mean and σ^2 is the variance.

The moment generating function can be expressend in terms of the moment-generating function of a normal distribution:

$$E(X^k) = E(e^{kY}) = e^{k\mu+\frac{1}{2}k^2\sigma 2}. \tag{7.146}$$

From Equation (7.146) follows that the mean of a lognormal distribution is

$$E(X) = e^{\frac{\mu+\sigma^2}{2}}, \tag{7.147}$$

and the variance is

$$\mathrm{Var}(X) = e^{2\mu+\sigma^2}(e^{\sigma^2} - 1). \tag{7.148}$$

The lognormal distribution has finite moments of all orders.

By exploiting the relationship between a normal and a lognormal distribution, some properties of normal distributions can be applied to lognormal distributions after an appropriate change of the parameters. For example, since the sum of normal random variables is still a normal random variable, it follows that the product of lognormal random variables is still a lognormal random variable. Formally, if X_1 and X_2 are two independent random variables with distributions $X_1 \sim LN(\mu_1, \sigma_1^2)$ and $X_2 \sim LN(\mu_2, \sigma_2^2)$, respectively, then

$$X_1 X_2 \sim LN(\mu_1 + \mu_2,\ \sigma_1^2 + \sigma_2^2). \tag{7.149}$$

Unfortunately, the sums of lognormal random variables are not easily tractable (Kleiber and Kotz 2003).

As we have seen, both the Pareto distribution and the lognormal distribution can be obtained from the exponential transformation of another distribution. Moreover, the CCDF in a double-logarithmic scale of the two distributions are very similar, sometimes indistinguishable, at least in the right tail (Mitzenmacher 2003).

For the Pareto distribution the behavior is exactly linear, while for the lognormal distribution the behavior will be almost linear for a large portion of the distribution. In fact, using the PDF, we know that for the Pareto distribution, the log of the PDF is:

$$\ln f(x) = (-\gamma - 1)\ln x + \gamma \ln x_0 + \ln \gamma, \tag{7.150}$$

while for the lognormal it is:

$$\ln f(x) = -\frac{(\ln x)^2}{2\sigma^2} + \left(\frac{\mu}{\sigma^2} - 1\right)\ln x - \ln\sqrt{2\pi}\sigma - \frac{\mu^2}{2\sigma^2}. \tag{7.151}$$

This fact implies that it is difficult to distinguish the Pareto distribution from the lognormal distribution using only a visual test. Some statistical tests used to distinguish between the two distributions will be discussed in the following sections.

Growth Distribution

In classical models, the logarithmic growth rates are assumed to be normally distributed, where the PDF of a normal random variable is expressed by Equation (7.144). In reality, empirical investigation has showed that the distribution of the growth rates is not normal but "tent-shaped." For this reason, the distributions used in this book to describe the growth rate exhibit a "tent shape" behavior. In particular, we used distributions belonging to the exponential power family. Since the family of exponential power distributions is a subset of the class of scale mixture of normal distributions (Kleiber and Kotz 2003), in the first part of this section we provide a brief description of the scale mixture of normal distributions. Then, we describe the exponential power family and some special cases of this family.

Scale Mixture of Normal Distributions

If Y is a random variable with density f_y and K is a positive random variable with density f_k, then the distribution of $X = KY$ is called a scale-mixture with a scale mixing density f_k and its PDF is given by

$$f_x(x) = \int_0^{\infty} f_x(x|k = h) f_k(h) dh = \int_0^{\infty} h^{-1} f_y(h^{-1}x) f_k(h) dh. \qquad (7.152)$$

Suppose that Y has a standard normal distribution, by substituting the density of a standard normal in Equation (7.152) we obtain the PDF of a scale mixture of Gaussian distributions (West 1987). Many unimodal and symmetric distributions can be derived from the class of the scale mixture of normal distributions (Andrews and Mallows 1974; West 1987). The precise shape of the distribution depends on the mixing density f_k. In particular, if we assume that f_k is exponentially distributed, we obtain an exponential mixtures of Gaussians, given by (Buldyrev et. al 2007):

$$f_x = \int_0^{\infty} \lambda e^{-\lambda K} \frac{1}{\sqrt{2\pi V K^{\psi}}} e^{-\frac{y^2}{2VK^{\psi}}} dK, \qquad (7.153)$$

where ψ is the scaling parameter. Some of the probability density functions that are obtained by varying the scaling parameter are summarized by (Buldyrev, Riccaboni, Growiec, Stanley, and Pammolli 2007) as shown in Table 7.1.

The Exponential Power Distribution

A random variable X is said to follow an exponential power distribution[8] if its density is given by

$$f(x) = \frac{1}{2\alpha^{1/\alpha}\sigma_\alpha \Gamma(1 + 1/\alpha)} \exp\left(-\frac{1}{\alpha\sigma_\alpha^\alpha}|x - \mu|^\alpha\right), \quad -\infty < x < \infty, \qquad (7.154)$$

[8] In physics literature, it is known as a stretched exponential distribution.

Table 7.1 *Probability density functions that are obtained by varying the scaling parameter. Φ denotes the cumulative distribution function (CDF) of the standard normal distribution.*

ψ	Probability density function (PDF)
$\psi > 1$	Exponential power with shape parameter $\alpha \in (0,1)$
$\psi = 1$	Laplace, $p(x) = \frac{1}{2}\sqrt{\frac{2\lambda}{V}}\ \exp\left(-\sqrt{\frac{2\lambda}{V}}\lvert x\rvert\right)$
$0 < \psi < 1$	Exponential power with shape parameter $\alpha \in (1,2)$
$\psi = 0$	Gaussian, $p(x) = \frac{1}{\sqrt{2\pi V}}\ \exp\left(-\frac{x^2}{2V}\right)$
$\psi < 0$	Emergence of power law tails
$\psi = -1$	$\sim x^{-3}$, $p(x) = \frac{\lambda}{2\sqrt{2V}}\left(\frac{x^2}{2V} + \lambda\right)^{3/2}$
$\psi = -2$	$\sim x^{-2}$, $p(x) = \frac{\lambda^2\sqrt{V}}{2\sqrt{\pi}x^2}\left(1 - \left(1 - 2\Phi\left(\frac{\lambda\sqrt{V}}{\sqrt{2}\lvert x\rvert}\right)\right)\sqrt{\pi V}\ \exp\left(\frac{\lambda^2 V}{2x^2}\right)\right)$

where $-\infty < \mu < \infty$ is the location parameter, $\alpha > 0$ is the shape parameter and $\sigma_\alpha > 0$ is the scale parameter (Kleiber and Kotz 2003), with

$$\sigma_\alpha = E\left[\lvert X-\mu\rvert^\alpha\right]^{1/\alpha} = \left[\int_{-\infty}^{+\infty} \lvert x-\mu\rvert^\alpha f(x)dx\right]^{1/\alpha}. \tag{7.155}$$

This distribution was named exponential power by Box and Tiao (1973) but it is known under different names since it was rediscovered several times in different contexts and with different parameterizations. The exponential power is often named Subbotin (1923), generalized Laplace distribution, generalized error distribution or generalized normal distribution of order p (Vianelli 1963; Kotz et al. 2001).

The exponential power is a family of unimodal and symmetric distributions. The shape of the distribution depends on the α parameter. In particular, the shape parameter α is linked to the thickness of the tails: for $0 < \alpha < 2$, a leptokurtic distribution is obtained, while for $\alpha > 2$, a platykurtic distribution is obtained.[9] By substituting, in Equation (7.154), $\alpha = 2$ we obtain the PDF of a normal distribution. For $\alpha \to \infty$, Equation (7.154) becomes the PDF of a uniform random variable, while, if $\alpha = 1$ we obtain

$$f(x) = \frac{1}{2\sigma}e^{-\frac{1}{\sigma}\lvert x-\mu\rvert}, \tag{7.156}$$

which is the PDF of a Laplace distribution, that will be discussed in the next section.

Due to its symmetry, the exponential power distribution has all its odd central moments equal to zero, while the k-th even central moment is defined as

$$\mu_k = (\sigma_\alpha \alpha^{1/\alpha})^k \frac{\Gamma((k+1)/\alpha)}{\Gamma(1/\alpha)}. \tag{7.157}$$

[9] A leptokurtic distribution has a kurtosis greater than three, while a platykurtic distribution has a kurtosis smaller than three.

Laplace Distribution

The PDF of a classical Laplace distribution is given by Equation (7.156), a new re-parametrization of this density is obtained by replacing $\sigma = S/\sqrt{2}$:

$$g(x) = \frac{1}{\sqrt{2}S} e^{-\sqrt{2}|x-\mu|/S}, \quad -\infty < x < \infty, \tag{7.158}$$

while the PDF of a standard Laplace distribution is, by setting $\mu = 0$ in Equation (7.158) and unit variance:

$$g(x) = \frac{1}{\sqrt{2}} e^{-\sqrt{2}|x|}, \quad -\infty < x < \infty. \tag{7.159}$$

The k-th even central moment for a classical Laplace distribution with density (7.156) is

$$\mu_k = \sigma^k k!, \tag{7.160}$$

whereas the odd central moments are all equal to zero. The central absolute moment of a classical Laplace distribution is given by

$$\nu_n = \sigma^n \Gamma(n+1), \tag{7.161}$$

and, in particular, the mean is $\mathrm{E}(x) = \mu$, while the variance is $\mathrm{Var}(x) = 2\sigma^2$.

The Laplace distribution admits many different representations characterized and summarized by Kotz et al. (2001), among these we want to remark the relationship with the exponential and the Pareto distributions. A standard Laplace distribution is also known as the law of the difference between two exponential random variables, since if W_1 and W_2 are two exponential i.i.d. random variables, then $X = W_1 - W_2$ follows a Laplace distribution. For this reason, the Laplace distribution is also known as double exponential distribution or two-tailed exponential distribution. Similarly, a Laplace distribution can be represented in terms of two independent Pareto distributions. Therefore, if P_1 and P_2 are two i.i.d. Pareto random variables, then $X = \ln(P_1/P_2)$ is a standard Laplace distribution.

The Laplace distribution can be also obtained as a mixture between a Gaussian distribution and an exponential distribution, as we have shown in Table 6.1.

Statistical Test of Goodness of Fit

In this section, we describe some statistical methods to assess whether a given distribution is suited to a dataset. In particular, we briefly introduce the most common nonparametric tests, tests based on the likelihood and tests for extreme values.

Nonparametric Tests

Statistical tests based on the empirical CDF can be divided into two strands: the simple goodness of fit problem and the composite goodness of fit problem (Dasgupta 2008). In the first problem, we have $X_1, \ldots, X_n$ observations from a distribution F and we want to test if $F = F_0$ where F_0 is a completely specified distribution. In this case, the null hypothesis is

$$H_0 : F = F_0. \tag{7.162}$$

In the composite goodness of fit problem, we want to test the hypothesis that F belongs to a certain family of distributions. We begin with describing the simple goodness of fit tests on the empirical CDF.

Goodness of Fit with a Completely Specified Distribution Nonparametric Tests

We want to test if an empirical CDF (ECDF) F_n is equal to a given, and completely specified, CDF F_0.

Given $X_1, \ldots, X_n$ i.i.d. observations from some distribution and the corresponding order statistics $X_{(1)} < X_{(2)}, \ldots, < X_{(n)}$,[10] the empirical CDF is given by

$$F_n(x) = \begin{cases} 0, & x < X_{(1)} \\ \frac{k}{n}, & X_{(k)} \leq x < X_{(k+1)}. \\ 1, & x \geq X_{(n)} \end{cases} \tag{7.163}$$

For large n, F_n is a consistent estimator of F, since F_n converges in probability to F as $n \to \infty$. Therefore, if the null hypothesis $H_0 : F = F_0$ is true, we should test H_0 by studying the discrepancy between F_n and F_0. A large collection of discrepancy measures has been proposed in the literature (Dasgupta 2008), among them we report the following:

$$D_n = \sup_{-\infty < t < \infty} |F_n(t) - F_0(t)| \tag{7.164}$$

and

$$Q_n = \int (F_n(t) - F_0(t))^2 \Psi(t) dF_0(t) \tag{7.165}$$

The first test, corresponding to the discrepancy measure D_n shown in Equation (7.164), is known as the Kolmogorov–Smirnov test, while from the discrepancy measure Q_n it is possible to obtain different tests by changing the weight function Ψ. The Cramer–von Mises test is obtained when $\Psi = 1, \forall (t) \in \mathbb{R}$. This test is a measure of the mean squared difference between the empirical

[10] Given any random variables, the order statistics are defined by sorting their realizations in an increasing order.

and the theoretical CDF. When $\Psi(t) = [F_0(t)(1 - F_0(t))]^{-1}$, the Anderson–Darling test A_n is obtained:

$$A_n = \int \frac{(F_n(t) - F_0(t))^2}{(F_0(t))(1 - F_0(t))} dF_0(t). \tag{7.166}$$

In this test, the tails are weighted more than the central part of the distribution. It can be shown that the expressions for D_n and A_n are equivalent, assuming that F_0 is continuous, to:

$$\begin{aligned} D_n &= \max \max_{1 \le i \le n} \left[\frac{i}{n} - F_0(X_{(i)}), F_0(X_{(i)}) - \frac{i-1}{n} \right], \\ A_n &= -n - \frac{1}{n} \left[\sum_{i=1}^{n} (2i - 1)(\ln(F_0(X_{(i)})) + \ln(1 - F_0(X_{(n-i+1)}) \right]. \end{aligned} \tag{7.167}$$

Under the null hypothesis that the sample comes from the hypothesized distribution F_0, we obtain

$$\begin{aligned} \sqrt{n} D_n &\Rightarrow \sup_{t \in [0,1]} |B(t)| \\ n A_n &\Rightarrow \int_0^1 \frac{B^2(t)}{t(1-t)} dt, \end{aligned} \tag{7.168}$$

where $B(t)$ is a Brownian bridge (Hida 1980). For the fisrt case, the CDF of the limiting distribution is given by:

$$\lim_{n \to \infty} P_{F_0}(\sqrt{n} D_n \le \lambda) = 1 - 2 \sum_{j=1}^{\infty} (-1)^{j-1} e^{-2j^2\lambda^2}. \tag{7.169}$$

The CDF of the limiting distribution of nA_n can be found as the CDF of the infinite linear combination $\sum_{j=1}^{\infty} \frac{Y_j}{j(j+1)}$, where Y_j are i.i.d. chi-square random variables with one degree of freedom (Dasgupta 2008). Tables of critical values[11] for both distributions have been published by (Pearson and Hartley 1972) and (D'Agostino 1986).

In the case of two samples, we can define a two-sided Kolmogorov–Smirnov test to asses whether the two data samples come from the same distribution. Let X_i, $1 \le i \le n$ i.i.d. samples with continuous CDF F_n and Y_j, $1 \le j \le m$, i.i.d. samples with continuous CDF G_m. In this case, the Kolmogorov–Smirnov statistic is

$$D_{n,m} = \sup_{0 \le t \le 1} |F_n - G_m|. \tag{7.170}$$

[11] The critical value is defined as the value of the test statistic beyond which we would reject the null hypothesis. The critical value is set so that the probability that the test statistic is beyond the critical value is at most equal to the level of significance if the null hypothesis is true.

Under the null hypothesis $H_0 : F_n = G_m$, the limiting distribution is

$$\lim_{n,m\to\infty} P_{H_0}\left(\sqrt{\frac{mn}{m+n}} D_{m,n} \leq \lambda\right) = P(\sup_{0\leq t\leq 1} |B(t)| \leq \lambda) = 1 - 2\sum_{j=1}^{\infty}(-1)^{j-1}e^{-2j^2\lambda^2}. \tag{7.171}$$

The limiting distribution of the two-sample KS statistic under H_0 is the same as that of the one-sample KS statistic.

Recently, Clauset, Shalizi, and Newman CSN proposed another method based on the KS statistics (Clauset et al. 2009).

Goodness of Fit with Estimated Parameters

In the previous section, we discussed some nonparametric tests used to asses if an empirical CDF F is equal to a certain CDF F_0 that is completely specified. Usually, it can be useful to test if an empirical CDF belongs to a certain family $\mathcal{F}_\theta$, where θ represents the vector of parameters that Indexes the family. For instance, if $\mathcal{F}$ is the family of all the normal distributions $N(\mu, \sigma)$, then $\theta = (\mu, \sigma)$. In this case, we no longer have the null CDF F_0. In fact, if the true value of θ is θ_0, the estimate of θ_0 is $\widehat{\theta_n} = \widehat{\theta_n}(X_1 \dots X_n)$. Then, F_0 must be replaced by $F(t, \widehat{\theta_n}) = P_{\theta=\widehat{\theta_n}}(X_i \leq t)$.

The adjusted statistics for D_n and A_n are (Dasgupta 2008):

$$\begin{aligned} \widetilde{D_n} &= \sup_{-\infty<t<\infty} |F_n(t) - F(t, \hat{\theta}_n)| \\ \widetilde{A_n} &= \int \frac{(F_n(t) - F(t, \hat{\theta}_n))^2}{F(t, \hat{\theta}_n))(1 - F(t, \hat{\theta}_n))} dF(t, \hat{\theta}_n) \end{aligned} \tag{7.172}$$

When the estimate $\widehat{\theta}$ is computed from the same sample, the critical values obtained from the limiting distribution in Equation (7.169), determined for the case of a completely specified distribution, are not longer valid (Lilliefors 1969). The limiting distributions of the statistics obtained under the null hypothesis H_0 are affected by a number of factors: the number of estimated parameters, the estimation method and the type of estimated parameters (Lemeshko et al. 2010). In such cases, Monte Carlo or other approaches may be required to find the critical values (Kac et al. 1955; Stephens 1955; Durbin 1975; D'Agostino 1986), but tables have been prepared for recurrent typical usual cases (Lilliefors 1969; Pearson and Hartley 1972).

The Likelihood Ratio Test

Suppose that a distribution F_1 depends on a set a parameters θ. Another distribution F_2 is said to be nested with F_1 if it is possible to transform F_1 in F_2 by imposing a set of constraints on the parameters. F_1 is called *unrestricted model* and F_2 is called *restricted* model. The likelihood ratio test is a method to compare the goodness of fit of two nested models. For instance, the normal distribution and the Laplace distribution are both nested with an exponential power distribution, since they can be derived from an exponential power PDF (shown in Equation 7.154) by setting the parameter α equal to 2 or 1, respectively.

The likelihood ratio test is based on the likelihood function. If x_i, $(i = 1 \ldots n)$ are n observations drawn from a parameterized family of distributions $f(x_i|\theta)$, then the likelihood function is the probability that $(x_1, \ldots, x_n)$ are drawn from this family given a specific value of θ:

$$L(\theta|x_1 \ldots x_n) = f(x_1 \ldots x_n|\theta). \tag{7.173}$$

If x_i are independent and identically distributed, then Equation (7.173) can be rewritten as:

$$L(\theta|x_1 \ldots x_n) = \prod_{i=1}^{n} f(x_n|\theta). \tag{7.174}$$

In many cases, it is easier to work with the so called log-likelihood given by

$$l(\theta|x_1 \ldots x_n) = \ln(L(\theta|x_1 \ldots x_n)) = \sum_{i=1}^{n} \ln f(x_i|\theta). \tag{7.175}$$

The likelihood ratio is given by:

$$\Delta(x) = \frac{\sup_{\theta \in \Theta_0} L(\theta|x_i)}{\sup_{\theta \in \Theta} L(\theta|x_i)}. \tag{7.176}$$

Under the null hypothesis that θ lies in a specified lower dimensional subspace Θ_0 of the total parameter space Θ, for $n \to \infty$, the statistic $-2\ln\Delta$ will be asymptotically distributed as a χ_r^2, where the number r of degrees of freedom will be equal to the difference in the dimensionality of Θ and Θ_0. In order to perform a likelihood ratio test, we need to estimate the parameters of both the unrestricted and the restricted model, and then calculate the log-likelihoods of the two models. If l and l^* are the log-likelihood of the unrestricted and the restricted model, respectively, then we can write the test statistic as follows:

$$D = -2\ln\Delta = -2l^* + 2l = 2(l - l^*). \tag{7.177}$$

Since the unrestricted model (with more parameters) will always have a greater log-likelihood than the restricted one, we are interested in determining if the difference between the two estimated log-likelihood functions is significantly large. If the difference is not significantly large, then the restricted model will be preferred over the more complex one.

Extreme Value Tests

The extreme value theory (EVT) is used to consider probabilities associated with extreme (and, thus, rare) events. EVT studies the statistical properties of the distributions of higher order statistics (Beirlant et al. 2006), which is equivalent to studying the behavior of the tail of a distribution. It is known that the extreme value distribution belongs to the domain of attraction of one of three family distributions, namely Fréchet, Gumbel, or Weibull (Embrechts et al. 1997; Kotz and Nadarajah 2000). The Type 1, Fréchet-type, distribution is defined as:

$$P[X \leq x] = \begin{cases} 0, & x < \mu \\ \exp\left[-\left(\frac{x-\mu}{\sigma}\right)^{-\epsilon}\right], & x \geq \mu \end{cases}, \tag{7.178}$$

where $\sigma > 0$, $\epsilon > 0$ and $\mu \in \mathbb{R}$. The Type 2, Weibull-type, distribution is defined as:

$$P[X \leq x] = \begin{cases} 0, & x < \mu \\ \exp\left[-\left(\frac{x-\mu}{\sigma}\right)^{\epsilon}\right], & x \geq \mu \end{cases}, \tag{7.179}$$

and the Type 3, Gumbel-type, distribution is defined as:

$$P[X \leq x] = \exp[-e^{(x-\mu)/\sigma}]. \tag{7.180}$$

The Fréchet-type distributions and the Weibull-type distributions are well identified by the respective definitions of the tails: heavy-tailed for the distibution of the Fréchet "family" and light-tailed for the distributions belonging to the Weibull "family." For the Gumbel-type distributions, the classification based on the tails is a bit more complicated, since they fall into the same domain of distributions characterized by tails that are usually defined as "heavy" (such as the lognormal distribution), and distributions with tails usually defined as light (like the normal distribution). This classification is all made more complicated by the fact that there are different definitions of heavy-tailed distributions (Embrechts et al. 1997).

The unifying feature across these distributions is the shape parameter ϵ, capturing the weights of the tail in the distribution of the variable X.

The three type of distributions can be represented as members of a generalized family of distributions (the Generalized Extreme Value Distribution) with the cumulative distribution function

$$P[X \leq x] = \left[1 + \epsilon\left(\frac{x-\mu}{\sigma}\right)^{-1/\epsilon}\right], \tag{7.181}$$

where $1 + \epsilon\left(\frac{x-\mu}{\sigma}\right)^{-1/\epsilon} > 0$, $-\infty < \epsilon < \infty$, and $\sigma > 0$. The distribution in Equation (7.181) is a Fréchet-type distribution for $\epsilon > 0$ and a Weibull-type distribution for $\epsilon < 0$. When $\epsilon \rightarrow \infty$ or $\epsilon \rightarrow -\infty$, the distribution in Equation (7.181) is a Gumbel-type distribution.

The EVT is the methodological reference for discriminating between a power law (Pareto) and a lognormal tail behavior.

Asymptotically, the behavior of a Pareto distribution is different from that of a lognormal distribution. The former converges to a Fréchet distribution while the latter converges to a Gumbel distribution, causing the two distributions to be mathematically distinguishable, at least asymptotically. As highlighted by Perline, however, the slow convergence of the lognormal distribution often causes the behavior of the two distributions to be indistinguishable for samples of a finite size (Perline 2005).

Various tests have therefore been proposed in the literature to distinguish between the Pareto and the lognormal behavior of a random variable. We mention here the Hill estimator (Hill 1975), the Uniformly Most Powerful Unbiased (UMPU) test based on the clipped sample coefficient of variation developed by Del Castillo and Puig (1999) and used by Malevergne et al. (2009), the Maximum Entropy (ME) test by Bee et al. (2011) and a test proposed by Gabaix and Ibragimov (2011).

The Hill Estimator

One of the most popular estimators for the tail index $\epsilon > 0$ was proposed by Hill (1975). The Hill estimator is the conditional maximum likelihood estimator for a Pareto distribution with CCDF $P(X > x) = Cx^{-\gamma}$, conditioning to $x \geq x_{min}$ for some fixed $x_{min} > 0$. This estimator can be applied to a wide variety of distributions, such as Type 2 extreme value distributions, whose tails are approximately Pareto (Hall 1982). Consider a random sample $X_1 \dots X_n$ and its order statistic $X_{(1)} \leq \dots \leq X_{(n)}$. The Hill estimator, based on the $k+1$ upper order statistic, is defined as

$$\begin{aligned} \hat{\gamma}_{k,n}^{-1} &= \frac{1}{k}\sum_{i=1}^{k} \ln \frac{X_{(i)}}{X_{(k+1)}} \\ \hat{C}_{k,n} &= \frac{k}{n} X_{(k+1)}^{\hat{\gamma}_{k,n}}, \end{aligned} \tag{7.182}$$

where $\hat{\gamma}_{k,n}$ and $\hat{C}_{k.n}$ are estimates of the parameters of the empirical distribution, γ and C, respectively. The primary weakness of this estimator is that we need to determine the size of the tail a priori.

Alternatively, as illustrated by Embrechts, since only observations larger than some unknown threshold x_{min} follow the Pareto distribution, it is possibile to estimate the treshold using a two-step procedure (Embrechts et al. 1997).

The importance of the choice of x_{min} is well illustrated by Clauset et al. (2009) who show that a wrong choice of the threshold will result in a biased estimate for the scaling parameters. We discuss the methodology proposed by Clauset and his coauthors to avoid this problem in the following section.

Clauset Test

The methodology used by Clauset and colleagues to estimate the lower bound x_{min} consists in choosing the value $\hat{x}_{min}$ of x_{min} that minimize the difference (distance) between the probability distribution of the measured data and the best-fit power law model (Clauset et al. 2009). Here the KS statistic is used as a measure to quantify the distance between the two probability distributions (but it is possible to use other measures as well). If $S(x)$ is the CDF of the data for observations $x \geq x_{min}$, and $P(x)$ is the CDF for the power law model that best fits the data in the region $x \geq x_{min}$, then our estimate $\hat{x}_{min}$ is the value x_{min} that minimizes the KS statistic D defined as:

$$D = max_{x \geq x_{min}} \mid S(x) - P(x) \mid . \tag{7.183}$$

Once we provide estimates for the scaling parameter and for x_{min} we cannot, however, say if the power-law fitting is plausible. To overcome this problem (Clauset et al. 2009), follow a semiparametric approach. The idea is to sample many synthetic data sets from a power law distribution with parameters $\hat{\alpha}$ and $\hat{x}_{min}$ and then compare these samples with the data.

Uniformly Most Powerful Unbiased Test

Suppose we sample from a population with a distribution that is completely specified except for the value of a parameter $\theta \in \mathbf{\Theta}$, and we test the null hypothesis $H_0 : \theta \in \Theta_0$ against the alternative hypothesis $H_1 = \theta \in \theta_1$, with $\Theta_0 \cup \Theta_1 = \mathbf{\Theta}$ and $\Theta_0 \cap \Theta_1 = \emptyset$. Let d be the decision function (test statistic) for an α-level test. Then, the power function[12] will be

$$\pi_d \leq \alpha, \ \ \forall \theta \in \Theta_0. \tag{7.184}$$

A test statistic d is a uniformly most powerful (UMP) test at the significance level α if d is indeed a level test and if for any other α level statistic $d*$

$$\pi_{d*}(\theta) \leq \pi_d(\theta) \ \ \forall \theta \in \Theta_1. \tag{7.185}$$

As highlighted by Bee and coauthors, the main problem of the UMPU testing lies in the fact that the reliability of this test depends to a large extent on the generating process of the data being tested, in particular from the sampling variation coefficient (Bee et al. 2011).

[12] The power of a statistical test is defided as the probability that the test will reject the null hypothesis when the null hypothesis is false.

The Maximum Entropy Test

The maximum entropy (ME) test was developed by Bee et al. (2011). The test entails maximizing the Shannon's information entropy under k moment constraints $\mu^i = \hat{\mu}^i (i = 1, \ldots, k)$, where $\mu^i = \mathrm{E}[T(x)^i]$ and $\hat{\mu}^i = \frac{1}{n}\sum_j T(x_j)^i$ are the ith theoretical and sample moments, n is the number of observations and T is the function defining the characterizing moment. It can be shown that the Pareto distribution is a ME density with $k = 1$, whereas the lognormal distribution is a ME with $k = 2$ (Bee et al. 2011).

For a complete description of the test and a discussion of the test performance when the distribution tested is neither Pareto nor Normal, refer to Bee et al. (2011).

Rank-1/2 Test

Gabaix and Ibragimov (2011) proposed a method (GI test) to estimate the Pareto exponent γ by running an OLS on a Zipf size-rank log-log plot. Recently, Bee et al. (2017) proposed a modification of the original GI test, according to which one must perform the OLS regression with two parameters γ and q:

$$\ln\left(r - \frac{1}{2}\right) = \text{constant} - \gamma \ln(X_{(r)}) + q[\ln(X_{(r)}) - \alpha]^2, \tag{7.186}$$

where γ is the Pareto shape, q is a parameter associated with the quadratic deviation from a Pareto distribution, r is the rank, $X_{(r)}$ is the r-th order statistic[13] and

$$\alpha \stackrel{\text{def}}{=} \mathrm{Cov}((\ln(X_{(r)}))^2, \ln(X_{(r)}))/2\mathrm{Var}(\ln(X_{(r)})) \tag{7.187}$$

is a recentering term needed for guaranteeing that γ is the same whether the quadratic term is included or excluded. Asymptotically, for the Pareto distribution, $q = 0$, and, therefore, a large value of $|q|$ points toward rejection of the null hypothesis of power law. Gabaix and Ibragimov (2011) show that, under the null hypothesis, the data follows a Pareto distribution and the statistics $\sqrt{2n}q(n)/\xi^2$ converges for $n \to \infty$ to a standard normal distribution, which can therefore be used to find the critical points of the test.

[13] If $X_1, \ldots, X_n$ is a random sample drawn from a certain distribution X, $X_{(1)}, \ldots, X_{(n)}$ are called order statistics if $X_{(1)} < X_{(2)}, \ldots, < X_{(r)} <, \ldots < X_{(n)}$.

References

Acemoglu, D. and Cao, D. (2015), "Innovation by entrants and incumbents," *Journal of Economic Theory* **157**, 255–294.

Acemoglu, D., Carvalho, V. M., Ozdaglar, A., and Tahbaz-Salehi, A. (2012), "The network origins of aggregate fluctuations," *Econometrica* **80**, 1977–2016.

Aghion, P. and Durlauf, S. N. (eds.) (1998), *Handbook of Economic Growth*, Elsevier, Amsterdam.

Aghion, P. and Howitt, P. (1992), "A model of growth through creative destruction," *Econometrica* **60**(2), 323–351.

Akcigit, U. and Kerro, W. R. (2010), "Growth through heterogeneous innovations," Working Paper 16443, National Bureau of Economic Research.

Amaral, L. A. N., Buldyrev, S. V., Havlin, S., et al. (1997), "Scaling behavior in economics: I. Empirical results for company growth," *Journal de Physique I* **7**(4), 635–650.

Amaral, L. A. N., Buldyrev, S. V., Havlin, S., Salinger, M. A., and Stanley, H. E. (1998), "Power law scaling for a system of interacting units with complex internal structure," *Physical Review Letters* **80**, 1385–1388.

Andrews, D. F. and Mallows, C. L. (1974), "Scale mixtures of normal distribution," *Journal of the Royal Statistical Society* **36**, 99–102.

Aoki, M. and Hawkins, R. J. (2010), "Non-self-averaging and the statistical mechanics of endogenous macroeconomic fluctuations," *Economic Modelling* **27**(6), 1543–1546.

Aoki, M. and Yoshikawa, H. (2012), "Non-self-averaging in macroeconomic models: A criticism of modern micro-founded macroeconomics," *Journal of Economic Interaction and Coordination* **7**, 1–22.

Arellano, M. and Bond, S. (1991), "Some test of specification for panel data: Monte Carlo evidence and an application to employment equations," *Review of Economic Studies* **58**, 277–297.

Argente, D., Lee, M., and Moreira, S. (2018), "How do firms grow? The life cycle of products matters," Working Paper, University of Chicago.

Arkolakis, C. and Muendler, M. A. (2010), "The extensive margin of exporting products: A firm-level analysis," Technical Report, National Bureau of Economic Research.

Arkolakis, C. and Muendler, M. A. (2012), "Exporters and their products: A collection of empirical regularities," *CESifo Economic Studies* p. ifs028.

Atalay, E. (2017), "How important are sectoral shocks?," *American Economic Journal: Macroeconomics* **9**, 254–280.

Autor, D., Dorn, D., Katz, L. F., Patterson, C., and Reenen, J. V. (2017), "Concentrating on the fall of the labor share," Working Paper 23108, National Bureau of Economic Research.

Axtell, R. L. (1999), *The Emergence of Firm in a Population of Agents: Local Increasing Returns, Unstable Nash Equilibria, and Power Law Size Distributions*, Center on Social and Economic Dynamics, Brookings Institution Washington, DC.

Axtell, R. L. (2001), "Zipf distribution of U.S. firm sizes," *Science* **293**(5536), 1818–1820.

Axtell, R. L., Gallegati, M., and Palestrini, A. (2008), "Common components in firms' growth and the sectors scaling puzzle," *Economics Bulletin* **12**, 1–8.

Axtell, R. L. and Guerrero, O. (2019), *Dynamics of Firms from the Bottom Up: Data, Theories and Models*, The MIT Press, Cambridge, MA. forthcoming.

Barabasi, A. L. and Albert, R. (1999), "Emergence of scaling in random networks," *Science* **286**, 509–512.

Barro, R. J. (1991), "Economic growth in a cross section of countries," *The Quarterly Journal of Economics* **106**, 407–443.

Barro, R. J. (1996), "Determinants of economic growth: A cross-country empirical study," Working Paper 5698, National Bureau of Economic Research.

Barro, R. J. and Jin, T. (2011), "On the size distribution of macroeconomic disasters," *Econometrica* **79**(5), 15767–1589.

Bee, M., Riccaboni, M., and Schiavo, S. (2011), "Pareto versus lognormal: A maximum entropy test," *Physical Review E* **84**, 026104.

Bee, M., Riccaboni, M., and Schiavo, S. (2013), "The size distribution of US cites: Not Pareto, even in the tail," *Economics Letters* **120**, 232–237.

Bee, M., Riccaboni, M., and Schiavo, S. (2017), "Where Gibrat meets Zipf: Scale and scope of French firms," *Physica A* **481**, 265–275.

Beirlant, J., Goegebeur, Y., Segers, J., Teugels, J., Waal, D. D., and Ferro, C. (2006), *Statistics of Extremes: Theory and Applications*, John Wiley and Sons, Hoboken, NJ.

Bernard, A. B., Redding, S. J., and Schott, P. K. (2010), "Multi-product firms and product switching," *The American Economic Review* **100**, 70–97.

Bottazzi, G., Coad, A., Jacoby, N., and Secchi, A. (2011), "Corporate growth and industrial dynamics: Evidence from French manufacturing," *Applied Economics* **43**(1), 103–116.

Bottazzi, G., Dosi, G., Lippi, M., Pammolli, F., and Riccaboni, M. (2001), "Innovation and corporate growth in the evolution of the drug industry," *International Journal of Industrial Organization* **19**, 1161–1187.

Bottazzi, G. and Secchi, A. (2006), "Explaining the distribution of firm growth rates," *RAND Journal of Economics* **37**, 235–256.

Box, G. E. P. and Tiao, G. C. (1973), *Bayesian Inference Statistical Analysis*, Addison-Wesley Publishing Company, Inc., Reading, MA.

Bremaud, P. (1981), *Point Processes and Queues: Martingale Dynamics.*, Springer Verlag, New York.

Brock, W. A. (1999), "Scaling in economics: A reader's guide," *Industrial and Corporate change* **8**(3), 409–446.

Brock, W. A. and Durlauf, S. N. (1999), "A formal model of theory choice in science," *Economic Theory* **14**, 113–130.

Brockwell, P. J. and Davis, R. A. (2009), *Time Series: Theory and Methods* (2nd ed.), Springer Verlag, New York.

Buldyrev, S. V., Amaral, L. A. N., Havlin, S., et al. (1997), "Scaling behavior in economics: II. Modeling of company growth," *Journal de Physique I* **7**(4), 635–650.

Buldyrev, S. V., Dokholyan, N. V., Erramilli, S., et al. (2003), "Hierarchy in social organization," *Physica A Statistical Mechanics and Its Applications* **330**, 653–659.

Buldyrev, S. V., Pammolli, F., Riccaboni, M., et al. (2007), "A generalized preferential attachment model for business firms growth rates II. Mathematical treatment," *The European Physical Journal B* **57**, 131–138.

Buldyrev, S. V., Riccaboni, M., Growiec, J., Stanley, H. E., and Pammolli, F. (2007), "The growth of business firms: Facts and theory," *Journal of the European Economic Association* **5**(2/3), 574–584.

Cabral, L. M. B. and Mata, J. (2003), "On the evolution of the firm size distribution: Facts and theory," *American Economic Review* **93**, 1075–1090.

Caldarelli, G. (2007), *Scale-Free Networks: Complex Webs in Nature and Technology*, Oxford University Press, Oxford.

Carsten, C. and Neary, J. P. (2010), "Multi-product firms and flexible manufacturing in the global economy," *The Review of Economic Studies* **77**(1), 188–217.

Carvalho, V. M. and Gabaix, X. (2013), "The great diversification and its undoing," *American Economic Review* **103**(5), 1697–1727.

Carvalho, V. M. and Grassi, B. (2015), "Large firm dynamics and the business cycle," Economics Working Papers 1481, Department of Economics and Business, Universitat Pompeu Fabra.

Castaldi, C. and Dosi, G. (2009), "The patterns of output growth of firms and countries: Scale invariances and scale specificities," *Empirical Economics* **37**, 475–495.

Caves, R. E. (1998), "Industrial organization and new findings on the turnover and mobility of firms," *Journal of Economic Literature* **36**, 1947–1982.

Chakravarti, I. M., Laha, R. G., and Roy, J. (1967), *Handbook of Methods of Applied Statistics*, Vol. 1, John Wiley and Sons, Hoboken, NJ.

Champernowne, D. G. (1953), "A model of income distribution," *The Economic Journal* **63**(250), 318–351.

Chandler, A. D. (1990), *Scale and Scope: The Dynamics of Industrial Capitalism*, Harvard University Press, Cambridge, MA.

Clauset, A., Shalizi, C. R., and Newman, M. E. J. (2009), "Power-law distribution in empirical data," *SIAM Review* **51**, 661–703.

Coad, A. (2009), *The Growth of Firms: A Survey of Theories and Empirical Evidencey*, Edward Elgar, Cheltenham, UK.

Cox, D. R. and Hinkley, D. V. (1979), *Theoretical Statistics*, Taylor & Francis, New York.

Cox, D. R. and Miller, H. D. (1968), *The Theory of Stochastic Processes*, Chapman and Hall, London.

D'Agostino, R. (1986), *Goodness-of-Fit-Techniques*, Marcel Dekker Inc., New York.

Darwin, J. H. (1953), "Population differences between species growing according to simple birth and death processes," *Biometrika* **40**, 370–382.

Dasgupta, A. (2008), *Asymptotic Theory of Statistics and Probability*, Springer Verlag, New York.

David, P. A. (1992), "Knowledge, property, and the system dynamics of technological change," *The World Bank Economic Review* **6**(1), 215–248.

De Fabritiis, G., Pammolli, F., and Riccaboni, M. (2003), "On size and growth of business firms," *Physica A* **324**, 38–44.

De Vany, A. and Walls, W. (1996), "Boseeinstein dynamics and adaptive contracting in the motion picture industry," *Economic Journal* **439**, 1493–1514.

De Wit, G. (2005), "Firm size distributions: An overview of steady-state distributions resulting from firm dynamics models," *International Journal of Industrial Organization* **23**, 423–450.

Del Castillo, J. and Puig, P. (1999), "The best test of exponentiality against singly truncated normal alternatives," *Journal of the American Statistical Association* **94**, 529–532.

Di Giovanni, J., Levchenko, A. A., and Rancière, R. (2011), "Power laws in firm size and openness to trade: Measurement and implications," *Journal of International Economics* **85**, 42–52.

Dokholyan, N. V., Buldyrev, S. V., Havlin, S., and Stanley, H. E. (1997), "Distribution of base pair repeats in coding and noncoding dna sequences," *Physical Review Letters* **79**, 5182–5185.

Dosi, G. (1988), "Sources, procedures, and microeconomic effects of innovation," *Journal of Economic Literature* **26**(3), 1120–1171.

Dosi, G., Pereira, M. C., and Virgillito, M. E. (2016), "The footprint of evolutionary processes of learning and selection upon the statistical properties of industrial dynamics," *Industrial and Corporate Change* **26**(2), 187–210.

Douc, R., Moulines, E., and Stoffer, D. (2014), *Nonlinear Time Series: Theory, Methods and Applications with R Examples*, CRC Press, Boca Raton.

Dunne, T., Roberts, M., and Samuelson, L. (1989), "The growth and failure of us manufacturing plants," *Quarterly Journal of Economics* **95**, 657–674.

Durbin, J. (1975), "Kolmogorov-smirnov tests when parameters are estimated with applications to tests of exponentiality and tests on spacings," *Biometrika* **62**, 5–22.

Durlauf, S. N. and Quah, D. T. (1999), Chapter 4: The new empirics of economic growth, *in Handbook of Macroeconomics*, Vol. 1, Elsevier, pp. 235–308.

Eaton, J., Kortum, S., and Kramarz, F. (2011), "An anatomy of international trade: Evidence from french firms," *Econometrica* **79**, 1453–1498.

Embrechts, P., Klüppelberg, C., and Mikosch, T. (1997), *Modelling Extremal Events: For Insurance and Finance*, Springer Verlag, New York.

Ericson, R. E. and Pakes, A. (1995), "Markov-perfect industry dynamics: A framework for empirical work," *Review of Economic Studies* **62**, 53–82.

Evans, D. S. (1987a), "Tests of alternative theories of firm growth," *Journal of Political Economics* **95**, 657–674.

Evans, D. S. (1987b), "The relationship between firm growth, size, and age: Estimates for 100 manufacturing industries," *The Journal of Industrial Economics* **35**, 567–581.

Feller, W. (1968), *An Introduction to Probability Theory and Its Applications*, Vol. I, 3rd edition, Wiley, Hoboken, NJ.

Fenton, L. (1960), "The sum of log-normal probability distributions in scatter transmission systems," *IRE Transactions on Communications Systems* **8**(1), 57–67.

Freeman, C. (1982), *The Economics of Industrial Innovation*, The MIT Press Cambridge, MA.

Friedman, M. (1992), "Do old fallacies ever die?," *Journal of Economic Literature* **30**, 21–29.

Fu, D. F., Pammolli, F., Buldyrev, S. V., Riccaboni, M., Matia, K., Yamasaki, K., and Stanley, H. E. (2005), "The growth of business firms: Theoretical framework and empirical evidence," *Proceedings of the National Academy of Sciences of the USA* **102**, 18801–18806.

Gabaix, X. (1999), "Zipf's law for cities: An explanation," *Quarterly Journal of Economics* **117**, 739–767.

Gabaix, X. (2009), "Power laws in economics and finance," *Annual Review of Economics* **1**, 255–294.

Gabaix, X. (2011), "The granular origins of aggregate fluctuations," *Econometrica* **79**, 733–772.

Gabaix, X. and Ibragimov, R. (2011), "Rank-1/2: A simple way to improve the ols estimation of tail exponents," *Journal of Business and Economic Statistics* **29**, 24–39.

Gambardella, A. (1995), *Science and Innovation: The US Pharmaceutical Industry During the 1980s*, Cambridge: Cambridge University Press.
Garibaldi, U. and Scalas, E. (2010), *Finitary Probabilistic Methods in Econophysics*, Cambridge University Press, Cambridge.
Garicano, L., LeLarge, L. C., and Van Reenen, J. (2013), "Firm size distortions and the productivity distribution: Evidence from France," Working Paper 18841, NBER.
Gibrat, R. (1931), *Les Inegalites Economiques*, Librairie du Receuil Sirey, Paris.
Gini, C. (1936), "On the measure of concentration with special reference to income and statistics," Working Paper 208, Colorado College Publication, General Series.
Greene, W. H. (2012), *Econometric Analysis (7th international ed.)*, Pearson, Boston.
Griffiths, D. (2005), *Introduction to Quantum Mechanics*, 2nd edition, Pearson Prentice Hall: Upper Saddle River, NJ, pp. 100–200.
Growiec, J., Pammolli, F., and Riccaboni, M. (2018), "Innovation and corporate dynamics: A theoretical framework, Eic working paper series," IMT School for Advanced Studies Lucca.
Growiec, J., Pammolli, F., Riccaboni, M., and Stanley, H. E. (2008), "On the size distribution of business firms," *Economics Letters* **98**, 207–212.
Gulisashvili, A. and Tankov, P. (2013), "Tail behavior of sums and differences of log-normal random variables," Working Paper 1309.3057, arXiv.org.
Hall, B. H. (1987), "The relationship between firm size and firm growth in the U.S. manufacturing sector," *Journal of Industrial Economics* **35**(4), 583–606.
Hall, P. (1982), "On some simple estimates of an exponent of regular variation," *Journal of the Royal Statistical Society* **44**, 37–42.
Harris, T. E. (1989), *The Theory of Branching Processes*, Dover Publication Inc., New York.
Hart, P. E. and Oulton, N. (1996), "The growth and size of firms," *Economic Journal* **106**(3), 1242–1252.
Hawkes, A. G. (1971), "Spectra of some self-exciting and mutually exciting point processes," *Biometrika* **58**(1), 83–90.
Hellerstein, R. and Koren, M. (2019), "Are big firms born or grown? preliminary and incomplete."
Henderson, R., Orsenigo, L., and Pisano, G. P. (1999), "The pharmaceutical industry and the revolution in molecular biology: Interactions among scientific, institutional, and organizational change," *in* D. C. Mowery and R. R. Nelson, eds, *Sources of Industrial Leadership: Studies of Seven Industries,* Cambridge University Press, pp. 267–311.
Henly, S. E. and Sanchez, J. M. (2009), "The U.S. establishment-size distribution: Secular changes and sectoral decomposition," *Economic Quarterly* **95**, 419–454.
Heyde, C. C. (1963), "On a property of the lognormal distribution," *Journal of the Royal Statistical Society, Series B* **25**, 392–393.
Hida, T. (1980), *Brownian Motion*, Springer, Berlin.
Hill, B. M. (1975), "A simple general approach to inference about the tail of a distribution," *Annals of Statistics* **3**, 1163–1174.
Hymer, S. and Pashigian, P. (1962), "Firm size and rate of growth," *Journal of Political Economy* **70**, 556–569.
Ijiri, Y. and Simon, H. A. (1964), "Business firm growth and size," *The American Economic Review* **54**(2), pp. 77–89.
Ijiri, Y. and Simon, H. A. (1975), "Some distributions associated with bose-einstein statistics," *The Proceedings of the National Academy of Sciences of the USA* **72**(2), 1654–1657.
Ijiri, Y. and Simon, H. A. (1977), *Skew Distributions and the Sizes of Business Firms*, North-Holland Pub. Co., Amsterdam.

Johansen, A. and Sornette, D. (2010), "Shocks, crashes and bubbles in financial markets," *Brussels Economic Review* **53**, 201–253.

Jovanovic, B. (1982), "Selection and the evolution of industry," *Econometrica* **50**, 649–70.

Kac, M., Kiefer, J., and Wolfowitz, J. (1955), "On tests of normality and other tests of goodness of fit based on distance methods," *The Annals of Mathematical Statistics* **26**, 189–211.

Kadanoff, L. P. (1991), *Scaling and Multiscaling: Fractals and Multifractals*, nonlinear phenomena in fluids, solids and other complex systems edition, Elsevier Science Publisher: Amsterdam.

Kalecki, M. (1945), "On the Gibrat distribution," *Econometrica* **13**(2), pp. 161–170.

Keith, H., Mayer, T., and Thoenig, M. (2014), "Welfare and trade without pareto," *The American Economic Review* **104**, 310–316.

Kendall, D. G. (1948), "On some modes of population growth leading to r. a. fisher's logarithmic series distribution," *Biometrika* **35**, 6–15.

Kesten, H. (1973), "Random difference equations and renewal theory for products of random matrices," *Acta Mathematica* **13**, 207–248.

Kleiber, C. and Kotz, S. (2003), *Statistical Size Distribution in Economics and Actuarial Sciences*, John Wiley and Sons, New Jersey.

Klepper, S. (1996), "Entry, exit, growth, and innovation over the product life cycle," *The American Economic Review* pp. 562–583.

Klepper, S. and Thompson, P. (2006), "Submarkets and the evolution of market structure," *RAND Journal of Economics* **37**, 861–886.

Klette, J. and Kortum, S. (2004), "Innovating firms and aggregate innovation," *Journal of Political Economy* **112**, 986–1018.

Koren, M. and Tenreyro, S. (2007), "Volatility and development," *The Quarterly Journal of Economics* pp. 243–287.

Koren, M. and Tenreyro, S. (2013), "Technological diversification," *American Economic Review* **103**(1), 378–414.

Kotz, S., Kozubowski, T., and Podgorski, K. (2001), *The Laplace Distribution and Generalizations: A Revisit with Applications to Communications, Economics, Engineering, and Finance*, Birkhäuser Boston.

Kotz, S. and Nadarajah, S. (2000), *Extreme Value Distributions: Theory and Applications*, Imperial College Press.

Lando, D. (1998), "On cox processes and credit risky securities," *Review of Derivatives Research* **2**(2-3), 99–120.

Lee, Y., Amaral, L. A. N., Canning, D., Martin, M., and Stanley, H. E. (1998), "Universal features in the growth dynamics of complex organizations," *Physical Review Letters* **81**, 3275–3278.

Lemeshko, B. Y., Lemeshko, S. B., and Postovalov, S. N. (2010), "Improvement of statistic distribution models of the nonparametric goodness-of-fit tests in testing composite hypotheses," *Communications in Statistics – Theory and Methods* **39**, 460–471.

Lentz, R. and Mortensen, D. T. (2008), "An empirical model of growth through product innovation," *Econometrica* **76**, 1317–1373.

Leonard, J. (1986), "On the size distribution of employment and establishments," Working Paper 1951, National Bureau of Economic Research.

Lewis, P. A. W. and Shedler, G. S. (1979), "Simulation of nonhomogeneous poisson processes by thinning," *Naval Research Logistics Quarterly* **26**(3), 403–403.

Lilliefors, H. W. (1969), "On the Kolmogorov–Smirnov test for the exponential distribution with mean unknown," *Journal of the American Statistical Association* **64**, 387–389.

Lotti, F., Santarelli, E., and Vivarelli, M. (2009), "Defending Gibrat's law as a long-run regularity," *Small Business Economics* **32**, 508–523.

Lucas, R. E. (1978), "On the size distribution of business firms," *Bell Journal of Economics* **9**, 508–523.

Lunardi, J. T., Micciché, S., Lillo, F., Mantegna, R. N., and Gallegati, M. (2001), "Do firms share the same functional form of their growth rate distribution? a statistical test," *Physica A: Statistical Mechanics and Its Applications* **299**(1), 188–197.

Luttmer, E. G. J. (2007), "Selection, growth, and the size distribution of firms," *The Quarterly Journal of Economics* **122**, 1103–1144.

Luttmer, E. G. J. (2010), "Models of firm heterogeneity and growth," *Annual Review of Economics* **3**, 547–576.

Luttmer, E. G. J. (2011), "On the mechanics of firm growth," *The Review of Economic Studies* **78**(3), 1042–1068.

Luttmer, E. G. J. (2012), "Technology diffusion and growth," *Journal of Economic Theory* **147**(2), 602–622.

Magazzini, L., Pammolli, F. and Riccaboni, M. (2004), "Dynamic competition in pharmaceuticals," *The European Journal of Health Economics* **5**, 175–182.

Malerba, F., Nelson, R. R., Orsenigo, L., and Winter, S. G. (2018), *In Innovation and the Evolution of Industries: History-Friendly Models*, Cambridge University Press, Cambridge.

Malevergne, Y., Pisarenko, V., and Sornette, D. (2009), "Testing the pareto against the lognormal distributions with the uniformly most powerful unbiased test applied to the distribution of cities," *Physical Review E* **83**, 036111.

Mansfield, E. (1962), "Gibrat's law, innovation, and the growth of firms," *The American Economic Review* **52**(5), 1023–1051.

Mantegna, R. N. and Stanley, H. E. (1995), "Scaling behavior in the dynamics of an economic index," *Nature* **376**, 46–49.

Matraves, C. (1999), "Market structure, R&D and advertising in the pharmaceutical industry," *Journal of Industrial Economics* **47**, 169–194.

Mc Kelvey, M., Orsenigo, L., and Pammolli, F. (2004), *Pharmaceuticals Analyzed thourgh the Lens of a Sectoral Innovation System*, Sectoral system of innovation edition, Cambridge University Press, Cambridge.

Mitzenmacher, M. (2003), "A brief history of generative models for power law and lognormal distributions," *Internet Mathematics* **1**, 226–251.

Mokyr, J. (2005), *Long-Term Economic Growth and the History of Technology*, number SUPPL. PART B *in* "Handbook of Economic Growth," suppl. part b edn, pp. 1113–1180.

Montroll, E. W. and Shlesinger, M. F. (1982), "On 1/f noise and other distributions with long tails," *Proceedings of the National Academy of Sciences of the United States of America* **79**(10), 3380–3383.

Montroll, E. W. (1987), "On the dynamics and evolution of some sociotechnical systems," *Bull. Amer. Math. Soc.* **16**, 1–46.

Morescalchi, A., Pammolli, F., Riccaboni, M., and Tortolini, V. (2019), "The firms size-growth relation. an econometric approach," Eic working paper series, IMT School for Advanced Studies Lucca.

Nelson, R. R. (1959), "The simple economics of basic scientific research," *Journal of Political Economy* **67**(3), 297–306.

Nelson, R. R. and Winter, S. G. (2002), "Evolutionary theorizing in economics," *Journal of Economic Perspectives* **16**(2), 23–46.

Newman, M. E. J. (2005), "Power laws, pareto distributions and zipf's law," *Contemporary Physics* **46**, 323–351.

Ogata, Y. and Vere-Jones, D. (1984), "Inference for earthquake models: a self-correcting model," *Stoch. Proc. Appl.* **17**, 337–347.

Orsenigo, L. (1989), *The Emergence of Biotechnology: Institutions and Markets in Industrial Innovation*, Pinter, New York.

Pammolli, F. (1996), *Innovazione e Concorrenza nel Settore Farmaceutico*, Guerini, Milano.

Pammolli, F., Magazzini, L. and Orsenigo, L. (2002), "The intensity of competition after patent expiry in pharmaceuticals. a cross-country analysis," *Revue d'Economie Industrielle* **99**, 107–131.

Pammolli, F., Magazzini, L., and Riccaboni, M. (2011), "The productivity crisis in pharmaceutical R&D," *Nature Reviews Drug Discovery* **10**, 428–438.

Pareto, V. (1896), *Cours d'Economie Politique*, Macmillan, London.

Pearl, J. (2000), *Causality: Models, Reasoning and Inference*, Cambridge University Press, Cambridge.

Pearson, E. S. and Hartley, H. O. (1972), "Tables for statisticians," *Biometrika* **2**, 117–123.

Penrose, E. T. (1959), *The Theory of the Growth of the Firm*, Oxford University Press, Oxford.

Perline, R. (2005), "Strong, weak and false inverse power laws," *Statistical Science* **20**, 68–88.

Perline, R., Axtell, R. L., and Teitelbaum, D. (2006), "Volatility and asymmetry of small firm growth rates over increasing time frames," *U.S. Small Business Administration, Office of Advocacy, The Office of Advocacy Small Business Working Papers*.

Petroni, A. M. (1992), "Why have a heuristic of scientific discovery?," *International Studies in the Philosophy of Science* **6**(1), 53–55.

Petroni, A. M. (1993), "Conventionalism, scientific discovery and the sociology of knowledge," *International Studies in the Philosophy of Science* **7**(3), 225–240.

Popper, K. R. (1961), *The Logic of Scientific Discovery*, Basic Books, New York.

Prais, S. J. (1976), *The Evolution of Giant Firms in Britain*, Cambridge University Press, London.

Quah, D. T. (1996), "Twin peaks: Growth and convergence in models of distribution dynamics," *The Economic Journal* **106**(437), 1045–1055.

Radner, R. (1993), "The organization of decentralized information processing," *Econometrica* **61**, 1109–1146.

Reed, W. J. (2001), "The pareto, zipf and other power laws," *Economics Letters* **74**, 15–19.

Reed, W. J. and Hughes, B. D. (2002), "From gene families and genera to incomes and internet file sizes: Why power laws are so common in nature," *Physical Review E* **66**, 067103.

Riccaboni, M., Pammolli, F., Buldyrev, S. V., Ponta, L., and Stanley, H. E. (2008), "The size variance relationship of business firm growth rates," *Proceedings of the National Academy of Sciences of the USA* **105**, 19595–19600.

Ricolfi, L. (2014), *L'Enigma della Crescita*, Mondadori, Milano.

Rossi-Hansberg, E. and Wright, M. L. J. (2007*a*), "Establishment size dynamics in the aggregate economy," *The American Economic Review* **97**, 1639–1666.

Rossi-Hansberg, E. and Wright, M. L. J. (2007*b*), "Establishment size dynamics in the aggregate economy," *The American Economic Review* **97**, 1639–1666.

Saichev, A., Malevergne, Y., and Sornette, D. (2009), *Theory of Zipf's Law and Beyond*, Springer Verlag, Berlin.

Schmalensee, R. and Willing, R. (1989), *Interindustry Differences of Structure and Performance*, handbook of industrial organization edition, North Holland, Amsterdam, pp. 951–1009.

Schumpeter, J. A. (1934), *Theory of Economic Development*, Harvard College, Cambridge MA.

Simon, H. A. (1955), "On a class of skew distribution functions," *Biometrika* **42**, 425–440.

Simon, H. A. (1968), On judging the plausibility of theories, *in* B. V. Rootselaar and J. Staal, eds., "Logic, Methodology and Philosophy of Science III," Vol. 52, Elsevier, pp. 439–459.

Simon, H. A. (1991), "Organizations and markets," *Journal of Economic Perspectives* **5**(2), 25–44.

Simon, H. A. and Bonini, C. P. (1958), "The size distribution of business firms," *The American Economic Review* **48**, 607–617.

Singh, A. and Whittington, G. (1975), "The size and growth of firms," *Review of Economic Studies* **42**, 15–26.

Slanina, F. (2014), *Essential of Econophisycs Modelling*, Oxford University Press, Oxford.

Solomon, S. and Golo, N. (2014), "Microeconomic structure determines macroeconomic dynamics. aoki defeats the representative agent," *Journal of Economic Interaction and Coordination* **10**, 5–30.

Solomon, S. and Richmond, P. (2001), "Power laws of wealth, market order volumes and market returns," *Physica A: Statistical Mechanics and Its Applications* **299**(1), 188–197.

Sornette, D. (2000), *Critical Phenomena in Natural Sciences*, Springer, Berlin.

Sornette, D. and Cont, R. (1997), "Convergent multiplicative processes repelled from zero: Power laws and truncated power laws," *Journal de Physique I* **7**, 431–444.

Sornette, D. and Conty, R. (1997), "Convergent multiplicative processes repelled from zero: Power laws and truncated power laws," *Journal of Physics I France* **7**, 431–444.

Stanley, H. E. (1971), *Introduction to Phase Transitions and Critical Phenomena*, Oxford University Press, Oxford.

Stanley, M. H. R., Amaral, L. A. N., Buldyrev, S. V., Havlin, S., Leschhorn, H., Maass, P., Salinger, M. A., and Stanley, H. E. (1996), "Scaling behaviour in the growth of companies," *Nature* **379**, 804–806.

Stanley, M. H. R., Buldyrev, S. V., Havlin, S., Mantegna, R. N., Salinger, M. A., and Stanley, H. E. (1995), "Zipf plots and the size distribution of firms," *Economics Letters* **49**, 453–457.

Steindl, J. (1965), *Random Processes and the Growth of Firms: A Study of the Pareto Law*, London, Griffin.

Steindl, J. (1987), *Pareto Distribution*, The new Palgrave: a dictionary for economics edition, The Macmillan Press: London, pp. 810–813.

Stephens, M. A. (1955), "Use of the kolmogorov-smirnov, cramer-von mises and related statistics without extensive tables," *The Annals of Mathematical Statistics* **26**, 189–211.

Subbotin, M. T. (1923), "On the law of frequency of errors," *Matematicheskii Sbornik* **31**, 296–301.

Sutton, J. (1997), "Gibrat's legacy," *Journal of Economic Literature* **35**(1), 40–59.

Sutton, J. (1998), *Technology and Market Structure*, The MIT Press Cambridge, MA.

Sutton, J. (2002), "The variance of firm growth rates: The scaling puzzle," *Physica A* **312**, 577–590.

Sutton, J. (2007), *Market Structure: Theory and Evidence*, Vol. 3 of *Handbook of Industrial Organization*, Elsevier, chapter 35, pp. 2301–2368.

Takayasu, M., Watanabe, H., and Takayasu, H. (2014), "Generalised central limit theorems for growth rate distribution of complex systems," *Journal of Statistical Physics* **155**, 47–71.

Teece, D. J. (1982), "Towards an economic theory of the multiproduct firm," *Journal of Economic Behavior & Organization* **3**(1), 39–63.

Teece, D. J., Rumelt, R., Dosi, G., and Winter, S. G. (1994), "Understanding corporate coherence: Theory and evidence," *Journal of Economic Behavior and Organization* **23**(1), 1–30.

Tukey, J. W. (1977), *Exploratory Data Analysis*, Addison-Wesley Publishing Company, Inc., Reading, MA.

Vianelli, S. (1963), "La misura della variabilità condizionata in uno schema generale delle curve normali di frequenza," *Statistica* **23**, 447–474.

West, G. (2017), *Scale: the Universal Laws of Growth, Innovation, Sustainability, and the Pace of Life in Organisms, Cities, Economies, and Companies* Penguin Press, London.

West, M. (1987), "On scaled mixtures of normal distributions," *Biometrika* **74**, 646–648.

Winter, S. G. (1984), "Schumpeterian competition in alternative technological regimes," *Journal of Economic Behavior & Organization* **5**(3), 287–320.

Wooldridge, J. M. (2010), *Econometric Analysis of Cross Section and Panel Data*, The MIT Press Cambridge, MA, Cambridge.

Wyart, M. and Bouchaud, J. P. (2003), "Statistical models for company growth," *Physica A: Statistical Mechanics and Its Applications* **326**(1), 241–255.

Yamasaki, K., Matia, K., Buldyrev, S. V., Fu, D. F., Pammolli, F., Riccaboni, M., and Stanley, H. E. (2006), "Preferential attachment and growth dynamics in complex systems," *Physical Review E* **47**, 35103–35106.

Yule, G. U. (1925), "A mathematical theory of evolution, based on the conclusions of Dr. J. C. willis, F.R.S.," *Philosophical Transactions of the Royal Society B: Biological Sciences* **213**, 21–87.

Ziman, J. M. (1977), *The Force of Knowledge*, Cambridge University Press, Cambridge.

Zipf, G. K. (1949), *Human Behaviour and the Principle of Least-Effort*, Addison-Wesley Publishing Company, Inc., Reading, MA.

Author Index

Subject Index